American Cuisine

ALSO BY PAUL FREEDMAN

Ten Restaurants That Changed America

Out of the East: Spices and the Medieval Imagination

Food: The History of Taste (editor)

Images of the Medieval Peasant

American Cuisine

AND HOW IT GOT THIS WAY

PAUL FREEDMAN

LIVERIGHT PUBLISHING CORPORATION

A division of W. W. Norton & Company

Independent Publishers Since 1923

For information about permission to reproduce selections from this book, write to
Permissions, Liveright Publishing Corporation, a division of W. W. Norton & Company, Inc.,
500 Fifth Avenue, New York, NY 10110

For information about special discounts for bulk purchases, please contact
W. W. Norton Special Sales at specialsales@wwnorton.com or 800-233-4830

Manufacturing by Versa Press
Book design by Ellen Cipriano Design
Production manager: Julia Druskin

Library of Congress Cataloging-in-Publication Data

Names: Freedman, Paul, 1949– author.
Title: American cuisine : and how it got this way / Paul Freedman.
Description: First edition. | New York, NY : Liveright Publishing Corporation,
A division of W. W. Norton & Company, Independent Publishers Since 1923, 2019. |
Includes bibliographical references and index.
Identifiers: LCCN 2019029642 | ISBN 9781631494628 (hardcover) | ISBN 9781631494635 (epub)
Subjects: LCSH: Cooking, American. | LCGFT: Cookbooks.
Classification: LCC TX715 .F8626 2019 | DDC 641.5973—dc23
LC record available at https://lccn.loc.gov/2019029642

Liveright Publishing Corporation, 500 Fifth Avenue, New York, N.Y. 10110
www.wwnorton.com

W. W. Norton & Company Ltd., 15 Carlisle Street, London W1D 3BS

For Bonnie. We've had some nice meals . . .

Contents

PART I
American Regional Cuisines and Their Decline

PART II
Modernity

LIST OF ILLUSTRATIONS

What Is American Cuisine?

Even in the twenty-first century, many people think that American cuisine does not exist. In contrast to other nations, the United States does not have a clear culinary dossier; what Americans eat reflects eclecticism and experimentation, not obedience to tradition or rules. Why not have guacamole or blue cheese with that burger, or maybe try some pineapple on that pizza? The consumer has many choices, from restaurant types (Chinese, Mexican, diner) to ice cream flavors, but only in recent years have people paid attention to quality as opposed to variety. What Alice Waters, the founder of Berkeley's Chez Panisse restaurant, termed "the delicious revolution" restored attention to primary products. This simple but truly revolutionary notion inspires today's farm-to-table cuisine. Rather than "How many things can I make with canned peaches," the question is "Where can I find a juicy, fresh peach?" Since the 1970s, there has been a stunning upsurge of attention to dining as pleasurable, so food is now a major subject of conversation and media attention. What follows, then, in *American Cuisine: And How It Got This Way* is a narrative discussing the recent innovations, but in order to understand our current cuisine, it is vital to look at what came before and how American food took the form it now has.

The anthropologist Sidney Mintz, one of the founding fathers of the serious study of food in history, once defined a cuisine as a cultural phenomenon that ordinary people discuss and about which they have strong opinions. He went on

Jell-O mixed vegetable flavor. From *Better Homes and Gardens*, 1965. Jell-O salad was usually made with lime or lemon Jell-O or unflavored gelatin, but this line of vegetable flavors was a feature of the 1960s.

to say that in the absence of such an intense culinary culture, America doesn't have a cuisine.[1] Writing in the 1990s, Mintz was hardly the first person to deny that the United States possesses what can legitimately be called a cuisine. In the 1870s, an offhand statement by a distinguished Russian visitor, the Grand Duke Alexis, set an example for a dismissive attitude toward American cuisine and provoked an uproar in the American press. In a book about his trip to the United States, Alexis wrote that there was simply no such thing as American cuisine.[2] Reproachful responses to this statement focused on the regional glories of the United States: What about our marvelous Western game, Pennsylvania sausage, Chesapeake Bay terrapin, and so forth? Deprecation of American cuisine was answered by pointing to the food of its regions, an assertion that would be repeated throughout the next century.

Foreign observers often assume, contemptuously, that people in the United States live exclusively on fast food—McDonald's is really what American cuisine amounts to. Allied to this is the common notion that Americans don't actually enjoy food, at least not in a thoughtful, leisurely way. As far back as the early nineteenth century, European travelers were appalled at how quickly Americans wolfed down their food: ten minutes for breakfast and twenty for other meals, according to one haughty British visitor in 1820. The pleasures of conversation while dining seemed to be unknown to Americans, who regarded eating as a task best accomplished as fast as possible.[3] Over a hundred years later, in 1937, the French diplomat Paul Morand was amazed at the speed of the American lunch and at what he saw as Americans' unwillingness to savor it. They seemed, he opined, to regard meals as intrusions rather than small pleasures. Morand was particularly upset that people often consumed lunch at their desks—*mon Dieu!*—giving the appearance of eating in a stable rather than in a civilized environment.[4]

In a classic essay entitled "An American Tragedy," written in 1930, the food writer and wine merchant André Simon identified three false gods of American dining: speed, sugar, and shows (e.g., singing waiters, dancing, and other distractions). He sadly observed that "bolting one's food [is] a crazy habit which ruins the health of millions of people, people who have no idea of what to do with the spare time on their hands and yet swallow a few sandwiches for lunch in five minutes instead of enjoying a proper meal in a rational manner."[5]

It seems unfair—Europeans denounce the United States for large portions and chronic overeating on the one hand and, on the other, claim Americans give no thought to the pleasures of dining. Unfortunately, haste and overeating are related, and both remain national traits even in this present era of food fascination. Some of this has to do with the food industry itself, which does better at providing low prices and convenience than high quality. Oversize restaurant portions are linked to the relatively low cost of food compared to other expenses such as rent, labor, and insurance. The restaurant needs to justify pricing at a certain level and is willing to throw in more food in order to charge a profitable amount. Another structural inducement to overeating is the snack food category. Snacking increases total food sales, and more money is made off barbecue-flavor potato chips than raw potatoes or even mashed potato mix. Advertising therefore encourages grazing.

As for Americans not liking food, there is a real variation in how seriously different nations regard dining, if not food itself. The French diplomat and bon vivant Prince Talleyrand said, "Show me another pleasure like dinner which comes every day and lasts an hour."[6] It would be hard to come up with an equivalent American quote. According to surveys, Americans see eating as a matter of individual preference and freedom, while the French regard dining as a special time of conviviality. Despite the pressures of everyday life, the French by and large regard meals as pleasant occasions set apart from the rest of the day, while Americans like to distract themselves while eating by, say, staring at their cellphones, with dining as a background activity. One of the French subjects in a recent sociological study of food habits, a woman of twenty-eight, said that sometimes she is so busy at work that she does not have lunch. She buys something at a *boulangerie*, adding, "I eat it in the street." In the US, this *is* lunch, but the French informant does not consider eating on the run to be an actual meal. The general rule, according to French responses, is no newspapers, no smartphones at the table. Contrary to common American belief, the French don't take three-hour breaks for lunch, but the meal, however simple, should be protected from the concerns of the day.[7]

Beyond love of fast food or eating in a hurry, Americans and their dining options now actually have some favorable images abroad, but this is new, almost unprecedented. Where our eclecticism was once evidence of a lack of culinary standards, the United States is now recognized as impressive, "awesome" even, for the variety of its "ethnic food" offerings. American culinary internationalism takes two forms. One is regional influence of immigration, such as German cuisine in Pennsylvania or Mexican in California. Second is the phenomenon of diverse restaurants reflecting many nations, which has extended to food trucks and multinational food courts. Such restaurant options used to be associated with large, polyglot cities like New York or Chicago, but the phenomenon is now everywhere. At one time, Europeans in particular regarded the prominence of foreign restaurants as proof that there is no true American cuisine, but now such places are tourist attractions and imitated abroad. It still doesn't get us very far, however, in identifying common food characteristics across the United States other than diversity itself.

Americans have always been reluctant to accept the common foreign attitude that there are no canonical American dishes. The quest for a core culinary experience began over two hundred years ago with a cookbook entitled *American Cookery*, which appeared in 1796. Its author, Amelia Simmons, identified simply and mysteriously as "an American Orphan," was the first to claim to be publishing a work presenting the cuisine of the newly independent nation.[8] As is often the case with cookbooks, *American Cookery* was less innovative than it claimed to be. Of its 192 recipes, 57 were copied—we would call it plagiarized today—from British recipe books, sometimes with slight variation in wording or ingredients. A further 81 recipes have no identifiable source but are firmly within a tradition of British cuisine. Only 23 dishes have no British antecedent. These exceptions feature cornmeal, cranberries, pumpkin, and turkey, all identified with colonial New England. *American Cookery* is also the first place the Dutch-derived word "cookie" appears in print instead of the English term "biscuit."[9] The book is certainly original, but it does not come close to laying out a distinctive cuisine.

Certain dishes would come to be associated with American identity, but not many and not forever. The phrase "as American as apple pie" implies that there is a recognizably American food dossier. Banal though it is, the saying about apple pie is significant because while the cliché remains in our minds, actual practice has changed. Few people actually make apple pies at home, and it has faded as a dessert, as fruit pies in general have. Even diners, where apple pie was once as common as a cup of coffee, seldom serve it anymore.

The search, then, for a set of classic American dishes continues. Almost two hundred years after Amelia Simmons's effort, Phillip Stephen Schulz in 1990 published a cookbook with the appropriate title *As American as Apple Pie*. In it he presents 20 dishes (including apple pie), each prepared 12 different ways.[10] A peculiarly American emphasis on options and variety informs this repertoire—one cannot imagine a French cookbook with twelve ways to prepare pot-au-feu or boeuf bourguignon.[11] Schulz's list includes pot roast, chili, fried chicken, baked beans, meatloaf, potato salad, and chocolate chip cookies. Ignoring for the time being the fact that chili is of Mexican-American origin and potato salad was introduced by Dutch and German settlers, these dishes are recognizable, but not all of them are commonly consumed anymore. When did you last eat pot roast or bread pudding, let alone prepare them at home? Many of these dishes are eaten predominantly at restaurants, often under the rubric of another distinctly American sobriquet, "comfort food"—i.e., foods you could cook at home but don't. Some, like fried chicken, are not whipped up in home kitchens to the extent that they were fifty years ago. For baked beans not from a can, one would have to go back to before the Great Depression.

AMERICAN DISHES

Apple pie	Cole slaw
Baked beans	Fried chicken
Barbecue sauce	Hash
Biscuits	Meat loaf
Bread pudding	Pancakes
Brownies	Potato salad
Chili	Pot pies
Chocolate cake	Pot roast
Chocolate chip cookies	Stew
Chowder	Waffles

From Philip Stephen Schulz, *As American as Apple Pie* (New York, Simon and Schuster, 1990)

What Americans consume in real life is less hearty or picturesque than hash or chowder: hamburgers, hot dogs, pizza, soft drinks, and French fries are the top five foods, with potato chips, chocolate chip cookies, and donuts not far behind.[12] This does not encourage the notion that American cuisine, if it exists, is particularly interesting.

Another way to identify American cuisine is to abandon the idea of a single national taste in favor of the diversity of the country's regions. Waffles or pot roast may not work as building blocks of a national cuisine, but Louisiana gumbo or New England clam chowder or Florida Key lime pie might claim regional origins and authenticity. We will examine the strengths and weaknesses of this point of view later on.

Three Ways of Looking at American Cuisine

Notwithstanding the difficulty of identifying it, there *is* an American cuisine. Americans have well-defined and consistent tastes, whether we are aware of them or not, which *American Cuisine: And How It Got This Way* attempts to figure out. Foreign travel makes many Americans long for peanut butter, something the rest of the world tends not to admire. Neither do people in other countries think much of American bottled salad dressings (which tend to be sweet), maple syrup, glazed ham, or sweet-and-sour pork (in China it actually is sour as well as sweet). Americans in fact love to mix sugar into sauces and dressings even if no one would actually sprinkle sugar on meat or fish. Barbecue sauce in its supermarket form reflects this love of sweet and piquant, and honey mustard is little known outside the United States.

Beyond specific products or a national fondness for sweet, spicy, and salty combinations, there are unmistakable American tastes. These fall into three categories. The first consists of the regional traditions that underlie the history of American cuisine, traditions that have weakened over the past 125 years with the onslaught of the second force shaping American food habits: standardization. This term includes related phenomena that dominated the twentieth century. Consolidation of the food industry created national brand names like

Gold Medal flour or Nabisco cookies. Industrial processing made such brands inexpensive, readily available, and capable of replacing homemade foods such as pickles (Heinz) or soup (Campbell's). National supermarkets became the natural home of these products. The result is a coast-to-coast uniformity that would be reproduced in the restaurant sphere during the golden age of fast food, roughly 1960–1990.

The third feature of American cuisine is variety. This may seem contradictory because standardization sounds as if it reduces choice, but it is easy to make different flavors of industrial foods, and this diversity distracts attention from underlying uniformity. Processed foods have built-in taste limitations because they are products made in factories. Even advances in flavor chemistry cannot effectively mimic fresh, artisanal, or home-cooked versions; Campbell's soup does not taste the same as homemade. People appreciate convenience, but you don't have to be a connoisseur to perceive the difference. In addition to offering ease of preparation, Campbell's soup, like many standard brands, is available in a bewildering number of varieties, which is also an American tradition. Similarly, both Dannon yogurt and high-end, preservative-free Chobani, are made in vast plants for shipment all over the country. They cannot have the same taste as what is created locally or at home, but you can choose among many flavor options.

Variety and choice obscure blandness. They compensate for the drawbacks of mass production, especially the mediocrity of primary ingredients and the chemical artificiality of processed foods. European visitors, "gourmets," chefs, and restaurateurs are among those who have at various times complained about American meat, fish, and produce. Henri Soulé, the brilliant, though imperious, owner of New York's Le Pavillon, lamented in the 1950s that even he could not obtain ingredients that middle-class French women buy every day: fresh butter and eggs from small farms, fish from local streams, pristine Breton oysters. American vegetables were "fresh" all year round and so never really fresh in a natural, seasonal way.[13]

Rather than approaching American cuisine from a list of specific national or regional dishes, *American Cuisine* looks at the interactions among regionalism, standardization, and variety. The first three chapters deal with regional food as both reality and as comforting myth in an era of increasing national standardization. That standardization, the product of a new food system based on technological advances and large business enterprises, is the subject of chapters 4, 5, and 6. These are intended to describe a process of homogenization, and to assess the technological, economic, and cultural reasons for this characteristically American but paradoxical enthusiasm for newness and sameness.

In the United States, the desire for novelty as well as predictability resulted in an exponential growth of food options. The variety of canned olives, pasta sauces, and cookies diverted attention from the ubiquitous blandness of industrial taste and the dominance by the same brands from coast to coast. Chapter 7 looks at proliferating choices in terms of corporate strategies, and Chapter 8 at how restaurants opened by immigrants catered to this same desire for low-risk novelty.

This trio of key features of American cuisine—region, modernity, and variety—changed beginning in the 1970s. As presented in Chapter 9, that

Hamburger Chop Suey or Chow Mein
Cooking time: 30 minutes   •   Yield: 6 servings

		THICKENING AND FLAVORING:
¼ cup butter	1½ cups water	
1 pound hamburger	1 can La Choy Mixed Chinese Vegetables, drained	2 tablespoons cold water
1 medium onion, chopped		2 tablespoons cornstarch
2 teaspoons salt	1 can La Choy Bean Sprouts, drained	1 tablespoon La Choy Soy Sauce
Dash pepper		1 teaspoon sugar
2 cups diced celery	1 can mushrooms, sliced	1 tablespoon La Choy Brown Gravy Sauce if Chop Suey is desired

Cook hamburger and onion in butter until lightly browned. Add salt, pepper, celery and 1½ cups water. Bring to boil. Cover; simmer 20 minutes. Add vegetables and heat until hot. Combine thickening and flavoring ingredients; add to meat mixture. Cook until slightly thickened, stirring constantly. Serve hot with cooked rice for Chop Suey or La Choy Noodles for Chow Mein. Flavor individual servings with La Choy Soy Sauce to desired taste. Garnish with sliced green onions and sliced hard-cooked eggs.

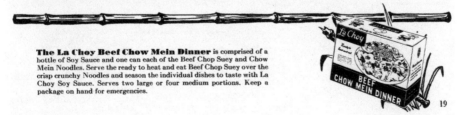

The La Choy Beef Chow Mein Dinner is comprised of a bottle of Soy Sauce and one can each of the Beef Chop Suey and Chow Mein Noodles. Serve the ready to heat and eat Beef Chop Suey over the crisp crunchy Noodles and season the individual dishes to taste with La Choy Soy Sauce. Serves two large or four medium portions. Keep a package on hand for emergencies.

19

La Choy, hamburger chop suey recipe, 1957. The aim is fusing the best of East and West.

decade saw the maximum extension of the modern corporate food system, but at the same time the beginning of a transformation. Everything the late nineteenth and early twentieth centuries had built as reproducible parts of a food system—from fast food to supermarkets—began to seem boring, environmentally damaging, and unhealthful. Beginning in the mid-1960s, California took the lead in counter-cultural ideas such as hippie communes and tie-dyed clothes. Some ideas that began on the fringe became mainstream—for example, yoga, environmental activism, and artisanal foods. It is a challenge to convey properly how American food and tastes have changed over the last five decades, but chapter 10 looks at the immediate origins of what Americans eat today. Trends include celebrity chefs, food television as entertainment, and the rise of farm-to-table eating.

The conclusion of *American Cuisine* peers at where we have ended up in the year 2020 (2020 hindsight, one might say). There is—as if inexorably—a genuine American cuisine, but it is, as the book points out, quirky and unpredictable in its historical unfolding.

PART I

American Regional Cuisines and Their Decline

CHAPTER 1

Flowering and Fading: American Regional Food

The premise of *American Cuisine: And How It Got This Way* is that there has always been an identifiable cuisine in this country. For much of United States history, that cuisine was divided into geographical and cultural regions, but around 1880, these distinctions began to blur. Some previously regional dishes, such as chili, became national; others, such as Southern possum and Rhode Island jonnycakes, became extinct. Depletion of habitat and overhunting undermined or destroyed mid-Atlantic terrapin and Midwestern prairie hens, while brand-name standardization meant that more people ate Nabisco cookies than Southern pralines or Arkansas fried pies. It is worth exploring how American regions developed characteristic ingredients and dishes and how these were supplanted by a national food system. Despite the progress of homogenization, the memory if not the reality of regionalism has been kept alive. Not all these memories are accurate, but all are important and most are entertaining.

All reasonably large nations are divided into geographical regions, but modernity has weakened their culinary borders. Many areas in America have lost their supposedly "typical" dishes, or they are retained more in recollection than in the kitchen. Various writers have struggled over the past century and a half to identify a typical American cuisine, whereas for Italy or India, there are obvious and famous dishes like lasagna or curry that everyone thinks of as typical. Anyone entering an Italian or Indian restaurant in New York, London, or Tokyo has clear expectations, but an "American Restaurant" could mean almost anything since the United States lacks even dubiously authentic unifying dishes such as lasagna or curry. The difficulty in creating an exportable American cuisine is due to our love of variety at the expense of tradition—and, sometimes, quality. As the nation matured, technological innovation obliterated culinary regions and made food standardized, while variety—the proliferation of supermarket products and restaurant options—made it hard to establish canonical dishes.

In the United States, the conformist modernizing tendencies started earlier than anywhere else and were embraced with more enthusiasm beginning in the late nineteenth century. Packaged food supplanted transitory regional cuisines. All this took place not because of some lack of virtue, but thanks to the relative newness of expansion and the constant movement of population. The history of regional cuisine in America is one of decline. As processed food took over, people tended to eat the same things across the country. Technology allowed food shoppers to ignore the seasons, so regional conditions ceased to be important. When fast food chains came to monopolize the highways, replacing the local and quirky with the rigidly predictable, the same burger or fried chicken could be purchased in Maine as in California. Such homogenization did not, however, entirely wipe out the sense of a place and the food preferences of the people living in that place. Vestigial souvenirs, such as sourdough bread for sale at the San Francisco airport or wild rice at the Minneapolis–Saint Paul airport, attest to the desire to interest outsiders in the local culinary imagination.

Geography and Culture

If the way to understand American cuisine is through its regions, just what are those culinary subsections? Some are clear and agreed on, although not in themselves internally consistent. There is a readily accepted idea of Southern food, with typical products such as grits and country ham. Specialties like barbecue, however, vary greatly across the southern states. In North Carolina and much of Tennessee, barbecue means pork shoulder cooked for a long time, shredded, and mixed with a vinegary sauce. Memphis barbecue, on the other hand, is baby back ribs rubbed with spices and served "dry" (without sauce). A special barbecue style confined to Decatur, Alabama, is smoked chicken with a mayonnaise-based white sauce. Mustard barbecue sauce is part of the lore of Columbia, South Carolina. In north-central Tennessee and south-central Kentucky, barbecue means pork shoulder steaks with a hot pepper sauce.[1] Owensboro, Kentucky, specializes in mutton barbecue. Texas uses beef brisket and sausages; its cooking method relies on indirect heat and the meat is sliced. Experts will tell you there are several other Texas styles besides this best-known Central Texas barbecue, including an East Texas version more like the North Carolina pork barbecue and a South Texas variety made with a thick, somewhat sweet sauce.

These proliferating variations can be dizzying, for both the customer and the historian trying to make sense out of traditions without repeating the usual cli-

chés. Notwithstanding subregional variation, outsiders as well as Southerners have a notion of what characterizes Southern food. The same is not true everywhere else, creating hurdles for anyone trying to codify American food. Products such as salmon and Olympia oysters identify the Pacific Northwest, but there are no region-specific ways there of making basic foods such as bread, in contrast to Southern biscuits, spoon bread, and cornbread, nor is there a distinctive, long-standing Northwestern cooking style.

Culinary maps of the United States show different foods by place of origin. The cover of the 1939 *New York World's Fair Cook Book* displays one or two items from almost every state: lobster in Maine, cheese in Wisconsin, and,

Cover of *New York World's Fair Cook Book*, 1939. The map of the states and their specialties wraps around the spine and the back cover.

Duncan Hines' Food Odyssey book jacket. The cover of this 1955 autobiography of the salesman and restaurant reviewer features a map with typical food items of different regions.

somewhat surprisingly, brandied peaches in Mississippi.[2] The latest edition of Jane and Michael Stern's history-making *Roadfood* has similar little drawings of biscuits, pie slices, or crabs accompanied by the name of a specific place that serves them, thus tamales at Taqueria Pico de Gallo in South Tucson and tacos at Rosita's in Scottsbluff, Nebraska.[3] Even here, however, the "iconic" dishes do not correspond consistently to regions: Nebraska is not as famous as Arizona for Mexican-American food.

How, then, were America's regions to be divided up? "America Eats," the federal government's project just before the Second World War to record American food customs, identified five geographic sectors: Northeast, South, Middle West, Southwest, and West. These divisions are too large to be meaningful when applied to food. While one can certainly imagine such a thing as Southern or Southwestern cuisine, the others are only territorial demarcations.

The wildly popular series of cookbooks that Time-Life published circa 1970 offers six volumes of regional American recipes and description: New England, the "Eastern Heartland," South, Creole and Acadian, West, and Northwest. The editors commendably devoted an entire volume to Louisiana, whose New Orleans and Cajun cuisines are perhaps the most vibrant traditional styles of cooking in America. On the other hand, we do not get any sense of what Northwest culinary style might amount to, and the heading "Eastern Heartland" encompasses types of cooking as diverse as those of the Pennsylvania Germans and the people around the Chesapeake Bay.

A current textbook of American regional cuisines addressed to students in culinary programs identifies fifteen divisions, based on geography, "homogeneous food culture," and particular defining dishes. Louisiana remains distinctive, as are now Hawaii and, interestingly, New York City, reflecting the city's status as a restaurant and immigrant capital more than as an inventor of a single style. "The South" consists of the entire region encompassing Chesapeake Bay Shore, the "plantation south," and southern Florida joined with Puerto Rico.[4]

Betty Fussell's *I Hear America Cooking* from 1986 presents an eccentric and diverting theory of regional identity. The chapter divisions do not claim to cover the entire United States but rather identify those pieces with qualities that affect cuisine:[5]

The Mexamerican Desert ("sun")
The Delta South ("water"—Cajuns and Creoles)
Southeast Dixie ("earth")
The New England Coast
The Great Lakes of the Midwest
The Ecotopian Northwest

The Northwest may have ecological aspirations, but these do not amount to a culinary identity. The recipes are grouped into clever and suggestive subheadings—thus for the New England chapter, "Bread and Breakfast," "Potboilers," "Garden Stuff," and "Pudding Pies and Cookie Cakes."

Notwithstanding the many ingenious ways of slicing the map, the fact remains that some American regions have an immediately recognizable identity, while others do not. And some are in between, as is New England with its small surviving culinary repertoire that includes well-known items like lobster and clams, but whose once rich food tradition has largely vanished. The void is partially filled by vacation items such as fried clam puffs or lobster rolls that, however delicious, would not have been familiar to colonial cooks and homemakers.

Another weakness in asserting that real American cuisine is regional is the difficulty of fitting in immigrants. The Time-Life editors solved this problem by issuing a separate volume entitled *The Melting Pot* that included cuisines brought to this country by different national and ethnic groups.[6] For example, traditional cooking in Pennsylvania, Wisconsin, or Texas is unimaginable apart from German settlement going back to the early nineteenth century. A trickier question is whether Italian food is part of national American cuisine or a particular phenomenon of cities such as New York, Boston, or San Francisco. Some of the same difficulty exists in Canada, whose regional culinary treatments often feature the dishes of immigrants: Chinese along the western railroad routes, German Mennonites in Ontario, Ukrainians in Saskatchewan. On the other hand, Canada has a clearly distinct French-influenced cuisine in Québec, its second-largest province in terms of population.[7]

Many regional culinary authorities have avoided the obvious immigrant inflection, associating the foreign-born with a few big coastal cities. According to this view, Germans and Scandinavians, for example, were not "really" immigrants, while the Chinese formed an enclave with no impact except for their popular restaurant cuisine. The situation of Mexican people was particularly hard for guidebooks to deal with. On the one hand, the Southwest, including much of Texas and southern California, is distinctively Mexican in its culinary character, yet older treatments of American regions, reflecting historical biases, preferred to speak of "Spanish" colonial legacies rather than recent Mexican influence. Newer regional food books try to have it both ways: the food of immigrants enriches and diversifies New England culinary traditions, according to a cookbook put out in 2002 by a consortium of art institutes; nevertheless, "the roots of the region run deep" (whatever that means).[8]

So, although regional differences still exist, it is best to think of them not as fixed characteristics but as mutable and fragmented. What survives is a patchwork quilt rather than a monochrome blanket.[9] In addition, the differential pace of change means that some dishes regarded as regionally typical are actually archaic survivals reborn as sentimental favorites. The pimento cheese sandwich, all the rage everywhere in the 1920s, is regarded today as a treasured Southern tradition, when in fact it is an archaism turned into a culinary point of reference.[10] Chess pie, which is like pecan pie without the pecans—sugar pie, essentially—is also supposed to be a uniquely Southern favorite, but it was made all over the United States in the nineteenth and early twentieth centuries and descends from fancy European sugar tarts.[11]

Three American Regions

What people think of as regional identity is as important as what is actually cooked. Newly invented traditions often outshine old ones—for example, Nashville hot chicken is celebrated even though it is a recent innovation and not an expression of the land or of home cooking, while spoon bread (cornmeal with a texture between pudding and bread) is a genuinely long-standing, but almost forgotten, Southern item. Both hot chicken and spoon bread show something about Southern food, and about the South as a larger entity. Throughout the country the proliferation of nontraditional "traditions" such as Buffalo chicken wings or blackened redfish tells us stories about changes in taste (bland to spicy), the diffusion of local inventions, and, above all, nostalgia for an America of diverse and unpredictable tastes. For most of the twentieth century, standardized brand names, and fast-food formed a drab background for a few stars of regional culinary variation and local distinction.

One way of considering historically the variation among regional cuisines is to look at the influence of slavery and the adaptations to the New World made by Africans.[12] At one extreme was the West Indies, the richest part of British colonial North America thanks to revenue from sugar. With the rapid extermination of the native population through disease and mistreatment, the sugar industry, which reached its peak in the eighteenth century, came to depend on slaves transported from Africa.[13]

Barbados, Jamaica, and Hispaniola were completely given over to sugarcane fields and factory-like refineries. The black population of the islands at the time was between 75 and 90 percent of the total. White plantation owners and colonial officials were not interested in making a permanent home in the Caribbean. They were investing, not emigrating in search of a new life, and they seldom brought over their families. Rather than settling permanently on the islands, which they considered unhealthful, their plan was to get rich quickly and return to Britain, resuming life on a higher social scale.

British members of the Caribbean elite made minimal efforts to create their own means of agricultural subsistence, let alone cuisine. At first, they depended largely on imported food, which was expensive and not especially tasty, items on the order of hardtack and dried fish. Even the harshest overseers knew that the slaves had to eat, and rather than attempt to import their food, it was more practical to allow the slaves to grow crops that would also feed their overseers and masters.[14] Lady Maria Nugent, wife of the Governor of Jamaica, kept a journal of her stay on the island from 1801 to 1805. She mentions fish and hog dishes, crab pepper pot with okra, turtle soup, another soup made from parrots, okra, and lots of spices (she particularly emphasizes allspice). This food, all cooked by slaves and reflecting their African origins, was not particularly attractive to her, but it was plentiful.[15] African slaves learned to grow Native American crops such as cassava and to catch and cook unfamiliar kinds of fish. They also cultivated African imports such as yams, sorghum, okra, and watermelon. Modern Caribbean cuisine, therefore, is based in large part on African-based adaptations.

New England was at the opposite extreme of the Caribbean in terms of settlement motives and patterns. Many of its European-born inhabitants were Calvinists disheartened with the incomplete Reformation undertaken by the English church and the suppression of their worship and doctrine. In the seventeenth century, the increasingly strident defense of the established church under King Charles I and his ministers, the disruption of the ensuing English Civil War, and the continuing religious controversies of the Restoration drew sectarian communities to the New England colonies. These people intended to subdue the wilderness, as they regarded it, supporting themselves by farming, fishing, or engaging in trade. They did not cultivate an export crop like Caribbean sugar or Southern tobacco.

This is not to say that the New England Puritans and other religious refugees had a consistent, principled objection to slavery, nor to deny that they were heavily involved as suppliers and commercial intermediaries for the wealth of the Southern and Caribbean colonies,[16] but their agrarian enterprises, as opposed to their shipping interests, did not depend on large-scale slave labor. Their food evolved according to a more European pattern than was the case farther south.

Freed from the English religious orthodoxy, the New Englanders were still happy with the food traditions of their home country. They considered American corn (maize) inferior to European wheat as a nutritive source. "The barbarous Indians, who know no better" might consider maize a good food, but, according to the botanist who made this observation just before 1600, it was more fit for swine.[17] The early New England colonists would have loved nothing better than to eat the familiar Old World combination of leavened wheat bread, dairy products, meat from cows and pigs, and familiar vegetables. Yet because of the soil and climate of the region, they were forced to learn about what they called "Indian corn," along with pumpkins, clams, cranberries, wild turkeys, and other natural bounty that they only grudgingly accepted. Gradually they were able to impose their familiar regime of row crops and domesticated animals on the new territories.

First Tolerated, Then Cherished: New England Cuisine

New England inevitably comes first in the story of American cuisine, not only because it created what Keith Stavely and Kathleen Fitzgerald called "America's Founding Food," but because along with that venerable if questionable status, New England cuisine came to be considered America's *standard* food. The influence of the Boston Cooking School in the late nineteenth and early twentieth centuries, and particularly of its most famous teacher, Fannie Merritt Farmer, made New England seem the custodian of "real American cooking." New England cuisine was presented as simple, frugal, and healthful, opposed to both French pretentiousness and immigrant complexity and spiciness. It would become the quintessential cuisine of the Protestant establishment.

Late in the year 1620, the pilgrim ship *Mayflower* made several landings on

Cape Cod prior to establishing the colony at Plymouth. During one of these preliminary stops, an exploratory party returned to the ship with several bushels of multicolored corn stolen from the indigenous inhabitants. From that moment, the colonists were compelled to take up what they referred to as "Indian corn" along with Native American ways of cultivation, fishing, gathering, and hunting. They deferred to the practical knowledge of native peoples during the first decades of their colonization, but with a certain discontent, shading over into the conviction that the savage Indians followed an unhealthful diet. The fact that Native Americans were dying from European diseases was attributed not to exposure to new infections, but rather to the natives' biological inferiority. Europeans in the Caribbean feared disease, while those farther north regarded themselves as tougher and better suited to the land than its original inhabitants.[18]

The British settlers were concerned not to copy too closely the Native American foodways lest they themselves became sick, uncivilized, or regarded back home in the British Isles as uncivilized. It was easier to grow corn than wheat, and easier to find shellfish than to pasture cattle, but that didn't make native products equal in status to British staples. To be civilized meant rejecting interspersing different crops in favor of European separate, geometric rows, and importing and then breeding domestic animals unknown to the native population. The Indians moved around with the seasons, changing their residence and field locations; this was, according to Western outlook, akin to the nomadic existence of barbarians.

New World foods included pumpkins, apples (and apple cider), cranberries, turkeys, clams and other shellfish, cod, beans, chowders, salt pork, and maple syrup. Indian corn was prepared in many ways, as cornbread, small cakes (cornpone), pancakes (what would become known as johnnycakes or hoecakes), pudding, various kinds of porridges, and mush that could also be evaporated and then fried. Hominy is another preparation of pounded corn kernels, as is what was referred to as "hasty pudding" made with milk and water and cooked relatively quickly to resemble porridge rather than regular, more solid pudding that required more time and effort. Corn could also be mixed with rye and baked into a bread known as "ryaninjun."[19] All were ubiquitous in early colonial America but were given little prominence in descriptions of the new lands because reliance on corn, clams, or cranberries rather than civilized wheat and livestock called into question the European superiority that justified dispossessing the Indians.

Corn exported to Britain was used there to feed livestock, not people. An English comic writer who went under the name of Ebenezer Cooke published a satire of colonial life entitled *The Sot Weed Factor* (i.e., the tobacco broker). The factor drinks hard cider and eats coarse food based on corn: hominy, cornpone, and cornmeal mush, flavored with molasses and bacon fat.[20] The American colonists might resent such characterization, but they accepted its premise. One early chronicler wrote in 1654 that many had found it hard to subsist on "Indian bread," yet they had no choice until cattle and plowed crops could be introduced. The renowned Massachusetts Bay minister Cotton Mather wrote that the poor depended on low-status food such as mussels, clams, and nuts.[21] Even when praising the teeming fish and wildlife of New England, observers such as the Plymouth Colony governor William Bradford regarded game, fish, and Indian corn as barely acceptable, clearly inferior to the butter, beef, sugar, and wheat bread of England. The colonists longed for rich gravy sauces, roast mutton, pies, and bacon. Doubtless Bradford would have preferred wine or even English ale to cider as well.

By the mid-eighteenth century, with increasing population and trade, moderately affluent Americans might approximate a comfortable English diet. New England had become prosperous, and its residents could afford refined sugar, spices, rum, and other luxuries. The Boston Tea Party, a protest in 1770 against British taxes, demonstrated the popularity of luxury imports. The mid-Atlantic region exported wheat to Europe, the West Indies, New England, and the South, and New England sent rum, molasses, and fish to a similarly diverse set of destinations. The American colonial economy as a whole grew at an annual average rate of 3.5 percent between 1650 and 1770, contrasting with England's 0.5 percent average growth. This advantage was due to the unremunerated labor of slaves, especially in the West Indies.[22] With the proceeds of economic expansion, Massachusetts bought wheat from agriculturally more favored colonies such as Pennsylvania and English-style white bread replaced ryaninjun and cornbread.[23] By the mid-eighteenth century, New England meals were closer to those consumed in Britain than at any time before—ironic given that the Revolution was about to take place. Molasses, clams, pork, and ryaninjun had given way to sugar, beef, and cake.

The American Revolution began a process of gradual disassociation of New England food, and American food generally, from English tastes. As with buckskin jackets and homemade whiskey, culinary ruggedness was partly for show, a means of celebration and a boast. The new republic's wilderness and roughness contrasted favorably with tired and decadent Europe. The frontier changed from embarrassment to advantage as Andrew Jackson in his electoral triumph of 1828 made so resoundingly clear. The mountains and forests of the West no longer signified nature's dominance over civilization, but rather democracy, the means by which American "yeoman" farmers could reap the rewards of their own labor instead of depending on the aristocracy for access to scarce land.

French food was widely imitated by some members of the American upper class, while attacked by others. A self-serving example of regional American food is what was referred to as "Knickerbocker Cookery," the good old plain cuisine of New York. In the late 1830s, when Delmonico's in New York established a high standard of elegance and fidelity to French cuisine, their "rare and unmentionable dishes" were ridiculed by Sandy Welsh, owner of a competing restaurant and catering business. Rather than the French so-called delicacies, Welsh exalted the food at his own Knickerbocker Hall, whose specialties were terrapin, roast beef "alamode" (braised beef), turtle soup, lobster, and pork.[24] The irony that the term "alamode" was derived from French was clearly lost on Welsh.

Another early example of praise of America's simple culinary virtues is Joel Barlow's poem "The Hasty Pudding," written in 1793. The author was an American of sufficiently radical credentials to receive French citizenship with the advent of the revolutionary government. He was inspired to write his encomium to American cornmeal pudding after eating a similar polenta in the French Alpine region of Savoy, where he was an unsuccessful candidate in elections for the French National Convention. "The Hasty Pudding" is a lasting if not immortal product of his efforts. It opens with an evocation of Gallic liberties and the death of kings, describes the moment of awakened memory, and extols the simple breakfast of egalitarian America.[25] Hasty pudding is healthful, simple, and democratic, but never does Barlow claim that it is particularly delicious. His only reference to taste is the ominous observation that hunger encourages enjoyment. Ignoring flavor while praising convenience ("hasty" means it doesn't require the bother of a full-fledged pudding), and healthfulness constitute signs of the American future, a virtuous, democratic austerity identified particularly with New England.

OLD AND NEW WAYS TO MAKE HASTY PUDDING

Indian Pudding

This is one of three recipes under the heading "A Nice Indian Pudding," and at a mere 1½ hours of cooking, the fastest. The second recipe requires baking for 2½ hours, while the third has to be boiled for 12 hours.

---

3 pints scalded milk, 7 spoons fine Indian meal, stir well together while hot, let stand till cooled. Add 7 eggs, half pound raisins, 4 ounces butter, spice and sugar and bake one and half hour.

From Amelia Simmons, *American Cookery or the Art of Dressing Viands, Fish, Poultry and Vegetables . . .*
(Hartford: Hudson & Goodwin, 1796), 36.

Hasty Pudding: Traditional Version

½ cup yellow cornmeal

1 cup cold water

½ teaspoon salt

2 cups boiling water

Mix cornmeal with cold water. Add with salt to boiling water. Reduce heat and cook 10–15 minutes, stirring frequently. Serve with cream and maple sugar, brown sugar, honey, or molasses. Chill unused mush, slice, dust slices with flour, and brown in butter or bacon grease. Serve with syrup.

From *The Old Farmer's Almanac*, https://www.almanac.com/recipe/hasty-pudding, accessed July 22, 2018.

Hasty Pudding: Fancier Modern Adaptation

INGREDIENTS

2–3 pints milk (or cream, depending on desired thickness)

1½ cups cornmeal

1½ cups melted butter

1 cup sugar

2–3 eggs

¼ tsp cinnamon

¼ tsp nutmeg

¼ tsp ginger

¼ tsp cloves

¼ tsp pumpkin pie seasoning (optional)

¾ cup raisins (optional)

1. Scald the milk in a pan, and stir in cornmeal while still hot. Continue stirring on the heat until the mixture thickens.
2. Remove from heat and let cool.
3. Stir together melted butter, sugar, and eggs in a separate bowl, and mix it in.
4. Add in spices and raisins as needed according to the taste.
5. Pour into cupcake tins or a pie tin and bake in the oven at 350 degrees for 30 minutes.

From the "Preservation Maryland" website, http://www.preservationmaryland.org/historic-recipe-hasty-pudding/, accessed July 22, 2018.

The cookbooks published in the independent United States were knockoffs of English recipe collections. As previously noted, Amelia Simmons's *American Cookery* of 1796 is regarded as the first American cookbook, but its contents are mostly derived (i.e., copied) from English classics such as Susannah Carter's *Frugal Housewife*. Lucy Emerson wrote the first recipe book that presents itself as regional, *The New-England Cookery,* published in 1808. Despite its title, this is an English cookbook with few gestures toward any American, let alone New England, style.[26]

The first evidence for a distinctive United States, as opposed to colonial, cooking style comes in an American version of the most popular English cookbook of the eighteenth century, Hannah Glasse's *Art of Cookery Made Plain and Easy*. Published in Virginia in 1805, this edition included a few "new receipts adapted to the American mode of cooking," including pumpkin pie, Indian pudding, cranberry tart, and pot pies. It was not just the ingredients but also the simplified manner of preparation that made these American. Contrast Glasse's recipe for English pork pie, which calls for layers of pork loin and apples with white wine poured over them, with her American recipe, which uses pork of any cut, chopped up and baked in a pie.[27]

Although the country became richer and its meals more ostentatious, the prevailing cookbook idea remained virtuous frugality. Sarah Hale's *Good Housekeeper* (1839) and *Miss [Catherine] Beecher's Domestic Receipt Book* (1846) praised the wholesome simplicity of the past, identified especially with New England, a region that resisted the profligacy shared by mid-Atlantic cities like New York and Baltimore, and the slave-owning, feudal South. Esther A. Howland's *New England Economical Housekeeper and Family Receipt Book*, published in 1844, offers "the most economical mode of preparing various dishes," but none of these is a New England regional specialty.[28]

New England's culinary preeminence in the late nineteenth and early twentieth centuries reworked an established image of thrift to encompass health as well. The Boston Cooking School, established by the Women's Educational Association in 1878, promoted "modern," progressive cooking that would uplift the poor and working classes. The school's public outreach effort, called the

New England Kitchen, was intended to teach ordinary people how to cook, instructing them in self-discipline and a healthful diet. Healthful, according to nutritional theories of the time, meant fewer carbohydrates, lots of protein and fat, and avoidance of wasteful expense—fatty, cheap kinds of meat were deemed equally nutritious as cutlets and steaks, or even more so. Spices and pickles were rejected as inducements to indigestion and alcohol consumption. As has often been the case, the nutritional problems of the poor were attributed to ignorance and improvidence rather than lack of money.[29]

For all their social activism, the New England Kitchen advocates did not succeed in convincing their intended working-class and immigrant targets to accept frugal recipes for bland food. The precepts of plainness and white food (in both literal and racial terms) were more successful with the middle class, interested as it was in being instructed in health and science and not overfond of rich or complex flavor.

Addressed to this new audience, a prosperous version of the school's teaching was effectively diffused by Fannie Farmer's *Boston Cooking-School Cook Book*, first published in 1896.[30] Farmer herself was not at first an advocate of regional New England cuisine, nor was she a dogmatic follower of so-called scientific cookery. She had grown up in Medford, Massachusetts, her youth marred by polio and her hapless father's declining printing business. After some experience as, in effect, a mother's helper, she became affiliated with the Boston Cooking School, becoming its principal in 1893. Farmer had red hair and bright blue eyes, took little care with clothes, and walked with a limp, an effect of polio. She described herself as more of a businesswoman than a particularly skilled cook, combining a genius for marketing with a sense of balance among often-contradictory demands for healthful, tasty, and practical recipes.[31]

In the first edition of her cookbook, Farmer included more Southern dishes than those from New England, and more French-derived, elegant recipes than from all American regions combined. She had a section for recipes using a chafing dish, a silver serving piece set over a small fire to keep the contents warm, a sign of bourgeois gentility.[32] The "Boston" in the title of the cooking school and the cookbook did not mean so much New England as big-city sophistication.

After the author's death in 1915, her nieces supervised subsequent editions of what was to prove the most popular cookbook in the United States until the late 1930s, when *The Joy of Cooking* replaced it. The new versions of what came to be known as *The Fannie Farmer Cookbook* featured simple ingredients and a straightforward manner of preparation, both extolled as morally virtuous. The French dishes were eliminated, and "Boston" now conveyed Yankee thrift and virtuous simplicity. This middle-class food was supposed to contrast with both the overelaborate French style of the elite as well as the feckless diet of the poor, who spent too much money on cheap salty, spicy, and sugary taste sensations.[33] Twentieth-century American food would be based on beef, dairy products, sugar, potatoes, white bread, and cake, eschewing spices and complexity. This plain but high-calorie culinary outlook took off from the idea of New England as the American model.

Home economists and others trained in the Boston School's precepts wanted Americans to adopt New England cooking. Specific recommendations, in line with the frugal ideal of the early American republic, were beef broth, creamed codfish, pressed meat, corn mush, boiled hominy, oatmeal, baked beans, cracked wheat, and Indian pudding. The school's nutritional teachings were almost the opposite of what is now recommended: Its faculty believed that white bread was much healthier than dark bread that retained the bran, although an exception was allowed for Boston brown bread. Vegetables were considered to be of little nutritional value, though acceptable if cooked for a long time; milk should be condensed (a new scientific process), which involves adding sugar, believed to be a great source of nutrition. Fiber was bad for you, and food should be soft to aid digestion.

New England's regional cuisine, connected with a genteel form of nativism and mistrust of foreign influences, became a model for the United States simultaneous with the colonial revival, a stylistic movement spurred by the 1876 centennial of the American Revolution that created a long-lasting vogue for the colonial look in houses and furniture. The Centennial Exhibition in Philadelphia featured a New England log house that included a reproduction of a colonial kitchen and a contrasting modern kitchen next door. The older kitchen served New England items such as Boston baked beans and brown bread. A permanent exhibition replaced the temporary fair, and it turned the

The "New England Log Cabin" from the Philadelphia Centennial Exhibition, 1876. This exhibit recreated colonial New England, presenting the region as exemplary of America's founding virtues.

log cabin into a restaurant featuring "Ye Old Tyme Meals" including "Ye Baked Beans, prepared as in ye fashion of ye Olden Tyme in ye Ancient City of Boston" with doughnuts and molasses gingerbread for dessert.

By 1900, New England marketed itself as a tourist-friendly repository of quaint and homey colonial furniture, décor, and food. What New Englanders had previously dismissed as remnants of an impoverished past—iron kettles, quilts, or William and Mary furniture—were now valuable antiques. Copper bed warmers and pewter tankards came down from attic storage to decorate the walls of inns, resorts, hotels, and restaurants. Abandoned fishing villages on Nantucket and Cape Cod became picturesque tourist destinations.

Foods of the past, formerly associated with poverty and hard winters, were part of the revival. Eighteenth-century baked beans and pumpkin pie were enthusiastically brought back, though in more luxurious fashion and with more sugar than their antecedents. A colonist magically transported to Boston's Durgin-Park restaurant or Mory's in New Haven would not have recognized their Indian pudding, replete as it was with sugar and spices. Maple syrup was now prized rather than regarded as inferior to cane sugar. Newly invented traditions such as clambakes, shore dinners, and New England boiled dinners became emblematic of New England seasons. Pot roast was hardly new, but the designation "Yankee Pot Roast" became a standard restaurant menu item.

Forgotten dishes, once considered rustic, were now patriotic. Rhode Island became passionate about its jonnycake, an unleavened corn pancake, which was originally baked before the fire but latter fried on a griddle.[34] In *The Jonny-Cake Papers* (1915), Thomas Robinson Hazard defended old-fashioned products and recipes against ill-advised innovation. He participated in a learned debate about the ingredients and cooking method for the generic New England "johnny-cake" versus the supposedly more artisanal (as we would now say) Rhode Island "jonnycake" (without the *h*).[35] In the 1890s, the Rhode Island legislature tried to define a recipe for this delicacy, but the session ended in fisticuffs. Later there was sufficient agreement at least to pass a law mandating the "jonnycake" spelling within state boundaries.

The Waning of New England Cuisine

New England food may indeed be sentimentally America's first cuisine, but it is also America's first forgotten cuisine. As late as 1960, the peripatetic food-reporter Clementine Paddleford described local disagreements over how to make jonnycake (scalded or cold milk? a spell in the oven after frying or not?), but today, even in close-knit Rhode Island, jonnycake appeals more to elderly tourists than to natives. In Boston, once commonly referred to as "Beantown," quesadillas and falafel play a greater role than the once-famous baked beans or brown bread.[36]

As with most parts of the country, New England has experienced a culinary revival in the last thirty years as respect for local ingredients and food traditions has become reestablished. Judging by export power, however (i.e., the degree to which a region's dishes are imitated elsewhere), New England lags far behind the

PERMANENT EXHIBITION

Log Cabin Restaurant.

RIGHT OF MUSIC STAND.

Y^E OLD TYME MEALS.

Y^E Baked Beans, prepared as in ye fashion of ye Olden Tyme in ye Ancient City of Boston, Brown Bread, Coffee or Tea	25
Cold Ham, Bread and Butter, Coffee or Tea	25
Cold Tongue, " " " "	25
Roast Beef, " " " "	25
Corned Beef " " " " Tuesdays & Fridays	25
Potatoes, boiled	10
Boiled Eggs (2)	10
Fried Eggs	15
Sandwiches	10
Oat-Meal and Milk	15
Bread and Milk	15
Pie	10
Doughnuts	5
Molasses Gingerbread	5
Sponge and other Cakes	5
Iced Tea or Coffee	10
Bread and Butter	10
Ice Cream	10
Soups	20

Menu from the New England Log Cabin, 1876. In pseudo "Ye Olde Tyme" style, the menu features Boston baked beans and other delicacies.

South, Southwest, Texas, and Louisiana. It is easier to get authentic gumbo or barbecue in Boston than to find a decent clam chowder in Austin or Santa Fe. The region has lost its authority, both as the creator of America's original food and as a model for modern, scientific cooking. Jasper White, author of a number of well-liked contemporary New England cookbooks, includes in his *Cooking from New England* "traditional Yankee cooking" but also recognizes the cuisines of immigrant groups.[37] Nearly one-third of his recipes are for fish and shellfish, the unique culinary treasures of the region according to White. These are mostly traditional preparations, although he includes mussels cooked in the

Portuguese fashion and North End–style fried squid (the North End being Boston's original Italian immigrant neighborhood). There are updated recipes for venerable meat dishes like red flannel hash (here stir-fried) and New England boiled dinner. Later White presents several johnnycake recipes, including one for "johnnycake polenta," along with Boston brown bread and even Boston baked beans. There are also instructions for Portuguese caldo verde and for the New Haven specialty white clam pizza.[38]

It is certainly appropriate to speak of a historical New England cuisine, but while the current food revolution has revived local products, it has not yet restored the region's cuisine.

Nostalgia and Appropriation: The South

The southern United States has a stronger, more enduring regional identity than New England, although who owns that identity is a contested subject. Everyone can name things that taste Southern: grits, collard greens, ham and biscuits, red-eye gravy, chess pie, barbecue. More than any other part of the United States, the South has preserved features of its distinctiveness, among them food. Okra, chitterlings, fried tomatoes, pork rind, sweet potato pie, catfish, boiled peanuts, and Moon Pies are Southern favorites eaten infrequently or not at all elsewhere.[39]

Some of these supposedly Southern dishes used to be prepared all over the country. Congealed salad (made with Jell-O) is the descendant of all the gelatin salads that triumphed at the beginning of the twentieth century and faded outside the South by the 1970s. Beaten and regular biscuits were once found in all rural environments. Banana pudding has disappeared in most of the United States but flourishes in the South. Other dishes such as pecan pie and fried chicken are well known nationally but identified with the South. Finally, some dishes are symbolic of Southern distinctiveness and not commonly found outside the South except among African Americans with Southern roots: grits and mustard greens are examples. The migration of African Americans from the rural South to northern cities that began just before the First World War spread Southern food and created new crosscurrents involving what came to be considered "soul food" in its urban setting.

SOUTHERN INGREDIENTS AND DISHES

Food mentioned in "That's What I Like about the South" (a Bob Wills number exemplifying the "Texas Swing" style, 1939):

Fried eggs	Cornbread
Ham	Absinthe (New Orleans)
Layer cake	Backbones
Baked ribs	Turnip greens
Candied yams	Ham hocks
Virginia ham	Butter beans
Black-eyed peas	

Thirty Southern dishes:

Grits	Chicken fried steak
Beaten biscuits	Chicken and dumplings
Baking powder or buttermilk biscuits	Chicken pilau (or perlew)
	Red-eye gravy
Cornbread	Hoppin' John
Barbecue (pork, brisket, mutton, etc.)	Red rice
	Fried green tomatoes
Country ham	Okra
Catfish	Greens (collard, turnip, poke salat, mustard, etc.)
Burgoo	
Brunswick stew	Yams and sweet potatoes
She-crab soup	Fried corn
Fried chicken	Black-eyed peas

Watermelon rind pickles

Congealed salad

Pecan pie

Sweet potato pie

Banana pudding

Chess pie

From John Egerton, *Southern Food: At Home, On the Road, in History* (Chapel Hill: University of North Carolina Press, 1987).

Thirty dishes mentioned by Edna Lewis:

Benne biscuits

Corn fritters

Herring with its roe

Early spring wild greens
(poke salat, wild mustard,
dandelion, lamb's quarter,
purslane, wild watercress),
boiled in pork stock and
served with cornmeal
dumplings

Wild asparagus, steamed and
served on toast with cream
sauce

Potted squab

Turtle soup

Guinea hen, cooked in a clay
pot

Fried chicken

Gumbo

Okra cornmeal pancakes

Deviled crabs

Chicken salad

Shrimp paste, served over grits

Barbecued pig with coleslaw,
baked beans, potato salad,
and hushpuppies

Peach ice cream

Ham in cream sauce,
served over biscuits and
accompanied by poached
eggs

Squirrel

Brunswick stew

Wild pig

Country steak, smothered with
onions and gravy

She-crab soup

Strawberry shortcake

Black walnut whiskey cake

Coconut cake

Fried apple pie

Blueberry cobbler

Iced tea

Mint julep

From Edna Lewis, "What Is Southern?" *Gourmet*, January 2008 (posthumously published), http://www.gourmet.com.s3-website-useast1.amazonaws.com/magazine/2000s/2008/01/whatissouthern_lewis.html.[40]

The South, however, does not comprise a single culinary habitat or tradition. Appalachia, with its complex, isolated microgeography and history of subsistence agriculture, has very different food from that of the flat, fertile country of the Mississippi Delta. Before the Civil War, the coastal and cotton South had large-scale slavery to rival the system of the British Caribbean, but members of the land-owning class did not consider England their literal home, and the plantations were meant to be permanent. Slaves cooked for the planters, but the latter had a cultural investment in putting forward an upper-class, Anglophile version of Southern food.

Coastal zones, such as the South Carolina Low Country or Virginia Tidewater, had large slave populations in order to grow rice, indigo, and tobacco. These areas developed different agricultural and industrial exploitation from those of the hilly backcountry. Rice was immensely important to coastal South Carolina, only slightly less so in Louisiana and East Texas, and not cultivated elsewhere.

A standard textbook of American regional food divides the South into five parts: Plantation South, Chesapeake Bay Shore, Louisiana, Appalachia, and South Florida.[41] The Deep South, given over to cotton, was different from the tobacco regions of Virginia and North Carolina. Northern Florida resembles the rest of the South, but southern Florida is both more Caribbean and more influenced by the northern United States. Immigration from Cuba, plus an affluent expatriate community, have created a Latino culture in South Florida unmatched anywhere else in the South. Seasonal residents ("snowbirds") as well as a substantial permanent Jewish population have likewise affected Floridian tastes.

Notwithstanding all this variety, there are common elements among Southern subregions. Historically they have shared three staples: cornmeal, molasses, and pork. Greens should be added to this list, although they might differ—poke salat and other wild plants in Appalachia and much of the African American rural South, collard or turnip greens in flatter agricultural regions.[42]

Southern culinary unity and identity are often sentimentalized. Damon Lee Fowler, a cookbook author, says, for example "Each time a Southern cook hefts a skillet to the stovetop, he or she is not alone. Trapped within the iron confines of these skillets and stewpots are the scents and secrets of a family's culinary history."[43] This is wishful thinking unless we actually believe that most people in the South routinely use cast-iron cookware and cook the way their ancestors did. In the 1980s, the North Carolina chef and restaurateur Bill Neal, a leader of the revival of Southern food, said, "We know we are Southerners because we do eat possum and grits and okra"; he maintained that once "we" no longer ate these things, we would no longer be Southerners.[44] The defiant implausibility of this statement is endearing, but it does not describe the reality of the South. What is identified most commonly and justifiably as Southern food is a rural cuisine of the past. The South was until recently agrarian, and its cities, except for New Orleans, were not gastronomically distinguished. This was mostly due to the absence of a restaurant culture, in itself related to lack of immigration and restrictive alcoholic beverage laws.

Southern Distinctions

There are inevitably a number of axes of contrasts in the South: black and white, rich and poor, rural and urban. Geography and historical events account for some culinary differences. For example, sorghum syrup supplemented molasses in parts of the South, particularly during the Civil War when sugarcane processing and transport were interrupted.[45] Likewise, the mullet and shrimp of coastal Carolina did not travel inland. And wild game remained important longer in Appalachia than elsewhere; *The Foxfire Book of Appalachian Cookery*, a 1980s book of old folks' memories collected by young people who interviewed them, has recipes for venison, raccoon, and possum, along with instructions for dressing and cooking game. Gladys Nichols, one of the informants, shyly acknowledged, "People say I make good squirrel dumplings."[46]

The Whitney Plantation, up the Mississippi River from New Orleans, today presents visitors with an unusually up-front emphasis on the lives of slaves. The site reconstructs the slave diet as largely cornmeal products, okra, field peas, rice, sweet potatoes, molasses, all spiced with peppers. Small amounts of pork were consumed, along with crawfish, turtle, garfish, and alligator.[47] Emancipation does not seem to have changed what was available. African Americans living around Tuskegee, Alabama, in 1895–1896 ate salt pork, molasses and corn meal, which was mixed with water, formed into the shape of small cakes, and baked in the fireplace on a griddle or the flat surface of a hoe. Black families in Eastern Virginia along the Chesapeake Bay around the same time were better off in terms of variety and nutrition than were the people in Alabama, being able to supplement the same regime of pork, cornbread and molasses with small game, fish, turtles and frogs.[48]

Whites in the rural South had a diet similar to that of African Americans. In largely white eastern Kentucky in 1902, the population ate fat bacon, corn bread, and a few vegetables. To combat this overreliance on unhealthful food, northern home economists aided by philanthropists set up a model school and kitchen in Hazard, Kentucky. The meals consisted of nutritionists' favorites of the time, such as meatloaf and croquettes made from canned salmon. Eventually the volunteers who ran the kitchen reluctantly complied with the students' desire for familiar cornbread served with molasses or sorghum syrup. Many years later, in 1960, blacks and whites in the Deep South still depended on pork, cornbread made with sugar or sorghum syrup, field peas cooked with fatback, buttermilk biscuits, turnip greens, and sweet potato cobbler.[49]

Such affinity between black and white keeps getting obscured and rediscovered. A recent *New York Times* article by Julia Moskin interviews Todd Richard, an African American restaurateur in Atlanta, and Virginia Willis, a white chef, photographer, and Southern cookbook writer. Willis notes that the black-and-white divide is "a huge piece smack in the middle of the Southern food conversation," an observation that has the effect, as Moskin puts it, of "putting the elephant in the room right on the lunch table." The participants in the interview agree that class influences more than race what people eat.[50]

Better-off Southerners have historically had access to more elegant and varied food, even if some of them waxed nostalgic about wholesome simplicity. The physician and humorist George Bagby in *The Old Virginia Gentleman* (published in 1877), remarked, "Few other things besides bacon and greens are required to make a true Virginian." This affected frugality is followed by other typical Virginia foods—ash cakes, fritters, barbecued shoat, cracklin' bread, fried apples, butter beans, and catfish are just a few examples. At the end of the long list, he reiterates that the only real requirement is bacon and greens.[51] Bagby's post–Civil War nostalgia exaggerates the folk elements of what wealthy Virginians actually consumed. Their meals were prepared by unfree labor, and their culinary cues were still defined by Britain. Imported wine, spices, pastry, trifle, and syllabub (a frothy drink made with cream and sweet flavorings) were more prestigious than catfish and butter beans.

If we look for the roots of a distinctive Southern cuisine in early cookbooks, we are likely to be mystified. *The Virginia Housewife* by Mary Randolph, published in 1824, is the first book of recipes printed in the South.[52] Randolph does offer instructions for catfish curry, black-eyed pea cakes, okra soup, beaten biscuits, and other dishes regarded as Southern.[53] Overall, however, the cookbook is less regional than the title would suggest and reflects the same English-influenced cuisine that well-off Northerners aspired to. Randolph's book bears a strong resemblance to the contemporaneous *The Cook's Own Book* by "a Boston Housekeeper"; both take their cues from English recipes, or really from French recipes as modified in England—things like beef à la mode, haricot of mutton, stewed duck, and fish à la matelote (with wine and onions).[54]

Only after the Civil War was Southern food presented as distinctly regional, part of a self-conscious effort at making the lost past luminous. Among the dining options at the 1876 Centennial exhibition at Philadelphia was the "Restaurant of the South." We don't know how regionally distinctive the food served there was, but one of the standard visitors' guides did mention that it featured an "old Plantation Darky band" that also reenacted "Southern plantation scenes."[55]

The most obvious feature of Southern distinctiveness was of course the mass enslavement of Africans and the continuing subordination of African Americans by the Jim Crow regime of segregation that reigned from the 1890s until the 1960s.[56] The history of the South is indeed inseparable from the history of its black population. Even now, after the Great Migration of 1910–1970 that brought so many African Americans from the South to northern and midwestern cities, eighty-eight counties in the states of the former Confederacy have a majority black population. No one would think to write about Southern music without including the blues, but it has been scandalously easy to obscure the origins and nature of Southern food—in essence, to whiten it. Though it required subterfuge, black people could be rendered invisible in the representation of Southern culinary identity.

Until relatively recently, tours of grand antebellum plantations failed to mention the presence of black slaves, and no effort was made to preserve remnants of slave quarters. It was as if the grand houses and grounds were magically devoid of material, economic foundation. When Colonial Williamsburg opened in the 1930s, slavery was not exactly denied, but it was downplayed.[57] There were no reconstructed kitchens except in the Governor's Palace, presided over by what a *House and Gardens* reporter described as "an honest-to-goodness Mammy."[58]

If pressed, the reenactors and local keepers of traditions admitted that Colonial Williamsburg, Monticello, and the Deep South plantations depended on bonded labor. Devoting on-site attention to that enslaved labor, however, was considered no more relevant than having an exhibit about steel workers at the Carnegie and Frick mansions, or railroad laborers at Biltmore, the Vanderbilt estate, or, for that matter, serfs at a European medieval castle.

The same syndrome of separating and obscuring is evident in how Southern cuisine was described after Reconstruction. Even the authoritative Library of Congress rules for book cataloguing group cookbooks that white people wrote under the rubric "Southern cooking," while what black people prepare is, depending on the period, "Negro cookery," "Soul food cooking," or "African American cooking." In a subject search, it is difficult to find black cooking within the category of Southern cooking, or to realize that they are even related.[59]

Nevertheless, any serious investigation shows that what people ate in the South was derived in large measure from ingredients and cooking methods brought over from Africa. Yams, okra, watermelon, and black-eyed peas, along with forms of cooking that would influence or create gumbo and barbecue in the New World—all originated in Africa. American ingredients could be substituted for familiar African styles of cooking: New World sweet potatoes supplemented African yams; millet was replaced by corn in various forms such as hominy, corn pudding, mush, or cornbread.[60]

TWO AFRICAN AMERICAN RECIPES

New Year's Black-Eyed Peas

1 pound dried black-eyed peas

1 ham hock, a piece of salt pork or bacon, or smoked turkey

1 cup chopped onion (optional)

Salt to taste

1 tsp Kitchen Pepper*

1 crushed fish or cayenne pepper or 1 Tb. Fish Pepper Sauce*

A few tsp. molasses (optional)

Fresh herbs of your choice

Sort your peas, making sure you check for pebbles or bad peas. Soak the peas for several hours or overnight, or if in a rush, soak them in boiling hot water for 30 minutes before cooking. Prepare a stock of salt meat and onion and season with salt, Kitchen Pepper, and a hot pepper. Boil these together for 15 minutes and add the black-eyed peas. Add enough water to cover. If you like, you can add some molasses for more flavor, or the fresh herbs. Cook for an hour and a half. Pair it with corn pone.

*Kitchen Pepper

1 cup coarsely ground black pepper

1 tsp ground white pepper

1 tsp red pepper flakes

1 tsp ground mace

1 tsp ground Ceylon cinnamon

1 tsp ground nutmeg

1 tsp ground allspice

1 tsp ground ginger

Mix together. Store in a cool place.

*Fish Pepper Sauce

15 to 20 fish peppers

Kosher salt

4 cups apple cider vinegar or
rum

Take fish peppers and cut off the tops and tips of the pods. A few peppers, say 5 or so, should be hopped to a pulp in a food processor. Add a pinch or two of salt. Take this pulp and place at the bottom of a jar. The rest of the peppers can be sliced down the middle, exposing the seeds, or left whole. Place them on top of the pulpy mixture and cover in the bottle with apple cider vinegar or rum. Shake well and let steep 2 to 3 weeks before using.

From Michael W. Twitty, *The Cooking Gene* (New York: HarperCollins, 2017), 380.

Candied Yams (using sweet potatoes)

1½ to 2 pounds small sweet potatoes

¼ teaspoon ground cinnamon

¼ teaspoon ground nutmeg

½ cup (1 stick) butter

½ cup firmly packed dark brown sugar

Peel the sweet potatoes and cut them in large wedges. Place the potatoes, cinnamon, and nutmeg in a large saucepan and cover with water. Bring to a boil, reduce the heat, and simmer until the potatoes are tender when pierced with the tip of a knife, 20 to 30 minutes. Drain them well.

In the same saucepan, melt the butter and brown sugar over medium-low heat, stirring until smooth. Add the sweet potatoes and stir to coat. Cook over medium heat until the potatoes are warm and the sauce bubbles, about 3 minutes. Serve warm.

From Adrian Miller, *Soul Food* (Chapel Hill: University of North Carolina, 2013), 184.

The old orthodox version of white Southern culinary history did acknowledge African origins for specific products while limiting the role of actual African Americans in creating the cuisine. The most common way of marking, even celebrating African American participation in Southern cuisine while assuring white intellectual property was to depict the mistress of the great house as the custodian of tradition and the black cook as executor of that tradition. The latter could be portrayed as supremely skilled but cooking in an instinctual and subliterate fashion, incapable of putting into writing or scientific measurement what she knew how to do. This attitude was common during the period of slavery. "The negroes are born cooks," a South Carolina plantation owner's daughter said, so much so that if one of the cooks fell ill, any field hand (male or female) could be called in as a reliable substitute. A guest at one antebellum feast in Louisiana's St. Mary's parish reckoned that one of the black Creole cooks could tempt the devil himself, but skillful as the cook might be, the dish still required "the inspiration of Madame," her mistress.[61]

This notion of cooks skilled because of race persisted even after the Civil War ended. A historian of Louisiana writing in 1880 remarked, "The Negro is a born cook" even though he could not read and so learn from books. It was sufficient that "the god of the spit and the saucepan had breathed life into him."[62] The stereotypic household cook was more often female. The "Mammy" was made enduringly and ignominiously popular by the Aunt Jemima brand of baking products, which typified Southern culinary heritage marketing. Toni Tipton-Martin, an authority on African American cookbooks, identifies the years 1900–1950 as the era of "Mammyism," when corporations created Aunt Jemima, Uncle Ben, and other images of subjugated but colorful cooking traditions. The black woman in the kitchen was credited with marvelous cooking powers. In the 1930s, *The Southern Cook Book of Fine Old Recipes* described "the old mammy, head tied with a red bandanna, a jovial, stoutish, welcome personage . . . a wizard in the art of creating savory, appetizing dishes from plain everyday ingredients."[63] In *200 Years of Charleston Cooking*, published in 1931, the (white) authors wonder if one of the black cooks is a genius or simply a divine gift to Charleston.

The untutored black expert could be regarded as exasperating, however,

Omega Flour cookbook, 1940s. Some sections are introduced by a black cook in the employ of a leading Southern local family. This dates from the period of what Toni Tipton-Martin calls "Mammyism," as described in her book *The Jemima Code*, pp. 54–55.

particularly when a white housewife attempted to obtain a recipe. The cook for John Rutledge, the first governor of South Carolina, responded to a question about what went into his roast oysters by saying "a little bit of this and a little bit of that." How long should they cook? Just long enough. What recipe did he use? His father had learned from the Chickasaw Indians.[64] One hundred fifty years later, in a Savannah cookbook (1933), Harriet Ross Colquitt resigns herself to the fact that "getting directions from colored cooks is rather like trying to write down the music to the spirituals they sing."[65] Recipes in the 1953 *Edgefield* (South Carolina) *Guest Book* feature a photograph of Aunt Mittie Wigfall, a cook for the Thompkins family who knows how to make "victuals beyond compare" but operates entirely "by ear."

Actually, she *does* measure everything, she is quoted as asserting, "right in de palm of my han."[66]

The voice of the black servant speaking in what purports to be authentic dialect is one way of finessing the putative difficulty of understanding the inspired knowledge of black female cooks. Many cookbooks of the Mammy Era were ventriloquist exercises in which a white cookbook writer interpreted or more often made up a black informant, much as "minstrel shows" depicted carefree and comical black people using white actors in blackface. *Aunt Priscilla in the Kitchen* (1929) is an infamous example of this peculiar masquerade. Like Betty Crocker, Aunt Priscilla was a fictional icon, invented by the *Baltimore Sun* newspaper to deal with readers' questions about cooking. Eleanor Purcell, a white employee at the *Sun*, answered inquiries in the guise of Aunt Priscilla, as in this response to a request for a crab cake recipe: "I'se bery glad to gib you de crab recipes Miss Katie, speshully as serbil mo' ladies done ast fo' de same. Try yo' crab cakes dis way."[67]

Not all Southern white people embraced the paternalistic imagery of black culinary creativity. Forward-looking women, members of civic clubs as well as home economists and food reformers, tried to substitute white female labor for black cooks whom they regarded as slovenly and insubordinate. Mrs. James A. Kirk, the president of the Fenelon Club in Birmingham, contrasted the intelligence and self-respect of poor white women with African American "dishonesty and utter disregard to morality and cleanliness." The former should be rescued from mill labor and taught domestic service. The wives of upper-middle-class notables wanted food in touch with what was considered scientific opinion about nutrition, with neither the grease nor the local color of the Old South: salmon patties with white sauce rather than fried pork with greens. The campaign to train poor white women did not succeed, and affluent Southern ladies continued to employ black domestic workers while their less affluent white sisters had to rely on their own resources.[68]

Under segregation, the fact that Southern food was cooked by African Americans was generally acknowledged, and even gratuitously celebrated. This changed after the Second World War. The struggle over Civil Rights eventually resulted in a legal victory for justice and integration, but the postwar decades also witnessed the mechanization of cotton and many other kinds of work formerly dependent on an African American labor force, isolating blacks and whites economically and socially. It was this era, more than the hegemonic Jim Crow period of roughly 1890–1950, that saw an effort to come up with a Southern cuisine separate from that of the African American population. If slavery or segregation could no longer be presented as advantageous for all concerned, then what black people cooked could be marginalized as "soul food" while whites reclaimed "Southern" food for themselves.

A collateral result of the Civil Rights era was that the South became an embarrassment to much of the rest of the country, so its culinary history and character were increasingly ignored. The cuisine and lifestyle magazine *Gourmet* in the 1940s and 1950s had depicted the South as a bastion of gracious hunt balls, stiff damask, ancestral silver, and elegant food. Black servants grinned in the background. By the 1960s, however, the magazine could no longer market this version of Southern hospitality and so tended to bypass the region altogether.[69]

John T. Edge has described the place of Southern cuisine and shared meals in the struggles for justice waged by black people in the South. He identifies the role of food in relation to the Civil Rights movement as exemplified by the careers of segregationist restaurateurs like Lester Maddox in Georgia and Maurice Bessinger in South Carolina.[70] Edge also outlines the marketing of a hokey, picturesque white South that reached its peak during the Jimmy Carter years, anticipated by the success of *The Beverly Hillbillies*, which began airing in 1962. In the years of the television programs *Hee Haw* and *Mayberry R.F.D.* (both began in 1969), when country music ascended into national popularity, Southern folkways and food were whitened. Appalachian hillbilly stereotypes were borrowed as the old plantation South receded. This version of the South had little space for black people—remarkably, Mayberry (a fictional town in North Carolina) was all white for its first seven years.[71]

Southern food retained certain ingredients like grits and country ham, but its cooking lost its former careful, craft aspect. *Being Dead Is No Excuse*, an entertaining and only slightly exaggerated guide for Southern women hosting "the perfect funeral," was written in 2005, but it reflects customs long in place. The authors, describing the folkways of white people in the Mississippi Delta, deride the notion that fresh food is preferable to casseroles. The naïve and pushy niece of one Delta lady flew in from California for a funeral and had the effrontery to suggest a Cobb salad, claiming she had consumed enough Velveeta and cream of mushroom soup to last until her own demise. The response to this suggestion was not favorable: "A *Cobb* salad? When someone has *died*? Frankly, none of us could believe our ears. Sarah wrote her niece out of her will. Somebody so un-Southern wouldn't have the foggiest notion what to do with the family silver."[72]

The 1970s also saw the solidification of soul food as a sign of African American identity. In the North and Midwest, what had formerly been referred to neutrally as "Southern," or more affectionately as "down home" food, was now the possession of black people rather than a transplanted, integrated style.[73]

SOUL FOOD DISHES

Fried chicken
  (oven-fried or corn
  flake–fried with
  cheddar waffles)
Nanticoke catfish
Creole broiled catfish
Catfish curry
Chitlins Duran
Deep-fried chitlins
Black-eyed peas
Purple hull peas
Macaroni and cheese
  (three recipes—
  the relevant chapter
title is "How Did
  Macaroni and Cheese
  Get So Black?")
Mixed greens
Sweet potato greens
Spoon bread
Candied yams
Candied carrots
Hot water corn bread
Minnie Utsey's "never fail"
  cornbread
Kool-Aid
Banana pudding
Peach crisp

From Adrian Miller, *Soul Food* (Chapel Hill: University of North Carolina, 2013).

Not all African Americans liked the exaltation of soul food, especially as many did not have recent Southern antecedents. Others regarded soul food as a heritage item but not a matter of present identity. In *A Date with a Dish*, the 1948 cookbook put out by the middle- to upper-class African American magazine *Ebony*, the first chapter is entitled "Collector's Corner" and includes chitterlings, pigs' tails and feet, collard greens, and opossum with sweet potatoes. Freda DeKnight, the author of *A Date with a Dish*, describes the book's intention as compiling and presenting "authentic Negro recipes," but she denies that such authenticity is limited to Southern clichés like greens, chicken, and cornpone. After all, Boston baked beans are a part of black culinary heritage as it was black cooks who often prepared it.[74]

African American cookbook authors in the era of soul food acknowledged the Southern context but distinguished between ingredients and experience. Bob Jeffries defined *soul* as inherent in the cook and the person eating, not so much in the food itself. All soul food might be Southern, but not all Southern food has soul.[75] A similar definition based on factors external to the actual dishes is a reworking of the old theme of black women cooking by instinct. "Vibration cooking" is what Vertamae Smart-Grosvenor called the inner knowledge of quantities without the need to follow directions.[76]

The separation of soul food from Southern food was fine with white custodians of Southern identity. Certain characteristic foods now were marked as exclusively African American. Pig extremities (jowl, tail, feet), small wild animals (snapper turtles, raccoon, opossum), and wild plants (poke salat, pawpaw) became black property. This was arbitrary and new. Mark Twain had included chitterlings in a list of foods he missed, and nineteenth-century plantation owners not only ate chitterlings with pleasure, but also got into altercations with their cooks about their preparation.[77] By the mid-twentieth century, however, the separation of black and white Southern cooking had become an agreed-upon fact.

After 1960 or so, apart from a few widely recognized and easily marketable dishes such as grits or ham and biscuits, Southern food was relegated to colorful lunch places, remnants of pseudo-gracious dining and special spots on the order of Doe's Eat Place in Greenville, Mississippi, for steaks, or Charlie Vergos in Memphis for barbecued ribs. A Southern culinary renaissance began slowly in the 1980s but always had a number of contradictions. It was hard to revive dishes from a rural past of the sort recollected by Edna Lewis from her Virginia childhood. The suburbanization and homogenization of the South and a sense of loss—the inability to find the flavors Lewis remembered from the farm of her childhood—led her in 1992 to predict the imminent extinction of Southern cuisine.[78]

Despite periodic moments of fascination with the South, the food as presented to non-Southerners became unappealing. The rest of the country—and indeed many Southerners themselves—perceived game, cornmeal baked goods, and vegetables cooked with pork as unpleasant or unhealthful. One approach to popularize or revive culinary memory was to use Southern ingredients to mimic the innovations of Mediterranean or California cuisine. Examples of peculiar reinterpretations and attempted modernization include hoppin' John risotto or egg rolls stuffed with tasso and collard greens.[79] A turning point came with restaurants like Frank Stitt's Highlands Bar and Grill in Birmingham, Alabama, which opened in 1982. Stitt and his followers based their cooking on a closer relationship with sources, ingredients, and traditions that were neither the monochrome food of the poor nor the eclectic, hard-to-describe tastes of the well-off. Recently, chefs such as Sean Brock at Husk in Charleston, South Carolina, have paid attention not just to locality but also to reviving the lost breeds and varieties of the past.[80]

I am not sure I agree with John T. Edge that the culture of the entire United States has come to look like that of the South. He is right, however, that the South has played a key part in the movement to reject industrial food and pay attention to tradition and the quality of basic ingredients. This is not so much because of the region's intrinsic virtue, but because it never went quite as far as other parts of the country in destroying its small farms, rural knowledge, and food traditions. These are more easily restored in the South than in places like New England or the Northwest, where they have had to be reinvented from scratch.[81]

New Orleans Creole Cuisine

No other part of the United States has preserved its regional cuisine to the degree that Louisiana has. This is both because of its French basis and because the southern part of the state has simultaneously a cosmopolitan immigration history (New Orleans) and a rural version of French cooking (the Acadian, "Cajun" parishes). There are two distinct culinary traditions here, Creole and

Cajun. Rice and gumbo are important to both, but Creole is an urban cuisine of New Orleans with more bread, butcher's meat, and fancy desserts, while the Cajun bayous have afforded more opportunity for game, crawfish, and alligator. Cajun food tends to be spicy, while Creole style is rich with butter and sauces. New Orleans Creole cuisine has a long history of exterior projection and tourism. Cajun food, first popularized by Paul Prudhomme in the 1980s, is often confused with Creole, partly because Prudhomme's K-Paul restaurant was in New Orleans, but they have distinct histories and aesthetic principles.[82] The

Austin Leslie's Creole-Soul cookbook cover. Leslie (1935–2005) became one of the most famous New Orleans chefs, first working for his aunt, who owned Chez Helene, and then buying the restaurant in 1975. He died in the aftermath of Hurricane Katrina, after having been trapped by floodwaters for two days in his stifling attic.

French who colonized New Orleans were immigrants directly from France, and later French refugees from the Caribbean, especially Saint-Domingue (Haiti), where, beginning in 1791 a slave revolt and revolution drove out the sugar planter class and its administrators. The Acadians, by contrast, were French Canadians expelled from the Maritime Provinces in a brutal act of ethnic cleansing by the victorious English after the mid-eighteenth-century Seven Years' War.

The distinctiveness of French cuisine created food traditions in Louisiana that were stronger than those of New England, the South, or anywhere else among American regions.

The key event in marketing Creole cuisine to the rest of the country was the 1884–1885 New Orleans "World's Industrial and Cotton Centennial Exposition." Before the Civil War, New Orleans had been the nation's second largest city, exporting the products of the South and Midwest that came down the Mississippi River. It was also the great entrepôt for slave trafficking in America.[83] By the 1880s, the combination of the Civil War's effects and the efficiency of the railroads had somewhat dimmed the exotic city's prospects. The Exposition, marking the supposed hundredth anniversary of the first cotton exported from New Orleans, was intended to boost commerce and tourism.

The fair of 1884–1885 drew national attention to the Creole food of New Orleans and resulted in a "Creole boom."[84] Two influential cookbooks came out of this occasion: *The Creole Cookery Book* by the Christian Women's Exchange, a Protestant charity, and *La Cuisine Creole* by Lafcadio Hearn, better known as a figure in literary history.[85] Neither cookbook was produced by a member of the actual French population of New Orleans. The Christian Women's Exchange consisted of American rather than Creole notables, since the latter were firmly Catholic. Lafcadio Hearn, of mixed Greek and Irish heritage and a versatile man of letters, had lived in New Orleans for only eight years; shortly after publication of *La Cuisine Creole*, he moved to Japan, taking on a Japanese name (Koizumi Yakumo) and achieving his greatest fame by introducing foreigners to the restrained perfection of the Japanese aesthetic.

There is nothing unusual or wrong about outsiders popularizing cultural artifacts. Paul Gauguin and Margaret Mead immortalized the allure of the South Seas; Lord Byron and then, over a century later, Patrick Leigh Fermor

CUISINE OF LOUISIANA

"Signature Dishes" of New Orleans

Sazerac (a cocktail)	Gumbo
French bread	Trout amandine
Shrimp remoulade	Red beans and rice
Oysters Rockefeller	Mirliton (chayote) and
Daube glacé (cold sliced	shrimp
and chopped meat	Creole tomato salad
with herbs, served in	Creole cream cheese
aspic)	Bread pudding
Turtle soup	Café brûlot

Typical Cajun Dishes

Maque choux (corn	Boudin (sausage made
stew)	with pork and rice)
Jambalaya	Tasso (dried smoked
Roux	meat)
Gumbo	Andouille
	Étouffée

From *New Orleans Cuisine: Fourteen Signature Dishes and Their Histories*, ed. Susan Tucker and S. Frederick Starr (Jackson: University Press of Mississippi, 2009); Marcelle Bienvenu, Carl A. Brasseaux and Ryan A. Brasseaux, *Stir the Pot: The History of Cajun Cuisine* (New York: Hippocrene Books, 2008).

made Greece the object of romantic reverence. Often it takes someone foreign to the culture to present it to an otherwise ill-informed public. This was the case for Creole customs; indeed, despite decades of literary production (in French, it is true), there was little interest in the peculiar history of New

Orleans during the years of its prosperity and expansion before the Civil War. The discovery of Creole food was part of an enthusiasm for French traditions in Louisiana, an enthusiasm that grew at the same time that the actual use of the French language in literature and journalism was disappearing.[86] The sunset was garish and splendid as the romantic French Quarter replaced the run-down French Quarter in the twinkling of an eye, and what American inhabitants of New Orleans had previously regarded as retrograde, superstitious, and foreign became a tourist attraction.[87] "Local color" proved to be marketable, and the Exposition of 1884–1885 created the modern tourism industry of New Orleans, based not only on architecture, history, and atmosphere but also on food.[88]

The two Exposition-era cookbooks comprise a small number of clearly region-specific dishes and a lot of generic upper-middle-class American food such as leg of mutton, oxtail soup, chicken curry, or veal and ham timbales. In introducing *La Cuisine Créole*, Lafcadio Hearn emphasized both the French basis of Creole cuisine and the influences of many nationalities and cultures, including West Indian and Mexican. Yet once one gets beyond gumbo and crawfish bisque, Hearn's recipes have no recognizable regional origin, and many were copied from standard cookbooks such as *The Improved Housewife* (first published in 1844) and *The Successful Housekeeper* (1882). *The Creole Cookery Book* borrows heavily from *The Buckeye Cookbook*, which is itself not particularly representative of Ohio, the Buckeye State.[89]

The Picayune's Creole Cook Book of 1900, sponsored by the New Orleans *Daily Picayune* newspaper, was more thoroughly local in content and inspiration.[90] It has lengthy introductions to chapters and dishes that discuss not only Creole cooks' recipes (a total of 1,560), but also the characteristic ways of preparing meat, what fish were taken from the Gulf, and the seasons and local geography of oysters. This cookbook saw sixteen editions through 1989 and remains a defining text for the regional style.

In publicizing the book, the newspaper claimed that Creole cooking was endangered by the gradual passing away of former slaves whose "secrets of the Louisiana Kitchen" were in danger of dying with them.[91] Many of the recipes had been gathered by visiting "the old Creole 'mammies'" who still tended the

kitchens of prominent families, but soon, white housewives would have to figure things out for themselves. Preserving cooking knowledge was portrayed as
a cultural rescue mission.

The Creole literary elite of the nineteenth century rejected black influence on anything having to do with bloodlines and genealogy, but the general
Southern truism was accepted: the black cook is the custodian of culinary tradition; not its creator, to be sure, but its executor. The first four editions of *The
Picayune Creole Cook Book* (the possessive "*Picayune's*" was dropped), published
between 1900 and 1910, emphasized the heritage created by black women in
the kitchen. This was maintained with varying degrees of emphasis until the
eighth edition in 1936, when the black role was minimized in favor of a male
and elite story of the diffusion of Creole cuisine through public settings such
as restaurants. In 1947, the ninth edition dispensed with the image of the black
woman with a headscarf in favor of a male chef with upturned mustaches, a
French auteur. Midcentury tourist promotions for New Orleans typified its
cuisine as that served by restaurants, finessing or ignoring the origins of the
particular cooking style under a rubric of New Orleans's appreciation for "the
finer things in life."

Insofar as the nature and formation of Creole food was treated during most
of the twentieth century, it was portrayed as the product of many influences,
restoring variety and mixture to the word *Creole*. A typical product of cautious
multiculturalism is a booklet from the late 1930s entitled *Louisiana's Fabulous
Foods and How to Cook Them*. Its brief preface refers to a French cuisine developed for "gentlemen of high rank" who came to the colony from France. The
influence of Spaniards, Italians, and American Indians is acknowledged, but
nothing is said about African Americans.[92]

The displacement of African Americans was never completely successful.
Lena Richard, an African American chef and restaurateur, achieved local fame
catering for the parties given by New Orleans socialites in the 1930s and, beginning in 1937, she taught classes in what was explicitly described as "Creole Cooking."[93] The *Times Picayune* correspondent remarked that Richard (referred to as
"Lena") seemed unfazed and unsurprised that a "negro woman" would presume
to teach "white folks" about Creole cooking. In 1940, Richard published 333

recipes under the title *New Orleans Cook Book* and, interestingly enough, reversed conventional discourse by describing her plan to reveal to a wide public "the secrets of Creole cooking which have been kept for years by the old French chef." In 1947, the same year that the *Picayune Creole Cook Book* eliminated its African American cover image, Lena Richard began hosting one of the nation's first television cooking programs. It's unfortunate that none of the footage from her biweekly show appears to have survived.[94]

As racially segregated and hierarchical as anywhere in the South, New Orleans sometimes allowed privileges to exceptional black figures, so Louis Armstrong, for example, was exempted from some rules about segregation. Lena Richard's restaurant Lena's Eatery, which opened in 1941, was allowed to go against local ordinances by serving black and white people together. Lesser-known representatives of the black Creole tradition tended to be ignored, although in 1971, the Time-Life cookbook volume on Louisiana featured black-owned Chez Helene with Helen DeJean Pollock and her family and African American chefs alongside the white owners of Brennan's, Antoine's, and Galatoire's. In 1978, the compendium *Creole Feast* presented recipes from fifteen black Creole chefs. The introduction notes the "curious effort to ascribe a

Lena Richard, television show set. Richard was one of the first
television chefs. Her program, *Lena Richard's New Orleans Cook Book*,
ran on WDSU in New Orleans from 1947 until her death in 1950.

secondary, lowly or nonexistent role to the Black hand in the pot," despite the fact that the most consistent aspect of Creole cuisine is "the Black element."[95]

From the time of its popularization in the late nineteenth century, New Orleans cuisine has been depicted as vibrant yet endangered, exceptional but beleaguered. Threats include the same infatuation with standard brands and processed food that undermined or destroyed other distinctive regional cuisines, but New Orleans could be offered up as resistant to the siren song of convenience, an exceptional place where taste and enjoyment were more important than efficiency and ambition. New Orleans's unique food was noted with approval by guidebooks and other tourist publications, and in many respects the golden age of the fine New Orleans restaurants of the Antoine's, Arnaud's, or Commander's Palace type coincided with what is usually identified as the nadir of American epicureanism from Prohibition to the 1970s.

Other perils to New Orleans have included population loss, a declining economy, ecological damage inflicted by the oil and chemical industries to its once rich environs, and the consequences of natural and human disasters of which Hurricane Katrina in 2005 was only the most notorious and severe. As with the rest of the South, New Orleans experienced several false starts in the 1970s and 1980s in its efforts to present a modern, sophisticated dining scene. New Orleans hosted another world's fair in 1984, the hundredth anniversary of the 1884 Cotton Centennial Exposition. While its effects were not as dramatic as those of its predecessor, the 1984 event coincided with a change in New Orleans gastronomy toward trendy New American fashions. As the luster of the traditional shrines of the French Quarter faded, new places sprang up offering something resembling the aesthetic pioneered in California: grilling, rejection of rich sauces (previously the great accomplishment of Creole restaurants), seafood from other regions (scallops, for example), more diverse ethnic influences, more pasta, and more spices.[96]

The personality who most dramatically affected both tourism and local image was Paul Prudhomme, a gifted chef with a contagious and charismatic enjoyment of life. His tastes formed by the spiced, smoked, and cured food of his Cajun farm home, Prudhomme brought a lustier cuisine to genteel New Orleans—this is the man who invented the turducken, after all. Additionally,

Prudhomme popularized an attitude of defiant, unkempt joyfulness that would be taken up by later luminaries like Anthony Bourdain, Guy Fieri, and Emeril Lagasse.[97]

No longer unique for its passionate gourmandise, New Orleans has had a difficult time negotiating twenty-first-century cuisine. The city has been affected by the decline of well-heeled tourism and elegance. The elegiac *Lost Restaurants of New Orleans* is such an accomplished work of historical nostalgia that even if one has no personal recollection of these monuments, the effect is still poignant.[98]

Maylie's Turtle Soup

Near the public markets, the big meal at Maylie's (closed in 1983 after 113 years) originally was lunch, served after the market closed. New Orleans turtle soup is traditionally of thicker consistency than elsewhere.

3 lb. turtle meat, veal shoulder, or combination, including any bones

3 bay leaves

3 whole cloves

Peel of 1 lemon, sliced

1 Tb. salt

½ tsp. black peppercorns

2 sticks butter

½ cup flour

2 ribs celery, chopped

2 medium onions, chopped

1 small green bell pepper, chopped

2 cloves garlic, finely chopped

½ tsp. thyme

½ tsp marjoram

1 cup dry sherry

2 Tbs. Worcestershire sauce

1 cup tomato purée

1 tsp. black pepper

1 Tbs. Louisiana hot sauce

2 hard-boiled eggs, chopped

1 bunch flat-leaf parsley, leaves only, chopped

Simmer the turtle meat and veal with bones in 1 gal. water, along with the bay leaves, cloves, lemon peel, salt, and black peppercorns. Keep the simmer going for about 2 hours.

Strain the stock, reserving the liquid and meat. If you don't have at least 3 qt. stock, add water or veal stock to get up to that quantity. Chop the meat into small shreds and set aside.

Make a medium-dark roux (the color of a well-used penny) with the butter and flour. When the roux is the right color, add the celery, onions, bell pepper, and garlic, and cook until the vegetables are soft. Add thyme, marjoram, sherry, Worcestershire, and tomato purée. Cook for one minute then add the stock.

Lower the heat and add the pepper, hot sauce, and meat. Simmer for a half-hour, then add the eggs and parsley and simmer for 10 minutes more. It's ready to serve now, but it gets better if you let it simmer 1 or 2 more hours.

From Peggy Scott Laborde and Tom Fitzmorris, *Lost Restaurants of New Orleans* (Gretna, LA: Pelican Publishing Co., 2012), 168–69.

Louisiana Creole and Cajun cuisine remain the most successful American regional survivals, even if the actual, everyday consumption of traditional dishes at home is modest. In 2005 and 2007, schoolchildren in New Orleans were asked to keep a food diary. The nine hundred responses show families eating the same things as Americans elsewhere, except for red beans and rice, gumbo, and shrimp for holiday meals. Only one family had daube glacé, and another made turtle soup.[99] Yet at least in terms of passionate interest and the expansion of an already-vibrant restaurant scene, post-Katrina New Orleans has defied expectations and gives reason for hope in the face of adversity.

✦   ✦   ✦

HAVING OFFERED NEW ENGLAND, the South, and New Orleans as examples of culinary heritage, next we will examine how journalists, writers of guides, cookbook authors, and even fiction writers have presented America's regional cuisine. The interplay between authentic and dressed-up history has already been shown in how New England's supposed frugal virtues were applied to teaching immigrants to cook American, or how legends of the Old South dealt with the legacy of slavery—or evaded it. In what follows, the emphasis will be on the idealizations and distortions surrounding the subject of American cuisine generally, and its regional variations in particular.

CHAPTER 2

Culinary Nostalgia

Was there ever a vibrant set of regional cuisines in the United States? There is a good case for the years leading up to the Civil War, when geographical variation in diet was as pronounced as it ever was going to be.[1] East of the Great Plains, the population had been settled long enough to create patterns of food consumption that varied with the particular climate and soil conditions. Communication and preservation technologies were not yet so far advanced, however, as to facilitate national distribution, so most Americans had no choice: they ate locally, in keeping with the seasons and the environmental constraints of where they lived. What people consumed differed according to relative proximity to the ocean, temperature range, rainfall, soil fertility, and population density.

Many established regional dishes of this earlier era did not survive the twentieth century. Some disappeared because of environmental degradation—for example, canvasback ducks are no longer a mid-Atlantic delicacy. Others declined into near oblivion because tastes changed—who expects succotash in New England anymore? A few regional specialties have flourished, transformed into clichés of mass culinary culture, but their success has unmoored them from any specific origin. Chili has long since cast off from its anchorage in Mexican American households. More recently, Texas-style barbecue has become fashionable everywhere, as have New England lobster rolls. Southern fried chicken is ubiquitous, but beaten biscuits, once a well-known Southern specialty, are almost extinct, preserved only on the food equivalent of wildlife refuges because they are hard to make and come out hard and cracker-like. Country ham and biscuits or grits have an intermediate status; they are so common in the South that chains like Arby's and Cracker Barrel feature them, but only occasionally are such foods found outside the region.

The decline of regional food was noticed long ago. In 1926, that curmudgeonly cynic and arbiter of American culture H. L. Mencken lamented that restaurants in the United States all adhered to the same mediocrity of "tasteless roasts, banal beefsteaks" and vegetables "with no more taste than baled shavings."[2] You could no longer find satisfying Boston baked beans and you would look in vain for good steamed crabs in Baltimore or catfish in St. Louis.

Real and Invented Food Traditions

For well over a century, food writers of a more optimistic temperament than Mencken's have denied the obliteration of regional gastronomy, celebrating what they see as the dazzling variation of American cuisines and seeing their mission as defending vibrant diversity against uniformity imposed by modernization. These writers cherish regional food, sometimes as an endangered species but more often as evidence of a "real" America that lives in the countryside and small towns, a safe distance from the soulless cities with their indifference to tradition. Stories about America's rich food traditions often exaggerate the extent and strength of regional gastronomy, but what is interesting is not their accuracy but their appeal to a nation whose official narrative bubbles over with enthusiasm for change and technology, but whose citizens feel displaced from the comforting, familiar, and handmade.

Food stories about regional cuisine express a hope for continuity amidst change and for diversity within technology-driven conformity. Culinary observers want to see a colorful and flavorful world of folk food culture—of clambakes, fish fries, pulled pork, and cherry pies—behind the numbing sameness of the big highways, downtown skyscrapers and exurban sprawl. Such persistent desire for heritage shows how Americans think about food, even if the warm images do not mirror reality. In the nineteenth and early twentieth centuries, regional dishes were catalogued or praised, but by the Great Depression, writers about American food assumed that the regional diversity was fading, imperiled by modern sameness and neglect of tradition, and this continues to the present day.

One way of exalting and preserving regional cooking is to portray it as an authentic expression of the people. Nostalgia for supposedly simpler, well-established customs, including those related to cuisine, encourages "invented traditions," things that seem old and venerable but in fact are modern creations. Invented traditions are pseudo-ancient habits or cultural artifacts that do not, in fact, date from time immemorial but rather derive from a datable, relatively recent, moment.[3] Classic examples include the Scottish kilt and tartan patterns (developed in the late eighteenth and early nineteenth centuries) and Confederate memorials erected many decades after the Civil War to reinforce racial segregation.

The purpose of calling attention to invented traditions is not to dismiss them as mere commercial ploys or political mythology: Manufactured traditions have a way of becoming genuine traditions, identifying regions and their people. The fish taco did not grow up with the city of San Diego any more than the West Virginia pepperoni roll is a folk product of the Appalachian Mountains and hollows, but both are now strong local symbols.

Places and things evoke collective memory and a sense of continuity with the past. The Gettysburg battlefield is one such place, but so are sites with emotional significance not associated with any particular historical event, such as the Empire State Building or the Grand Canyon. Memory and place function together to respond to rapid social change and the disorienting acceleration of history.[4] I write this during the fiftieth anniversary of what was called the Summer of Love, the hippie renaissance (if that is the word) that in 1967 converged on San Francisco. In the wide world, this event has only minor historical significance, but in my own life it has a transformative meaning.

Food provides many such points of personal recollection, not just Marcel Proust's famous madeleine that summoned forth a multivolume work of art and memory, but the sense of time and place evoked by the first lobster roll tasted on a Cape Cod vacation or Grandma's homemade biscuits. Collective as opposed to individual food memories make the lobster roll emblematic of New England or the biscuits a symbol of the South. Identifying American foods with particular regions is more than just a convenient organizing device or an answer to the widespread derision of the very idea of American cuisine. It involves statements of cultural significance, putting together individuals with comparable experiences in a setting that is emotionally meaningful. You do not really have to enjoy grits in order to be authentically Southern, but the fact that such a belief is so widely shared is important.

Food is particularly powerful at attracting legends. Specialties thought to spring from the age-old habits of a region's peoples often turn out to be relatively recent and traceable to a particular inventor. So, for example, New England fried clams were popularized nationally by Howard Johnson's; Key lime pie was invented in 1941, based on a Magic Lemon Cream Pie recipe put out by Borden's condensed milk; Cincinnati chili, which can include spaghetti, grated cheese, onions, and kidney beans, was developed in 1922 by Tom Kiradjieff, a Macedonian immigrant.[5]

Meticulous accuracy is less important than what people think regional cuisine is. That grits, pork barbecue, or collard greens are unknown in many parts of the South such as Appalachia or southern Florida matters less than how these dishes mark a space and create an attachment.

Indeed, invented traditions infuse regional cuisines just about everywhere, and many "traditional" foods are not as old as most people believe. Italians only started using tomatoes in sauces in the nineteenth century. *Maultaschen*, filled pasta squares larger than Italian ravioli, are a beloved regional specialty in Swabia (southwestern Germany) and enjoy protected status from the European Union. Far from being a food whose origins are lost in the mists of ancient days, however, *Maultaschen* originated in the nineteenth century: their first appearance in a written source is 1831 and the first printed recipe dates from 1850.[6]

Haggis first appears in a Scottish source in 1747, not all that long ago for an Old World culinary landmark. Its fame is due to the Robert Burns poem "Address to a Haggis," penned in 1786. Not only was haggis unknown to the Scottish hero Robert Bruce in the Middle Ages or the Stuart kings of the seventeenth century, it seems to have been invented by the English. At least it comes up in a household and recipe book entitled *The English Hus-Wife* published in 1615.[7]

What follows is based on writings praising American regional food, invented and authentic. In the nineteenth century, food writers saw their mission as exalting American cuisine to refute explicit or implied foreign contempt or ignorance. After World War I, writing about America's culinary regions became an effort to preserve traditions increasingly threatened not by haute cuisine, but by the combination of progress, efficiency, and uniformity that made it easier for someone in Vermont to find Southern fried chicken than New England boiled dinner. H. L. Mencken was famous as a malcontent, but there were many less grumpy observers who shared his anguish over the demise of regional diversity.

Most of the writers described here cheerfully (or hopefully) denied that decline and blurring of distinctions. Explicitly or not, they extolled the culinary wealth of the United States, finding it in its small towns and farms, not in the big cities with their fancy French restaurants, and certainly not along the highways.

The first sustained defense of American cuisine in general and the culinary wealth of its particular places came after the Civil War. This conflict accelerated industrial food processing, expanded railroads, increased telegraph and newspaper circulation, and opened up the Western mountains and Great Plains to white settlement. For many Americans, these developments created a sense of gastronomic promise. The United States may have been made up of many different climates and habitats, but now modern communications could bring oysters to Montana and oranges to Boston. There was some sensitivity to the common charge that Americans really did not care about food or lack a real cuisine, but as yet no feeling of any loss of traditional foods of particular places.

Refuting Grand Duke Alexis, 1874

Mention has been made of a visit made in 1871–72 by the Russian Grand Duke Alexis. His offhand remark that there was no such thing as American cuisine, from a memoir of his trip published in 1874, was greeted in the United States with vigorous protest. It is worth looking at the incident in more detail here not because of Alexis himself, but for the ways in which the perceived insult was answered, especially in relation to a defense of America's regional specialties.

Some of the responses may have been triggered by a sense of the duke's ingratitude. After all, he had been fêted everywhere on his itinerary, met with President Grant, celebrated Mardi Gras in New Orleans, and shot buffalo on the plains.[8] A banquet at Delmonico's in New York featured a consommé named in his honor, followed by a dozen additional courses including California salmon with Genevoise sauce (a red-wine preparation made with the fish's head), venison cutlets in pepper sauce, and a complicated presentation of woodcocks in aspic.[9] No doubt this impressed the duke, but not as a particularly American meal.

Some version of the prince's casual observation continued to echo in the succeeding century and a half: there might be fine food available in the United States, but it was French. This opinion would be widely shared until the 1980s, and you didn't have to be a foreigner to see it. Craig Claiborne, editor of the first *New York Times* restaurant guide to New York City in 1964, gave three stars to only eight restaurants, seven of them French. In the 1972 edition of the *New York Times Guide*, the scale went up to four stars, and four out of those seven were French. Four years later, in Seymour Britchky's guide, all four four-star restaurants were French.[10]

Among those who responded indignantly to Duke Alexis, asserting that there was indeed a brilliant American culinary repertoire, was James Parkinson, a chef and restaurateur from Philadelphia. Parkinson had begun as an ice cream seller, but by the time of the Russian duke's visit in 1871, he was running a nationally famous restaurant. Parkinson's reputation was boosted by a David-versus-Goliath triumph over New York's Delmonico's in 1851. Parkinson was unexpectedly victorious over the most esteemed restaurant in the country with a seventeen-course dinner that lasted until dawn, convincing both New York and Philadelphia bon vivants to award him the laurel garland.[11]

The haste with which American hoteliers agreed with the duke's dismissal of American food annoyed Parkinson; he said, "The admission is well-nigh universal that the French 'Made Us' and that we are 'the sheep' of the French 'pastures.'" In fact, he went on, we have our own specialties and styles of cookery of which we should be proud, and as proof, he begins with American fish: shad and sturgeon, trout, lobsters, and oysters. Parkinson then points to the classic pair, canvasback ducks and Chesapeake Bay terrapin, as examples of uniquely American haute cuisine (both had in fact been included in the Delmonico's dinner for Alexis). In the nineteenth century generally, American gourmands offered wild animals such as ducks at the high end or opossum and raccoon at the low, as uniquely characteristic dishes, while vegetables unknown in Europe, such as pawpaw or sweet potato, were ignored.[12] Parkinson himself went beyond the conventional boasts about game to praise New England chowders, baked pork and beans, buckwheat cakes, and Jersey sausage. The greatest glory of the United States, according to Parkinson, is its ice cream, for which he, a confectioner by training, had a particular affection.[13] In his response to Prince Alexis's dismissal of American cuisine, Parkinson made regional styles together constitute a proud national cuisine. His remarks, published in response to an article about Alexis's memoir in the *Philadelphia Press*, were made in anticipation of the celebration in Philadelphia of the nation's centennial in 1876, which would provide, Parkinson hoped, evidence that would convince Alexis to withdraw his calumny.

Mark Twain, 1880

Another late-nineteenth century essay in praise of American food was written by Mark Twain. The celebrated author of stories about American life, particularly its humorous and self-deluding aspects, was not indifferent to elegant meals, but he appreciated the Southern-inflected food of his Missouri boyhood and the culinary wealth of far-flung parts of the United States. At the close of the 1870s, he wrote a comical but plaintive conclusion to his travel book, *A Tramp Abroad*, expressing culinary homesickness during his travels in Germany and listing American foods that he particularly longed for.

Many of these objects of gustatory nostalgia were identified with a particular city, state, or region: Boston bacon and beans and Philadelphia terrapin soup, for example. Eleven items are Southern, including fried chicken and hot hoe-

Chefs preparing terrapin at the Maryland Club, 1948. Terrapin remained the quintessential mid-Atlantic luxury dish well into the twentieth century. The Maryland Club kept live terrapin in zinc-lined pens until they were to be cooked.

cakes (there is a surprising amount of bread typified as Southern). Fried chicken would subsequently become available everywhere without completely losing its regional identity, while possum remained a Southern specialty.[14]

Apart from the fact that Twain missed foods that are now unfamiliar because of species depletion (prairie hens, for example), his list has some surprises. In a few instances, the food is still eaten, but the ideal place of origin has changed: Who would look for San Francisco mussels now? Twain had tastes different from those prevailing today, although steak and potato chips would still turn up in a contemporary American's list. Missing American coffee and cream might reflect the normal attachment to breakfast as comforting routine, but still there is something unlikely about it. The United States has never had

MARK TWAIN'S LIST OF MOST-MISSED AMERICAN FOODS

Radishes

Baked apples, with cream

Fried oysters

Stewed oysters

Frogs

American coffee, with
real cream

American butter

Fried chicken, Southern style

Porterhouse steak

Saratoga potatoes [i.e., potato
chips]

Broiled chicken, American style

Hot biscuits, Southern style

Hot wheat bread, Southern style

Hot buckwheat cakes

American toast

Clear maple syrup

Virginia bacon, broiled

Blue points, on the half shell

Cherrystone clams

San Francisco mussels, steamed

Oyster soup

Clam soup

Philadelphia terrapin soup

Oyster roasted in the shell,
Northern style

Soft-shell crabs

Connecticut shad

Baltimore perch

Brook trout, from the Sierra
Nevadas

Lake trout, from Tahoe

Sheep-head and croakers [types of
fish], from New Orleans

Black bass, from the Mississippi

American roast beef

Roast turkey, Thanksgiving style

Cranberry sauce

Celery

Roast wild turkey

Woodcock

Canvasback duck, from Baltimore

Prairie hens, from Illinois

Missouri partridges, broiled

Possum

Coon

Boston bacon and beans

Bacon and greens, Southern style

Hominy

Boiled onions

Turnips

Pumpkin

Squash

Asparagus

Butter beans

Sweet potatoes

Lettuce

Succotash

String beans

Mashed potatoes

Catsup

Boiled potatoes in their skins

New potatoes minus the skins

Early Rose potatoes, roasted
in the ashes, Southern style,
served hot

Sliced tomatoes with sugar or
vinegar

Stewed tomatoes

Green corn, cut from the ear and
served with butter and pepper

Green corn, on the ear

Hot corn pone, with chitlings,
Southern style

Hot hoe cake, Southern style

Hot egg bread, Southern style

Hot light bread, Southern style

Buttermilk

Iced sweet milk

Apple dumplings with real cream

Apple pie

Apple fritters

Apple puffs, Southern style

Peach cobbler, Southern style

Peach pie

American mince pie

Pumpkin pie

Squash pie

All sorts of American pastry

Fresh American fruit

Ice water

From Andrew Beahrs, *Twain's Feast: Searching for America's Lost Foods in the Footsteps of Samuel Clemens*
(New York: Penguin, 2011)

much of an international reputation for coffee compared to, say, Austria or Italy. You would think Germany could come up with more-than-adequate cream, but Twain hated all European cream, denouncing it as pale and fake, made from overworked cattle or diluted condensed milk. German coffee, too, Twain complained, was unconscionably weak. He never learned German but thought he ought to practice German phrases equivalent to "This tea isn't good" and "Isn't that something in the butter?"[15] Some of Twain's problems are attributable to living in hotels. Europe did not lack farms or agricultural traditions, and a

European staying in American hotels would hardly be exposed to the raccoon or corn pone with chitterlings Twain so missed.

Twain clearly believed there is an American cuisine composed of regional specialties. Some of these required local ingredients—Virginia bacon or Mississippi River black bass, for example—even if there were other places that produced these things. More often, regionalism is a style of preparation. It might appear as if you could easily fix bacon and greens or fried chicken outside the South according to a Southern recipe, but in his *Autobiography*, Twain expressed contempt for all Northern attempts to reproduce Southern fried chicken or cornbread.[16] According to Mark Twain, the best regional dishes in their authentic forms are not readily exportable.

In James Parkinson's critique of the Russian prince and Twain's homesickness for American food, the enemy is Europe. In the twentieth century, the opinion of foreign snobs became less important, and the real forces undermining American regional cuisine were domestic: technology and homogenization of tastes in particular. Against this background, culinary regionalism represented a real, hearty, no-nonsense America whose charming diversity was a counter to the featureless modern food landscape.

Duncan Hines, 1935: The First National Food Guide

It is more than a chronological jump from the post–Civil War world of Mark Twain to the America of the 1930s. The title of the definitive book on food in the period 1880–1930, *Revolution at the Table* by Harvey Levenstein, describes a true transformation.[17] The automobile became nearly universal, electricity as well. Although harshly restrictive anti-immigrant legislation of the 1920s had altered the dynamic of American population growth, waves of earlier migration had changed the gastronomic as well as sociological picture of the United States. Cooking based on the science of nutrition had replaced the opulent practices of the Gilded Ages, and the temporary but blighting triumph of Prohibition had allied with the ethos of efficiency and modernity to create a less sensuous culinary standard. Meals were smaller, advice on how to diet was ubiquitous, and the marketing of female beauty emphasized a slim and sporty look.

Environmental decline meant that many things from Twain's list were scarce (terrapin) or no longer cheap (oysters). Above all, the end of the nineteenth and the beginning of the twentieth centuries saw the triumph of large food companies that standardized old commodities such as flour (Pillsbury; General Mills) and created new ones like canned pineapple (Dole). A national cuisine—or at any rate, nationally distributed processed and packaged products—replaced regionalism, rural cooking methods, and basic ingredients.

Duncan Hines, 1880–1959. Hines had been famous as a national restaurant reviewer for many years when, in the early 1950s, he licensed the use of his name to various products, most famously a line of cake mixes owned by Nebraska Consolidated Mills, now Conagra.

What we eat now is hardly the same as during the Depression, but the food of the 1930s forms a recognizable substratum to contemporary American dining. In contrast, what Americans ate in Mark Twain's era amounts to another world for us today, but it was also alien during the interwar period. Massive social and cultural changes make the 1920s and 1930s a turning point in the history of American cuisine.

A once-famous restaurant guidebook writer exemplifies how regional cuisine was praised in the modern period of American history.[18] Insofar as his name is familiar today, Duncan Hines (1880–1959) is identified with a brand of cake mix, a sign of corporate homogenization and the opposite of regionalism. For anyone who grew up in the 1960s, Duncan Hines inhabited a category of possibly fictitious brand spokespersons, like Betty Crocker. But before he lent his name, late in life, to a variety of consumer products, he was a food celebrity.

Hines began as a traveling salesman for printing companies but, unlike most salespeople, he regarded the occupational hazard of finding good meals in unfamiliar places as a game rather than a tedious chore. At first, Hines undertook his restaurant research on weekends, driving around the Midwest with his wife, Florence (an odd way, one might think, to spend time off from a job that involved constant automotive travel). Changes in American life that eroded regional distinctions did not bother Hines, but he was very much aware, from hard experience, that a lot of bad food was served along the nation's roadsides. As he crisscrossed the country, at work or leisure, Hines was dismayed at the ubiquity of dirty restaurants with rancid food and so kept a record of what he considered to be exceptional places that offered wholesome food at a time when that was not easy to find.

In 1935, under the rubric "Adventures in Good Eating," Duncan Hines put together a list of 167 favorite restaurants and sent it to friends and business associates along with his Christmas cards. Already he had a reputation as a food expert, the result of a Chicago newspaper interview a year earlier, but the newsletter touched off what we would now call a "viral" response from others frustrated with the plethora of unhygienic restaurants serving awful food.[19] In June 1936, at his own expense, he published *Adventures in Good Eating for the Discriminating Motorist*, the first such national directory. Its success led him to update the guide, soon simply called *Adventures in Good Eating*, until his death. It continued publication for a few years after, until 1962.

Hines did not embark on a mission to salvage American regional food. Despite the title of his guide, he actually offered *respite* from adventure. The point was to make dining predictable. He was more interested in good steaks than in esoteric local specialties, though he did say he liked wild fiddlehead ferns as a New England specialty and praised California Chinese food.[20]

Hines organized his guidebooks, logically, by geography, and thus became the most visible prewar food writer to praise American cuisine in terms of its regions.[21] The dustjacket for his 1955 autobiography, *Duncan Hines' Food Odyssey*, is a colored stylized map of the US showing a lobster in Maine, orange trees in Florida and California, and leaping salmon in the Northwest. The automobile and the development of a network of highways had changed the culinary and physical landscape of the country, making it appear more accessible than previously, and Hines created a model for how to look at the United States as full of interesting corners once you left the main roads.[22]

Hines balanced expert judgment with reassuring folksiness. His guide was sufficiently critical to be useful, but he represented himself as a person just like the reader—an enterprising everyman rather than a hard-to-please snob. He was a cheerful mentor to those inclined to keep on the sunny side of life, much in the manner of Will Rogers, an even more famous figure whose dictum "I've never met a man I didn't like" exemplifies the era's ethos of positive thinking.

Born and raised in Bowling Green, Kentucky, Hines portrayed himself as a farm kid, a fan of food that was simple and honest but skillfully prepared. He maintained a wry attitude of sheepish appreciation mingled with "what will they think of next?" toward luxury dining and European cuisine. He was proud to be a member of the elite Lucullus Circle ("one of the greatest honors ever paid to me"), a group of prominent gourmands established by Claudius Philippe, better known as "Philippe of the Waldorf." Hines considered Philippe to be, like himself, a great judge of food. On the other hand, his response to wine connoisseurship was that he was more of a bourbon-on-the-rocks man, and he took care to state that he attended only a few of the Lucullus dinners, thus assuring the reader of his regular-guy bona fides.[23]

Of all the American culinary regions, Duncan Hines most admired New England because of the unadorned simplicity of its food and its traditions of frugality. As for his own Border South, as well as the Deep South, he acknowledged "Negro cooks" as the creators of Southern cuisine. He found it less satisfying, though, because it was too much given over to fried foods.[24]

Hines did not see himself as particularly expert in regional cuisine, but he did believe that the natives themselves unjustly ignored their local ingredients. After all, "Why should I stuff myself with chicken in California, when the whole Pacific Ocean, full of seafood, is right offshore?" It was appropriate to eat chowder in New England, soft-shelled crabs in Maryland, okra and shrimp in South Carolina, and "Spanish" dishes in Texas and California.[25] In a *Life* magazine article of 1946, Phyllis Larsh observed that for many years, Hines had tried to persuade restaurant owners to serve their region's food—on the Gulf Coast, for example, they should pay more attention to red snapper than ordinary chicken and steak.[26]

Despite these recommendations, Hines focused on criteria other than food. His reviews emphasized cleanliness and good organization more than any picturesque, let alone crafted qualities. From the start, Hines and his wife used a checklist by which they made a preliminary judgment: Does the restaurant look clean? Is the smell from the kitchen appealing? How fresh are the table furnishings? Are the floors clean and are the waiters or waitresses neat?[27] What made Hines's compendium successful was that it offered predictability, the same feature that roadside chains such as Howard Johnson's and Stouffer's were implementing.

Although he included short restaurant descriptions, Duncan Hines was not particularly interested in describing actual food. Sometimes he merely lists a few dishes without comment: "Boneless shad, roast capon, filet mignon are some of the dishes on the dinner menu" at the Fountain House in Doylestown, Pennsylvania. Of the famed Cloister Inn resort on Sea Island, Georgia, he outlines the available activities and then adds merely, "very good food." Hines claimed that brevity was necessary in order not to make the book too unwieldy, but he was able to fill each edition with his own words of wisdom, quips, and proverbial observations:

> ABOUT one man in a hundred will stand up and admit he likes ice cream soda. The other ninety-nine will stand by and envy him [ice cream soda being considered a women's beverage].

> MUCH of our cooking falls down through the fact that too many cooks are still trying to discover something that will take the place of good butter, fresh eggs, rich milk and a loving touch. It just hasn't been done yet.

What made an establishment truly outstanding was not its food but a heartwarming story. He approved of the Lowell Inn in Stillwater, Minnesota, because its owners were former actors made unemployed because of the Depression. They took over a failing hotel and determined to become "the best hotel people they possibly could." Similar grit and devotion to quality characterized the Smorgasbord in Stow, Ohio, and the Stockholm in Detroit.[28]

In his 1955 autobiography, Hines acknowledged regret that "a strictly regional dinner is becoming a thing of the past," but this was not especially disastrous. The innate restlessness of Americans and their mobility inevitably meant a lack of firm roots in a particular location. Rather than complain, Hines was happy to praise the changes that had taken place since his childhood, greater variety and technological innovation in particular.[29] He missed

THE GREEN BOOK

In 1936, the same year as Duncan Hines's debut, a parallel guide issued for African Americans first appeared. The guide was given different names but was familiarly known as the *Green Book*, and was addressed to the "Negro Motorist" or the "Negro Traveler."[30] Issued until 1966, it listed places where African Americans traveling by car could find accommodation and not risk rejection, ridicule, or worse. This was necessary not only in the "sundown towns" of the South, which prohibited the presence of nonwhite people after dark, but also in the rest of the country. It was quite possible that a black motorist would be turned away in New York, Minnesota, or some other officially integrated state.

The *Green Book* resembled the Duncan Hines guide in its national scope and state-by-state organization, but given the lack of choice imposed by segregation, it did not rate or discuss individual establishments. The fact that a motel, restaurant, garage, or other business catered to African Americans was sufficient for inclusion.

the large breakfasts of the past and had a number of peeves and even rants, but in public at least, his regrets did not contradict his avuncular, aw-shucks persona.

RESTAURANTS MENTIONED IN DUNCAN HINES'S ORIGINAL 1936 GUIDE STILL OPEN AS OF 2019

Deer Path Inn (Lake Forest, IL)

Beaumont Inn (Harrodsburg, KY)

Antoine's (New Orleans, LA)

Mrs. K's Toll House (Silver Spring, MD)

Dearborn Inn (Dearborn, MI; now affiliated with Marriott)

The Krebs (Skaneateles, NY)

Nittany Lion Inn (University Park, PA)

Skye's Inn (Smithfield, VA; now the Smithfield Inn)

Williamsburg Inn (Williamsburg, VA)

Mader's Restaurant (Milwaukee, WI)

Red Circle Inn (Nashotah, WI)

Nero Wolfe, 1938

Nero Wolfe, a fictional detective created by Rex Stout, might seem an odd choice as a defender of American cuisine, but he fits our discussion of belief in America's regional culinary virtue. Between 1934 and 1975, in over fifty novels and numerous short stories, Rex Stout fused the detective as genius genre established by Arthur Conan Doyle's Sherlock Holmes with Raymond Chandler and

Dashiell Hammett's detective as American tough-guy.[31] Unlike Holmes, Nero Wolfe is a fat and rather lazy genius, a New York City private detective whose two passions are cuisine and orchids. Solving murders is not an obsession or even a diversion, but merely a talent that finances his expensive tastes. Wolfe's associate, Archie Goodwin, is a genial, cynical, street-smart sleuth who narrates the stories. Like Conan Doyle's Dr. Watson, Goodwin does not figure out in advance the tricky solutions to the murders, but he is not as naïve as Watson. Goodwin is a shrewd commentator, wise to the petty crooks, irritable cops, and shady hotel detectives that populate this urban landscape.

Nero Wolfe dislikes women and evinces little emotion other than pride and irritability. He loves food and passes his happiest hours in the company of his Swiss cook, Fritz Brenner. Unusual for the mid-century era, Nero Wolfe and his author were staunch advocates for American food and its traditions. In *Too Many Cooks* (1938), a murder mystery that takes place at a resort hotel much like the Greenbrier in West Virginia, Wolfe passionately defends American cuisine in the face of the contempt of one of the chefs in an elite group gathered at the resort. The French-Catalan chef Jerome Berin says he has heard tell of New England boiled dinner, corn pone, clam chowder, and milk gravy, all of which are probably good in their modest homemade settings, but certainly not international gourmet material. Wolfe asks the arrogant master-chef if he has ever tasted terrapin stewed with butter, chicken broth, and sherry. Or planked porterhouse steak with parsley, limes, mashed potatoes, and slightly undercooked mushrooms? What about the Creole tripe of New Orleans?[32] The list goes on: Tennessee opossum, Philadelphia snapper soup, and chicken in curdled egg sauce.

These might not be what we first think of when defining classic American regional cuisine. Some, like the opossum, although lauded too by Mark Twain, were already rustic eighty years ago, at the time of the story. Others, like the Maryland terrapin (also a Twain favorite), were in decline. The emphasis on local ingredients, simplicity, and authenticity, however, does accord with today's locavore and seasonal trends. Wolfe's is a lonely but confident voice raised in defense of America's ability to compete internationally and, obliquely, in support of its regional cuisine.

Cover of Rex Stout, *Too Many Cooks*, 1938. The original "who killed the celebrity chef" mystery includes recipes and a defense of American food against European snobbery.

As with Duncan Hines, there is a sense in the Nero Wolfe mysteries that what threatens the excellence of American regional traditions is simultaneously upper-class infatuation with French cuisine and middle-class infatuation with modern convenience and insipid food. This is only a minor problem for Wolfe, who clearly does not care about the tastes of anyone else. Modernity does not threaten his carefully controlled world; he just spends money to go around any difficulties. Comfortably established in an old brownstone townhouse on West

35th Street in New York, Wolfe has a roof garden full of orchids, a skilled chef, and a friend who owns the best restaurant in the city.

Having casually endowed his detective with extraordinary gourmandise, Rex Stout was forced, by the success of his creation, to learn about food and to keep up the appearance of his own culinary expertise and interest. *Too Many Cooks* is the only mystery that places food at the center of the action, so much so that there is even an appendix of recipes.[33] The regional cuisine expert Sheila Hibben put together the recipes and provided advice on other American culinary aspects of the book, for which Stout paid her two thousand dollars (the equivalent of thirty-five thousand dollars today).[34]

Although Nero Wolfe frequently expresses contempt for popular culture in the United States, he is devoted to its traditional cuisine. He dissents from the orthodox opinion of American gourmets that only French cuisine has real distinction. Stout does allow his detective to admit that France is in first place when it comes to high-end cuisine, but Wolfe goes against the grain in preferring beer to wine, mashed potatoes to pommes frites, and Chesapeake Bay turtles to French frogs.[35] Even for the 1930s, the specialties of Wolfe's kitchen were a bit old-fashioned—spoon bread, shad roe mousse, and corn pudding—but in another way Wolfe's creator was ahead of his time, anticipating by fifty years or so the revival of American local and regional cuisine.

The mystery stories are off-hand in their mention of what Wolfe served at his table. Archie Goodwin, the narrator, merely witnesses an argument between Wolfe and Fritz over juniper in the marinade for venison loin chops, or comes back home to sample some headcheese. On another occasion, in a hurry to go out, Goodwin is unhappy about missing braised wild turkey with celery sauce and corn fritters. That is usually as much as we hear about these tantalizing possibilities, the fleeting citations making the dishes seem all the more attractive.

In 1973, Rex Stout and Barbara Burn assembled *The Nero Wolfe Cookbook*.[36] It reflects Wolfe's preference for mid-Atlantic cuisine, featuring crab, shad, terrapin, scrapple, and clams. There is a reasonable amount of game, plenty of duckling, and specialties from other regions, such as Georgia country ham, Kentucky burgoo, and blue grouse from Montana that have fed on mountain huckleberries. There is a James Beard sensibility here, minus outdoor cooking or home entertainment, neither of which interests Wolfe.

In *Too Many Cooks*, Wolfe announces the solution to the mystery of who murdered the much-disliked Chef Philip Laszio as a dramatic addendum to a talk on *"Contributions Américaines à la Haute Cuisine."* We do not learn the details of his impassioned praise, but the menu for an American dinner accompanying Wolfe's address is provided:

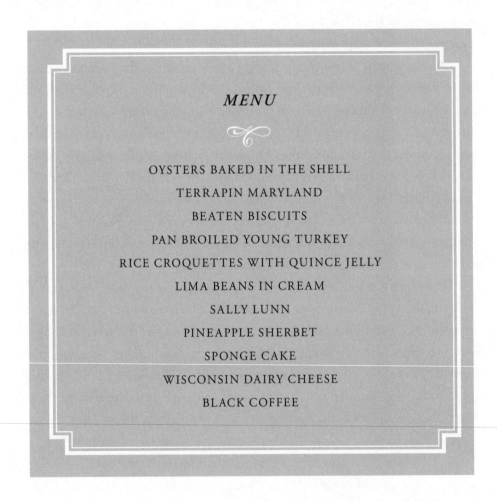

MENU

OYSTERS BAKED IN THE SHELL

TERRAPIN MARYLAND

BEATEN BISCUITS

PAN BROILED YOUNG TURKEY

RICE CROQUETTES WITH QUINCE JELLY

LIMA BEANS IN CREAM

SALLY LUNN

PINEAPPLE SHERBET

SPONGE CAKE

WISCONSIN DAIRY CHEESE

BLACK COFFEE

The reader is assured that the international group of chefs was appropriately ecstatic.

Shad Roe aux Fines Herbes

2 pairs fresh shad roe

½ cup butter

2 Tb chopped fresh chives

1 tsp. fresh chervil

1 tsp. fresh tarragon

1 tsp. minced shallots

Salt and pepper to taste

Blanch the roe in salted water, simmering it for about 5 minutes. Drain and separate the pairs. In a large skillet, heat ¼ cup of the butter and add the shad roes. Cook for a minute on each side over a medium flame, turning the roes very carefully.

Cover the skillet and reduce the heat. Cook for 10 minutes longer. Remove the roe to a heated platter. Add the remaining butter and the herbs to the skillet and heat for 2 minutes. Correct the seasoning and pour over the roe. Serve immediately.

From *The Nero Wolfe Cookbook* (New York: Viking, 1973), 63–64.

"You and your Nero Wolfe Recipes!"

Cartoon: "You and your Nero Wolfe recipes!" Rex Stout's detective, Nero Wolfe, is a gourmand whose other extravagant pleasure is growing orchids. He has a preference for hearty, fairly elaborate American dishes.

"America Eats," 1939–1941

"America Eats" is the name of a massive but unpublished collaboration that explored American cooking, another example of the search for real, American folk cuisines of diverse region. More systematic than the impressionistic Nero Wolfe mysteries, less consumer-oriented than Duncan Hines, the project looked at American food traditions through collective manifestations such as New England clambakes, cemetery-cleaning picnics in the South, or cattle roundup barbecues in the West.[37] The federal government announced the project in 1939 and set up a central editorial committee charged with distilling the data compiled from interviews across the country. Unfortunately, the work only started in earnest at the beginning of 1941, the deadline for submission of the chapters coincided with the Japanese attack on Pearl Harbor, and the results never appeared in print.[38]

America Eats grew out of the Works Progress Administration (WPA) efforts to put the unemployed to work on public projects during the Great Depression. The Federal Writers' Project (FWP) hired several thousand intellectuals to explore American life and culture, recording the customs and attitudes of ordinary Americans. The results were an anthropology or sociology of life in a regionally diverse and largely rural country.

The FWP reflected both the desperation and optimism of the New Deal, exalting the fundamental strength of the American people and commending their unity in diversity and in adversity. Behind this banal but meaningful idea was another one: that America had a great tradition of democratic culture and an ever-expanding technology even if the Depression of the present was a daunting challenge.[39] The socialist-realist WPA murals in post offices and other public buildings during the 1930s exalted old crafts, sturdy pioneers, and hard-working farmers, while celebrating the construction of great public works, such as dams and highways, that would bring about a bright future. Before that bright future arrived, as things turned out, the United States had to fight abroad. In early 1942, the FWP became part of the war effort, and in 1943, the WPA itself came to an end.

America Eats favored the nostalgic more than the futuristic agenda of the

WPA. It showed off a tradition of cooking threatened by mass production, amounting to a storytelling exercise rather than a confident leap into an electrified tomorrow. The problem, according to the thinkers behind the project, was housewives' infatuation with convenience products. The male organizers of America Eats claimed that women were uninterested in food as a sensory experience, distressingly eager to give up wonderful, old-fashioned if labor-intensive food. With the individual household lost to the mediocrity of modernity, the focus of the research was on communal dining experiences that preserved the customs of the past. After all, surely no one would bring cobbler made with canned peaches to an Alabama church supper.

The project organizers identified five regions: Northeast, South, Middle West, Southwest, and West. Within each, one state was a representative and the subject of a detailed research program. For the Northeast, New Jersey was the exemplary state, Louisiana for the South, Illinois for the Middle West, Arizona for the Southwest, and Montana for the West. The files of the project, now in the Library of Congress, show variation in how far the research got before it was abandoned and how much survives. There are hundreds of pages of notes for Virginia, for example, but nothing for West Virginia.[40]

African Americans were included, but most often as culturally subordinate to whites. Following a pattern established by Southern food writers, black women were shown as skillful cooks, but were usually instructed by their white employers. America Eats handled foreign-born Americans inconsistently: European white immigrants were prominent in the Eastern cities and the Midwest, as were "Spanish" and Mexican people of the Southwest. On the other hand, the Chinese and Japanese were regarded as not really part of the American melting pot. Chinese immigration had been severely restricted since the 1882 Chinese Exclusion Act, and when the America Eats project was underway, the Japanese were not far from the implementation of the wartime internment orders.[41] Older traditions, like those of the Germans and Scandinavians, received more favor than the contributions of more recent immigrants. There was a debate over whether a Middle-Western Scandinavian *lutfisk* (fermented cod) dinner was sufficiently American, and it was eventually decided that this customary meal had enough reverberation beyond a single ethnic community to qualify. A Chinese christening party, however, was supposedly too localized within a single ethnicity to be considered of national significance.[42]

The writers and directors of America Eats did not look forward to or advocate the imposition of American industrial standardization. Regional festivities marked by hot dogs and soft drinks, were lamented or at most tolerated. More than with other examples of 1930s regionalism, America Eats saw food traditions as threatened by modernization and evoked a degree of culinary nostalgia.

The people who conceived of America Eats were not much interested in restaurants fancier than the Automats. An exception to the prevailing populist tone is a group of observations by one of the contributors, Allan Ross MacDougall, on American dishes that originated in New York restaurants, items such as Waldorf salad, lobster Newburg, and vichyssoise, the latter invented by Louis Diat at the Ritz-Carlton Hotel.[43] Equally exceptional is a Mississippi article by Eudora Welty, who would go on to become one of the greatest American short-story writers of the twentieth century. Here she presents recipes from the mistresses of grand, antebellum homes. None of the dishes is very fancy. Included are such modest regional staples as beaten biscuits, lye hominy, and two kinds of gumbo, but her assertion that the guardians of gastronomic tradition are members of the upper classes is at variance with the overall democratic tone of the collection.

The Midwestern section is attributed to the Chicago writer Nelson Algren, another writer who was just starting on the path to literary fame.[44] It begins with the Native American populations and gives considerable space to immigrants, ranging from the Dutch in Michigan to Serbians in Illinois. They are all rural people, which it at odds with the urban tough-guy image for which Algren would later be celebrated. This is one reason among others for doubting Algren's authorship, a claim based on very shaky assumptions and the unsupported assertions of unreliable witnesses.[45] The most interesting item here is an early recipe for shakshuka, now a well-known Israeli dish via North Africa.[46]

America Eats dwells on disputes over sacred regional specialties. "The Mint Julep Controversy" includes several contributions relating to how to properly make this bourbon cocktail served over shaved ice and garnished with mint. A discussion of jonnycakes begins by noting that for natives of Rhode Island, "the ability to differentiate between genuine, honest-to-goodness jonny cakes and the palate-insulting commercial substitutes is a natural inheritance." The dishes described by the writers are eaten in company, on the job (at ranches, or a fish fry for levee workers), at community gatherings, or at an appropriate time of year, as with a South Carolina barbecue for the end of the tobacco season. The project reported on events such as an African American "chitterling strut" in North Carolina, and obtained elderly people's memories, such as a 90-year-old Oregon woman's account of pioneer reunion dinners.

There is an elegiac tone to the America Eats project as it has come down to us, both because it was unfinished and because it attempted to assert that regional cuisine was flourishing in the face of a considerable amount of contrary evidence. It was undertaken at a time when it was obvious that American food habits were becoming standardized through the marketing of industrial food products such as sliced white bread and bottled salad dressing. The modern world was taking over family life, and it was not likely that traditional communal celebrations could restore regional and homemade virtues. With touching optimism, however, these customs were conceived as representing the underlying strength of the American people.

The *World's Fair Cook Book*, 1939

At the same time that the writers for America Eats were out collecting field notes, a Broadway producer was in charge of another way of looking at American regional food with a tie-in to the 1939–1940 New York World's Fair. Crosby Gaige's *New York World's Fair Cook Book*, published in 1939 when the fair opened, is in its way as thorough as America Eats, but for his research, Gaige relied on home economists from every state rather than touring the interior himself.[47] Gaige (1882–1949) was more man-about-town than amateur anthropologist. An authority on cocktails and French cuisine, he served as president of the New York Wine and Food Society. The *World's Fair Cook Book* is surprisingly authentic and intriguing—surprising because one would expect sponsorship from a fair whose theme was "The World of Tomorrow" to require processed ingredients.[48]

The home economists furnished Gaige with a good sampling of traditional recipes from their states. Home economists have a bad image in recent scholarship that portrays them as shills for the food industry, prejudiced against African Americans and immigrants, infatuated with hygiene and technology, mistrustful of flavor, and contemptuous of tradition.[49] Indeed, the evidence for all these charges is extensive. In this instance, however, the women contacted by Gaige were respectful of local customs and offered regionally specific dishes and menus.

Large divisions organize the book: New England; New York and Pennsylvania; South, Middle West; South and Southwest, then subdivided by states. Little overt threat from modern conveniences or standardization of taste is discernible; there are few mentions of cans or other processed foods. The reader is assumed to be undaunted by making pastry dough without instruction, splitting raw turkeys, and skinning opossums. Authenticity means effort: a beaten biscuits recipe from Maryland includes 25 minutes of beating the batter with a club; a Kentucky version requires rolling it through a kneader 150 to 200 times.

The *New York World's Fair Cook Book* includes more than just routine regional dishes on the order of fried chicken or tamales. A chapter on "oddities" from New York and Pennsylvania offers Albany corn fritters, Philadelphia pepper pot (tripe soup), and Empire State pandowdy (apples baked under a crust, which is then removed and crumbled into the finished dessert).[50] Unlike America Eats, here regional cuisine sometimes incorporates immigrants' food, or at least American adaptations. A California section on Chinese and Japanese recipes mentions chop suey, chow mein, and beef sukiyaki. Most of the Southwestern chapter consists of Mexican or Mexican-influenced dishes, including turkey molé, New Mexico kid cooked with blood, and chili con queso.

Perhaps the most interesting part, however, is a set of dinner menus from each state as well as Puerto Rico. Care was taken to present regional fish, produce, and signature dishes: diamondback terrapin in Maryland, broiled pompano in Louisiana, succotash and Boston baked beans from Massachusetts. Even more intriguing is a clear pride in local, not just regional ingredients. Mildred King, an instructor in Institution Management at the University of Minnesota, recommends Lake of the Woods wall-eyed pike, mushrooms from caves near St. Paul, russet potatoes from the Red River Valley, and smoked ciscoes (a cousin of whitefish) from Lake Superior. Margaret Terrell of the School of Home Economics at the University of Washington provides a long list of local products, including salmon from Puget Sound, turkey from the Yakima Valley, peas from the San Juan Islands, and Walla Walla asparagus tips. North Dakota has two menus: one is what a typical restaurant would offer, while the other emphasizes the state's regions and resources. The restaurant menu could be from anywhere: tomato juice, fruit cup, tom turkey, tenderloin steak, pineapple and cottage cheese salad. The state-focused menu, however, includes specific varieties of produce, such as dishes made with Bliss Triumph potatoes and Mary Washington asparagus tips, and regional wildlife such as buffalo and mallard ducks.

These menus show an aspirational regional cuisine that reflects traditions and specialties. The North Dakota menu pairing makes it clear, if one needed further evidence, that a restaurant experience would be generic rather than local, with no sense of where the establishment was situated. National standardization, here characteristic only of restaurants, would accelerate in the postwar years, reducing variation to a bland sameness until the development of "California cuisine" in the 1970s. Old dishes, recipes, and style would at least partially reemerge as the twentieth century ended and the twenty-first began.

Dixie Chicken Shortcake

1 large chicken
1 lb. mushrooms
Salt and pepper
1 pan cornbread
2 Tb flour

Cook the chicken until very tender. Cool and remove the skin and bone. Cut in medium-sized pieces. Make a sauce using the chicken stock and thickening with the flour. Sauté the mushrooms in butter. Now add the chicken to the sauce and season to taste.

Cut the cornbread into four-inch squares and split. Cover the bottom half with the chicken mixture. Lay on this the top crust and cover with more gravy and chicken mixture.

From Crosby Gaige, *New York World's Fair Cook Book* (New York: Doubleday Doran, 1939), 92.

The *Ford Times* Guides, 1950–1968

The outbreak of war in Europe interrupted but did not close down the 1939–1940 World's Fair. The greatest culinary legacy of that event was not Crosby Gaige's book but rather the founding of the greatest midcentury French restaurant, Le Pavillon. It was opened in Manhattan by French restaurant personnel at the Fair, stranded as refugees after the fall of France to Hitler in the grim spring of 1940.[51] After the war ended, an economic boom gathered strength and resulted in a dramatic change in social mobility and middle-class affluence. The result was to open up opportunities for leisure tourism, but also to speed up homogenization of America's food and blot out its regional distinctions. As the average standard of living improved in the postwar period, the Ford Motor Company began publishing a series of brief notices about restaurants across the country in its monthly magazine, *Ford Times*. The end of gas rationing and the ability of the average wage earner to afford a car meant that Duncan Hines no longer monopolized guides for dining away from home. Although a few of the restaurants listed in the Ford guides were in cities, most were way stations convenient for family trips. The material was collected in a series of books, beginning in 1950 and ending in the late 1960s. They show the same sort of open-road search for diversion in a vast country as Duncan Hines and America Eats, but with little or no sense of authentic regionalism and an unnerving enthusiasm for ersatz food.

A painted drawing and a recipe accompany the listing for each restaurant. The pictures collectively provide impressions of midcentury modern décor—the knotty-pine motel look—as well as of historic inns. The parking lot is often in the foreground to show off an assortment of Ford, Mercury, and Lincoln automobiles. Many of the restaurants are in small towns or the countryside, but there is little to evoke rural folklore or tradition.

Unlike the WPA and World's Fair guides, this series focused on restaurants, so it affords a good view of "nice" but not especially fancy establishments at the time. The Ford books are explicitly regional only to the extent of grouping restaurants into related driving destinations. New England and the Mid-Atlantic tend toward antique hostelries or former coaching stations; the South

KING COLE RESTAURANT

A large collection of original 19th century paintings add interest to this restaurant which features an open hearth charcoal broiler.

Lunch and dinner served daily. Reservations necessary. Closed Sunday and major holidays.

34 West Second Street (3 blocks west of U.S. 25), Dayton

Breast of Turkey—King Cole

2 pounds broccoli, cooked and drained

12 slices turkey breast

½ cup Parmesan cheese

Arrange broccoli on a platter; place turkey slices on top and cover with sauce. Sprinkle with Parmesan cheese and place under broiler for a few minutes until golden. Serves 6.

Sauce

6 egg yolks

1 lemon, juice

½ pound butter, melted

1 cup heavy cream

Salt and cayenne pepper, to taste

Beat egg yolks and lemon juice in a double boiler. Add butter slowly in small pieces; continue beating. Blend in cream in at the last minute. Remove from heat and season.

From *The Ford Treasury of Favorite Recipes from Famous Eating Places*,
vol. 3 (New York: Golden Press, 1959), 142.

is either folksy or plantation-gracious; the West is modern or cowboy. When they are not in historic buildings, the restaurants are often zany: two California restaurants with natural streams running through the dining room, a "fascinating view of traffic" from the Glass House built over a highway in Oklahoma, and plenty of hotel rooftop restaurants and tiki huts.[52]

The food could be anything. Recipes mention lobster in Maine and fried chicken in the South, but usually the dishes bear no relation to place. The first compendium presents a "New England pecan pie" as served at the Old Mill Inn in Bernardsville, New Jersey, located in neither New England nor the South. Pecan pie also shows up in Northampton, Massachusetts, at Wiggins' Old Tavern, and at Brad Ryan's Lake Breeze Lodge near Nicolet National Forest in Wisconsin.[53] In the first collection, there are only a few entries that reflect the region: Pennsylvania Dutch "fastnachts" (doughnuts) at the Shartlesville Hotel, poached Colorado rainbow trout at the Indian Grill in Colorado Springs, and abalone beurre noir at the Harbor Restaurant in Santa Barbara are among the scarce examples.[54]

Odd juxtapositions are common. Red snapper gumbo is a specialty of the Boston Oyster House in Chicago; the second volume highlights cheese blintzes at a Hollywood restaurant "famous for its chuck-wagon dinners." Baked pork chops "Southern style" accompany the entry for the Bud Lake Café near Missoula, Montana.[55]

In the first collection especially, restaurant owners present recipes for bizarre, "creative" postwar foods: corned beef supper salad from the Riverton Inn in Connecticut; salad with tomato soup dressing from the White Drum in Orange, Massachusetts; lime gelatin and cottage cheese salad from the Barrows House in Dorset, Vermont; banana meat rolls from the Gold Eagle in Beaufort, South Carolina.[56] The later volumes tone down the frightening innovation, but the food is still in no sense regional—lots of fruit salads, baked noodles, nut breads, Swiss steak, and the like. There is plenty of variety, but it is unrelated to geography, let alone terroir. Many of the dishes were fashionable, but not from any particular part of the country. The 1968 guide contains three recipes for crab imperial (crabmeat mixed with mayonnaise and other ingredients, then

RAND'S ROUND-UP

Ray Rand is the owner and manager of this spot, famous for its chuck-wagon dinners.

Lunch, dinner, after-theater supper daily. Sunday morning brunch.
7580 Sunset Boulevard, Hollywood, California

Cheese Blintzes

2 eggs

2 cups water

⅛ teaspoon vanilla

2 cups flour

⅛ teaspoon nutmeg

4 tablespoons sugar

¾ teaspoon baking powder

⅛ teaspoon salt

Beat eggs and add water and vanilla. Blend dry ingredients and combine with egg mixture with a few strokes. Heat a 5-inch skillet and grease with a few drops of oil. Add small amount of batter and tip skillet to spread batter over bottom. Brown on one side only and turn out on a plate brown-side up. Fry all the blintzes.

Filling

Combine 6 ounces dry cottage cheese and 6 ounces cream cheese and place a spoonful of this mixture on each blintz. Fold blintz edges toward middle so they lap over filling. Return blintzes to skillet and sauté in butter on both sides until lightly browned. Serve with powdered sugar and sour cream. Makes about 15 blintzes.

From *The Second Ford Treasury of Favorite Recipes from Famous Eating Places*
(New York: Simon and Schuster, 1954), 211.

baked or broiled): from the Glasgow Arms in Glasgow, Delaware, the Harbour House in Annapolis, and Kaplan's in Houston.[57]

The ingredients are usually simple and, unlike with women's magazines recipes, butter still edges out margarine and there is not much in the way of Jell-O or cream of mushroom soup. True, the gumbo from the Old Carriage House, located in the antebellum Stanton Hall in Natchez, Mississippi, calls for frozen okra, corn, and shrimp and a can of tomatoes, but this is exceptional.[58] There is no attempt in these guides to highlight older regional cuisine, but this was not the end of the insistence that "out there" there were not only odd, modern concoctions like the banana meat roll, but real food of a diverse past.

RECIPES FROM THE THIRD FORD RECIPE COLLECTION

Cranberry Chiffon Pie
from the House by the Road (Ashburn, Georgia)

1 envelope unflavored gelatin

¼ cup cold water

1-pound can cranberry jelly

1/8 tsp. salt

1 tsp. grated lemon rind

2 tsp. lemon juice

2 egg whites

2 Tb. sugar

8-inch pastry shell, baked

Whipped cream (optional)

Place gelatin in a custard cup. Add cold water and let stand 2 minutes. Place custard cup in pan of boiling water until gelatin dissolves. Add to jellied cranberry sauce (crushed with a fork) or whole sauce. Add salt, lemon rind and lemon juice; chill until mixture begins to set. Beat egg whites until stiff and beat in sugar. Fold into cranberry mixture. Pour filling into baked pastry shell and chill until firm. Top with whipped cream if desired.

Green Bean Casserole
from the Hotel Manning (Keosauqua, Iowa)[59]

4 cups French-style green beans (split)

½ cup cooked mushrooms, diced

1 Tb. onion, chopped

1 tsp. salt

¼ tsp. pepper

4 Tb. butter

1 cup toasted buttered breadcrumbs

Combine cooked green bean, mushrooms, onion, salt, pepper and butter and cook together for 15 minutes. Pour mixture into baking dish and cover with breadcrumbs and dots of butter. Bake in moderate 350° oven for 25 minutes or until nicely browned.

From *The Ford Treasury of Favorite Recipes from Famous Eating Places*, vol. 3 (New York: Golden Press, 1959), 84, 121

Clementine Paddleford, *How America Eats*, 1948–1960

When the Ford guidebooks started to appear, the newspaper reporter Clementine Paddleford (1898–1967) had already created a uniquely lyrical form of writing about American food. The height of her fame was simultaneous with the publication of the Ford series, and she covered a similarly wide range of American heartland territory, but with more of an eye for authenticity—and she did not follow the Ford recommendation to drive everywhere. Among her achievements was learning to fly her own plane; by her own estimation she

Clementine Paddleford, 1898–1967. Paddleford had many interests, from flying her own plane to enjoying the companionship of cats. She wrote over 800 articles about restaurants, home cooks, and food as an expression of creativity, tradition, and fellowship.

logged 800,000 miles in her Piper Cub. Raised on a Kansas farm, Paddleford moved to New York City as soon as she graduated from college and became the leading newspaper food writer in the postwar era.[60] She made her way confidently out of the confines of the women's pages of several newspapers to travel the world and bring attention to the survival of American culinary diversity.

Paddleford merits the overused term "indefatigable" for her verve and curiosity about food and the people who make it, and for surviving cancer of the larynx, contracted at the age of thirty-three, just as her career was taking off. The treatment was successful, but it forced her to depend on a voice box in order to speak, and she always wore a throat ornament to hide the disfiguring result of the grueling operation. Characteristically, she saw some advantage in her strange, hoarse, artificial-sounding voice: "People never forget me," she often said.[61]

Over the course of a dozen years, from 1948 to 1960, 845 columns of "How America Eats" appeared in the *Herald Tribune* and the nationally distributed Sunday supplement *This Week*. By her own account, Paddleford interviewed 2,000 cooks, mostly homemakers. Restaurants figure in only 10 percent of her columns. She was a great fan of Antoine's in New Orleans, however, and she managed to coax previously secret recipes out of its owner, Roy Alciatore.[62]

In 1960, Paddleford published a large selection of her culinary travelogues in a book entitled *How America Eats*, a bestseller that was reviewed widely and favorably. The essays accompanying the recipes depict a country whose roadside restaurants give a pallid and inauthentic impression of the true riches of its regional variety, ingenuity, and sensuality. Defending her native Midwest, Paddleford remarked that the region's food is unjustly criticized by tourists who "pass through at sixty miles an hour, eating en route in public places, and seldom of the best" without ever sitting down at a family table to enjoy the real food of the bountiful countryside.[63]

Paddleford was interested in the food of American regions, not just in pleasant dining while traveling, the focus of the Duncan Hines and Ford guides. She deliberately used the word "regional" to describe the different adaptations settlers and immigrants created with what was available. An unexceptional idea at the opening of the twentieth century, by the time Paddleford wrote, the notion of American cuisine varying by geography was unorthodox given the prevailing acceptance of uniform, modern taste.[64]

Clementine Paddleford employed what now seems an arch and fatiguingly flowery writing style. A description of Alabama begins:

> I was Alabama-bound to Birmingham. The day of my arrival the glory of the Old South lived anew. It was Confederate Memorial Day below the Mason-Dixon Line. . . . Menus were planned in the colonial manner; lace tablecloths came out of blue-paper wrappings; heirloom silver and glass came down from the high cupboards to do the day honor.[65]

Or the prologue to "Lobster is the Maine Thing:"

> June lay gently on the shoulder. The fragrance of balsam mingled with the ocean's salty breath. Walter Stanley, fifty years a lobsterman, had invited me down to the bay to see how it goes, tending 125 traps. A long, lean Yankee, with scraggly gray eyebrows and deep-set blue eyes cool with salt distance. He pulls his living from the sea at the end of 360 feet of warp. Come hell or high water, war or peace, Walter Stanley goes trawling.[66]

Unlike Walter Stanley, the typical informant for *How America Eats* tended to be a woman of high social position, identified by her husband's name—Mrs. Floyd L. Rheam, Mrs. Ezra Taft Benson, and the like. Regional cuisine was the repository of old families, especially in the South, where the culinary heritage was entrusted to the owners of antebellum homes. What unites the diverse cooking of the South, Paddleford says, is the "lavish tradition of plantation days."[67]

There is almost no mention of African American cooks, even as servants of the plantation grandes dames. In her newspaper column, Paddleford did praise Lena Richard, the African American chef from New Orleans. Writing about Richard's *New Orleans Cookbook*, Paddleford said Richard had saved "delicacies originated by the Negro cooks of the past generation" from oblivion.[68] Occasionally Paddleford credited immigrants with contributions to regional culinary traditions, but she was considerably more enthusiastic about Scandinavians in Minnesota or the Pennsylvania Dutch than about home cooks who had grown up in Mexico or China. Representatives of fine "old Spanish" California families were consulted, but not recent immigrants from Mexico.

Perhaps it is churlish to criticize Paddleford for sins common in her era. It is not as if the Ford Guides are particularly multicultural either. Paddleford wanted to show that American regional food still flourished in the homes of regular, if usually well-off, people. As she told a columnist for the *Saturday Evening Post*, we all have "hometown appetites," longings for the simple but vivid tastes of the farm or hometown left behind.[69] The comforting idea that America is not, appearances notwithstanding, a land of mediocre, mass-market food, guided Paddleford. Her relentless curiosity about American dining and its regional variations confirmed at least some of this optimistic picture.

Regional specialties were not merely curious survivals, nor was Paddleford an ethnographer in the manner of the Federal Writers' Project researchers. Her columns involved recipes designed for readers to try out, and represented an effort to bring the variety and wholesomeness of American regions to the attention of urban and suburban cooks. Regional cuisine is often built around local ingredients hard to find elsewhere—crayfish in Louisiana or shad on the East Coast—but Paddleford brushed away such limitations. She breezily asserted that Philadelphia scrapple was available in cities "everywhere," which does not seem likely.[70] Indeed, the planked shad festivals and clambakes would have been hard to imitate in a 1950s GE Electric "Wonder Kitchen"; the emphasis in her book was on practical fare such as pies, cakes, hearty stews, meatballs, and potato salads. Paddleford intended her recipes for "the quick-cook artists, who love doing things the easy way."[71]

Paddleford was hardly unaware that modern home cooking based on mixes, cans, and frozen food was at least as important as American regional practices. She saw her mission as publicizing and preserving culinary history and diversity. With her characteristic optimism, Paddleford was not bothered by the fish sticks and cottage cheese of expanding suburbia.

The *Time-Life Cookbooks*, 1968–1971

Clementine Paddleford died in 1967, by which time she had been displaced in the food-writing world by Craig Claiborne of the *New York Times*. Claiborne was from as authentically rural a background as Paddleford, in his case the Mississippi Delta, but he was only intermittently interested in American cuisine and became famous as an arbiter of restaurants and a Francophile *bec fin*. The inheritor of Paddleford's celebration of American regions was not Claiborne, but the *Time-Life Cookbooks*, a corporate effort that exhibited a similar faith in the persistence of American folkways behind the façade of mediocre casseroles and ubiquitous cheeseburgers. The *Time-Life Cookbooks* present an enthusiastic and thorough treatment of American regional food that was nevertheless almost comically unconvincing. The official name of the series was "*Foods of the World*," but everyone called them the "*Time-Life Cookbooks*." Issued in 27 volumes beginning in 1968, they were long and narrow in format, with beautiful color photographs. Intended for display, the illustrated books contained a few exemplary recipes, while a separate spiral-bound volume for each country or region gave the full complement of recipes. Gravy and grease would spatter the notebook in the kitchen, while its lavish companion reposed on coffee tables or in living room bookcases.

The editors of this series devoted eight volumes to America, a culinary treasure trove as important as Europe and a repository of intact folk traditions. An introductory volume about American cooking generally summarizes the regional styles of the country, dividing it into 12 parts.[72] There are then separate books devoted to six regions: New England, "Eastern Heartland," South, Creole and Acadian, West, and Northwest. In a nod to the immigrants' influence, there is also a *Melting Pot* volume.

The cookbooks were a commercial success even before they were issued: half a million people (my mother among them) signed up for an initial subscription. The fervid interest says something about the paradoxical culinary passions of the time. As the food writer and restaurant expert Mimi Sheraton complained in 1968, enthusiasm for cuisine coincided with the degraded state of food actually available. While the public was fascinated by great Parisian restaurants like Maxim's and the Tour d'Argent, not a single unwaxed cucumber could be had, she pointed out, and American meat was bred to be tasteless.[73] The Time-Life editors ignored this kind of pessimism.

Popular as it was, the *Time-Life* series was recognized as exaggeratedly "authentic," even fantastic in its portrayal of regional cuisines. More than with Paddleford, the effect was picturesque and archaic: yeoman farmers and doughty fishermen, the age-old culinary traditions of people wedded to the land and sea. With regard to both magnificent and folklorish aspects—game dinners in Austrian castles and market women in Mozambique—the series was perceived even at the time as over the top. The satiric magazine *National Lampoon*, another cultural phenomenon of the 1970s, created a memorable takeoff with "Welcome to the Cooking of Provincial New Jersey," perfectly mimicking the graphics, illustrations, and tone of the original.[74] The *Lampoon* article lovingly contrasted those parts of the state where frozen foods were especially beloved with other regions that based their cuisine on powdered foods and mixes. Canned goods and "food helpers" were also prominent: "21 cuisines; one great taste" was the conclusion about the cooking of the so-called Garden State.

The assumption that the young, mass-market readers of the *National Lampoon* would be familiar with the object of the parody is an indication of the popularity of the *Time-Life* series, but also of the general understanding that the world it portrayed was largely fictional. Few suburban cooks were going to reproduce Mrs. Norman Walker's old family recipe for Boston baked beans requiring ten hours in the oven, or the recipe for Maryland terrapin stew, part of an elaborate description of terrapins in the Southern volume. The florid language is similar to Paddleford's, but with none of her ambition to make the regional heritage easy for the home cook.

These volumes were written according to a breathless corporate style that makes Clementine Paddleford read like Ernest Hemingway for concision. A

From an article, "Welcome to the Cooking of Provincial New Jersey," in the *National Lampoon*, June 1974. This is a takeoff on the precious and reverential tone of the *Time-Life* series *Foods of the World*.

picture caption from a chapter in the Southern US book is typically entitled "Juleps, Jiggers and Jillions of Colas." The chapter begins thus:

> The South attempts to sate its insatiable thirst with potables ranging from iced tea to fruit punch, mint juleps and straight bourbon whisky. In true Southern style, Mrs. John Marston, on the porch of Termite Hall in Mobile, attends to some mending while keeping a comfortable pitcherful of minted iced tea close at hand.

Time-Life writers seldom used words like *drinks* when *potables* was available.

As regards the United States, the tone of the series is optimistic, even triumphant, celebrating America's natural wealth: "a huge natural larder" (the farms and shorelines of the East), "the cornucopia of California," "the bounty of the Pacific

Northwest." The word *bounty* is almost a mantra, and the tone is established in James Beard's introduction to the general American volume, "take equal parts of bounty, diversity and ingenuity." The books purport to show the food traditions of ordinary people, but these traditions are so venerable that in fact they were about to disappear. The result is a museum of dying techniques: "the old craft of molding ice cream still keeps its cool in Philadelphia," a way of cooking trout "learned from oldtime fishermen" on the shore of Lake Superior, an "old-fashioned harvest" of nuts in Ohio.[75] It is as if the automobile is a new-fangled machine. Sorghum syrup is made in western North Carolina using a horse turning a press and an open boiler. Horses also bring New England maple syrup out of the woods. Even Clementine Paddleford, no foe of the quaint, acknowledged that tractors did the work in transporting maple-tapping equipment in Vermont.[76]

Jane and Michael Stern, *Roadfood*, 1977–, and the End of Traditional Regionalism

The *Time-Life* series represents the last gasp of American regionalism portrayed as if unaffected by agents of homogenization such as interstate highways, shopping malls, and McDonald's.[77] As the 1970s advanced, such a perspective became even more implausible, especially with the rise of fast food chains. Diners, Howard Johnsons, and local hamburger stands gave way in the 1970s to fast food with its stripped-down, automated, and formulaic offerings. In 1970, Americans spent 6 billion dollars at quick-service establishments (the official name for fast food). By 2000, the figure was $110 billion. In 1963, there were 40,000 fast food outlets. Twenty years later, the number had tripled to 122,500.[78]

With their first food travel book, *Roadfood,* in 1977, Jane and Michael Stern became the inadvertent leaders of a movement of culinary preservation and celebration.[79] They met when they were both graduate students in art history at Yale University and shared an enthusiasm for pizza, New Haven's great specialty. *Roadfood* served as a guide to the endangered genus of family-run dining spots that until sometime in the 1960s had been routine and unremarked. Once ordinary, ubiquitous, even nondescript chili parlors, barbecue joints, and seafood shacks now were minor national monuments worth memorializing. *Roadfood* was an immediate and long-term success, and has been through ten editions.

The Sterns' formula relates only tangentially to regionality. Their original intent was to compile a practical traveler's guide, a hipper Duncan Hines enterprise, pointing out places that made traditional but generic, small-town food such as pancakes, fried chicken, pies, or meatloaf. By the second edition (1980), the cover advertised *Roadfood* as offering regional selections within ten miles of a major highway. The idea was still to find sustenance on long-distance trips, but *Roadfood* now could serve as a tour of American cuisine that had a local coloration. *Roadfood* extends the twentieth-century practice of searching for a real, nostalgically recollected America, but with an updated, realistic attitude of salvage and conservation in the face of freeway standardization.

Over the years, *Roadfood* has been augmented by dozens of books by the Sterns about American popular culture, including different takes on regional cuisine, ranging from a national survey of chili in every state to how to plan cross-country trips stopping at local rather than chain restaurants.[80] Some of these other books put regional traditions in the foreground. In 1983, with *Goodfood*, the Sterns looked at the same sorts of restaurants as in *Roadfood*, but with an eye to regional specialties, including many geographically restricted dishes such as barbecued mutton in northern Kentucky, or buttermilk and sugar-cream pies in Indiana, or stuffed ham in St. Mary's County, Maryland. In *Eat Your Way across the U.S.A.* (1997), the organization is similar to that of the earlier *Roadfood* and *Goodfood* books, but sidebars rank restaurants by specialties that might be national (hot dogs), or regional (New England fried clam shacks), or a combination of ethnic and regional (Midwestern Polish restaurants). As before, however, the primary purpose is to find homey food that may or may not have a regional identity or variation.[81]

Later versions of *Roadfood* have placed regions in the foreground. The book became a series of routes and destinations to explore authentic as well as unexpected items. Not only did it describe well-known offerings such as lobster or barbecue, but it also presented obscure specialties such as chicken-fried steak in Texas or fried pies in Arkansas and Louisiana to a national audience. For the 2002 edition, according to a brief introduction, the purpose was to "point the way to meals that uniquely express the soul of their region."[82] Looking at the tenth edition, however, the guide, after nearly forty years, remains a collection of individual rather than regional places, what the introduction now refers to as "a melting-pot cuisine where tradition, creativity, and devil-may-care resourcefulness swirl to create meals that, like the population, are boundlessly diverse."[83] Variety is more important than regional authenticity.

Unlike previous guides, *Roadfood* exalts the quirky rather than the deeply traditional. The Sterns are not interested in picturesque but extinct colonial traditions of the jonnycake or Boston baked beans sort, nor the plantation hunt breakfasts of the antebellum South. They are fond of local inventions like deep-fried hot dogs in Connecticut. The Sterns' dossier of "regional specialties" in *Goodfood* emphasizes peculiar and not necessarily rural treats such as celery seed salad dressing in the Midwest, cheese steak from Philadelphia, and beef on weck (roast beef on a salt-crust and caraway-seed roll) in the area of Buffalo, NY. Recently developed examples of such "vernacular" (i.e., nontraditional) regional specialties include Nashville hot chicken (chicken fried in a crisp, spicy batter) and Hawaiian poke.

Foods brought over by immigrants are only indirectly important for the Sterns. Cornish pasties in Michigan's Upper Peninsula or Texas barbecue owe their existence to immigrants, but the Sterns have always focused on individual restaurants more than collective ethnography.[84] Kolache, a breakfast pastry like a fruit Danish, came to Texas with Czech immigrants, and sausage, a key constituent of Texas barbecue, is the result of German influence, but in the foreground is the nature of the particular establishment serving them. Ridgewood Barbecue in Bluff City, Tennessee, for example, is among the Sterns' favorites, not because of any intensive local customs but just place-specific genius. Sometimes the Sterns triumphantly find an almost extinct local practice, as with a persimmon pudding now limited in its habitat to Indiana's Brown County.[85] Indeed one of the Sterns' recent books is an extensive directory of endangered dishes such as Memphis-style barbecued spaghetti and sour-cream raisin pie from the northern Midwest.[86]

The threat of homogenization and the disappearance of individuality has receded in certain respects—the success of the Sterns or of Guy Fieri's Food Network show *Diners, Drive-Ins and Dives* suggests that fast food chains will not swallow up everything. Calvin Trillin's assertion "the best restaurants in the world, of

Menu cover from Charlie the Butcher's Kitchen, Buffalo, New York, featuring the local specialty "beef on weck" (sliced roast beef on a salt-crust and caraway-seed roll).

course, are in Kansas City" may not compel universal agreement, but what was a reckless and daring remark in 1979 when Trillin published *American Fried* is now the cornerstone of a new pride in culinary regionalism.[87]

SOME "VERNACULAR" ITEMS

Deep-fried hot dogs: A specialty of New Jersey, New York, and Connecticut, with some slight variations. Deep-frying makes the skins very crisp (pages 84–88).

Taylor ham (also known as Taylor pork roll): Invented in 1856 and confined to New Jersey. A large pork sausage that resembles baloney, but is usually fried and served as a sandwich or breakfast dish (pages 111–12).

Garbage plate: Rochester, NY. Invented in the 1930, this is a mixture of hot dogs, sausage, onions, chili sauce, and mustard accompanied (on the same plate) by macaroni salad, home fries, and baked beans (pages 88–89).

Beef on weck. A specialty of Buffalo, NY, and surroundings. Sliced roast beef on a salt and caraway-seed roll (pages 72–73).

Mutton barbecue: Served in western Kentucky, especially Owensboro (pages 182–83).

Barbecued spaghetti: Memphis, known also for other kinds of barbecue (pages 132–33).

Italian beef: Chicago. Doesn't seem very Italian. . . . Roast beef sandwich with gravy (pages 261–63).

St. Paul sandwich: St. Louis. An egg foo yong sandwich with lettuce, tomato, mayonnaise, and optional cheese (pages 278–79).

Pasties: Michigan, Upper Peninsula.[88] A pastry stuffed with seasoned meat. This is an example of a relatively simple transmission of an immigrant dish—tin miners from Cornwall were recruited to work the mines in the nineteenth and early twentieth century. Cornish pasties are well known throughout Britain (pages 270–71).

Chicken-fried steak: Texas (particularly the Hill Country). A thin steak breaded and fried in oil, served with white gravy. Now widespread throughout Texas and the South (pages 309–11).

Frito pie: Texas and New Mexico. Perhaps invented in Santa Fe, and now the object of struggle for ownership between Texas and New Mexico. In its simplest form, just chili with a Fritos topping, but more elaborate versions have layers of cheese, lettuce, and other essentially taco ingredients (pages 320–23).

Fish tacos: Originating in Baja California, once confined to San Diego but now popular everywhere in the US. Easily the most widely diffused item on this list (pages 384–86).

From Jane and Michael Stern, *500 Things to Eat Before It's Too Late* (New York: Houghton Mifflin Harcourt, 2009).

Problems of Regionalism

The Sterns' *Roadfood* marks a fork in the proverbial road of regional food writing. In the nineteenth century and up to the 1920s, it was a reasonable assumption that American regions differed in their food as well as their landscape and climate. Defenders of American food like James Parkinson or Mark Twain pointed to the wealth of American regional specialties, but did not deem necessary any preservation effort. While individual specialties might decline—prairie hens were scarce by 1900 and the passenger pigeon was on the verge of extinction—there was little sense of a larger threat from economic consolidation.

By the 1920s, denunciations of American dining were becoming more common. Now the deficiency was not that Americans hurried over their food or did not know how to enjoy conversation over meals, but that the people of the United States had forgotten what food was supposed to be; that convenience, efficiency, and corporate marketing had convinced them that industrial food was tasty and good for them. A common response to this apparent triumph of corporate brands and national sameness was to claim there was a living tradition of regional food in America and you just had to get out of the ugly cities and off the main roads to find it. This view was strongest in the 1930s, an expression of Depression-era uplift and folklore.

After the Second World War, some food guides such as the Ford books accepted the new world of tuna noodle casserole and gelatin cottage cheese salads. The *Mobil Travel Guides*, another auto-related series, seemed to award stars to restaurants based on décor, restrooms, or price point rather than food, and there was never any concern for local authenticity. On the other hand, popular surveys such as those by Clementine Paddleford and the Time-Life editors achieved success because they presented a nation still in touch with its rural roots and varied home cooking.

By the time of the Sterns' *Roadfood*, the late 1970s, there was still a fascinating undiscovered country out there. Its culinary wealth was not in vanishing folk tradition but rather in a combination of once-ordinary things like homemade pie and odd but appealing local specialties on the order of upstate New York white hots (like a bratwurst or Weisswurst with chili) or date shakes in the California desert region.

The Sterns do not quite represent the end of the story of American regionalism. Food writers and explorers have refused to give up American regional cuisine. Two books published in 2017 show that the threatened and slightly implausible genre remains alive. *The Mad Feast* by Matthew Gavin Frank, a state-by-state inventory of local and odd specialties, is perhaps more manic than actually mad.[89] The book is about the joy of discovering food traditions, many of them unlikely items like brined and baked beaver tail in Arkansas, or elk stew in Montana. There are tarnished delicacies whose genuine ancestry has been obliterated by mass-market imitation, such as Florida Key lime pie, as well as passionate controversies involving loosemeat sandwiches in Iowa ("loosemeat" is unmolded, crumbled ground beef) or different kinds of Sheboygan (Wisconsin) bratwurst.

America: The Cookbook, edited by Gabrielle Langholtz, is a lavish collection of recipes from all fifty states, and more sedate in tone than *The Mad Feast*.[90] The editor's motto is "Discover America," and here once more regionalism is the answer to the widespread belief that American cuisine is an oxymoron. The editor organizes things in the usual cookbook manner by courses, each labeled by appropriate region and state. There follows an extensive state-by-state discussion by chefs and food writers that serves as a detailed account of fifty food experiences. Most of them are personal rather than focused on tradition, but they represent a new kind of regionalism based on ingredients, such as cedar oil and pine tree tips (Idaho) or chanterelle mushrooms with hazelnut velouté (Oregon).

Regional culinary traditions survive in the United States, especially in parts of the South and Southwest. The latter has been a success story in that a version of its food, from chili to burritos to salsa, has established itself in popular dining everywhere in the country.[91] For New England and the mid-Atlantic, on the other hand, there are just memories of a formerly flourishing cuisine; only a few dishes like clam chowder remain famous. Some other factors, however, make it difficult to assess what regionalism means for American food practices. Are ingredients such as salmon or lobster sufficient markers of Northwestern or New England cuisine, or do such cuisines need actual methods of preparation and specific dishes? Are immigrant foods and recipes part of a regional cuisine? Southwestern and Texas cuisine are obviously influenced by Mexico, but various European enclaves such as Scandinavians in Minnesota or Germans in Wisconsin have had strong effects on what can be presented as Midwestern. Invented traditions and vernacular regionalism of the Cincinnati chili or Nashville hot chicken variety have created delightful culinary options, but these further blur the nature and identity of regional cuisine—or at least its similarity to more firmly rooted rural practices in other parts of the world.

The result is a "lite" regionalism whose most effective realization is in California. Much of California cuisine combines some local ingredients, such as abalone or sourdough bread, nationally available produce (but perhaps fresher), a semi-Mediterranean style (Spago's pizza varieties or Chez Panisse's baked goat cheese salad), and a respect for locality mingled with a climate that makes seasons indistinct. Lite regionalism has the advantage of flexibility. California specialties such as fish tacos or ingredients such as alfalfa sprouts move out nationally, while imports such as poke or bubble tea show up all over the state. The national diffusion of shallow forms of regional cooking gives effervescence and variety to cuisine in the United States; after all, kaleidoscopic shifts and options are a basic feature of American taste.

LITE REGIONALISM IN CANADA

Canada has one distinct and complex regional cuisine, that of Québec, but the rest of the nation is even vaster than and equally as homogenized as the United States, with an ambivalent list of what passes for regional recipes. The following menus depict one effort at evoking a modern sense of regionalism.

British Columbia: "A Picnic in Stanley Park" (page 22)

Wine-pickled salmon with pumpernickel and crème fraîche

Caramelized onion and prosciutto tart *or* Summer tossed sushi salad

Raspberry Nanaimo bars and fresh fruit

The Prairies: "A Prairie Brunch" (page 61)

Brie and prosciutto bread pudding

Mixed green salad with mustard vinaigrette

Tea-infused winter fruits with prune brandy cream

Apricot coffee cake with butterscotch walnut filling

The North: "A Midnight Sun Supper" (page 75)

Wild rice pancakes with sour cream and (whitefish) caviar

Grilled arctic char with orange-onion salsa

Wild rice and cranberry salad

Cheddar jalapeño cornbread

(Wild) Blueberry bread pudding with whiskey sauce

Ontario: "A Midsummer Grill" (page 125)

Antipasto platter (marinated artichoke hearts, shrimp, salami slices, olives)

Focaccia

Lemon-raspberry grilled lamb

Garlicky Portobello mushrooms

Sage new potato kebobs

Honey-grilled pears with ginger Mascarpone cream

Hazelnut biscotti

Québec: "A Sophisticated Supper" (page 184)

Quick brandied chicken liver pâté with baguette slices

Toasted garlic soup

New world coq au vin with buttered fingerling potatoes

Baked chèvre on mesclun with fig vinaigrette

French lemon tart

The Maritimes: "A Maritime Company Buffet" (page 246)

Spicy shrimp with fresh coriander and lime

Seafood pot pie

Steamed fiddleheads served cold with mustard vinaigrette

Sesame wheat biscuits

Rhubarb red wine mousse with poached rhubarb

Newfoundland and Labrador: "Christmas Dinner" (page 249)

Cod and potato ovals with spicy lemon mayonnaise

Roast turkey and gravy, wild mushroom and leek stuffing

Mashed potatoes

Rutabaga and pear "crisp"

Shredded sprouts sautéed with pancetta

Individual mincemeat cheesecakes

White Christmas pudding

Chocolate pecan fruitcake

From Rose Murray, *A Taste of Canada: A Culinary Journey* (North Vancouver: Whitecap, 2008).

CHAPTER 3

Community Cookbooks

Some guides to American regional food, like Crosby Gaige's *World's Fair Cook Book*, are organized around recipes—in this case, state by state. Others consist of mostly narrative punctuated by recipes—the *Time-Life* books, for example. Still others, as with Duncan Hines's *Adventures in Good Eating* series or the Sterns' *Roadfood* guides, do not include recipes at all. To what extent do cookbooks that are not also guidebooks reflect regional variation? National cookbooks—those purporting to cover American food in general—tend to include an assortment of regional dishes, such as gumbo, "Yankee" pot roast, or pecan pie, just as they usually present a few Americanized versions of foreign dishes on the order of gazpacho and lasagna. Two categories of cookbooks seem likely, at first glance, to orient their contents around a particular place: those with a regional title, such as *New-England Cookery* and *The Picayune's Creole Cookbook* and others we've looked at already, and community cookbooks, recipe collections put out by local notables, usually to support a charitable cause. Community cookbook recipes are often contributed by the women of the church, club, school, or other group that organized the effort.

It turns out that both types of cookbooks reflect time and class better than the local cuisine of a particular community, revealing its chronological moment and the social level of the anticipated audience more than the cooking of the place of origin. *Marion Brown's Southern Cookbook* is an authentic compendium of what Southern white, upper-middle class families ate in 1951 when it was published, and in 1968 when it was updated. Brown includes a few folksy Southern ingredients, such as wild greens and pawpaws, as well as traditional dishes, such as chitlins and Kentucky burgoo, but her book is oriented more to the eclectic tastes of the mid-twentieth century exemplified by shish kebab, lasagna, and "perfection salad" (celery, pimento, and cabbage in gelatin).[1] Her recipes are taken mostly from community cookbooks put out by Junior League members of various Southern towns. These tended to contain a few old-fashioned, "heritage" items, but mostly reflect trends at the time: chafing-dish recipes or silver cake around 1900; fifty years later, some form of "oriental" chicken (grilled with soy sauce and a sweet Chinese restaurant–style duck sauce) and Jell-O salad.

Comparing Marion Brown's version of Southern regional food with John T. Edge's similarly organized collection of Southern charitable cookbook recipes published in 1999 shows changing tastes and standards of authenticity over nearly fifty years. Edge's *A Gracious Plenty* dispenses with both old Plantation and new suburban styles and gives more weight to African American recipes and rural traditions.[2] Edge does not include Brown's genteel Robert E. Lee cake or anything from the vaguely international category, which for Brown includes tabbouleh salad and Spanish rice.

In this respect, regional and community cookbooks are disappointing but also fascinating, because while less evocative of a particular regional cuisine than one might hope, they offer an excellent impression of what was actually being cooked when the book was published.

Regional Cookbooks

Searching nineteenth-century cookbooks to find authentic American regional traditions tends to be futile. In the first place, there are few regional cookbooks from before the twentieth century, the emphasis being rather on national recipes. The nation's hundredth birthday in 1876 was the occasion for the publication of *The Centennial Cook Book and General Guide,* whose nearly one thousand recipes show almost no hint of regionalism.[3] *The Centennial Cook Book* organizes its recipes in a fashion typical for the period, emphasizing bread, cakes, and pies more than salads, paying more attention to beef and mutton than to lamb or pork. Game is well represented. Several recipes are identified as American, sometimes in contrast to others. American biscuits are on the same page as English biscuits, the difference being that the US version calls for butter, milk, and cream of tartar along with flour and sugar, whereas the English (and French) recipes rely simply on eggs, flour, and sugar. A German variation includes cream. Other dishes are simply stated to be American: American Christmas pudding, American chicken salad, or American waffles. Only a few recipes have a local identification: Boston brown bread, fried oysters Washington style, and Philadelphia roast (an oyster dish).

The titles of a few nineteenth-century cookbooks do seem to promise a regional orientation, but they have the same core as other recipe collections, with only a few additional local touches. Mary Randolph's *Virginia House-Wife* of 1824, Lettice Bryan's *The Kentucky Housewife* (1839), and Sarah Rutledge's *The Carolina Housewife* (1847) gesture at their authors' milieux but follow, for the most part, prevailing Anglo-American standards of the comfortable classes.[4]

Buckeye Cookery (better known as *The Buckeye Cookbook*) began as a fundraising effort undertaken by the women of the First Congregationalist Church in Marysville, Ohio, but they did not aim to produce a regional compendium. The editor and coordinator, Estelle Woods Wilcox, did not live in Ohio but rather in Minneapolis and published the cookbook there in 1877.[5] Its practicality and household advice made *The Buckeye Cookbook* popular beyond the normal range of the new genre of community cookbooks. Wilcox and her husband created the Buckeye Publishing Company and marketed *The Buckeye Cookbook* along with other regional titles such as *The Dixie Cookbook*, creating a franchise. *The Buckeye Cookbook* was updated constantly, and even a German translation appeared. "Buckeye" did not mean Ohio in a culinary sense, but was merely a brand name with an overtone of Midwestern wholesomeness.[6]

After the Civil War, the South set the pattern for the self-consciously regional cookbook. This was a product of genuine Southern distinctiveness, which became more pronounced as the North industrialized and the Southern ruling classes increased their domination over the nominally free black population. Exalting Southern culture was part of the rehabilitation of the Confederacy's historical reputation. Sentimentalized as a gallant "lost cause," the Old South was pictured as an era of gracious living, an image that would be widely diffused in the 1930s by the novel and movie *Gone with the Wind*.

Coinciding with the end of Reconstruction was the publication of *Housekeeping in Old Virginia*. The operative word in the title is *old*, connoting antebellum times.[7] As with *The Buckeye Cookbook*, this is a collective effort, here of 250 women from Virginia and "sister states." One of the contributors is an African American servant listed as "Mozis Addums" (with the quotation marks). His recipe for field peas cooked with bacon is presented in what was supposed to be black dialect.[8] Despite such picturesque touches, the cookbook is more concerned with the standard repertoire than with anything particularly Southern. Cornbread or biscuits were not yet identified with the South, and there are recipes that are national or from other regions, such as beef à la mode and terrapin salad. What makes this book Southern is not culinary style, but rather the mythology of plantation hospitality, the Virginia Cavalier largesse brought over by the aristocratic adherents of the deposed King Charles I and reflected in a society of honor, courtesy, and romance.[9]

The Bluegrass Cook Book, published in 1904, is more aggressively regional in tone than in cuisine. It doesn't try to evoke a chivalric Kentucky past in the manner of the Virginia gentry or the French Creoles of New Orleans, but rather praises the resourcefulness of "Aunt Dinah," a black cook without whose magical skills the master's hospitality would have been logistically impossible. The cookbook uses "Kentucky" and "Bluegrass" in the titles of recipes for corn pudding, burgoo, Catawba (grape) punch, roast quail, and chowchow.[10] *Dishes and Beverages of the Old South* (1913), a more general regional book from the same era, also employs the trope of "old" to recall antebellum elegance and Mammy as the loyal and skilled keeper of the kitchen.

The old South and its culinary glories form an entry in the ledger of what Stephen Schmidt has called "sampler histories"—sentimental cookbooks that resemble those old stitched alphabets and expressions of virtue that adorn the walls of bed-and-breakfast inns. Schmidt subdivides culinary sampler categories into Yankee New England, Southern hospitality, Pilgrim, Pioneer/Prairie, Old Charleston, and so forth. Such cookbooks play on the sense of a lost world of virtue and skill that might include quilting circles, grandmother's pies, butchering animals, produce grown from "heirloom" seeds, and cooking over a hearth fire with iron pots. You may not know how your ancestors cooked, but this is no more important than the absence of cowboys or Yankee maple syrup tappers in your family tree.

Nostalgia for a past you did not experience leaves open the possibility for mistakes, even by experts. A recipe for "Nantucket Cranberry Pie" was a favorite of the distinguished novelist and food journalist Laurie Colwin. A posthumous article in *Gourmet* for November 1993 reported her fruitless search through New England cookbooks to locate the origins of this cranberry dessert with a cake-like crust. As it turns out, far from being an old dish, Nantucket cranberry pie was invented in the 1950s by a home economist for the National Cranberry Association, intending it for home cooks who didn't like making piecrust. The toponym "Nantucket" lent New England authenticity, but no one during Nantucket's whaling days was anticipating digging into this cranberry dessert while carving scrimshaw or weaving baskets.[11] The "sampler" model can be used apart from direct nostalgia to present a narrative of virtuous sustainability. The food writer Michael Pollan's well-known advice to not eat anything your great-grandmother would not have recognized fits into a category Schmidt refers to as "the seasonal/local, farm-to-table Vermont farmhouse sampler."[12]

Community Cookbooks

Having completed this brief and admittedly cynical account of regional recipe collections, let's look at community cookbooks, a genre that reflects simultaneously symbolic regional identity and the irresistible diffusion of national trends like layer cakes and casseroles. Community cookbooks, sometimes called charitable or compiled cookbooks, first appeared during the Civil War. They are put together by church-goers or members of charitable and professional organizations. Until recently, the contributors were almost all female. First designed to raise money for the relief of wounded soldiers, after the war the cookbooks aided other charitable purposes—to fund a church building or to help a hospital, library, or other institution. In the late nineteenth century, these gatherings were so popular that entrepreneurs offered prepackaged text ready to customize with local recipes and advertising.[13] More often, however, the community cookbooks list specific women as the authors of recipes, conferring on them a public-spirited social prominence.

In Canada, a large national community cookbook was issued in 1877 by prominent women to raise money for a children's hospital. The compilers of *The Canadian Home Cook Book* lifted recipes from *The Home Cook Book of Chicago.* Subsequently, many Canadian localities and associations published community cookbooks, but *The Canadian Home Cook Book* remained ubiquitous and is still in print, with many alterations since the original publication.[14] There is nothing to match this in the United States, where charitable cookbooks have always been local rather than national compilations. There are an immense number of these books: over three thousand just from 1861 to 1915.[15] In a bibliography of all cookbooks published between 1860 and 1960, 558 of the 4,447 listings are for community volumes.[16]

They are still being published, but the golden age of the charitable cookbook was from about 1890 to World War II, a prosperous period for small-town America. The community cookbooks offer glimpses of regional cuisine across the United States, but this is a little like panning for gold—a lot of mud has to be sloshed around in order to find the precious flecks. Most community cookbooks have a few regional dishes, but they tend to offer mostly food that was fashionable or at least common nationally. Their authors did not set out to preserve folkways but rather to offer reasonably easy, new recipes—goals that, by definition, were incompatible with the labor-intensive preparations of the past.

From the Civil War until the 1920s, contributors to community cookbooks were usually prominent women affiliated with Protestant churches. The standard bibliography by Margaret Cook, ending in 1915, has 314 Presbyterian listings, 289 Methodist, 220 Congregational, and 151 Baptist. Episcopalians have a modest representation of 77, and there are 22 Jewish synagogues and organizations. At this point, almost no cookbooks were put out by Catholic groups.[17]

Contributors were for the most part white—the absence of African American compendia does not reflect any scarcity of organizations of this period.[18] Exceptions include *The Federation Cook Book,* issued in 1910 by "the colored women of the state of California," who were members of women's clubs, and later African American community cookbooks come from Milwaukee (1968), West Oakland (ca. 1969), and the Sea Islands of South Carolina (1987).[19]

The women who shared their recipes were not, for the most part, members of the town's first families but rather belonged to the upper middle class; the attorneys' wives of Lincoln, Nebraska, for example, in 1976 issued *Tort Pleasers*.[20] Until about 1930, the word *Ladies* in bibliographies is an indication that the listing is for a community cookbook. "Junior League" is a keyword for a subsequent more civic and secular period. Social standing was important, because these women saw themselves as representatives of a particular place yet also as up-to-date with fashions coming from the sophisticated cities—at least as transmitted by women's magazines. It would be interesting to go through a large number of community cookbooks to trace the rise and slow decline of Swedish meatballs, or of salads made with gelatin. The decline would be slow, because while contributors to these books were quick about picking up new dishes, they abandoned them with reluctance. By the 1970s, Jell-O and canned peas were no longer versatile recipe staples in New York City or Chicago but were still important in upstate New York or downstate Illinois. *Church Suppers* is a 2005 collection of recipes from various churches, and it still offers a few gelatin salads and 1950s-vintage casseroles, but its editor Barbara Greenman writes that her favorite aspect of the book is the regional diversity and authenticity of its recipes. In fact, diversity actually blurs culinary authenticity: chicken fajitas from Vermont, "Honolulu Chicken" from Michigan.[21]

Organizers of community cookbooks did not regard themselves as the anointed custodians of regional cuisine in the way that Clementine Paddleford's plantation mistresses and farm wives did. These women admired and sought to preserve certain local culinary ingredients and dishes—chowders in New England, game in the South, or salmon on the West Coast—but they were enthusiastic about nationally familiar foods, for which they offered a version that was "tried and true," often a title for the collections or a recipe subheading. In the early years of community compilations, that enthusiasm extended to copying recipes from published sources. The compendium published in 1901 by the ladies of St. Paul's Episcopal Church in Waco, Texas, included more than forty recipes from *The Century Cookbook* put out in 1895.[22]

Community cookbooks usually mixed several components: traditional recipes reflecting the region of origin; trendy American items; and easy, convenient things such as casseroles or inexpensive takeoffs on elegant dishes—hamburger Stroganoff was a favorite. Far from endeavoring to share difficult recipes, the contributors wanted to appear helpful, thrifty, and resourceful. Creativity was encouraged as long as it didn't spoil the grading curve by calling for esoteric ingredients, hours-long cooking time, or tricky techniques.

Desserts were always prominent. An Emporia, Kansas, cookbook of the early 1960s devotes only six pages to meat, fish, and vegetables but twenty to desserts and cookies.[23] Desserts resisted the relentless twentieth-century drive for convenience. They require labor and time, and things can easily go wrong in baking, nevertheless, when it came to cakes, pies, and puddings, the community cookbooks tended to reject shortcuts and packaged ingredients. It was fine to use canned string beans for a vegetable course and employ canned cream soup as a sauce base, but until the late 1950s, baking from scratch was expected from contributors to local compendia.[24]

In a sample of thirty-three community cookbooks from the Great Plains, all dating from the 1970s, half the space is taken up by desserts.[25] Not surprisingly, the only fish in this region came in the form of canned tuna or salmon. Casseroles equal or outnumber straight meat and poultry recipes. Salad meant something in gelatin, rarely mixed greens or raw vegetables.

A 1974 cookbook from the Upper Florida Keys resembles those of the 1970s Great Plains.[26] There are some fish recipes, including Bahama conch chowder and Keys fish chowder, but cakes, cookies, and desserts make up half the listings. Gelatin salads abound, and there is a recipe for "Five Cup Salad," a community cookbook staple: one cup each of mandarin oranges, chopped pineapple, miniature marshmallows, shredded coconut, and sour cream. Casseroles are not as prominent as in the Plains states, but ground beef is ubiquitous, not only in four varieties of chili but in "Jiffy Beef Stroganoff," sloppy joes, and "Savory Burger Stew." These findings can be generalized to the rest of the country, although by the 1970s, home cooks from well-off communities were starting to lose enthusiasm for processed ingredients.

The degree of borrowing from immigrants or nonwhite people varied. The Southwest dealt with its Hispanic heritage more openly than with the influence of its contemporary Mexican population. Thus, books often referred to the legacy of the "Spanish," represented as conquistadors. The word *Mexican* as applied to tamales or enchiladas was unavoidable, but while Spanish and Mexican were conflated, actual Mexican Americans were marginalized. In general, so-called ethnic foods were sought after as long as they fell within the Americanized repertoire: chop suey, spaghetti, chili con carne. Some foreign dishes like Swiss fondue or Wiener schnitzel were not considered ethnic at all but just chic European.

Local patriotism notwithstanding, the women who assembled these projects were usually more interested in recipes that were homey but contemporary, quick and easy rather than heirlooms. Some of the community cookbooks would be impossible to locate geographically if you opened them without looking at the cover, but more often there is an attempt to balance a culinary sense of place with modern trends. In this way, community cookbooks are points of access to the ambiguous, or maybe multifaceted, attitude toward regional culinary traditions.

Because community cookbooks show the tastes of particular times regardless of place or region, we present them chronologically, with some repeated editions emanating from the same or similar circles offered to show change over time.

Canyon and Randall County, Texas, 1903–1940

The town of Canyon (known as Canyon City until 1911) is the county seat of Randall County, in the middle of the Texas Panhandle. It is the home of West Texas A&M University, on whose campus is the Panhandle Plains Historical Museum and its marvelous library, which includes several local community cookbooks. The oldest, from 1903, is *C. P. Workers Cookbook* (C. P. refers to Canyon City's Cumberland Presbyterian church). In 1909, the Home Mission

Society of the Canyon City Methodist Episcopal Church, South, issued a collection of recipes, and that same year the *Amarillo Cookbook* was published by women of the First Baptist Church in that nearby, relatively large city. As is usually the case, none of these books claims to be purely or authentically regional.

The Presbyterian cookbook of 1903 has a few colorful items, such as "Old Texas Corn Pudding" and "Panhandle Preserves," the latter actually a standard apricot or plum preparation.[27] There is an unusual recipe for okra crullers and an aspirational oyster soup reflecting East Coast standards of elegance. By the opening of the twentieth century, it was possible to ship live oysters anywhere, and they were also available canned.[28] New Orleans is the inspiration for two kinds of gumbo, one specifically referred to as "Creole Gumbo Soup." There is Georgia plum pudding as well as a New England plum pudding. Some of the puddings and the single ice cream recipe involve packaged gelatin, one of the few processed foods included. Desserts are prominent, including such church ladies' favorites as Scripture cake, which gives only the biblical references to ingredients: Nahum 3:12 (figs), Numbers 17:18 (almonds), II Chronicles 9:9 (spices), and so forth.

A peculiarity of the time as well as place of publication is a recipe for "Free Silver Cake." Normal silver cake, made with egg whites and so resembling angel food cake, was well known, so the distinction here is the adjective *free* to describe silver, referring to a goal of the Populist movement that reached its peak in the 1890s: to have the national government renounce the gold standard and to allow unlimited coinage of silver at a ratio artificially high in relation to gold. The intended effects of free silver would have been inflationary, benefiting debtors like the ranchers and farmers in Texas, the South, and the Midwest while reining in the profits of banks and other creditors, mostly in the Northeast. Deflation had followed the severe economic contraction after the panic of 1893, so debts were particularly onerous. The defeat of "the Great Commoner" William Jennings Bryan in the presidential elections of 1896 and 1900 meant the failure of free silver. Accordingly, the Methodists ladies of 1909 omitted any form of silver cake, but two slightly different versions appear again in the Amarillo Baptist cookbook, but only as regular silver cake, the political impetus having spent itself.

Sociopolitical movements aside, the 1909 *Canyon City Cookbook* is more ambitious and hortatory than the Presbyterian effort of six years earlier.[29] It opens with an admonition to teach young girls how to cook so that when they are old their husbands will not stray. The collection is notable for the surprising number of oyster dishes, not just a single soup but patties, croquettes, pie, escalloped oysters, two stews (one Creole), and oyster cocktail. The evocation of New Orleans continues with gumbo and "Creole Hash." This book also has a recipe for spaghetti, which was quite unusual at this time. Two innovations that later cookbooks would elaborate on are salads made with gelatin, in this case a tomato aspic, and Mexican American recipes, here chili con carne, chicken tamales, and baked tamales.

Although Amarillo was and remains a considerably larger town than Canyon, the Baptist cookbook, also dating from 1909, is unpretentious, perhaps an indication of the relative social status among Protestant churches.[30] There are no gelatin salads, but chili and tamales appear, along with the regular silver cake. There are recipes for five types of fruit cake and one for "Mexican Loaf Cake."

The next collection from the area is *Favorite Recipes of the Women of Randall County,* put out during the Second World War.[31] This is not the product of a specific religious or charitable effort and may fall more aptly into the genre of handbooks for dealing with rationing. Meatless dishes are offered, but there are, as usual, many desserts despite sugar rationing. "Italian" spaghetti is made with veal and American cheese. Mexican-inspired dishes and gelatin salads, two innovations in the two 1909 cookbooks, come into prominence: tamale loaf, Mexican chicken, and *albondigas* (meatballs) are accompanied by lime-apple salad, jellied supper salad, and ginger ale salad.

The Panhandle cookbooks show a combination of Texas particularities and national tastes. There was an effort at the beginning of the twentieth century to present Texan cuisine as Southern or related to New Orleans Creole cookery. Gentility gave way to modernism as evidenced by the rise of salads in general and gelatin salads specifically. The presence of Mexican people and cuisine was at first ignored and then Americanized. A 1949 Texas cookbook emphasized Texas as part of the West rather than the South, or at least the South here signaled by possum and sweet potatoes, not upper-class items.[32] Game includes goat, rattlesnake, barbecued armadillo, and even crows. There are also recipes for spaghetti and meatballs, chop suey, and curry.

This Western ranching image of Texas, however, did not dominate. In 1964 the Favorite Recipe Press, which made a business of collecting and publishing state and local recipes, published a book of nine hundred recipes from female club members in Texas.[33] The introduction tells us that the Lone Star State offers dishes of Southern, Mexican, and cosmopolitan big-city origin. There are, alas, no armadillos, and regional identification is mostly unconvincing. "Texas Salad" is made with lemon or lime gelatin, canned pineapple, pimentos, nuts, cottage cheese, and heavy cream. It appears alongside national classics such as 7 Up salad, cola salad, Coca-Cola salad (different from regular cola salad), congealed salad, and oriental salad (with mandarin oranges). The national taste of the 1960s is acknowledged by a casserole with tuna and elbow macaroni called "Tuna Mediterranean." Cosmopolitan influences are distilled in a "foreign favorites" section that includes Mexican enchiladas, tacos, chiles rellenos, and the like.

Spaghetti

Put on to boil in salted water the required amount of spaghetti, add a little garlic. Boil thirty minutes and drain. Butter baking dish, put in layer of spaghetti, layer of cheese, dash of cayenne pepper, sprinkle with catsup, repeat until dish is full. Put on top a layer of cracker crumbs, put milk to nearly cover. Bake in moderate oven one-half hour.

From *The Canyon City Cookbook* (Canyon City, TX: no publisher listed, 1909), 32.

East Hampton, New York, 1948, 1975

Moving across the country to New York's Long Island, we leave behind the tumbleweed, armadillos, and the free silver movement. The differences between the sophisticated Hamptons and the agrarian and industrial Texas Panhandle are only partially manifested by their community cookbooks.

Now part of the swank Long Island summer resort area, East Hampton dates back to 1648, and for centuries its inhabitants supported themselves by agriculture and fishing. Eastern Long Island was famous for its potatoes as well as for scallops and oysters. The East Hampton Ladies' Village Improvement Society sponsored a cookbook in 1898 to raise money for its activities and continued to collect recipes and publish them periodically thereafter. Looking at two of these, from 1948 and 1975, shows the change from an established year-round town to a sophisticated summer resort, although still an artistic and slightly bohemian one compared to posh Southampton.

The 1948 cookbook marked the three hundredth anniversary of the founding of the town.[34] As with its predecessors, the 1948 collection tried to be historically authentic, rejecting appetizers because "our forefathers" had little need of them, but including all manner of clam preparations along with menhaden (a fish related to herring, now seldom seen), eels, and bread made with what was considered inferior-grade flour ("canaille"). The women were enterprising enough to cook steaks cut from two porpoises that had washed up on the beach in December 1947. Porpoise tastes just like beef, *The Three Hundredth Anniversary Cookbook* reports, as long as you take care to remove the layer of blubber covering the meat. Still, with gelatin salads, Swedish meatballs, casseroles, and "peatunia" (canned peas, cream of mushroom soup, and tuna), we are clearly in the postwar era.

Nothing quite as wild or local as porpoise appears in *The East Hampton Cookbook of Menus and Recipes* issued by the same Ladies' Village Improvement Society in 1975.[35] The book opens with an introduction by Craig Claiborne, the *New York Times* food writer who lived primarily in East Hampton. The assumed reader was the owner of a second home, although the editor made an effort to retain native traditions like clam pie (three varieties) and beach plum pudding. In keeping with the needs of a summer house constituency, this eleventh cookbook of the LVIS is arranged by menus for brunches, buffet lunches, holiday barbecues, and the like, although there are a few cold-weather ideas as well. Unlike the older cookbooks, the recipes are anonymous, gathered together by an editor. No economical or timesaving tips here—the food is not elaborate, but it is up-to-date—fresh vegetables, risotto rather than spaghetti—and replete with

East Hampton community cookbook cover, 1948. Put out by the East
Hampton Ladies' Village Improvement Society.

1970s staples like arugula, steak tartare, white bean salad, and Boursin cheese. It
is also, so to speak, negatively harmonious with the sophisticated world, so there
is no salad made with gelatin, only one casserole (made with vegetables), and no
canned soup concentrate. The cookbook's emphasis on seafood indicates something about the location, and the ubiquity of fresh vegetables suggests summer,
but for the most part this cookbook, as with most other community compendia,
is a better indicator of class and sophistication than place.

Apple Pandowdy

4 cups sliced apples

½ to ¾ cup sugar

½ tsp cinnamon

½ tsp nutmeg

2 Tb molasses

2 Tb butter

pastry

Arrange alternate layers of apples, sugar, spices, and molasses in greased baking dish. Dot with butter and cover with lid of pastry. Cut slits in top and bake in hot oven 450 degrees for 15 minutes. Then lower temperature to 375 and continue cooking until the apples are soft.

From *The Three Hundredth Anniversary Cook Book* (East Hampton: Ladies Village Improvement Society, 1948), 47.

Rawalpindi, Pakistan, 1955

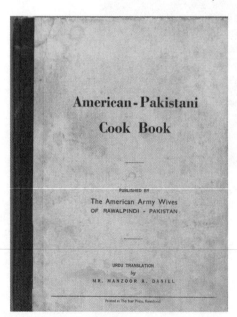

American-Pakistani Cook Book cover, ca. 1955. The book contains recipes in English and Urdu assembled by "American army wives" in Rawalpindi, Pakistan.

The *American-Pakistani Cook Book* put out by "American army wives" affiliated with the United States base in Rawalpindi captures the tone of midcentury community cookbooks, but for an exotic locale and in an unusual format.[36] As with Texas and Long Island, there is a sense of place, but even more a pattern of recipes common to a certain moment in American culinary history. In this sense, the American women in 1950s Pakistan were au courant with US food trends.

No charitable purpose was announced for this collection, which was probably intended to offer guidance for new arrivals and others who needed to adapt dishes from home to an unfamiliar environment.

The recipes are given in English accompanied by Urdu translations in order that the household cook could be shown what the American family wanted. That said, it is hard to imagine a Pakistani chef who could interpret US enchiladas, no matter how good the translation.

Unlike the majority of community cookbooks, specific recipes were not identified with particular women. Nevertheless, the collective effort resulted in a typical group of American recipes. Only two Jell-O salads are presented—lemon-lime pineapple salad and pear salad that uses lime-flavored Jell-O—but the main courses and desserts are thoroughly representative of home. Fried chicken, pot roast, New England boiled dinner, and chicken à la king are there, as are the usual lightly international standards such as Spanish rice and chili con carne. Twenty-six out of 130 pages are devoted to desserts such as cobbler, coffee cake, apple betty, pie, and brownies.

An extensive and detailed section describes how to make bread, rolls, and biscuits. The chapter on canapés reflects the entertainment duties of military wives and includes such tips as using chocolate pudding as a tea sandwich filling. The compilers of this cookbook were not obsessively focused on creating a fortified island of American familiarity. The book includes Pakistani dishes because of the "keen interest shown in the specialties of this area" and as a souvenir of service: when the army wife returns home, she will be able to amaze her friends. Some southern Indian dishes, such as *idli* and *dosa,* find their way into this section as do, strangely, arroz con pollo and angel food cake. The northern India/Pakistan dishes are mostly standard—chicken curry, stuffed chapattis, dal, kebabs, and mango pickles—but they are the result of firsthand observation.

The cookbook has the cheerful tone found generally in community compilations. Rawalpindi was much safer for Americans in the 1950s than it is now, but also more remote before commercial long-distance jets went into service. The persistence of standard community cookbook recipes is not surprising, given the distance, at least mild homesickness, and the need to please a gastronomically unadventurous family. What makes the American-Pakistani collection unusual is the perhaps timid but real curiosity about where the contributors are actually living and, of course, the effort of the Urdu translator.

Garam Masala (Curry Powder)*

1 chhatank jeera [i.e., cumin
   seed]

1 chhatank large black
   cardamom

½ chhatank cinnamon bark

10 whole cloves

1 chhatank dry dhaniya [i.e.,
   coriander]

1 oz bay leaves

1 oz black pepper

Grind spices together.

*In fact, garam masala is not curry powder but a different, sweeter spice mixture found in many parts of India and Pakistan. The local measurements in *chhatank* (approximately 2 ounces) may be for spices to be bought by household servants, while pepper and bay leaves are given in ounces since the housewife presumably could buy these from the American PX (the military store).

From *American-Pakistani Cookbook* (Rawalpindi: Red Star Press, ca. 1955), 105.

Harkers Island, North Carolina, 1987

Harkers Island is in a section of the southern coast of North Carolina known as Down East that lies between mainland North Carolina and the southernmost portion of the Outer Banks, so not exposed to the open ocean. During most of its 350-year history, Harkers Island has been isolated, dependent on fishing, hunting, and farming for sustenance. Today, the island's population includes vacationers and retired people who have moved from elsewhere. *Island Born and Bred*, a cookbook put out by the Harkers Island United Methodist Women in1987, has a greater than normal degree of local distinction but is not a reflection of a completely self-sufficient place. It shows the tension or, put more positively, complementarity between local cooking and national influence.[37]

The Harkers Island cookbook offers a few "traditional recipes" for loon, whale, turtle, and robins, all illegal to hunt now and so included only for historical reference. More realistic local recipes are provided for oysters, crabs, mullet, May peas, blackberries, and blueberries. The book also describes how to dry and cook fresh mullet roe.[38]

No recipes for preparing game appear in the Harkers Island collection, nor do we find other specialties described by culinary researchers such as Muscadine grape-hull pie.[39] Harkers Island dishes include the slow-cooked seafood characteristic of the region: stewed oysters, drum, hard crabs with gravy, stewed crabs with cornmeal dumplings, slow-roasted jumping mullet, baked menhaden roe, roasted conch. Shrimp recipes are well represented, and shrimp is so much a local specialty that people take off from work and school when the shrimp are plentiful.[40]

Although it presents authentic seafood recipes and offers a lyrical portrait of island life through stories and historical accounts, *Island Born and Bred* is at heart a typical community cookbook. The reader is regaled with recipes for guacamole and party dips featuring Lipton onion soup mix with sour cream and cream cheese. As is often the case, the salad section is in tune with mainstream trends. Insofar as marshmallow salad and "Heavenly Hash" (canned pineapple, Cool Whip, coconut flakes, maraschino cherries, and milk) were old-fashioned in 1987, their inclusion can be attributed to Harkers Island lagging twenty or thirty years behind the rest of the country rather than to a desire to preserve unique coastal Carolina traditions.

Stewed Clams

2 pecks chowder clams
5 lbs. potatoes
1 bunch scallions
3 slices fat pork
6–8 cornmeal dumplings
salt and pepper to taste

Gut and wash clams—wash about 3 times. Chop clams into bite-size pieces. Fry-out fat pork in cooking pot; add clams and enough water to cover. Add salt and pepper to taste. Boil for about 1 hour. Add chopped scallions; boil about 1 hour more until tender. Add potatoes; then cornmeal dumplings. Cook for another ½ hour.

From *Island Born and Bred* (Atlantic Beach, NC: Weathers Printing Company, 1987), 193.

Jackson, Mississippi, 1971

Jackson is as authentically Southern as Harkers Island, but its self-conception, at least as communicated by its white upper-middle class, is that of a cultivated city that consumes the bounty of the rural South but is not involved in producing it. The 1971 *Jackson Cookbook*, put out by the Jackson Symphony League, begins with a memoir by the venerated Mississippi writer Eudora Welty noting the limited options for dining out during her childhood and the importance of entertaining at home.[41] Among other things, she recalls the belief that two "well-traveled bachelors" (which would have been understood to refer to a gay couple) had brought mayonnaise to Jackson sometime early in the twentieth century. The contributors here are socially prominent white women; there is no explicit recognition of African Americans. Unusual among such collections, there is a substantial and separate section of recipes offered by men.

The first section, "Heirloom," consists of recipes from "several of Jackson's first families," mostly never before shared. Unlike remote Harkers Island, there is no old-fashioned food being caught or foraged here. Most of the supposedly traditional recipes are for nonregional desserts such as Neapolitan pudding (which involves meringue and macaroons), and eggnog cake. The contributions by the majority of the participants, esteemed if not quite first-family level, tend toward popular national dishes such as quiche Lorraine, vichyssoise, and beef Stroganoff. The South is represented by grits and hoppin' John, but moussaka appears just a page away from the latter. Desserts have the greatest number of recipes, and they don't involve mixes or canned ingredients. Coca-Cola congealed salad and ginger ale salad are clearly Southern, but more by reason of enthusiasm for what would no longer have been fashionable in the North, unlike quiche or moussaka.

Contributors to the "Men's Recipes" chapter were identified as occasional cooks, and their recipes fit into the common notion that men prefer hearty, spicy food. Many of the dishes are complicated, because they reflect cooking as a weekend hobby—lasagna, beef bourguignon with nineteen ingredients, and a recipe for the Midwestern noodle, meat, and cheese combination known as Johnny Marzetti. (The founder of Marzetti's restaurant in Columbus, Ohio, gave the recipe to the contributor's father.) Wild duck and quail represent game. The men give directions for a few desserts, notably grasshopper pie, made with crème de menthe and crème de cacao.

Ginger Ale Salad

1 tablespoon gelatin

2 tablespoons cold water

¼ cup heated ginger ale

¼ cup lemon juice

1 cup ginger ale

½ cup seedless grapes

½ cup drained crushed pineapple

½ cup chopped preserved ginger

¼ cup chopped celery

Soak gelatin in cold water. Dissolve in heated ginger ale. Add lemon juice and remaining ginger ale. When mixture begins to set, add grapes, pineapple, ginger, and chopped celery. Congeal and serve on lettuce with mayonnaise.

From *The Jackson Cookbook, Compiled by the Symphony League of Jackson, Mississippi* (Jackson, MS: Symphony League of Jackson, 1971), 38.

White Trash Cooking, 1986

In the same genre, but at a considerable sociological distance from East Hampton and Jackson, is *White Trash Cooking*, published in 1986, a defiant takeoff on the standard community cookbook.[42] The women who contributed their recipes were not members of the Junior League and deliberately highlighted their poverty and resourcefulness. The book is a mannered snapshot of rural, white, poor-folks' cooking of its time, incorporating a self-reliant tradition of hunting and dressing small animals from squirrel to "cooters" (land turtles), but one also

White Trash Cooking, 1986. A different kind of community cookbook, this one represents a class of Southern women rather than a specific town.

based on margarine (referred to as "oleo"), Bisquick, and canned beans. The juxtapositions are stunning: Four-Can Deep Tuna Pie, calling for canned green beans, canned or frozen French-fried onion rings, Campbell's cream of mushroom soup, and canned tuna fish, is followed by the considerably more traditional and less convenient Cooter Pie baked in the turtle's shell, an intimidating recipe that begins "Drop live cooter in a pot of boiling water. . . ."

Not every recipe has someone's name attached to it, but the author, Ernest Matthew Mickler, collected recipes from women in small towns of the South as well as acquaintances from North Florida, where he grew up. Contributors and informants include Big Reba Culpepper of Burnt Corn, Alabama; a woman identified as Miz Ina from Sandfly, Georgia; and Nelda Welch of Hot Coffee, Mississippi. The collection is prefaced with a series of endorsements that testify to its ambiguous tone and impression: both comic and tragic, serious and spooky, mouth-watering and off-putting: Mark Holburn, the editor of a photography magazine called *Aperture*, said, "It is the funniest book I have seen in years." "But surely people don't eat that stuff?" remarked the South African–born American geophysicist Athelstan Spilhaus. On the other side, Arkansas Senator J. William Fulbright said, "How did you know that Trashin Cookin is my favorite of all cuisines?" Harper Lee, author of *To Kill a Mockingbird*, found the photographs of houses, people, and kitchens "shattering" and said the book was "a beautiful testament to a stubborn people of proud and poignant heritage."[43]

The recipes are not immediately identifiable as white as opposed to African American, demonstrating our earlier findings about Southern cuisine generally. The white author recalls helping his mother make dinners of chitlins, turnip greens, hoecakes, swamp cabbage stew, and Scripture cake to raise money for some local unfortunates whose trailer had burned.[44] Mickler acknowledges the similarity between black and white cooking and then moves quickly on, contenting himself with the observations that soul food is spicier (true) and that white rural cooking has more variety than black (probably not). *White Trash Cooking* received praise from Vertamae Grosvenor, an African American expert on soul food and the author of *Vibration Cooking*.

The current popularity of Rachael Ray as an unpretentious, homespun cook is in some ways a manifestation of the same outlook as *White Trash Cooking*, which in contrast lacks Ray's cheerfulness or mainstream emphasis on convenience. This cookbook does not assume its readers are stressed about time, or at least that is not a major obstacle in their hard lives. Much more than anything Rachael Ray comes up with, the recipes evoke something closer to poverty than shopping at Costco and keeping to a budget. One, "Pore Folk Soup," is simply soda crackers crumbled in warm milk. Potato chip sandwich and "Kiss Me Not Sandwich" (mustard and onion or, alternatively, peanut butter and onion) are not much fancier. There are, however, plenty of elaborate recipes—Brunswick stew calls for twenty ingredients and, as with most community cookbooks, the desserts are luxurious, after a fashion. "Big Reba's Rainbow Ice-Box Cake" requires a cup of sugar, pecans, egg yolks, four boxes of Jell-O (lime and cherry), canned pineapple, oleo, and graham crackers. *White Trash Cooking* balances dishes made from scratch with those dependent on processed ingredients. There are two chicken casserole recipes, one involving thirteen ingredients beginning with a stewing hen, and the other explicable by its title: "Freda's Five-Can Casserole" using canned boneless chicken.

The three basic ingredients of this cuisine are the rural Southern trinity: molasses, cornmeal, and salt meat (pork), but condensed soup and margarine also appear frequently. Certain categories, such as cakes and game, are presented in a straightforward and traditional manner. Of the eleven cake recipes, only two suggest using a mix, and obviously there is no quick 'n' easy way to make rabbit pie, roast possum, or gator tail. The salads, on the other hand, reflect the bygone gentility of aspic made with Jell-O, mayonnaise and additional flourishes involving marshmallows, coconut, bananas, and even cinnamon candies. This section is not so different from the corresponding chapter of the Jackson Symphony League compilation. Both have "Five-Cup Salad," for example.[45]

As is often the case with American cookbooks, the story behind *White Trash Cooking* is more complicated than it first appears. The upper-crust authors of the 1950 *Charleston Receipts*, as ladylike a compendium as can be imagined, claimed that Mickler had copied at least twenty recipes from their book, including roast possum hung from a hook.[46] They seem to have been right, although they could not obtain relief from the courts because recipes do not have copyright protection. That the rich and poor of the South should have such a close connection is noteworthy, showing that class boundaries as regards cooking are less firm than they look to be at first.

Today, more than thirty years after the publication of *White Trash Cooking*, rural white America is in more desperate condition than ever. The tone of *White Trash Cooking* seems comparatively optimistic, its wryly stoical contributors presenting a hardscrabble but still viable way of life. Their self-irony, reminiscent of the 1981 Barbara Mandrell song "I Was Country When Country Wasn't Cool," reflects a sly take on rural food habits, preferable to the currently widespread notion that such people are completely captured by fast food and are mostly obese. The women in this book express a combination of self-mockery and contempt for outsiders' patronizing stereotypes.

Goldie's Yo-Yo Puddin

1 stick oleo margarine (¼ lb)

2 egg yolks

1 cup nut meats (your choice)

1 cup white sugar

1 small can pineapple

2 small boxes Nabisco
   vanilla wafers

Cream the oleo, sugar, and egg-yolks together and add your Nabisco vanilla wafers, pineapple, and nuts. Beat egg whites stiff. Serve topped with Cool Whip.

From Ernest Matthew Mickler, *White Trash Cooking* (Berkeley: Ten Speed Press, 1986), 102.

Cabbagetown, Georgia, 1976

Cabbagetown Families, Cabbagetown Food, like *White Trash Cooking*, is a community cookbook of poor, Southern white people, but from a former textile town, now part of greater Atlanta. A group biography of female mill workers and their recipes, it is a more serious storytelling production than *White Trash Cooking*.[47] The lives of these women, as well as their cooking tips, are told in their own voices. The recipes are frank about poverty. Nancy Roden, born in 1915 and mother of nine children, has a "cheap casserole" recipe involving pork, canned tomatoes, macaroni, and cheese. Corncob dumplings are a more traditional inexpensive dish offered by Azilee Edwards, and imitation coffee made with meal bran is presented by Levie Bratcher, who grew up as the daughter of sharecroppers.

No picturesque game recipes here, although people recall eating raccoon with their rural relatives. There are memories of foraging for pokeweed, blue mustard, and wild cabbage when Cabbagetown bordered on open country, and there are four recipes for making cooked poke salat and one for wild sumac. There are no preparations involving Jell-O. Processed food is not completely absent—canned salmon and oatmeal are the basis for a casserole.

Beatrice Dalton's Stewed Chicken

I love to cook anything that's good, I just love to cook. I love to cook cakes and I love to cook pork and stew beef and I like to stew chicken and make dressing.

Put water in the boiler and put [the chicken] in there and boil it till it's real good and tender. You can put it whole or cut it up just however you want it. I take cornbread and biscuit, crumble them all up together real good and put butter and eggs and some sage and onions and stir it up real good. I have my broth a' boiling in the pan. I'm going to cook it in and put all the things in there, stir them real good. Sometimes I put it in the stove and bake it and sometimes I just stir it up and boil it. I love the boiled dressing the best. [When] the chicken's done I take most of it and just cut it up or tear it up and put it in the dressing. I made some Sunday and it sure was good.

From *Cabbagetown Families, Cabbagetown Food* (Atlanta: Patch Publication, 1976), 11.

Southern Appalachia, 2015

Appalachia is not the setting for the people featured in either *White Trash Cooking* or *Cabbagetown Families*, but its inhabitants have been affected by the same contemptuous language and imagery as their Deep South kin receive. The English chef and television personality Jamie Oliver visited Huntington, West Virginia, in 2010 and tried to teach its citizens and their public school kitchen personnel how to get out of first place in the demography of obesity.[48] In a distillation of the culinary representation applied to rural America as a whole, Appalachia went from colorful hillbilly (backyard chickens, moonshine, hunting critters, home canning) to dystopian modern (opioids, fast-food addiction, smoking, obesity) without stopping at any intermediate stations.

In fact, there is a culinary renaissance underway, with increasing attention paid to small farms and local breeds that never disappeared from the Eastern mountains. At first glance, Ronni Lundy's *Victuals*: *An Appalachian Journey, with Recipes* might seem like an homage to the *Time-Life* cookbooks.[49] The photographs show a dreamy landscape with no strip mining or even automobiles. Tools, houses, and for that matter people are worn, but in an attractively weathered fashion. No cans or mixes here, although Lundy does have a recipe for West Virginia Pepperoni Rolls.[50]

This is a species of community cookbook, albeit one lavishly produced and organized by an author, not a mere editor. It names Appalachian cooks, farmers, and restaurant owners as recipe authors. Instead of treating the region as a shrinking reserve of dying customs, Lundy is optimistic about the expansion of interest in preserving seeds, the revival of wild greens, and little-known domestic vegetables like Candy Roaster squash. She is proud of dishes confined to Appalachia such as apple stack cake (a layered cake made with sorghum syrup). She notes the presence of an African American population and attributes to it many common foods and preparations like sauerkraut, and shuck beans (beans dried in their casing, soaked, and cooked with smoked pork).[51]

Buttermilk Brown Sugar Pie

Single unbaked pie crust

1½ cups (packed) light brown sugar

¼ cup finely ground cornmeal

½ tsp salt

3 large eggs at room temperature

4 Tb butter, melted and cooled to room temperature

¾ cup whole buttermilk, at room temperature

1 tsp vanilla extract

Preheat oven to 350° F. Place crust in 9-inch pie pan and refrigerate while making the filling.

In a medium bowl, combine brown sugar, cornmeal and salt.

In a large bowl, beat eggs until frothy. Beat in melted butter. Add the dry mixture and stir vigorously until the brown sugar dissolves. Add buttermilk and vanilla.

When all is well combined, pour mixture into pie crust and bake for 45 minutes, or until the center is set.

Allow the pie crust to cool until just barely warm before slicing.

From Ronni Lundy, *Victuals: An Appalachian Journey, with Recipes* (New York: Clarkson Potter, 2016), p. 129.

MORE RECIPES FROM COMMUNITY COOKBOOKS

Traditional/Regional

Baked Beans with Maple Sugar

1 quart of beans, either soldier or pea beans. Soak in water overnight. In the morning drain and parboil, boiling in fresh water until the skins curl when a few beans are picked up in a spoon and blown upon.

Place beans in a bean pot, or a kettle may be used.

Add to the beans:

    1 cup soft maple sugar

    3 tsp. salt

    1 tsp. ginger

Cover with boiling water and put in the oven to bake.

In the meantime, put 1 lb. of lean salt port on to parboil, first having scored the rind each way in small squares, cutting down into the meat. Let the pork come to a boil. Drain, discarding the water in which it cooked and bury it in the hot beans with the rind showing.

Bake the beans 5 or 6 hours in a slow, slow oven until the water has been absorbed but the beans are still moist and juicy. Add more water if needed. Toward the end of the baking, remove the cover and let the pork brown.

From *A Bicentennial Book of Recipes from Pownal, Vermont* (Pownal, VT: no publisher listed, 1976), 34.

Green Tomato Pie

3 green tomatoes, sliced

½ cup water

½ cup seedless raisins

Pastry for 2 (9-inch) layers

1 cup sugar

2 tablespoons flour

¾ teaspoon cinnamon

½ teaspoon ginger

¼ teaspoon nutmeg

2 tablespoons unsalted butter

Grated zest of 1 lemon

1½ tablespoons lemon juice

¼ cup brandy or whiskey

Preheat the oven to 450°. Select firm green tomatoes about 8 ounces each. Pour the water over the tomatoes in a skillet and simmer five minutes or until they have absorbed most of the water and seem tender. Add the raisins and cook a little longer. Drain the skillet, reserving the liquor, and place the tomatoes and raisins in a 9-inch pie pan lined with uncooked pie dough. Mix the sugar and flour together and sprinkle over the tomatoes. Sprinkle with the cinnamon, ginger and nutmeg. Dot the surface with the butter. Add the grated zest and lemon juice. Pour the brandy over the top. If there is room, add a few tablespoons of the reserved tomato liquor. Top with a slashed solid crust or with strips of dough. Bake for 15 minutes. Reduce the heat to 375 and bake 30 minutes longer, or until the crust is golden brown.

From *Out of Kentucky Kitchens*, reprinted in John T. Edge, *A Gracious Plenty: Recipes and Recollections from the American South* (New York: HPBooks, 1999), 109.

Raccoon (Caldwell Terry's recipe)

1 raccoon
1 large onion, quartered
water to almost cover
salt and pepper to taste
sage
meal and flour, mixed half and half

Clean coon and put in pan with water, salt and onion. Boil until tender. Remove from liquid and drain. Rub in sage, salt and pepper as desired. Roll in mixture of half meal and half flour. Bake in oven at 350° until brown. Serve with sweet potatoes and corn bread.

From *Not by Bread Alone, Moodyville Missionary Baptist Church: Recipes for Life, Byrdstown, Tennessee* (Collierville, TN: Fundcraft, 2018), 17.[52]

Modern/Eclectic

Surprise Tuna Potato Bake

3 (7 oz.) cans chunk tuna fish

3 (2½ oz.) cans shoestring potatoes

1 (14½ oz.) can evaporated milk

1 (10½ oz.) can of mushrooms

1 (4 oz.) can pimentos

Mix all together. Put in greased two-quart casserole. Bake in 375-degree oven about 45 minutes.

From *A Bicentennial Book of Recipes from Pownal, Vermont* (Pownal, VT: no publisher listed, 1976), 30.

Tater Tot Casserole (Levi Hand's Recipe)

ground beef

1 large can cream of mushroom soup (undiluted)

½ lb. Velveeta cheese, grated

1 pkg. Tater Tots

Brown ground beef; drain and season with salt and pepper. Spoon soup over ground beef with spatula. Spoon Velveeta cheese on top. Cover top with Tater Tots. Bake until brown at 350°.

From *Not by Bread Alone, Moodyville Missionary Baptist Church: Recipes for Life, Byrdstown, Tennessee* (Collierville, TN: Fundcraft, 2018), 37.

American Regional Cuisine in Legend and Reality

As we have seen, then, several generations of twentieth-century writers examined regional cuisine and were resourceful in their battle against numbing culinary homogenization. Journalists like Clementine Paddleford, food writers like the authors of the *Time-Life* volumes, and field workers like the America Eats researchers preserved knowledge about endangered local and regional dishes, but the march of processed foods, national brand names, fast-food hamburgers, and convenience products seemed inexorable. A sense of the obstacles advocates of American regional traditions faced is provided by two cookbooks by Sheila Hibben (1888–1964), an Alabama native who was raised in Europe and served during the First World War as a nurse. She was mentioned earlier as providing Rex Stout with culinary information for his Nero Wolfe mystery, *Too Many Cooks.* When she was helping Stout in 1936 and 1937, she was food columnist for *The New Yorker,* for which she eventually wrote more than 350 articles.[53] She was also well known as the author of *The National Cookbook*, published in 1932, which went through multiple printings notwithstanding the country's economic collapse.[54] Hibben said she wrote the book in reaction to a *New York Herald Tribune Magazine* article on March 25, 1928, which featured a tableau of whipped cream in the shape of a terrier paddling in a dish of soup. This couldn't really be what America had come to, could it? If only, she wrote, the American housekeeper would pay attention to how things taste, and set aside novelty, frivolity, convenience, efficiency, supposed healthfulness, science, and all the other distractions that interfere with the enjoyment of food. Given its natural wealth, the United States ought to have wonderful cooking and indeed, there are regional traditions that, if attended to, would restore not just its cuisine but its soul.[55]

The name of the cookbook was not intended to convey a single, unified culinary path but rather to celebrate regional variety found within a single nation. It fits into the pattern discerned as far back as James Parkinson's riposte to Grand Duke Alexis that America's regions are the source of its best and most authentic food. Most of the recipes in *The National Cookbook* are given a state or city identification: broiled soft-shell crabs are from Baltimore; baked chicken pie is identified with Missouri; French pancakes are a New Orleans specialty. Because the cookbook is organized by type of dish (soups, fish, poultry, game, and so on), one has to use an index giving each state's contributions in order to discern any regional pattern.

True to her intentions, Hibben offers the reader a sensuous compendium, including recipes of foreign settlers, Germans particularly. Some attributions seem mysterious, however: Why is Welsh rarebit a San Francisco treat, or date pudding a specialty of Colorado, or tutti-frutti ice cream supposedly from South Carolina? Unlike some of the collections looked at earlier, such as America Eats, *The National Cookbook* is not descriptive of ways of life, nor is it an anthropological document. Hibben's purpose was to restore cooking based on enjoyment. She hoped that America's regional culinary reserves would be revived and that national taste might be rescued.

The National Cookbook fit the mood of rediscovering the innate strength of the country despite the epic crisis of the Great Depression, a feeling also expressed by the WPA artistic and intellectual projects, including America Eats. The need to cut back on household expenditures also meant that a previously affluent class had to cook more often at home, and its members responded to the call for enjoyment of inexpensive pleasures. All this notwithstanding, the Depression and the power of the government to influence food policies and practices meant that food became more centralized and advice even more blandly nutritionist in orientation. Eleanor Roosevelt, whose greatness as a moral and political leader did not include fondness for culinary pleasures, flirted with the idea of making Hibben a consultant for reviving American food at the White House. Not long after the beginning of Franklin Roosevelt's first inauguration, however, the official line had become almost ludicrously frugal and the result flavorless.[56]

The Second World War did not aid Hibben's vision of a pleasurable, regional cuisine based on simple but high-quality ingredients. At the end of the conflict, she published *American Regional Cooking*, which, despite its contrasting title, is actually very similar to the national cookbook.[57] It too is organized by type of dish, with forty-three states and a few localities associated with the recipes. Shorter than its predecessor, *American Regional Cookery* was not as widely noticed.

Hibben was the first permanent food writer for *The New Yorker*, but at that time staff writers were almost anonymous, and Hibben had a cause that was not, unfortunately, in step with its era. She was aware, she claimed, that the currents of the period ran against her advocacy. "Peace and Freedom have come to us riding on a tide of Ready-Mixes." Could not there be room for a fresh take on the old ways, a reconstruction of taste after years of rationing? If the nation is not to succumb to the food manufacturers' blandishments for "dreary synthetic foods," the simple pleasures of the table must be cherished.[58] The fact was that in 1946, and for quite some time after, American food was not defined by the bountiful traditions of its regions but by a thrifty, playful, bland, and modern cuisine.

Chili con Carne (Texas)

2 cups Mexican beans
3 Tb beef suet, chopped
1 large onion, chopped
4 chili peppers, ground
2 cloves garlic, mashed
1 lb lean beef, cut in pieces
1 Tb flour
2 cups chopped tomatoes
Salt

Wash the beans and set to soak in cold water overnight. Drain and simmer until tender in unsalted water. Heat the suet in a deep pot, add vegetables and beef and fry to a deep brown. Stir in flour and when well-blended add chopped tomatoes and a cup of the water in which the beans have been cooked. Simmer, covered, 1 hour; season with salt, and add the drained beans. Cover 30 minutes longer, stirring constantly. Put aside for 12 hours; reheat and serve.

Murray County Corn Meal Dodgers in Pot Licker
(Tennessee)

In Middle Tennessee, these corn dodgers or dumplings are called "poorsouls."

1 cup white corn meal
¼ tsp salt
1 large Tb melted lard
cold water

Mix the meal and salt and add the melted lard and enough cold water to form with the hand into small cakes about the size of a biscuit. Drop into boiling pot licker [normally the liquid left after boiling greens such as collard or turnip greens, but here the greens stay in the pot] on top of the greens, and cook for twenty minutes with the cover on the pot. Serve around the greens.

From Sheila Hibben, *American Regional Cookery* (New York: Crown, 1946), 59, 185.

PART II

Modernity

CHAPTER 4

The Golden Age of Food
Processing, 1880–1970

The title of this chapter is taken from Harvey Levenstein's book, *Para-dox of Plenty*.[1] He uses the heading to denote the postwar United States, particularly the 1950s, but it can be more broadly applied to American food

Unpacking shopping on kitchen counter, a photograph taken in 1958 and circulated by the United States Information Agency. The Cold War was waged in part by showing off the superior living standards of average Americans.

Soviet premier Nikita Khrushchev visiting an American supermarket, 1959. The leader of the USSR was aware that providing consumer goods to his people was proving more difficult than winning wars, achieving technological feats like the orbiting satellite Sputnik, or expanding Soviet influence across the world.

from the advances in technology and corporate consolidation at the end of the nineteenth century to the first signs of fatigue with the industrial model in the 1970s.[2]

That model dramatically increased food production and lowered prices. For most of the twentieth century, the sheer quantity of food available to the average American was a basis for national pride, particularly with the rest of the world engulfed in war and social conflict. American food might be unexciting, but it was plentiful at a time of food shortages elsewhere. If you grew up in postwar middle-class America, your parents will undoubtedly have admonished you to finish what was on your plate because people in other countries went hungry (e.g., anachronistically, "Think of the starving Armenians").

The Cold War era offered opportunities to demonstrate American abundance, a weapon in the arsenal of the Free World. For the Zagreb Trade Fair of 1957 in what was then Yugoslavia, the US Department of Commerce embarked on what it considered psychological warfare, exhibiting a ten-thousand-square-foot model supermarket with dairy product coolers and rows of precut meats wrapped in cellophane. Penn Fruit, a supermarket company, paid to airlift fresh produce. The most impressive proof of America's bounty, however, was the thousands of processed items: frozen foods, instant coffee, baby food in jars, boxes of cake mix. So sensational was the reception of this display that the Soviet pavilion, with little in the way of food to show off, presented helicopter rides as a distraction from the American exhibit.[3]

Two years later, at the Moscow Trade Fair, the American exhibit included a model house with a kitchen featuring General Electric appliances as well as packaged food and other kitchen goods. It was at this display that Vice President Richard Nixon and Soviet Premier Nikita Khrushchev got into a famous discussion about standards of living in the USSR and US, what came to be known as the Kitchen Debate. The communist leader alternated between boasting that workers in his country had the same things and claiming that the house was a fraud because American workers could not possibly afford to live in such comfort.[4]

Such episodes are worth recalling because they show that at one time, the American diet, supermarket, and processed foods were the envy of the world—or at least Americans were confident they were. Current preoccupations with natural taste and sustainability were ignored in the 1950s. Whether or not Wonder Bread tasted anything like homemade bread or Velveeta like real cheese was considered unimportant, as was the effect of cattle-rearing practices or fertilizer runoff on the environment. The publication in 1962 of Rachel Carson's *Silent Spring* would mark the beginning of a slow awakening to environmental costs of industrialization. For most of the twentieth century, however, the bottom line was that Americans enjoyed the world's highest standard of living as demonstrated by an opulent and varied food supply. A balance of social egalitarianism and capitalistic innovation, according to the prevailing American view, benefited ordinary people more effectively than was the case in rigidly guided socialist economies.

American Modernity

Modernizing the food system meant increasing the distance between producer and consumer and the homogenizing of taste. The price of plentiful, inexpensive, mass-produced food products was that local farms and provisioners disappeared in favor of large, centralized enterprises. These large companies, like Nabisco for cookies or Del Monte for canned tomatoes, undermined the bakeries and small farms that gave literal and metaphorical flavor to particular places. When consumers could buy these factory-made products at any market anywhere in the country, distinctions among regions and places were obliterated.

Today opinion has turned against homogeneity; nevertheless, the industrialized food system has had a favorable impact on everyday life in many respects and it is best to be up front about this, especially since much of what follows will

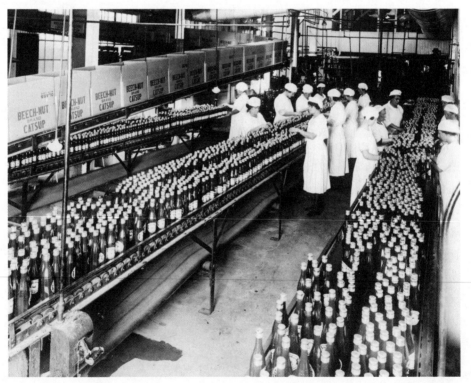

Beech-Nut catsup factory, early twentieth century. White-uniformed inspectors give the impression of clean and scientifically managed production.

be devoted to the dangerous and aesthetically displeasing aspects of corporate domination.[5] What we eat is radically cheaper than in the past when calculated as a percentage of household expenditures. In 1900, more than 40 percent of an average family's income was spent on food, and in 1950, the figure was 30 percent. In 2016, it was 12.6 percent, which is actually not the lowest it has been.[6] And despite all the justified lamentation about obesity, type 2 diabetes, and circulatory diseases brought about by highly processed and fast foods, life expectancy has increased from forty-nine in 1900 to seventy-eight today.[7]

The percentage of people engaged in agriculture has fallen so that now it employs less than 1 percent of the population. Nostalgia for a vanished rural way of life notwithstanding, this long-term development freed people from the basic task of ensuring enough to eat. The industrial revolution of the nineteenth century and the growth of the service sector in the twentieth would have been impossible without the consolidation of farms and food supply and the consequent decline in agricultural employment.

Abundance has been accompanied by more choice and exemption from seasonal fluctuation. Advances in transport and preservation not only reduced the cost of food, but they also made previously rare or unknown products available. By the early twentieth century, the banana, previously an unusual bit of exotica, was commonplace. While farmers' markets have gained attention in recent decades, most people in the United States buy lettuce, oranges, and pineapple in all seasons. In late summer, everyone impatiently awaits local tomatoes and sweet corn, but few people are faithful to seasonality in winter, preferring non-local lettuce or asparagus to parsnips or turnips.

The most serious adverse consequences of the modern food system are not aesthetic but environmental. Industrial agriculture, characterized by immense farms and feedlots, massive irrigation, large "inputs" of pesticide and fertilizer, and monocultures (growing a single crop, such as wheat or corn), have eroded the soil, depleted water tables, polluted rivers and coasts, and destroyed wildlife habitats and natural systems of renewal. Modern agriculture, processing, and distribution have also contributed to deforestation and climate change, created dietary problems, wiped out plant and animal species, and undermined culinary diversity, including regional cuisines. As a result of the scaling-up of the food system's complexity and volume, the distance between the producer and consumer has become so great that individuals have no idea where their food comes from, and even food producers and processors often merely assemble ingredients from global suppliers about whose practices they are conveniently ignorant.

One effect of the large-scale modern food system is to make everything part of a mass market: the same supermarket layout, the same fast-food drive-thru lanes, the same varieties of fruit, the same breakfast cereals across the land. The economics of scale and complex national distribution patterns encouraged uniformity in raising both plants and animals. Fruits and vegetables were bred for hardiness in order to withstand mechanical harvesting and long-distance transport. A small number of animal breeds were developed to maximize size and the preferred animal parts sold to consumers (chicken breast meat, for example). Taste was a secondary consideration.

The history of the apple in the United States effectively displays this decline in diversity.[8] In 1905, the US Department of Agriculture listed an astounding fourteen thousand varieties of apples grown between 1804 and 1904.[9] In the colonial era and well into the nineteenth century, a large proportion of harvested apples went to make cider and applejack brandy. In the early twentieth century, they suddenly came to be regarded as healthy snacks, and "an apple a day keeps the doctor away" became one of the most successful commodity advertising slogans ever created. The need to appeal to consumers meant selecting apples for their color, regular shape, and durability. Technological innovation made it possible to increase yields, store apples for months, and transport them beyond the harvest regions. Whatever its taste, the ideal apple was hardy, attractive, and prolific. By the 1960s there were essentially only three kinds of apples sold in supermarkets: McIntosh from the Northeast, and golden and red Delicious from Washington State. Consumers didn't vociferously complain about their lack of taste and spongy textures, but apple consumption started to decline.

The history of the apple is symptomatic of a larger trend toward sameness. In mid-nineteenth-century South Carolina, thirty-two kinds of beans were grown and thirty-eight varieties of cabbage.[10] By 1970, Americans had perhaps ten kinds of beans and at most two sorts of cabbage available at supermarkets.

Whatever the recent inroads of organic vegetables, artisanal bacon, or free-range chicken, the evidence of triumphant uniformity is still visible everywhere. It remains impossible to tell whether a Kroger supermarket or a Popeyes is in Maine or Arizona. Not only are boxes of Green Giant frozen peas or cans of Hunt's tomato paste the same from coast to coast, but so are the meat and fresh produce that come from far away and are impervious to seasons. What differentiates retail food establishments and restaurants is not climate or geography but class. A branch of Whole Foods Market is immediately distinguishable from the food section of a nearby Walmart or Target. Markets like Wegman's and Trader Joe's occupy particular niches and have enthusiastic followers, but they too are not regionally distinct.

The sameness that we perceive as boring or artificial would have been regarded at one time as advantageous. When most roadside food was available from dubious truck stops and "greasy spoons," the reliability of the standardized Howard Johnson's was cherished. At a time when grocery stores routinely sold unhygienic and spoiled food, packaged crackers or hot dogs made by nationally recognized companies were considered preferable to what now might be prized as crafted local products. The perceived advantages of uniformity were hygienic safety, consistency, affordability, and, overall, a rising standard of living.

According to mid-twentieth-century opinion leaders like *Time* and *Life* magazine publisher Henry Luce or newspaper columnist Walter Lippmann, America was a model of progress, efficiency, and equitable distribution of benefits, notably that the average person had more than enough to eat. Until 1970, at least, the detriments of the food system were either unrecognized or regarded as minor or as the preoccupation of a few unreconstructed, Francophile snobs. The first substantial dissent from this point of view, in the 1970s, coincided with growing disenchantment with political institutions and social norms. The old faith depended on application of new technologies and, even more importantly, widespread belief in the dramatic benefits of applied science.

The modern food industry was enabled by technological progress, but it was not simply its inevitable result. Certainly, railroads made it possible to transport food across the country, and the development of refrigerated cars meant that California fruit could be sold on the East Coast, or Maine lobsters in Montana.

The Bonneville Dam project commissioned Woody Guthrie in 1941 to write songs celebrating the use of the Columbia River to bring water and electricity to the rural Northwest, in part to power factories making war planes.

Improvements in flour milling, hydrogenation, freezing technology, dehydration, and chemical preservatives changed the nature, price, availability, and convenience of most of what Americans routinely buy and eat. Consumer technology has also had a profound influence on what people cook, from the development of indoor stoves in the nineteenth century to the microwave oven in the 1970s.

Technology, however, is not the sole explanation for the modern food system, because technology does not drive change by itself. Other countries adopted American food science—and invented much on their own—yet they did not end up with the same food landscape as America. Canning in glass containers was invented in 1809, in the middle of the Napoleonic age, by a Frenchman in the service of a German prince. The French chemist Louis Pasteur discovered the process known as pasteurization. Dehydrated meat soup (the bouillon cube) was developed by a chemist working with the Swiss Nestlé company near the turn of the nineteenth century, and this processing method was applied to vegetables and legumes by the German Knorr company beginning in 1912.[11]

So while European countries embraced technology, their varied food traditions were firmly rooted, and regional cuisines survived there while Americans, enraptured with technologically driven convenience, neglected or completely forgot their past. Germany may not be renowned for its gastronomy (unfairly underestimated in my opinion), but to this day each German town has its own sausage type, beer, and local specialties. Germany has thirteen hundred breweries, with the largest ten companies controlling about half of what is consumed. In the United States, eleven companies control 90 percent of the beer market, even with the success of microbreweries and the popularity of imports.[12] In France, the erosion of national gastronomy and of rural culture is a source of constant lament, but even now France has not arrived at the American degree of sameness and predictability.

Technological progress has been closely related to changes in society. The average American middle-class household had at least two live-in servants in the 1880s but none in the 1920s, so demand grew for the simplification of meals and kitchen labor-saving devices. The interstate highway system changed dining while traveling and paved the way, as it were, for the expansion of fast food chains.

American consumers did not simply absorb technological change passively. Their existing cultural attitudes meshed with scientific improvements in preservation, packaging, and transport. Among these ingrained attitudes was a preoccupation with health, in terms of not only nutrition but also the desire to conform to a thin and fit ideal body image. Additionally, Americans as far back as the late nineteenth century took an interest in foreign food cooked in restaurants opened by immigrants. The infatuation with science and progress, as well as a cult of efficiency and time-saving, manifested themselves in the ready accep-

"Eat and Grow Slim" pamphlet by Gertrude Austin, 1948. Slimness became an ideal female body image by the 1920s, and efforts to market restricted but satisfying diets proliferated in subsequent decades.

tance of products offering convenience, even at the sacrifice of flavor (canned vegetables, cookie dough, and frozen waffles, for example). All of these are human as opposed to purely technological factors that have affected how we eat.

How Modern Food Conquered

The conquest of modern food was the product of consolidation in large, corporate units. Consolidation here means radical growth in size and standardization of food production and consumption. Thus, to take the best-known example, the fast food industry, McDonald's was originally a single hamburger stand in San Bernardino, California, and now is one of the world's largest corporations, with over fourteen thousand branches in the United States and another twenty-three thousand worldwide. The brand is so familiar that its symbols are better known globally than the Christian cross. McDonald's hires more than one million people a year, and something on the order of one in eight people in the United States have worked for the company at one time or another. Its food differs slightly internationally (beer and wine are available in some parts of Europe but not the United States), but its burgers and fries are made according to infinitely reproducible formulae.[13]

The story of modern American food can be described through similar patterns of consolidation of production—factory farms and national food companies—and expansion in retail markets and restaurants. In 1900, Americans bought food from small neighborhood grocery stores, and even the first successful chain of stores, A&P, sold only a few hundred items. By the 1960s, a large majority of the population shopped at supermarkets that carried tens of thousands of products. The few chain restaurants that existed in the early twentieth century served urban workers and travelers. In the 1960s, the hamburger and hot dog were just being introduced. Howard Johnson's, with waitresses and a substantial menu, had around a thousand branches; its replacement in leading the truly fast food expansion, McDonald's, went from a mere hundred stands in 1960 to five thousand worldwide in 1978.[14]

The American food industry in the twentieth century was dominated by a few major companies. In most people's minds, cookies meant Nabisco, cereals meant Kellogg's and canned soup meant Campbell's. None of these was a monopoly—Keebler also makes a lot of cookies, and Post is a gigantic cereal manufacturer—but a few giants owned processed food. Similarly, McDonald's battled for market share with Burger King and Wendy's, leaving independently owned burger stands as quaint vestiges by the 1970s.

Any history of how Americans consumed food has to include some version of the growth and consolidation of the food industry, and that story is one of creating perceived advantages and expectations. Food companies could present their products as reliable, inexpensive, convenient, and available everywhere. Every store offers Oreo cookies, and every one of the millions of Oreos consumed every day will be the same. In an age where "handmade" and "artisanal" are selling points, it has to be remembered how reassuring predictability used to be. How and when companies expanded is not exclusively about relentless corporate appetite, but a history of what American consumers preferred. True, the tremendous advertising budgets of these enterprises were intended to influence the behavior of shoppers, and companies were successful in this, but not every need their products answered was created by them: consumers really did want the convenience of frozen vegetables. Companies have often convinced people that food—whether milk or coconut water—was healthful when it wasn't, or not very, or not for everybody. It is a long-standing preoccupation with the moral qualities of food rather than enjoyment that made Americans receptive to advertising claims based on health. The history of the food industry is not simply a business narrative, but also an account of hard-wired American attitudes.

The twenty-first century has seen challenges to standardization as well as consumer resistance to even the most famous products of the industry, ranging from breakfast cereal to Kentucky Fried Chicken, but there's no evidence that the food paradigm that reached its peak in the late twentieth century is about to collapse.

How American Companies Grew

At first, technological progress tends to encourage competition as it lowers costs and disrupts monopolistic guilds and craft knowledge. For example, the price of sugar refining equipment fell between 1840 and 1870; consequently, so did the cost of sugar to consumers. The competitive phase is usually succeeded by concentration, so that by 1892, the American Sugar Refining Company (maker of Domino sugar) held 90 percent of the American retail market.[15] Likewise, Americans were great fans of soda crackers and biscuits, and until the late nineteenth century stores sold them from barrels. Technological advances in production and packaging, along with intensive marketing and advertising, allowed the National Biscuit Company (later shortened to Nabisco) to buy its competitors so that its share of the cracker market reached 70 percent by 1900.[16] Aided by the Sherman Antitrust Act of 1890, the government broke up the great monopolies, but certain companies continued, in effect, to own manufactured food product categories. To this day, the most recognized ketchup manufacturer is Heinz, founded in the post–Civil War era; Kraft, which dates from 1903, remains the best-known maker of packaged cheese products.

More common than flat-out monopoly was division of the pie into large slices. The meatpacking industry in the early twentieth century was dominated by the "Big Five:" Swift, Armour, Morris, Hammond, and Cudahy. Similarly, Pillsbury and the company that eventually became General Mills were the largest flour and later cake mix manufacturers. Sometimes there was a clear leader but an equally well-known number two: Coca-Cola and Pepsi or Oreo and Hydrox chocolate sandwich cookies are classic examples.

Technology and corporate consolidation radically lowered prices. One dollar bought fifteen pounds of flour in 1881 and thirty-four pounds in 1897. In the same period, coffee, tea, pork, milk, and rice also saw price declines on the order of 30 to 40 percent.[17] The increasing purchasing power of the average household created opportunities for food companies but also problems. The chief obstacle was that Americans by and large already had enough to eat. True, there was significant hunger and malnutrition, its existence coming as a periodic surprise to experts and the public throughout recent American history. Periods of handwringing over deprivation in a country so apparently rich were prompted by health concerns—for example, anxiety over national malnutrition from 1907 to 1921, or the current attention to obesity. On occasion, the rediscovery of poverty was the result of economic downturns, as during the Great Depression,

Packing and Weighing Crystal Domino Sugar.
Copyright 1912 by The American Sugar Refining Company.

Domino Sugar factory, 1912. Women were employed to handle the last stages of sugar production and packing. Even after the breakup of monopolies with the Sherman Antitrust Act of 1890, the American Sugar Refining Company controlled most of the industry.

but it also occurred in expansive economic times, as with President Lyndon Johnson's 1965 "War on Poverty." Isolated rural regions or impoverished inner cities were targets of food aid programs, often launched on the premise that the solution was more educational than economic.

Food companies don't regard efforts to improve the lot of the poor as great opportunities for expansion, preferring to concentrate on middle-class consumers who tend to embrace self-improvement that involves buying things. In 1900, such a potential consumer was eating according to a particular set of preferences, and the companies had to convince her or him to change—to substitute one thing for another. At the end of the nineteenth century, manufacturers persuaded consumers to break with long-established practices and assumptions. By means of a combination of advertising, availability, and low prices, companies producing what were soon to become universally familiar brands convinced people to stop making many things themselves. Nabisco marketed cookies and other foods previously made at home. Heinz made its mark on the American retail food scene by offering pickles, relishes, sauces, and other piquant foods previously prepared in household kitchens and stored in basements.

Another form of substitution involves creating added-value products to replace the basic item. Processed food can be marketed as a convenience and, sure enough, Pillsbury makes more money selling cake mix, cookie dough, and frozen biscuits than flour. The price is higher than the basic ingredients, but still not expensive. It is quicker to make chocolate cake from a mix than from scratch, and it is easier to microwave Lean Cuisine Mushroom Mezzaluna Ravioli than to make the pasta, filling, and sauce yourself. As the price of food as a percentage of total household budgets has declined, many food experts have been upset that its cheapness translates to poor nutrition and little profit to actual farmers. The perceived values of convenience are such that people dine out, order in, serve already prepared foods, or use mixes more than they buy raw commodities such as sugar, flour, meat, and eggs.

A third impetus for substitution is the development and marketing of previously unknown products that you didn't know you needed. The classic example is dry breakfast cereal, invented by William R. Kellogg for invalids at his Seventh Day Adventist (hence vegetarian) health resort in Battle Creek, Michigan.[18] His brother, Dr. John Harvey Kellogg, and a former Battle Creek patient, C. W. Post, came up with ways to sell their corn flakes and toasted wheat-barley mixture as healthful breakfasts to people who were not sick. Until the end of the nineteenth century, Americans usually ate bread, meat, and eggs or occasionally hot porridge for breakfast. To replace this array of possibilities with a nearly flavorless processed grain required an extraordinary degree of ingenuity. Snappy brand names, health claims, the addition of sugar, and aggressive advertising changed how Americans came to regard the most predictable meal of the day.

The growth of the food industry can be traced by stages of technological and marketing progress—for example, from fresh to canned to frozen peas, or the discovery of previously unknown needs such as low-calorie soda (Tab, Coca-Cola's first diet line, appeared in 1963), or entirely new products such as canned Chinese food in the 1920s, or Flav-R-Straws, which were supposed to save the bother of mixing chocolate into milk, in the 1950s. In the first decades after the Second World War, certain brands were ubiquitous: almost everyone had

Wise Potato Chip factory, from a 1957 booklet, *Recipes That Pep-Up Meals with Wise Potato Chips*. "Scientific conditioning" makes the chips fresh and flavorful.

Crisco shortening, Mott's applesauce, and Chef Boyardee ravioli in their pantry, and everyone knew the jingles to their television advertisements. Many of these products were not mere humdrum staples—they became symbols of the American way of life. Coca-Cola is probably the most famous emblem of the United States because it was aggressively marketed abroad. Kellogg's cereals were not as successful in opening up new territory, and so Bing Crosby's song title "What's more American than corn flakes?" has a slightly defiant resonance as opposed to Coke's imperial universalism—something dear to Americans and no one else, just as baseball used to be.[19]

Beginning around 1980, as the value of conformity diminished, the big food companies were challenged by local, niche products with healthier ingredients. Large food companies have kept their profits and position either by embracing trendy foods, such as granola or health bars, or by acquiring small, hip natural or organic enterprises. In the last few years, Naked Juice was acquired by PepsiCo, Honest Tea by Coca-Cola, and Kashi by Kellogg's. Garden Fresh Gourmet, a Berkeley upstart salsa maker with an image of artisanal quality, has been bought by Campbell's. General Mills now owns Annie's Homegrown, maker of naturally produced macaroni and cheese mix, snacks, and condiments.

Not all such transactions have worked. It is expensive to buy other companies, and sometimes the parent company is too clumsy to run the small acquisition or its own image adversely affects the progressive, healthful vibe. Snapple is an example of a diluted image. It was bought first by Quaker Oats, then by Cadbury Schweppes, and finally by Keurig. Started as a small natural juice company, Snapple has become a manufacturer of supermarket and vending machine drinks that are no trendier than V8 juice. Ben & Jerry's was originally a locally produced ice cream with lots of attractive graphics and a story that combined love-sharing entrepreneurship, quality, and superior taste. It is now owned by Unilever, and a new independent ice cream brand, Halo Top Creamery, has recently become wildly popular, appropriating the simultaneously indulgent but healthful image of Ben & Jerry's. Part of the reason for the success of Halo Top is its skillful use of social media and other marketing unrelated to taste. People no longer want to be associated with standard, middle-class brands, a symptom of corporate malaise related to the hollowing-out of the middle class in basic demographic, sociological terms. They want a brand with a story—a quest, even.

Challenged as they are, the large food companies are not in mortal danger. Their control of the supermarket aisles is not as serene or assured as it was fifty years ago, but they are not disappearing quite yet. But of course, the supermarket itself may not be around forever.

The Slow Death of the Family Farm

The most dramatic changes leading to the gigantic, integrated food industry occurred with farms, the beginning of food itself. For a time, farms lagged behind food processing in consolidation. By 1900, efficiencies already implemented to create large-scale food companies had been applied to farming experimentally, but the overwhelming majority of farms were small family enterprises, and 40 percent of the nation's population worked in agriculture. There were signs of future consolidation, but only for cereal crops on vast acreage.[20] The Great Plains offered lots of cheap land, and farmers found that despite the region's aridity and temperature extremes, it was profitable to grow wheat in very large units. Most of America, however, was not organized this way in the early twentieth century. The Midwest, with good soil and adequate rainfall, was still diversified. An average farm did more than grow one crop. Its owners raised chickens and hogs and the corn to feed them. They used horses and mules to pull agricultural implements, and grew oats and other grains to feed these animals.

Specialized agriculture attained early success with fruit in California. Technological advances such as refrigerated railroad cars, introduced in the 1890s, made it possible to centralize and scale up fruit production for a national market. While Georgia would remain famous for its peaches and Florida for its oranges, California increasingly produced most of the country's fruit. Large-scale, subsidized water from the government, plus migrant labor, made the fruit cheap to grow and harvest. While early picking and refrigeration undeniably detracted from flavor, low price and a long season of availability started to make growing peaches, strawberries, melons, and eventually almost all produce uneconomical anywhere else.

For the time being, large-scale, single-crop farming was exceptional. Much to the annoyance of agricultural scientists at state universities and extension services, farmers resisted being pushed toward greater productivity. Some of this was simply technological lag; tractors did not become feasible until the 1910s and 1920s. The industrialization of agriculture got under way massively only in the 1920s in response to a crisis in prices and profitability brought about by the end of World War I and by competition from Canada, Argentina, and Australia, whose wheat, meat, and other basic products undermined what had been profitable American exports. Other important steps included electrification, roads, irrigation, and technologies of mass production such as incubators, as well as changes in seeds and animal breeding.

Ironically it was not economic or technological progress that really accelerated the consolidation of farms, but the Depression. The prolonged downturn drove farmers off the land and radically increased government intervention in the economy, including farming. In the 1930s, planning, science, and a democratic, even socialist, model of egalitarian productivity meant immense public investments in basic infrastructure that dramatically affected agriculture. In 1930, perhaps 10 percent of farms had electricity. Created by the federal government in 1935, the Rural Electrification Administration made subsidized loans to electricity co-ops that doubled electrification in five years and by 1950 brought almost every farm onto the grid.[21]

Emblematic of this era was the Tennessee Valley Authority, an economic development scheme of the federal government that combined flood control, electric power generation, fertilizer manufacture, and the growth of agricultural productivity. The new dams, generators, model farms, and towns of a multistate region were for generations examples of the effectiveness of massive government intervention at raising standards of living. The fact that farmers were displaced by the dams was regarded as less important than lifting a huge, impoverished territory out of misery.[22] Scientific agricultural management replacing isolated, unproductive homesteads on eroded land was supposed to be ecologically beneficial, a contrast to the poor planning and short-sightedness that had created disasters like the Dust Bowl of the Great Plains.[23]

Few people questioned the beneficent effects of such modernization projects. Today, food writers are inclined to mourn the loss of small-scale, diversified agriculture, and well-paid executives abandon Wall Street to grow garlic in the Hudson Valley.[24] Chefs like Frank Stitt in Alabama or Sean Brock in South Carolina, who are leading a revival of lost seed varieties and animal breeds, grew

Tennessee Valley Authority, fertilizer comparison. The TVA's mission was to build dams to bring electricity and development to the impoverished Upper South.

up with mule-driven plows and home preparation of everything from butter to bacon. Edna Lewis in Virginia, and the young authors of *The Foxfire Book of Appalachian Cookery,* reveal the well-preserved memories of an almost vanished way of life.

In the mid-twentieth century, however, any regret for the rural past, advocacy of small farms, or opposition to hydroelectric development was the property of reactionaries like the Southern Agrarians, a group of literary figures who mourned the decline of the rural virtues of the South at the hands of Northern capitalism. In 1930, they released a book of essays with the tendentious title *I'll Take My Stand* (taken from the song "Dixie").[25] The book's attack on the numbing brutality of industrial modernity had no visible effect on policy, though for decades it influenced American belles lettres. Contributors included the great poet and novelist Robert Penn Warren, the literary critic John Crowe Ransom, and the poet Allen Tate. Neither in the South nor elsewhere was there much of a response to this or any other denunciation of industry, technology, or the seductive belief in progress.[26]

Jeffersonian ideals and piety toward family farms notwithstanding, Americans for most of the twentieth century agreed that farms should be more productive and food should be cheaper. To accomplish this required equipment, irrigation, fertilizer, pesticides, and, above all, scale and specialization. Rather than combining subsistence and market operations, modern farms were supposed to imitate the efficiency of factories. They would produce large quantities of one crop at low cost for a national market.

The supposed advantages of size, technological inputs, and maximum exploitation of the land for productivity were taken for granted until the 1970s and transcended the Cold War ideological divide. Marxism and Capitalism agreed on the necessity and inevitability of agricultural consolidation. Planners in the Soviet Union waged a brutal war on their own peasants, exterminating them by the millions in order to create huge collective units. Their methods were certainly distinct from those of the governing authorities of the United States, but the goals were similar: agriculture was to be organized like industry into large units producing for a national market. The Soviet rulers admired American farm consolidation and invited American experts in the 1930s to come and advise them.[27]

In the United States the plan worked according to easily measurable results. In 1900, an acre of planted corn yielded about 24 bushels and now produces 160 bushels per acre.[28] Such astronomical gains in productivity have meant fewer farms and, for the consumer, lower prices. As mentioned earlier, the percentage of disposable income Americans spend on food has declined to under 13 percent. For decades advances in technology, consolidation of agriculture, and cheap food seemed like an all-win combination.

American agriculture's efficiency has grown to the point where it now requires an almost negligible proportion of the population, while producing immense quantities of food. Agriculture has lost its former importance within the overall United States economy, but that is further evidence of its astonishing productive efficiency, which allows the rest of the population to engage in other pursuits.

AGRICULTURE'S SHARE OF US LABOR FORCE[29]	
c. 1750	75%–80%
1800	75%–80%
1850	55%
1900	40%
1950	12%
2013	00.67%

AGRICULTURE'S SHARE OF US GNP	
1800	46%
1870	33%
1900	18%
1930	8%
1945	7%
1970	2%
2012	1% ($395 billion, the greatest ever in terms of absolute market value)

From Peter Cochlanis, "Is Industrial Agriculture a Success or Failure?," in *Food Fights: How the Past Matters to Contemporary Food Debates*, ed. Charles C. Ludington and Matthew M. Booker (Chapel Hill: University of North Carolina Press, in press).

That America's technologically enhanced productivity allows it to feed itself and to export food was deployed by the postwar reconstruction of Europe, the creation of international aid, and development projects in the 1950s. Maximizing yield and production through increased size was the policy of successive secretaries of agriculture. Earl Butz, President Nixon's appointee in the 1970s, famously urged famers to "get big or get out." Land grant state universities and agricultural extension services devoted themselves to large-scale agriculture, ignoring their original mission of helping small, family-run farms.[29]

Federal subsidies for export marketing, price supports, and paying farmers to take land out of cultivation were all supposed to enrich agriculture, but things didn't work out so favorably. Except for the largest landowners, the financial picture for farming darkened. A major problem with monoculture is susceptibility to price fluctuations in volatile international commodities markets, so concentrating on one crop means exposure to considerable risk, which then requires massive government offset. A free market ideology in Congress and the farmers' declining political power meant that the farm economy became even more fragile. A grain agreement with the Soviet Union in 1973 seemed to vindicate breakneck productivity, but its cancellation in 1980 in the wake of the Russian invasion of Afghanistan caused a collapse. The backdrop to the farm crisis also included escalation in oil prices after the first energy crisis of 1973 and soaring interest rates. It was essentially, however, the result of a free-market approach to a sector that could not survive in a free market. Price fluctuations, uncertain weather, and political events affecting trade all have a disproportionate impact on farmers, and these are magnified when they are no longer diverse cultivators but completely dependent on one crop.

The 1980s witnessed the desertion of a countryside already in decline, courthouse auctions of bankrupt farms, and the Farm Aid concerts organized by Willie Nelson, John Mellencamp, and Neil Young in 1985. American agriculture has since continued its extraordinary productivity, but with very few people actually involved in the rural economy. Climate change and international tariff retaliation are the latest manifestations of its built-in weakness.

Parallel with consolidation of consumer manufacturing and of farms in the twentieth century was the coming together of large agricultural supply companies like Monsanto and Archer Daniels Midland. These companies profited from monoculture and large-scale farming, selling fertilizer and pesticide required by size, lack of diversity, and cultivation based on cheap land prices, not on actual soil fertility. As prime farmland was lost to suburbanization, the remaining farms on mediocre but empty land achieved their productivity goals only with massive inputs and reliance on unsustainable water resources.

The result is a concentration of farms to a degree that even other areas of the food economy can't match. Today just three commodities—corn, soybeans, and wheat—account for most of American agriculture. America remains capable of feeding itself and exporting harvests, but this depends on long-term environmental costs that cannot continue. Half of the country's water supply goes just to concentrated animal feeding operations (CAFOs). Almost all meat consumed in the United States is from these crowded lots, where animals are fed on corn and soybeans that account for almost 40 percent of the pesticides used in agriculture. Unless demand for meat declines, this system cannot be sustained as population increases.[30]

TOP 20 AGRICULTURAL PRODUCTS BY VALUE (WITH METRIC TONS GIVEN ALONGSIDE)		
1	Corn	256,900,000
2	Cattle meat	11,736,000
3	Cow's milk	78,155,000
4	Chicken	15,006,000
5	Soybeans	65,800,000
6	Pork	8,574,000
7	Wheat	63,590,000
8	Cotton	3,968,000
9	Eggs	5,141,000
10	Turkey	2,584,000
11	Tomatoes	12,275,000
12	Potatoes	20,820,000
13	Grapes	6,126,000
14	Oranges	10,473,000
15	Rice	9,034,000
16	Apples	4,242,000
17	Sorghum	10,446,000
18	Lettuce	4,490,000
19	Cottonseed	6,073,000
20	Sugar beets	27,760,000

From Peter Cochlanis, "Is Industrial Agriculture a Success or Failure?," in *Food Fights: How the Past Matters to Contemporary Food Debates*, ed. Charles C. Ludington and Matthew M. Booker (Chapel Hill: University of North Carolina Press, in press).

Buying Food: The Supermarket

Once all the food from farms and from food-processing industries is trucked out of factory depots, it is sold mostly in large food stores. Supermarkets are another link in a chain of technology- and corporate-driven convenience and offer what most consumers perceive as reasonably good food, lots of choices, and lower prices than either farmers' markets on the high end or convenience markets like 7-Eleven on the low end. There is a relatively new corporate initiative to present food in more intimate and attractive spaces, but most supermarkets remain as they have been for sixty years or so: cavernous, warehouse-like buildings surrounded by parking areas, featuring lots of stuff and okay service.

The supermarket is a large realm of bewildering choice. The average place now stocks some fifty thousand items. It has a standard layout, with dairy products usually at the back, produce on one side, and meat on the other. The middle aisles have processed food and nonfood items like cleansers, aluminum foil, and cat litter. The organization is for reasons of both logistics—refrigerated cases are easier to place alongside walls—and marketing—making shoppers see as much as possible even if they were planning to buy only a few items. Size, choice, and of course parking are key elements to the appeal of such markets. Aesthetically dull, they have become necessities, manifestations of the food industry's consolidation and uniformity at the retail end of the long food chain. The history of supermarkets exemplifies points made throughout this book, such as the connection, not contradiction, between dizzying variety and the domination of a few brands and breeds. At the height of twentieth-century uniformity, which we are taking to be somewhere around 1970, everyone knew Minute Rice, Birds Eye frozen peas, and Tropicana orange juice. Of course, eccentrics could buy Schweppes tonic water, but Coca-Cola and Pepsi ruled the soda aisles. All sorts of imported fruits were available, but there were only a few hardy, tasteless varieties of peaches and apricots, and exactly one kind of banana.

The kaleidoscope of offerings distracts attention from the fact that by their nature, supermarkets limit food choice. They displace picking up food daily on the basis of last-minute decisions or on what looks tempting today, habits that persist in Europe because people there are more likely to live near stores and markets and travel to and from work by public transport. In the American suburbs, it is distressing to run out of milk or another single item, because it may be miles to the nearest market, where you then have to deal with parking and checkout lines. Savvy households shop once a week, making processed, canned, jarred, frozen, and other durable products necessary. What is prepared at home, therefore, is influenced by where home is in relation to food sources. Suburbanization itself was encouraged by cultural attitudes, bank lending practices, and government tax policy. This long-established pattern has changed marginally with delivery services such as Fresh Direct, but this only offloads the logistical problem and still means buying food well in advance of use. The situation is also influenced by online shopping possibilities, but these tend to increase further the range of products and convenience, though not necessarily their quality.[31]

All the negative factors about supermarket shopping notwithstanding, in the first part of the twentieth century, the national chain market was seen as another benefit of progress and better living, much as the chain restaurant was, and for similar reasons: a guarantee of consistency in pricing and ambience and efficient if impersonal treatment that might be an advantage to people who felt (often with reason) cheated or held in contempt by independent owners.[32] The evolution of the supermarket was actually slower than was the case with related developments, such as chain restaurants or food industry consolidation. The Great Atlantic and Pacific Tea Company (for most of its history known as A&P) was the first major grocery chain. As its name implies, the company began as a retail seller of tea, followed shortly by coffee. It entered the diversified grocery business after the Civil War, and by 1880 it had 150 stores. The key to transforming a specialty business into a chain of stores selling all kinds of food was the cheap canning processes and the cardboard box, both invented toward the end of the nineteenth century.[33] Cans and boxes made it possible for national food companies to deliver products in uniform sizes with factory-graded quality and industrial quantity. Retail distribution was increasingly in the hands of large stores, of which A&P was the largest, consisting of sixteen thousand branches by 1920 with more sales than any other retailer in the world.[34]

A&P may have dominated the selling of food, but it was still some years away from our concept of a modern supermarket. The stores were numerous, but each was no larger than what would later be referred to as "Mom and Pop" groceries. Even more important, A&P was slow to adopt a self-service format: instead, you gave an order for items that clerks would bring to the counter. In 1916, Clarence Saunders opened the Piggly Wiggly in Memphis, Tennessee, the first self-service market, and by 1925 there were more than a thousand branches. Saunders convinced shoppers to accept his innovation not only on the basis of speed and allowing you to see what you were getting but on cleanliness—cutting out the clerk's handling of your edible merchandise. It did take some instruction in how to use the wooden baskets and to find your way around, and although it now seems like an immediately graspable innovation, the self-service idea did not quickly supersede the full-service practice. How the chain got the name Piggly Wiggly remains a mystery. Saunders was always evasive about this, but perhaps the very fact of the name being unusual gave the stores recognition.

The Piggly Wiggly self-service model was adopted in Southern California, where the term *supermarket* seems to have first appeared, sometime in the 1920s. Despite these glimpses of the future, self-service shopping for food didn't become common until the 1930s, helped along by the metal shopping cart (introduced in 1937) and the development of electric commercial refrigeration. Expansion of the size of home refrigeration units from a small "ice box" to an electric-powered refrigerator made it possible to shop infrequently and take advantage of the suburban landscape and its increasingly large stores. The full flowering of this system had to await the end of the Second World War and the suburban explosion.

Allowing customers to find their own requisites from an array of shelves radically expanded food company advertising directly to consumers. Now that the customer was wandering the aisles and able to choose what brand to buy, companies could attract and compete via newspaper ads, coupons, radio, and later television jingles. Packaging was no longer utilitarian but used color, design, and slogans to make sure the brand was memorable and appealing. The Campbell's soup kids and the red-and-white labels were instantly recognizable, as was the blue and orange box of Ritz crackers with the mock apple pie recipe reliably on the back.[35]

A snapshot of a moment in retail food history is provided in Michael Ruhl-

Piggly Wiggly, early self-service market. First tried out in Memphis in 1916, the self-service grocery store changed the experience of shopping. Clarence Saunders invented the supermarket as we know it, decades after chain grocery stores had started.

man's book *Grocery*, a reconstruction of the scene on Coventry Road in suburban Cleveland Heights between the two World Wars. The street was then still made up of independent stores selling dairy products, produce, meat, and baked goods. Along Coventry Road there were *two* A&P stores, with a third in the vicinity. An A&P of this size could stock a few hundred items, amounting to a mere half an aisle's number of products in a modern supermarket. Already, however, the supermarket of the future was hesitantly taking shape elsewhere. Jumping ahead of A&P and expanding the size of the self-service store, King Kullen opened in 1930 in Queens (New York). King Kullen was a three-thousand-square-foot store located not on a main street but in a factory warehouse neighborhood you had to drive to. The stand-alone location, free parking, large size, and a variety of products at inexpensive prices established a pattern for what would dominate the United States after 1945. By 1956, supermarket chains accounted for 62 percent of grocery sales, leaving the rest divided among smaller independent markets.[36]

As with many of the trends already discussed, 1970 marks the apogee of modern corporate dominance. By that date small retail food stores were limited to poor urban neighborhoods and rural backwaters, and on the flip side, gourmet shops for the wealthy. Local supermarket chains were being bought out by large regional or national corporations like Kroger or Safeway. Critiques of the homogenization of America and the standardization of food that surfaced among advocates of alternative lifestyles and politics in the 1970s meant that organic foods and specialized stores to carry them made some slight inroads in the hegemony of the supermarket. The first dramatic challenge, however, came from Walmart, whose decision in 1988 to carry food ratcheted big-box suburban consolidation up a notch. That same year Whole Foods began to expand from its home state, Texas, offering high-quality and more-or-less-organic food. Whole Foods appealed to affluent, health-conscious, and mildly gourmand shoppers, whose numbers have increased over the past thirty years. For a time, at least, Whole Foods offered the reassuring virtue of hippie organic food stores in an upscale ambience. Thus the conventional midlevel supermarket was being squeezed by Walmart on the low economic end and Whole Foods at the high end.

More recently there has been a shift in what consumers want, to the detriment of supermarkets. The decline of the middle class and its standardized tastes has led to a sales crisis in the supermarkets' middle aisles. The perception that processed food is unhealthy, and the increased prevalence of families eating dinner at different times and often on the run, together provide opportunities as well as upheavals. Markets have expanded their produce and other fresh food offerings, as well as prepared foods that can be brought home and eaten immediately. Trying to sell to new customers who don't conform to the "traditional" image of the suburban family, Bumble Bee tuna now offers single-serving cans; Duncan Hines mix comes in single-cupcake size, prepared in a mug using a microwave.[37]

The supermarket industry has thus become fragmented. The threat to traditional midrange giants such as Kroger or Albertson's was increased by Amazon's purchase of Whole Foods in 2017. The immediate slash in prices disrupted the assumed economic levels of the supermarket hierarchy. Additionally, Amazon's retail mastery of the internet opens up opportunities for delivery services that have already made the suburban shopping mall obsolete. The suburbs themselves are changing, even declining, as a result of millennials' preference for urban living. Their shopping habits eschew large weekly purchases of processed foods in favor of more immediate decisions about food and, in many cases, abandonment of all but the most rudimentary cooking at home.

Modern Dining: Fast Food

The same nexus of technology, convenience, cost cutting, and soothing uniformity visible in the growth of supermarkets also affected the ways in which Amer-

Carhops at Carl's in Los Angeles, 1953. Like its close postwar relative, the drive-in movie, hamburger stands with carhops now seem quaint more than actually convenient.

icans took meals outside the home. The fact that meals could be provided by large chain restaurants quickly and cheaply increased the percentage of money spent on dining out in proportion to cooking at home. Until well after the Second World War, restaurant meals were for special occasions. Travelers were the original impetus for the development of chains providing predictable food and quick service. People on the move usually do not to want to linger over their meal, but also, by virtue of the fact that they are often in unfamiliar territory, tend to prefer an efficient predictability. The highways of America were at one time full of inexpensive luncheonettes, hash houses, and truck stops, but beginning in the 1920s, Howard Johnson's was able to prosper by creating a formula of clean, friendly, and efficient roadside restaurants with consistent standards and an eminently reliable menu.

The first far-flung restaurant chain had been organized by Fred Harvey, an English immigrant who, beginning in 1876, created nice, reliable railroad station restaurants.[38] This was a bigger accomplishment than it might at first seem. From the time of the first trains, there had been notoriously bad depot "eating houses" that gave captive passengers terrible food. Trains couldn't run more than a hundred miles or so without needing water and coal, so stops lasting at least a half hour were necessary. Trains sometimes carried dining cars, but until the introduction of vestibules connecting cars in 1887, it was not possible to move from one car to another. If there was a restaurant car at all, and usually there wasn't, diners had to remain in it until a station stop. This was not a serious problem in the eastern part of the United States, where there were frequent stops, but in the sparsely populated West, the only alternative to being trapped for hours in the dining car was what were called hotel cars, offering sleeping quarters and a restaurant. The problem with hotel cars was their high price, as well as the proximity of the kitchen and its fumes and fire.[39]

As a freight agent for the Chicago, Burlington, and Quincy Railroad, Fred Harvey obtained sufficient experience with unpleasant options and the particular problems of travel in the West. His first dining establishment, a hall in the Atchison, Topeka, and Santa Fe terminal in Topeka, opened in 1876. Soon he had an empire of station restaurants, to which were later added newsstands, hotels, and shops, mostly in the western United States. As with any fast food chain, Harvey House restaurants routinized and streamlined service. Standardization imposed a degree of quality: it was immediately obvious that Harvey restaurants were cleaner and the food was better than what they replaced. Instead of regarding passengers as victims who would not be coming back, Harvey created loyalty and brand identification. He also paved the way for later restaurant chains based on automobile travel by instituting centralized buying and detailed instructions for service (portion size, speed standards) and supply (how much meat, butter, eggs, and everything else to keep on hand).

Among the innovations was that Harvey employed female waitstaff, particularly notable given that the West had few females to start with. The morals, looks, and affect of what were known as "Harvey girls" were monitored and standardized along with everything else. In the popular media, Harvey girls were the equivalent of the plucky lads of Horatio Alger novels celebrating social mobility. In the 1946 movie *The Harvey Girls*, Judy Garland played a young woman who works at a Harvey House in a small New Mexico town, looking for love and trying to get the townspeople to patronize the respectable establishment rather than the local saloon, while Angela Lansbury played a cynical, streetwise ally of the saloon.

In the early years of Harvey House, the train conductor would make an inventory of those intending to eat in the restaurant and telegraph the results an hour before a train came to the station. First courses were placed on the tables as the passengers entered. Their drink requests were taken by waitresses, who then placed glasses or cups in certain positions so that the drinks servers would know what was wanted. The meal usually took no more than a half an hour and was generally considered quite satisfactory.

Fred Harvey set the example for future restaurant chains, with modes of transportation dictating the particular location and type of restaurant. As highways and automobiles first supplemented and then largely replaced passenger rail traffic, quick-service restaurants were first strung along the two-lane US highways, often just outside the towns they went through, later at the rest stops of parkways and turnpikes such as the Pennsylvania Turnpike or the Blue Ridge Parkway, and finally on the ramps leading to and from the interstate highways.

Predictability was a key selling point of all the restaurant chains, enforced with ruthless zeal.

What differentiated post–World War I practices from what Fred Harvey had accomplished was franchising and a progressive limitation of the menu, itself an aspect of efficiency and predictability. These innovations were developed by Howard Johnson's, which started out in 1925 as an ice cream stand in Quincy, Massachusetts, just outside Boston, and became a full restaurant in 1929. During the 1930s, Howard Johnson's expanded on the basis of franchising, by which the costs of construction were shared with the franchisee, who also paid a percentage of sales to the company. The franchisee benefited from brand identification and, in this case, Howard Johnson's quickly gained fame for its instantly recognizable look and reasonably priced and carefully monitored food. It became a fixture of the highways, and by the 1960s, with something on the order of a thousand branches, served more meals than any other American institution with the exception of the US Army.[40]

Howard Johnson's had a menu with many choices compared to what would later become the stripped-down fast-food norm. The chain became famous for its twenty-eight different ice cream flavors and for a number of disparate but cherished dishes such as fried clams, Boston baked beans, date-nut bread, and chicken pot pie. The problem with franchising is that it limits the company's ability to maintain control over what is now referred to as the "customer experience." Constant supervision and evaluation are necessary to counteract the tendency for branches to deteriorate either because of cost cutting, inattention, or logistical problems delivering the product. Howard Johnson's pioneered concepts such as centralized commissaries and the use of frozen foods. It imposed exhaustive regulations for everything from how much water to pour into glasses before opening time to thawing instructions for each item. By the 1950s, Howard Johnson's and its imitators offered what was considered an ideal atmosphere that was family-friendly, clean, and wholesome. The menu presented enough choice to accommodate a range of customer tastes, but the economies of scale made the branches profitable.

In the 1960s and 1970s, Howard Johnson's started to decline in quality and profitability and was replaced by what we are familiar with still, the fast-food chains like McDonald's, KFC, and Taco Bell. These did away with the two-hundred-item menus of places like Howard Johnson's, replacing them with a few variations on a single food such as burgers, fried chicken, or tacos. No longer did waiters come to a table; a behind-the-counter liaison with a largely automated kitchen was the extent of customers' personal interaction with the establishment. Eventually such impersonality was offset by kids' play areas and free toys, but originally operational efficiency was not perceived as detracting from the experience of dining—quite the contrary. By 1952, McDonald's was featured on the cover of *American Restaurant* magazine because of its unheard-of efficiency (the article was entitled "One Million Hamburgers and 160 Tons of French Fries a Year") and low labor cost of 17 percent of total expenses. What most impressed Ray Kroc, who in 1961 took over the business and expanded it to dominate the fast-food world, was not these metrics, but the pleasure of diners, many of them in their cars. In his memoir, honestly if lugubriously enti-tled *Grinding It Out*, Kroc describes his life-changing epiphany, seeing a young woman in a yellow convertible "demolishing a hamburger . . . with a demure precision that was fascinating." He goes on to say it was not her "sex appeal" that made his heart pound wildly, but the "obvious relish with which she devoured the hamburger. . . . Her appetite was magnified by the many people in the cars that filled the parking lot."[41]

Sensuous enjoyment would later be forgotten as McDonald's became a stan-dardized experience, a necessity or routine rather than a special treat. Much of this was Kroc's doing. The McDonald brothers had wanted to concentrate on their single site and make it as speedy as possible; Kroc wanted to expand by franchising, so the hands-on supervision of the owners was unimportant. Howard Deering Johnson, who had made important innovations in franchising during the Depression, always regarded other people running restaurants with his logo as an irritating necessity rather than a benefit, but franchising was so central to Kroc's expansion of McDonald's that its real revenue growth stemmed from rent. The company's chief financial officer, Harry J. Sonneborn, famously remarked, "We are not technically in the food business. *We are in the real estate business*. The only reason we sell fifteen-cent hamburgers is because they are the greatest producer of revenue, from which our tenants can pay us our rent."[42]

The success of the fast food industry has been well chronicled. Eric Schlosser's *Fast Food Nation* is particularly wide-ranging in looking at the consequences of this success on the entire food system, from farms and ranches to nutrition and food-related disease.[43] Fast food chains even shaped American tastes: before Kentucky Fried Chicken and Popeyes, fried chicken was not eaten much outside the South. In addition, already common American foods, like the hamburger, became identified with a particular, universal brand. Hamburgers were already ubiquitous, but consolidation by McDonald's and other chains created uniformity in what a fast food hamburger was and the disappearance (until a recent rebirth) of non–fast-food burgers. There were still many thousands of independent hamburger stands across the United States in 1968, when McDonald's had a mere thousand or so branches nationally. This particular form of growth and consolidation came long after the agglomeration of food producers and decades after the development of the supermarket. It also extended chronologically well beyond the 1970s, when American food gigantism started to reach its limits. Fast food establishments lost their sense of delight and coolness, however, before the opening of the twenty-first century, becoming little more exciting than filling a car with gasoline.[44] It is only recently that there are signs of crisis in the entire industry, attributable in part to health concerns, but also to changing demographics and inflexible corporate strategies.

✦   ✦   ✦

TODAY, EVEN WITH THE IMPACT of farm-to-table and seasonal dining and the vogue for "artisanal" everything, American supermarkets are busy and filled with tens of thousands of manufactured food items. Well-established products made by large food companies may be fading in popularity, but entire categories that purport to be healthful but are just as industrially produced as Doritos flood the aisles—high-end pancake mix, gluten-free pasta, energy drinks, breakfast bars, coconut water, and kale chips are just a few examples. Tastes have become significantly more sophisticated as restaurants proliferate and diners seek out authentic and flavorful foods. Still, the fast food industry is not disappearing, and as dining outside the home increases, much of that service is provided by standardized eateries. The food scene today differs from the dreary homogeneity of fifty years ago, but the patterns established in the twentieth century remain recognizable, and the familiar, "iconic" brands names are still ubiquitous.

CHAPTER 5

Why Americans Welcomed
Industrial Food

The triumph of modern food was not simply the inevitable outcome of technological progress. It was a human, cultural phenomenon based on prevailing twentieth-century American attitudes toward health and convenience. How food tasted became less important than whether it was good for you and how quickly it could be put on the table. And "good for you" was not just about preventing disease but increasingly meant thinness, optimism, and physical fitness—components of what now would be called "wellness." Going beyond the merely negative absence of illness to the positive sense of well-being meant seeing food as partly resource and partly threat, a daily challenge to be mastered by science, not a form of pleasure.

Through advertising based on scientific nutrition claims and new images of beauty and health, the processed food industry convinced consumers that canned vegetables, frozen orange juice, and cake mixes represented modernity. Industrial processed food products were marketed as nutritious, convenient, and, by the way, tasty (or at least tasty enough). They kept longer than fresh ingredients and saved time and effort in preparing. Attractively packaged, they were advertised with memorable jingles. Anyone of a certain age remembers the tune to "In the valley of the jolly (Yo! Ho! Ho!) Green Giant."[1]

Processed food was emblematic of modernity, when it was common to anticipate the world of tomorrow with eagerness. The difficulty then and now is that the manufacturing process diminishes flavor, and consumers were never quite willing to sacrifice completely the satisfaction of appetite even to slimness, novelty, convenience, or health. Although food from pills featured in science fiction writing, this was never a mainstream expectation. The food identified with scientific progress was supposed to be hygienic, simple, and fortified with vitamins and minerals, but also attractively flavored or enhanced. The enhancement might be sugar, as with bread or spaghetti sauce, or corn syrup as with Miracle Whip imitation mayonnaise

Green Giant "Jolly Green Casserole," 1985. An offer for a Belgian enameled cast-iron pot came with recipe ideas using corn and other Green Giant frozen vegetables.

or chemicals for Tang orange-flavored drink powder. The consumer might even find the packaged product tastier than the natural version—for example, canned or bottled tomato juice is often preferred to fresh. Or the natural product might taste too strong—triple-crème cheese versus Swiss Knight triangles; fresh mackerel versus breaded fish sticks.

Wonder Bread is a good example of the attractiveness of a standard national brand regarded at one time as convenient, healthful, and in the vanguard of progress.[2] That the brand eventually became an emblem of tasteless conformity does not detract from decades of popularity after it was introduced in 1921 by the Taggart Baking Company in Indianapolis. In the 1930s, Wonder was the first to retail sliced bread, a convenience that seemed so marvelous that the phrase "the greatest thing since sliced bread" became a popular expression of praise after the comedian Red Skelton in 1952 used this locution on television.[3]

Processed white bread destroys many of the nutrients found in ordinary bread, a deficiency Wonder Bread turned to its advantage by enriching its product and then advertising that "Wonder Bread helps build strong bodies eight ways." This 1950s slogan, made famous by Buffalo Bob, host of the *Howdy Doody* television show, was expanded to "twelve ways" in the 1960s. The soft, spongy texture and cottony taste were acceptable; what sold the product was a combination of convenience and health.

Modern packaged foods such as Wonder Bread became so entrenched that formerly routine tasks such as bread making seemed hopelessly archaic. Buying bread from a bakery, meaning an extra stop and a higher price, did not seem worthwhile to most consumers. The unquestioned popularity of industrially produced food for much of the twentieth century was accompanied by mass forgetfulness. The taste of the past might remain dimly attractive, but it was made to seem unmanageably difficult and time-consuming to achieve in the contemporary, fast-paced world. Indeed, modern products offer peculiar images of history. Country Time Lemonade, a powdered mix, advertised itself in the late 1970s and early 1980s with the jingle "Tastes like that good old-fashioned lemonade." The folksy old man enjoying a pitcher of Country Time with his grandson evoked an appealing past, as if making fresh lemonade would require picturesque, out-of-date skills, not to mention trouble, commensurate with dressing game or churning butter. A persistent message of food advertising for packaged products is that the artisanal alternative is hopelessly laborious, something from a lost civilization.

The cultural sway of modern food started at the end of the nineteenth century and beginning of the twentieth. Its primary appeal was based on a Jetsons-like celebration of technological progress, but it could be extended to claim equivalence with a homemade past implicit in the Country Time ad campaign. Either way, national brands of industrial foods took over everyday life. Even if Hostess, the parent company of Wonder Bread as well as Twinkies, declared bankruptcy in 2012, even if Spam long ago lost the middle-class suburban mar-

Wonder Bread advertisement, 1956. The campaign, based on building strong bodies first eight then twelve ways, was aimed at parents. The company gave away thousands of wooden measuring sticks to chart children's growth.

Northwestern Yeast Company pamphlet for New York World's Fair, 1939. The pamphlet advertises a traditional home-baking product in conjunction with the futuristic imagery of the New York World's Fair.

ket, modern food and its famous brands are still with us.[4] Having shed their Tomorrowland allure, they nevertheless retain advantages of size and the ability to offer low-priced and well-known products. The accompanying ideas of health and convenience induced Americans to ignore flavor and tradition and to embrace what looked like progress.

Modern Food Is Good for You

To this day foreign observers are surprised by how much attention Americans give to dieting, particularly because we simultaneously demonstrate a propensity to overeat. Nowhere else are so many books and articles of advice published about how to eat healthfully, yet no other country has such large restaurant portion sizes. Notwithstanding the popularity of so-called superfoods like kale and quinoa, preoccupation with the healthfulness of food is generally negative. A more positive conception of diet is found in Chinese and Indian theories of human equilibrium and the belief that eating certain foods at certain times brings good luck. Americans succumb to successive food phobias whose optimistic side is that if you just give up whatever is the enemy of the moment, your life and health will be radically improved. The current gluten-free scare is a classic example, extending a very real problem of celiac allergy to a population that is unaffected but that, nevertheless, has decided to avoid a basic component of many foods in their natural state. At various times in American history the enemy has been vegetables, spices, saturated fats, carbohydrates, GMOs, butter, eggs, or red meat. The solutions to weight loss have included drinks (diet shakes), medicine (amphetamines), meditative or hypnotic therapies, or concentration on one element, as with low-calorie products or various high-protein, no-carbohydrate diets such as paleo and ketogenic.

Dr. Crum's Donut Reducing Diet, 1941. It would be nice if this worked especially well with chocolate and glazed donuts.

What all these diet recommendations have in common is that they identify most delicious foods as bad for you. An unlikely but widely believed explanation for this phenomenon is that the Puritan heritage of the northern colonies created a lasting mistrust of pleasure. It won't do to blame Protestantism, however, not only because its influence is only a small part of what has formed American culture, but also because the Puritans enjoyed dining and did not practice much in the way of fasting, nor did they come up with medicalized theories of

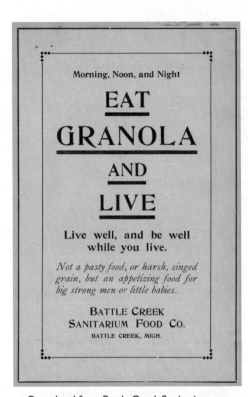

Granola ad from Battle Creek Sanitarium, ca. 1880. Granola was an early breakfast cereal experiment of Dr. Harvey Kellogg, combining wheat, oats, and corn.

diet.[5] Other Protestant sects such as the Mennonites (Amish) have quite a repertoire of delightful food with lots of meat, pie, and pickles. Anxiety about dietary health dates only to the late nineteenth century, not to seventeenth-century New England, and is the result not of religion, but of popular belief in science, or pseudoscience.

Americans' preoccupation with food and health has both an optimistic and a fearful side. The belief that science will tell us what to eat and make it appealing comes from popular attitudes toward technological progress and self-improvement. Food-related health claims join mental with physical well-being. The positive psychological effects attributed to eating properly range from optimism to increased intelligence. "Lightness," energy, and focus are important promises of American dietary fads. The downside is that not only are many tempting foods bad for you, but that they lead to moral degeneracy. A bad diet causes disease, but is also an encouragement to alcoholism, wastefulness, laziness, and other social deficiencies.

The belief that around the corner is the perfect diet recommendation (paleo, gluten-free, vegan) relies on nutritional science but also partakes of the language of religious cults. Americans are not uniquely infatuated with technology; the rest of the world is equally familiar with its benefits. In the late nineteenth century, when nutritional health concerns began to gain public attention, Europe too had railroads, electricity, steamships, and the telegraph. What was different about the United States was a belief in the advice of scientific experts and popularizers. The pursuit of health accompanied a secular gospel of enterprise and personal accomplishment. Preachers of this gospel include the brothers John Harvey and William Kellogg, who invented and popularized their corn flakes as health products, but also motivational experts like Dale Carnegie (author of *How to Win Friends and Influence People*) and Norman Vincent Peale (author of *The Power of Positive Thinking)*. Celebrity nutritionists also offered similar promises. Examples of such charismatic figures include Adelle Davis, an early advocate of whole grains and vitamin supplements, and Robert Atkins, inventor and eponym of the high-protein diet that swept the country in the 1990s.

The nutritional gospel of self-care often included quasi-religious components, such as temperance or moral improvement. These aspects reflect the fear of moral decay implicit in even the most optimistic American diet advice. Beginning in the 1830s, food reformers urged Americans to change their diet radically with programs of self-restraint based on moral, economic, and scientific ideas. Eating the wrong things would have personally debilitating and socially damaging effects.[6] Such advice fit in with the egalitarian ethos of the new republic and the personal struggle to achieve recognition in a society without well-established upper-class standards. Innovation and opportunity encouraged an entrepreneurial rather than pleasure-centered attitude toward food, regarding it as something to be tamed rather than enjoyed.

After the Civil War, with progress in the understanding of digestion and nutrition, but also in response to social Darwinism, the agitation for dietary change took on racial and competitive urgency. During the Gilded Age, the application of science to social analysis, religion, and everyday life became a framework for economic competition and success. Another program for transforming society was Christian Science, which held that medicine was useless because health and illness were the results of individual attitude. The educated public was eager for scientific teachings about what foods were good or bad for you, irrespective of whether you liked them or not.

The key factor that divorced consumption from taste in the late nineteenth century was the discovery that foods have invisible properties that affect health. The German chemist Justus von Liebig in 1847 identified proteins, fats, carbohydrates, and minerals as constituents of food, and although their exact effects were debated, their physiological uses and abuses became established facts.

Rather than all food being more or less like undifferentiated fuel feeding a fire, it was understood that some foods were better for you or answered specific needs. The taste and look of a particular food were less important than its function: proteins strengthened the body's tissue, while carbohydrates provided energy.

The nutritionists who studied the new science, and especially those who popularized it, regarded the human body as a machine requiring efficient fuel. They differed about what "efficient" meant in practice, but they unanimously taught that a lot of what most people ate was either useless or adverse. Reformers bemoaned the food habits of immigrants, as well as the stubborn carelessness of the native working-class population with regard to diet. The nutrition scientist Wilbur Atwater, who promoted calories as the basis for measuring the efficiency of diet, and Edward Atkinson, an entrepreneur and anti-imperialist, criticized the widespread fondness for sweets and the wasteful preference for finer cuts of meat. Because they believed that all protein was alike, scientific reformers were confident that a healthful diet could be had for much less money than the laboring poor were spending. It was ridiculous to buy oysters for two or three dollars when a pound of cod or mackerel costing a mere 38 cents provided the same amount of protein.

Such statistics were designed to aid economic efficiency and improve morals, but the poor proved to be recalcitrant. For food reformers, the fact that ordinary people loved oysters simply demonstrated their fecklessness. Because the lower classes waste their money on the pleasures of food and drink, the reformers argued, they neglect hygiene, orderly housekeeping, and their children's education.[7] Reworked in various guises, this notion of the poor as irresponsible, even immoral, has endured—feeding sugary drinks to children and addiction to fast foods are parts of the most recent version of the idea that nutritional sins manifest themselves as social and public-health crises. Consistently, experts have wanted to posit a link between diet and moral degeneration instead of considering poverty itself as the cause of poor nutrition. Rather than eating poorly because they were poor, the lower classes were believed to suffer nutritionally because they were uneducated and stubborn.

One problem for the reformers was that they disagreed as to what constituted good nutrition. While Atwater extolled protein, the chemist Russell Chittenden, director of the Sheffield Scientific School at Yale University from 1898 to 1922, thought that proteins were being consumed to excess. Chittenden was converted from protein advocacy by Horace Fletcher, another popularizer of science, who maintained that chewing food until it was completely tasteless, a hundred times or so, would get rid of protein and make digestion so easy that solid excrement would have no smell. He was happy to prove this assertion by sending stool samples in the mail to Chittenden and other acolytes.[8] Fletcher's followers, who included such luminaries as the novelist Henry James and his brother, the philosopher William James, regarded "Fletcherizing" as a miraculous relief from colds and dyspepsia as well as from psychological ennui.

The most radical and long-lasting food reform idea was the denigration of taste. According to the food reformers, ignorant people are guided by what tastes good—a harmfully deceptive criterion for deciding what to eat. The nutritionist Mary Hinman Abel bemoaned the tyranny of the allegorical "King Palate," whose misrule led to moral decay as well as physical degeneration, as evidenced by epidemics of indigestion, liver disease, and delirium tremens. The corrupt sway of King Palate was enabled by the uneducated preference of taste over science, as suggested by the foolish credo "I like this, so it must be good for me." In exasperation, another leading nutritionist imagined a poor woman saying "I'd rather eat what I'd rather. I don't want to eat what's good for me."[9] The food reformers' argument was a two-part doctrine that is still with us: (1) I like this, so it's probably bad for me; and (2) Eat this—you may not like the taste, but so what? It's good for you.

The Progressive Era, the first decade of the twentieth century, accepted the scientific, moral, and aesthetic critiques of flavor. The aesthetic part was a new fashion for a slim and athletic body. Instead of denoting prosperity or a good-natured temperament, a plump look now suggested self-indulgence. To be thin and to exercise was to be modern, meaning in this instance living in accord with science, self-control, and personal autonomy.[10]

Nutritionism really took off with the discovery of vitamins. The fact that laboratory rats fed theoretically balanced diets sickened and died suggested there were some vital elements to food besides carbohydrates, proteins, and fat. The isolation of vitamin B in 1912 was followed by a series of discoveries of other vitamins and their relation to terrible diseases. Scurvy, the curse of sailors, turned out to be caused by a lack of vitamin C, rickets by insufficient vitamin D, and pellagra by reliance on corn deprived of niacin (vitamin B_3). The startling consequences resulting from deficiencies of invisible substances made nutrition more than merely a calculus of efficient or economical management but a matter of public health. It was now clear that the taste of food was in no sense an adequate guide for personal health.

The discovery of vitamin deficiency as a cause of disease should have been of particular importance to the poor, people like the Southern tenant farmers whose children suffered pellagra. The middle classes, however, became the strongest proponents of the new nutritionism even though they did not, in fact, suffer from vitamin deficiency scourges like beriberi. This enthusiasm to solve a nonproblem would constantly recur. Iron tablets or foods rich in iron were supposed to combat anemia, another disease rare among decently nourished people. Calcium deficiency became another exaggerated middle-class concern.

In the late nineteenth century, nutritionists focused their attention on American-born workers, but also on immigrants whose eating habits seemed all wrong, although in a different way from the native poor. Southern and Eastern Europeans liked sharp flavors, like spices and garlic, which, as everyone knew, encouraged alcoholism. Immigrants were foolishly fond of vegetables, which had little nutritional value according to the then-standard theories, and were profligate in buying expensive imported goods like olive oil. The nutritionists believed in what they regarded as simple, pure foods like beef broth. Protein was to be emphasized over carbohydrates; pressed cod cakes were thus better for you than eggplant parmigiana.

Well-intentioned social workers and home economists of this period tried to make the insipid, frugal food of New England into the gastronomic model for poor people, especially immigrants, in order to get them to eat like "real Americans."[11] They employed contemporary scientific ideas, including racial and eugenic theories, whereby the culinary preeminence of New England was part of the overall Anglo-Saxon superiority to other peoples. Beef, breakfast cereal, store-bought bread, milk, and white sauces were the hallmarks of what purported to be a well-balanced diet. Ingredients should not be mixed together in

BROOKLYN SANITARY FAIR, 1864.
NEW ENGLAND KITCHEN.

A lithograph of the Brooklyn Sanitary Fair from 1864. Sanitary fairs were held across
the Northeast to raise funds for the Civil War. At this fair, the staples of the
New England Kitchen are on full display.

any complicated fashion. A dish like Italian lasagna that layered meat, cheese, and pasta was considered unhealthful—scientists said that digestion was vastly improved and nutrients better distributed when foods were eaten separately and with minimal amounts of sauce.[12]

The doctrine of scientific nutrition was put into effect by home economists, a profession that flourished beginning around 1900, along with other higher education fields open to women such as teacher training. The new progressive cuisine was taught at high schools, universities, and institutions such as the Boston Cooking School, founded by the Women's Education Association in 1878. In keeping with his notions of nutritional efficiency, Wilbur Atwater had praised New Englanders for relying on small amounts of fatty pork in relation to healthful, high-protein beans and for eating protein-rich cod and mackerel. The origins of this regional diet were partly in Scotland, whose inhabitants ate ideal combinations such as oatmeal with haddock or herring.[13]

If immigrants and the American-born poor seemed uninterested in the boring austerity of the reformers' New England cuisine, the middle classes were more receptive. Beginning in the 1890s, the faith of educated and affluent people in science and self-improvement allied itself with a desire for good health in terms of peak performance and good spirits. This same attitude still informs diet fads, mindfulness practices, and the consumption of food supplements to provide not just nutrition, but positive energy.

At the Chicago World's Fair of 1893, the New England model was put on display at what was called the Rumford Kitchen, which served brown bread, pea soup, escalloped fish, gingerbread, and other constituents of a sensible diet. No longer were immigrants or American-born laborers the intended audience for dietary propaganda. The Rumford Kitchen was appropriate for the "intelligent, thinking citizen" who wishes to improve himself, as opposed to the "incorrigible poor."[14]

Not only did dietary simplicity seem healthful, but it was also appropriate for a household without servants, a trend that would accelerate in the twentieth century. Scientific cooking also fit into a society whose population mostly purchased food at a store and then cooked it at home rather than engaging in hunting, cultivation, or preserving. Modern domestic activities centered around child care and socializing—piano lessons and dinner parties—not chopping wood, gutting animals, or home canning.

In the early twentieth century, the food industry figured out how to exploit Americans' fears of eating badly and their hopes for wellness. By the 1920s, food companies were attracting investors such as J. P. Morgan and E. F. Hutton, and their size and profits started to exceed even those of steel and textiles.[15] The food giants faced the already-mentioned problem of substitution, that in order to sell one kind of food, you had to get people to change their habits because they already had enough to eat. One way to do this was to convince people that new foods conferred nutritional as well as convenience advantages—in particular, targeting the role of the wife and mother as guardian of the family's health. This was a logical outgrowth of nurturing children, but in the early and mid-twentieth century, nurturing extended to husbands, too. If left to themselves, men would neglect or ignore their own best interests in favor of inappropriate foods, irregular meals, and excessive eating. Exalting the housewife as health expert made her the ideal target for advertising and fit in with the prevailing image of her subordinate but vitally sustaining role.

Home economists' classes and testimonials, magazine articles, radio advertisements, and food company brochures were the vehicles by which women were persuaded to try new products, serve more of a certain food group, or make use of food routines and perceive them as necessary—orange juice every morning, hot soup for lunch, milk for kids and teenagers. Companies manufacturing ordinary products made audacious health claims. Welch's grape juice was not only rich in vitamins and minerals but contained "laxative properties you can't do without." Fleischmann's yeast, whose sales declined because fewer people were baking bread at home, marketed itself as an ideal source of vitamins; Morton's salt helped make children energetic.[16] Government regulation of scientific claims was not rigorous.

Once food came to be regarded as a means to deliver nutrients rather than as a pleasurable necessity, it's not surprising that food companies boasted about vitamins and other supposedly beneficial ingredients that they added to "fortify" foods. The addition of vitamin D to milk by means of irradiation is a classic example of this practice.[17] Processing grain, meat, and vegetables removes nutrients, but along with retrofitting with vitamins and minerals, companies defined what was lost as useless or even dangerous. Today it is common knowledge that whole grains are better than processed, but before the Second World War, Cream of Wheat cereal advertised that it was healthful because the manufacturers had stripped away the "harsh" and "indigestible" parts of wheat.[18]

Beginning in the 1920s, food companies advertised in women's magazines like *Good Housekeeping, Family Circle, Ladies' Home Journal,* and *Better Homes and Gardens* and used nutritional information and misinformation to sell their products. Campbell's was a pioneer, presenting soup not only as appropriate for cold weather, but, as early as 1916, as food the woman of the household should deploy to keep her husband and children in "warm-blooded and vigorous" health. Hot breakfast cereals were not far behind. A 1920s advertisement shows a housewife saying, "I know I've done my best for Bill with good hot Quaker Oats."[19] Advertisements attributing to women the responsibility for the health of their husbands were particularly important for marketing fruits, vegetables, and other foods men were supposedly loath to consume: "He really ought to eat more green things and fruit." The way to overcome this reluctance was through the tastes added by prepared foods—such as sugar and spices added to Miracle Whip dressing to make salad appealing to men, according to a 1938 advertisement.[20] Women were thus enlisted to campaign for an adjustment of food intake in favor of health-enhancing industrial products.

Going beyond vaguely scientific promises of foods that promoted health, companies tried to increase market share by claiming beneficial effects for dubious or damaging ingredients. In the 1950s, breakfast cereals touted the fact that they came with added sugar. Kellogg's Sugar Frosted Flakes and Sugar Corn Pops advertisements claimed that sugar provided added energy and a taste kids loved. For Sugar Frosted Flakes, Tony the Tiger reminded children, "They're grrrrreat!!" Sugar Pops had a memorable television commercial featuring its prairie dog mascot Sugar Pops Pete singing, "Oh, the Pops are sweeter and the taste is new, they're shot with sugar, through and through!"

When sugar came under a cloud in the 1980s, Kellogg's dropped the word *Sugar* from the names of their cereals, so they are now simply Frosted Flakes and Corn Pops. Even so, cereal manufacturers resisted the notion that sugar was damaging to children's health, using a set of interlocking arguments: sugar in moderation is fine, balance among things consumed is better than renunciation, and, finally, if people don't eat a balanced diet, it's their own fault.[21]

Enlisting science and health to sell food began during the waning nineteenth century and continues in the present. In recent decades, companies and their experts have made health claims for sugar-free foods, labeled Froot Loops and Lucky Charms as "smart choices," and stretched the definitions (or nondefinitions) of words like *natural* and *organic*.[22] Weak and evasive government policies reinforce the impression that nutrition is an uncertain discipline whose recommendations keep on changing: eggs are bad for you one year and good the next; oat bran is a cure-all and then not, because now flaxseed has become the darling of the health food world. In fact, respectable nutritional advice has not varied that much over the past fifty years: don't consume so many calories; exercise; eat fiber, vegetables, and whole grains; limit the intake of sugar—don't drink soda in particular; and avoid processed foods in favor of actual cooking. None of this is popular because people want an easy, magic-bullet solution.

The "fat time of day:" you're starving and want to stuff yourself. Read how sugar comes to the rescue.

Sugar ad, 1968. Sugar companies pushed back against the notion that sugar is fattening.

Modern Food Is Good for Society

Food advertising is usually addressed to the white middle class. For much of the twentieth century, companies were aware that their products were bought by workers, poor people, and racial minorities, but they were afraid to target them lest they lose affluent consumers who didn't want to imagine that they had much in common with those they considered below them. Standard products can lose social prestige and acceptance, as happened with Kool-Aid, for example, an instant drink once considered part of middle-class child-rearing. It requires tons of sugar to make Kool-Aid, but then again, white suburban kids are raised on drinks like Capri Sun, whose manufacturers boast that they have gotten rid of high-fructose corn syrup in favor of "organic natural sweeteners" (i.e., sugar).[23]

Corporate attention to the middle class tended to distract public awareness of hunger and malnutrition except to the extent that it was recognized that poor diet leads to diseases such as diabetes, representing a public health financial burden. This concern was not an expression of communal solidarity but rather of notions of individual responsibility and the inducement to blame health problems on the victims. A hundred years earlier, the apparent irresponsibility of the poor was a frightening development, not because of medical costs, which in the absence of government insurance was not a public problem, but because poor nutrition was undermining the white race. Immigrants threatened the moral as well as physical vigor of America, according to popular and expert opinion of the 1890s to 1930s. Dietary vigilance would help defend America as a bulwark of white European civilization.

Nutrition, science, and public health were enlisted in the service of a geopolitical construct. Scientific tendencies toward measuring and managing society provided justifications for racism. The moral and intellectual superiority of the Anglo-Saxon race, Wilbur Atwater remarked, is related to their superior "frugal but rational diet."[24] The supposed menace to the Anglo-Saxon racial category came from imagined threats such as the "Yellow Peril" of China's large population, from racial intermarriage, and from a reworking of age-old prejudices in scientific language. Racial theorists, nutrition scientists, and home economists all worried about the self-indulgent diet of ordinary people, who seemed incorrigibly devoted to unhealthful food and alcohol. Ellen Richards, the first woman to graduate from MIT and a founder of nutritional science, warned that overeating threatened the future of the white race: "In all the discussion of the infertility of the higher branches of the human race, how little attention is paid to the weakening effect of the pampered appetite." As a complement to the emerging "science" of eugenics, the improvement of the (white) race through heredity, what Richards called "euthenics," would forward race improvement by manipulating the family environment, beginning with reforms to household management and cooking.[25]

According to influential "thought leaders" of the late nineteenth and early twentieth centuries, the Caucasian race was superior, and only northern European Protestants were really Caucasian, so Jews, Irish, and Italians were at an inferior level. Real whites were threatened by a declining birth rate, while the inferior races were having more babies and taking over the world. Solutions included better nutrition, physical fitness, stemming the flow of immigration, and developing a eugenic regime to regulate who could have children in order to maintain the healthy stock of the superior race. As with the discovery of natural selection or vitamins, the advances in genetics created a host of dangerously popular, pseudoscientific social teachings.

Not surprisingly, there were paradoxes and contradictions in the prevailing view of race, cuisine, and civilization. The rich, too, it was observed, ate badly. Their desire for elegant and exotic food was lamented by nutritionists. No less an authority than Dr. John Harvey Kellogg warned that "the decline of a nation commences when gourmandizing begins."[26]

Despite the prevailing paranoia about preserving Caucasian purity and fecundity, it was conceivable that other races might participate in social reform through nutritional betterment. Northern philanthropists urged progressive elements of the black race to adopt the civilized diet of the Boston Cooking School as a path to social and moral uplift. Indeed, at the Tuskegee Institute, Booker T. Washington arranged for beef to be served in the dining hall. Normally beef was rarely consumed in the Deep South, and some students reported that they had never eaten it before coming to Tuskegee. Washington urged them to reject the traditions of grits, pork, and cornbread. Students would be "five times healthier" if they adopted "clean, fresh beef." Under the direction of Anita J. Atkinson, a white domestic scientist, Tuskegee menus in the 1890s featured roast beef, rare steak, Boston baked beans, codfish balls, graham gems (made with graham crackers), and johnnycakes. The neurologist George M.

Beard opined that "savages who eat poor food are inferior to beef-eaters of any race," thus the improvement of the Negro might begin from within, as a matter of diet and digestion.[27]

Food reform leaders created an idealized picture of Americans as devotees of a plain, frugal, and healthful diet. Not for them the fancy sauces of the French, the highly spiced cuisine of Mexico, or the garlic and oregano of Italy. Digestive health and sensible economizing required blandness and austerity, but this image of plainness has never been accurate. Americans love sugary and piquant flavors—things like barbecue sauce, "Chinese" sweet and sour pork, and thick, sweet, vinegary "French" dressing. We are more interested in discussing diet than in healthful eating. Our food as it has evolved might be lacking in natural flavor, but it is far from plain.

LEARNING TO BE HOME MAKERS
A cooking class, canning fruit at Hampton Institute. The girls are learning the art of becoming good housewives.

Classes for future homemakers, Hampton Institute, 1917. The institute was founded by a Union general in 1868 to educate recently freed African Americans.

Convenience

They went into the kitchen and Mrs. Bridge looked into the refrigerator.
"Strawberries and whipped cream?" she suggested. "These are frozen,
of course. They don't really taste the same as the fresh, but they certainly
are a time-saver."

EVAN S. CONNELL, *MRS. BRIDGE* (1959), CHAPTER 97

In addition to healthfulness, the main selling point for modern, processed food is convenience. In contrast to the on-again, off-again preoccupation with health, American love of convenience has been consistent. For the century between 1870 and 1970, and to a great extent before and after, human progress could be measured by innovations that made the repetitive task of preparing meals easier. Efficiency and convenience are closely related, and in the food practices of Americans, both are seen as maximizing time. Heating up a can of soup or making a sandwich using packaged sliced baloney is faster than cooking something, and in that sense more efficient, just as eating at your desk is "better" than wasting time having lunch at a restaurant. Silicon Valley pioneered the practice of providing free meals on the office campus so that employees will work more hours.

All this assumes that more important things than food clamor for your attention. The dossier of American contempt for France includes its citizens' supposed fondness for interminable lunches. People who consider themselves native-born Americans also sometimes complain that immigrants seem to be cooking all the time. Certain ingrained attitudes about health and time were reinforced by advertising on the basis of wellness as well as efficiency. Americans tend to regard meals as necessary tasks to be accomplished as quickly as possible, so ideal food products were those, like breakfast cereal, that were both time-savers and good for you.

Efficiency is not quite the same as convenience. Efficiency is accomplishing things quickly while convenience is oriented toward ease. A slow cooker is convenient, but neither quick nor particularly efficient. In the passage quoted from the fiction writer Evan Connell's unflinching portrayal of affluent suburban Kansas City in the middle of the twentieth century, the frozen strawberries aren't really a "time-saver," but they appear to be less trouble.

The frozen strawberries also exemplify the context of convenience. They had the advantage of being always available in the Midwest in 1959, when fresh strawberries from California or Mexico were not yet a year-round supermarket fruit. This is not so much convenience as getting around seasonality, one of the big accomplishments of American culinary modernism. The reason they are introduced by the author of the Mr. and Mrs. Bridge books, however, is the false ease they offer. Boredom and empty days oppress Mrs. Bridge, so that even if the frozen product did save time, it wouldn't matter since she is not busy. The attraction is that it avoids what seems like the tedium of washing, trimming, and cutting, or perhaps it is simply the modern way of doing things.

Since the current rhetoric of the sustainable food movement is oriented toward a past of honest, healthful, and loving food preparation, it is a good idea to acknowledge the real advances in speed and comfort conferred by basic technological innovations. Indoor plumbing, refrigerators, gas, and electricity have radically reduced the drudgery and time needed to prepare meals over the past three centuries. In a book about the origins of American food, James E. McWilliams describes what it took to get ready a routine evening meal on a prosperous Maryland farm around 1650.[28] Corn kernels had to be soaked and ground. To obtain six cups of cornmeal required at least an hour of grinding with a large mortar and pestle. Pickled beef was relatively easy to take from storage, but as with smoked pork that the farm also produced, it was hard rearing and slaughtering the animals as well as butchering, processing, and preserving their meat. Milk and butter would be provided by a dairymaid, a hired skilled worker. Everything had to be perfectly clean or else not only would the milk sour, but the possibility of fatal diseases would be radically increased. The maid could milk a cow in ten minutes, and in McWilliams's reconstruction, seven cows had to be milked. The cream was skimmed off for butter. On a dry, warm, but not hot day, butter churning could be accomplished in perhaps two hours, more if the weather was cold. The cornmeal was cooked with milk and could be made into a porridge, bread, or pancakes and served with butter. Dinner could also include carrots and beans requiring their own harvesting and treatment, everything washed down with cider made with crushed apples, again necessitating considerable labor.

The effort and time saved in making the same meal today with ingredients bought from a store and cooked on an indoor appliance rather than an open fire is obviously substantial. It is also obvious that with the exponential growth in convenience over more than 350 years comes de-skilling. The ordinary household no longer includes anyone who knows how to churn butter or grind corn. Advertisers usually avoid saying explicitly that modern food products mean you don't have to know anything, but especially in appealing to inexperienced cooks and also in the rich field of "gourmet" meals with processed ingredients, convenience means that it is not necessary to be adept at anything complicated, like making a cake from scratch when a mix will do just fine. You can even make "Hungarian Goulash" out of packaged salami, sweet-and-sour cabbage from a jar, canned potatoes, and onions.[29]

Not all convenience products are craven or silly. Dried pasta, a real savings in terms of both time and effort, was adopted eagerly in Italy as well as the United States. Making fresh pasta is one of those seemingly simple but difficult and time-consuming tasks, so if there has been a mass falling-off in this skill, it is not completely lamentable. In other cases, the convenience is equally clear, but the taste consequences are substantial and unavoidable. Few people make bread at home even though the bread available from supermarkets is not very good. There aren't many bakeries, and even they have trouble with bread. France itself has had to restore this particular craft, and it has not been easy.[30] Thus, even if one rejects the extreme artificiality of Wonder Bread, the alternatives do not compare with what used to be routinely available, albeit with someone (baker, homemaker, servant) going to considerable trouble.

The heyday of marketing food on the basis of convenience coincided with the postwar era, when advertisers made it appear as if all women were housewives. Companies wanted their brands associated with a moderately prosperous way of life rather than directly appealing to women for whom convenience products were particularly useful, the roughly one-third of American women who worked outside the home during the 1950s.[31] Publications like *Mademoi-*

selle, directed at young women, portrayed working at a job as a temporary condition before marriage. In a limited fashion, advertisers acknowledged the reality of women in the workforce and sold all manner of modern food to this market, but single women over twenty-five and career women were largely ignored. The ability to prepare meals quickly or to show children how to fend for themselves during Mom's absence was actually important, and once working women were too obvious to ignore, the usefulness of condensed soup and microwavable meals was directed to them. For the period before 1970, however, the size of this category, demonstrable by census figures, did not tempt advertisers.

Speed is as important as convenience. A nostalgic look back assumes that once upon a time, before the many demands of modern life intruded, there was plenty of time for everything. No one would imagine the Maryland colonial family described by McWilliams trying to save corn-grinding time in order to binge-watch a television series. The demand for speed, however, is venerable in the United States, allied as it is to images of efficiency and modernity. If the time spent eating meals is itself regarded as irritating, how can its preparation escape an even more intensely negative image? It's all very well to try and cheer up whoever is responsible for cooking meals at home—the most popular cookbook between Fannie Farmer and Julia Child was entitled *The Joy of Cooking*—but the tedium is undeniable.

Convenience food advertising portrays the female head of household as stressed because it is to the food companies' advantage to show women as busy with demands other than cooking. As women's tasks became severed from the economic enterprise of the family, the significance of child-rearing and leisure became greater. Over the course of the twentieth century, women were increasingly involved in their children's lives, and those children became less self-sufficient in providing their own entertainment and determining their extracurricular options.

Even without the frazzled schedules, the ideal image of married life was no longer a kind of functional alliance, the oldest European paradigm being that men took care of agricultural labor in the fields and women supervised the house, its gardens, and animals. Part of modern life is the evolution of marriage from a partnership of different skills to a companionship with shared interests.

Men might seek out a wife who would be a domestic servant and mother of children, but they actually wanted her, within limits, to enjoy life as well. Already in the 1920s, Frank Shattuck, the founder of the Schrafft's restaurant chain, remarked:

> When I talk about the pies mothers used to make, it means something that is really excellent. Mothers today do not make such pies. They aren't particularly interested in pies. Their time is taken up with other things: movies, bridge parties, automobile rides. A young man contemplating marriage no longer asks whether a girl is a good cook; he wants to know whether she is a good sport.[32]

Of course, the young man does not plan to do the cooking, nor is he going to be happy if his wife doesn't provide him with regular meals, but their preparation shouldn't consume all her effort.

The time it takes to make dinner has decreased radically in recent decades. In the 1970s, the French-born New York restaurant chef Pierre Franey put out two cookbooks with the theme "the 60-minute gourmet." Surely, it seemed, no one could want anything faster! Decades later, before it folded in 2009, *Gourmet* magazine featured a column entitled "10-minute mains" (i.e., main courses).[33]

All this assumes that the family still eats together, which is obviously not usually the case. Meal preparation has fragmented, not just because most women work paid jobs, but because of the different schedules and priorities of family members and the fact that households do not uniformly conform to the married-couple-with-children-at-home model of yesteryear. The ultimate result of the seduction of convenience is to make cooking at home the exception rather than the rule. As restaurants, fast food, and takeout have taken over more of the landscape of consumption, the kitchen has been, if not abandoned, at least depopulated during most of the day, far from the perpetually burning hearth of the rural past.

Before the twentieth century, that hearth, as well as everything else having to do with preparing food in a middle-class household, would have been the responsibility of servants. Depending on time and place, these might have been slaves, indentured servants, recent immigrants, refugees from farms, or others displaced by economic progress. Reliance on servants came with its own inconveniences. Household advice, which made up a substantial portion of American cookbooks before the Civil War, included tips on managing lazy, unruly, or unreliable household help.

In the early twentieth century, the pool of potential servants evaporated as women were attracted to factory or clerical jobs. The demand for employees during the First World War and the economic expansion of the 1920s attracted women away from domestic service, and because of restrictive federal legislation, new immigrants were not numerous enough to make up the difference. In 1917, a writer for the magazine *Printer's Ink* reported that the scarcity of domestic labor on the West Coast was due to a falloff in the supply of Mexican, Chinese, and Japanese workers. Even in the South, the "colored population" was migrating northward in considerable numbers, making wages for domestic labor rise to "undreamed of levels."[34]

The clampdown on immigration that followed the end of World War I further reduced the number of people seeking domestic work. "The servant problem" was a constant theme of women's magazines, and this term covered both the scarcity of servants and the unsatisfactory nature of those who were available. To some extent, the South experienced less upheaval, as many African Americans remained domestic workers until well after the Second World War.[35]

The disappearance of servants was an opportunity for the makers of electronic appliances and convenience foods. Small kitchen machines like toasters, waffle irons, and coffee percolators were promoted as reliable replacements for clumsy or easily fatigued servants. Although good personal service has become hard to find, a 1923 article in *Sunset* claimed, electricity has freed the housewife from both labor and the annoyance of dealing with people. Another article from the same year in *The Country Gentleman* praised the new "hired girl on the farm," who is swift, neat, silent, untiring, and never needs to be paid. Electricity and the appliances it powers meant that "fragrant coffee, golden-brown waffles or toast" appear at the table, piping-hot and effortlessly.[36]

Food companies offered contradictory blandishments. On the one hand, cooking was extolled as fun and an opportunity to show skill, love, and inven-

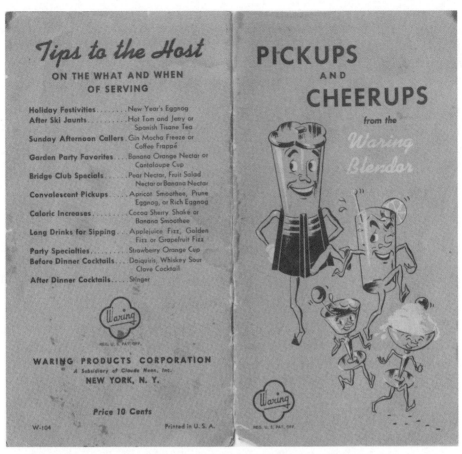

Waring blender pamphlet, "Pickups and Cheerups," 1950s. This is an example of the "home technology is fun" genre.

tiveness. This gave some glamor to prosaic items like instant pudding mix and encouraged women to experiment and buy things they had not used before. Even at the height of anti-immigrant sentiment in the 1920s, foreign food, albeit adjusted for American tastes, was promoted by magazines and companies. Soy sauce, water chestnuts, canned chili con carne, and ravioli all benefited from the popularity of international cuisine as a change from routine.

On the other hand, in opposition to "cooking is fun" was the repeated message that cooking is boring and oppressive. When just leaving the work for servants became impossible, the major selling point of convenience was not all the new things you could do with a blender, but the time and effort it saved.

Cover of Peg Bracken, *The I Hate To Cook Book*, 1960. This is a popular example of the practical, realist cookbook type.

In order to pitch enhanced products, companies emphasized that cooking is drudgery. In the mid-twentieth century, women were told that their time was too valuable to waste in cooking, not because of work demands, but to take advantage of leisure. Wasn't tennis or a card game with friends preferable to labor in a hot kitchen for hours over meat, sauces, and pies? Cookbooks and women's magazine articles were based on the notion that cooking is *not* joyful, at least not on a daily basis, but rather something to cope with. In 1960, the humorist Peg Bracken, who wrote about housekeeping and women's lives, published what would become a classic, *The I Hate to Cook Book*. She offered simple recipes, many with amusing titles (lamb shanks tra-la and hushkabobs, for example), to women looking for reliability, speed, and ease rather than challenge or novelty.[37]

The mainstream message of food publications directed at housewives was a balance between pride in cooking and the desire to reduce its tedium. Real figures like the food writer Poppy Cannon and fictitious icons like Betty Crocker offered simultaneously cheerful acceptance of the obligations of cooking and practical ways to cope with its constant demands. Betty Crocker was a vehicle for General Mills to sell cake mixes and other convenience products that made it possible to provide pleasurable food without too much effort. Poppy Cannon was a leading postwar representative of the ersatz gourmet movement. Instead of just settling for obvious, simple, or readymade food, she taught housewives to put together sophisticated meals using canned, frozen, and powdered ingredients. A recipe for "Roast Canned Chicken Flambé with Black Cherries" exemplifies this approach to creating elegant dishes that saved time and trouble. It calls for rub-bing the chicken with salad oil, rum, and Kitchen Bouquet (a commercial herb mixture), then baking it. The chicken is served surrounded with canned cherries, doused with more rum, and set on fire. Flambé dishes were seen as an important feature of the Continental repertoire that Americans wanted to mimic.[38]

Poppy Cannon did not monopolize this amalgam of European tradition and American know-how. Food companies tried to promote ordinary products like packaged cheese to create fondue or canned oysters for seafood bisque. In 1969, Campbell's issued *Great Restaurants Cookbook, U.S.A.*, giving recipes from 74 fancy restaurants, all of them using canned condensed soup. The introduction notes that the recipes are adaptations of restaurant specialties, thereby exempting the restaurants from appearing to use shortcuts in their kitchens. For the home cook, time and patience are no longer required, "for this is the day of the truly useful, truly valid short-cuts—without short-cutting quality."[39] This cookbook calls for condensed soups to make elaborate productions like "Pork Tenderloin Cordon Bleu à la Maria Christine" at Karl Ratzsch Restaurant in Milwaukee, or Frogs' legs Provençale from Ernie's in San Francisco.[40]

Baked Shrimp and Lobster Papillote (adapted from Perdita's, Charleston, South Carolina)

1½ Tb French-style prepared mustard

¼ cup sour cream

1½ tsp chopped chives

¼ cup Chablis or other dry white wine

3 cups cooked medium shrimp, fresh or frozen, shelled and deveined

3 cups diced cooked fresh lobster pieces or cooked frozen South African rock lobster tails

6 pieces heavy-duty aluminum foil cut in 12-inch squares

6 Tb butter

1 large lemon cut into twelve slices

1 can condensed Cheddar cheese soup

Nutmeg, salt, pepper

In a saucepan combine mustard, sour cream, chives and wine. Stir to blend; heat just to boiling point. Remove from heat; cool.

Combine shrimp and lobster. Place 1 cup on each square of foil. Top each with 1 tablespoon of the butter, 2 lemon slices, 3⅓ tablespoons Cheddar cheese soup, 1½ tablespoons of wine-mustard sauce. Sprinkle with nutmeg, salt and pepper.

Fold together 2 edges of the foil in a drugstore fold.* Seal ends tightly. Place packets on cookie sheet. Bake in a preheated 450° oven for 10 to 15 minutes or until packets are puffed.

Serve in foil by slitting each side of the center fold; pull up center fold to shape a handle, push back sides to shape a basket.

*A drugstore fold means folding over ¼ to ½ inch several times leaving some air space, then rolling up each end the same way to keep in the steam.

From *Campbell's Great Restaurants Cookbook, U.S.A.* (New York: Rutledge, 1969), p. 125.

The Limited Postwar Triumph of Convenience Foods

The great transformation of American kitchens and American home cooking took place in different stages and at different speeds between the 1890s and the outbreak of the Second World War. The real efflorescence of modern food came with postwar, middle-class prosperity, when the average standard of living rose dramatically, along with the expansion of suburban housing, limited-access highways, and television advertising. The period 1954 to 1964 has been dubbed the "Populuxe" decade. Between the end of the Korean War and the beginning of the Vietnam War, there was an explosion of mass-market luxury manifested by stylistic innovations such as automobile tailfins, wood-grain Formica, Naugahyde, and dinette sets. Populuxe (popular luxury) goods were produced in a lightweight, multicolored, streamlined style, available to all, or at least most.[41]

The war spurred the development of products whose convenience and ease of preparation met urgent military necessities such as eating meals at the front. In some sense, postwar convenience foods were a way of selling modified army field and combat rations to sedentary, comfortable civilians. Taken over from army kitchens, frozen food succeeded in the Populuxe era as homes now had freezer space, first as free-standing units and later adjoined to a refrigerator. Frozen food was superior to canned because the process better preserved natural color and texture, and frozen food was free from depressing, thrifty associations.

Notwithstanding the cornucopia of durable, inexpensive and ready-to-eat products, the food industry did not quite fulfill its ambition to turn kitchens into assembly points for meals from mixes, and canned or frozen ingredients. Frozen orange juice and lemonade concentrate, widely available from 1945, swept the nation, as did frozen fish sticks, which were introduced in 1952. The latter were all many people knew about fish—minced and breaded so as to come out crisp and "without that fishy taste." Swanson's TV dinners, introduced in 1953, became an even more famous symbol of the goofy, low-quality prosperity of the postwar era, but successful as they were, they were a limited novelty, seldom served to the entire family, let alone to guests. TV dinners, envisaged as replacing cooking altogether, were usually reserved for children when their parents were going out for dinner. Children were mesmerized by the futuristic look—the aluminum tray with its compartments—but few parents shared this enthusiasm.

Swanson's frozen TV dinner. Although enduringly famous, the 1950s TV dinner is most important as an ancestor to the 1970s diffusion of the microwave oven.

Many seemingly surefire innovations failed to engage consumers. Why did frozen orange juice supplant the canned product, while tomato juice concentrate never displaced canned tomato juice? Companies were ingenious, even devious, in manipulating consumer attitudes. For example, well into the 1950s, most women stubbornly regarded cake mixes as unacceptable. Housewives might routinely toast Wonder Bread and toss salads with Wish-Bone dressing, but cake-making was off limits for shortcuts. Surveys of housewives showed that certain conveniences were associated with slovenly and uncaring housekeeping, and cake mixes were right up there with instant coffee.

Manufacturers responded by offering the female homemaker a sense of achievement in baking that would be compatible with the convenience of using a mix.[42] By taking out powdered eggs and milk and calling for adding fresh eggs and milk to the recipe, Pillsbury, Duncan Hines, and their competitors restored enough of the feeling of individual creativity in cake-baking to convert large numbers of home cooks. The advertising slogan "Nothin' says lovin' like somethin' from the oven, and Pillsbury says it best" communicated the idea that what counts is baking, not how the batter was mixed.[43] If the promise of convenience alone was not sufficient, invoking family satisfaction was.

The cake mix example shows not so much an ambivalent attitude toward convenience as the adjustments of the food industry to a persistent desire to cook. A national contest, which began in 1949, demonstrated that masses of women were enthusiastic, at least about breads and desserts. The official name of this competition, designed to advertise Gold Medal Flour, was "Pillsbury's Grand National $100,000 Recipe and Baking Contest," but from early on everyone called it the "Pillsbury Bake-Off." It was an annual event for which recipes were submitted to a committee that selected one hundred of them for the final round of the contest, held at New York's Waldorf-Astoria Hotel. There each contestant was furnished with a General Electric stove (which would be sent to their home after the event), and they all simultaneously made their cake, bread, or other dish using the company's flour. As the title indicated, a total of $100,000 in prize money was distributed. In 1949, the first prize of $25,000 (over $260,000 today), awarded by former First Lady Eleanor Roosevelt, went to Theodora Smafield of Detroit for her "No-Knead Water Rising Nut Twists."

Laura Rott of Naperville, Illinois, won second prize and $10,000 for her "Starlight Mint Surprise Cookies."[44]

The Pillsbury Bake-Off is an early example of the ability of corporations and the media to attract interest in food competition, an innovation later dramatically exploited by the Food Network, beginning with the first *Iron Chef* broadcasts in 2005. The image of the Bake-Off was that of wholesome creativity, a marriage of Pillsbury products and home-town savvy. Almost all the finalists were women, though Andrew A. Wilson of Saint Paul, a "bachelor educator," was recognized for his wild rice turnovers at the sixth competition in 1955, and Ray Sharp of Hopewell, Virginia, made his coconut cake for the event the next year. The "junior" category of entries saw a few male finalists—for example, Robert Koren in 1956 learned to cook when he was seven, and his head shot shows him wearing a chef's toque. His jelly ripple cake had a vanilla frosting with jelly

Pillsbury's Fifth Grand National recipe book, 1954. The annual "Bake-Off" booklets featured the 100 contest finalists and their recipes.

drizzled over it, complementing the red jelly layers in the cake. More often, the adult contestants were married women, identified by their husband's name—Mrs. Budd. D Jackson, Mrs. G. Howard Kirk. Their short blurbs sometimes referred to their families, but it is clear that they had a local reputation and that their friends had encouraged them to enter the Bake-Off. The tone of the teenagers' competition is different. These are prodigies, not having the years of experience and so relying on sheer talent and insight. Some young women set out to impress guys, as with Renny Powell, a Chicago teenager whose "Blueberry Boy-Bait" cake recipe won the $2,000 second prize in the 1954 junior competition.

FIRST- AND SECOND-PLACE RECIPES FOR THE PILLSBURY BAKE-OFF, 1949–1955

1949—No-Knead Water Rising Nut Twists
   Starlight Mint Surprise Cookies

1950—Orange Kiss-Me Cake
   Peanut Crust Pie

1951—Starlight Double Delight Cake (chocolate)
   Chocolate Marble Bars

1952—Snappy Turtle Cookies
   Two-Crust Slice o' Lemon Pie

1953—"My Inspiration" Cake (vanilla and chocolate layer cake)
   Cinnamon Nut Crisps

1954—"Open Sesame" Pie (sesame seeds in the crust with a date chiffon filling)
   Butter Cream Orange Cups

1955—"Ring-a-Lings" (orange-glazed sweet rolls)
　　　Regency Ribbon Cake (mocha and orange layer cake)

From *100 Prize-Winning Recipes from Pillsbury's Grand National $100,000 Recipe and Baking Contest* (Minneapolis: Pillsbury Mills, Inc., 1951) and successive years' booklets with slightly varying titles.

The Bake-Off did wonders for sales of Pillsbury's flour, but as cake mixes became respectable, the contest admitted a category of "Busy Day" recipes using convenience products like mixes and refrigerated cookie dough or biscuits. The entire event was renamed the "Pillsbury Busy-Lady-Off" in 1958, recognizing the allure of convenience.

The contest is still held, though now entirely online, with a maximum of eight ingredients and a thirty-minute time limit. No longer is it possible to make something from scratch. Recipes must include one Pillsbury convenience product such as cookie dough or refrigerated biscuits. Taste counts for only 25 percent, and the contestant's "story" is part of the competition in addition to the actual recipe. First prize comes with $50,000, a fraction in consistent dollars of what was offered in 1949.[45] Part of the reason why the Bake-Off is no longer a major occasion is that the Internet affords endless opportunities for baking blogs, recipes, and exchange of information, so amateur experts from all parts of the country share their techniques, ideas, and recipes. Anyone looking to make Boston cream pie or caraway-seed rolls has plenty of options beyond the resources offered by any single corporation.

✦　　　✦　　　✦

SOME FOOD INDUSTRY inventions did not succeed: frozen coffee was marketed after the Second World War but failed. So did Pyquick, a pie crust mix sold with dehydrated apples to make apple pie.[46] The Automat, a chain of restaurants with a self-service component, was a memorable novelty, but it never influenced experiments in cutting restaurant labor costs. Frozen orange juice concentrate replaced what seemed like the laborious task of squeezing fresh oranges, but powdered artificial orange drinks such as Tang, promoted as the drink of astronauts, never really took off.

Of course, the fact that the food industry could convince people to buy their mediocre but convenient products shows the triumph of taste homogenization. By the 1970s, most families shopped in supermarkets, bought large quantities of processed foods, ate at McDonald's and would soon acquire microwave ovens.

CHAPTER 6

Women and Food in the Twentieth Century

The cultural movements that brought about the simplified, industrial, and convenient foods of the modern era were led by women. It is logical that change would reflect the desires—made up or real—of those who prepared food for their families, and they were overwhelmingly female. But beyond this obvious social fact, women for much of the twentieth century were regarded as the proponents of modern food, not merely passive recipients of corporate dictates. The success of the nutritionist movement, which marks the beginning of modern cuisine around 1900, was due to female home economists.

Male critics of the decorative blandness of what passed for cuisine in the early twentieth century often blamed lack of flavor on women's dislike of "real food." Our old friend H. L. Mencken denounced "female professors of what is called domestic science" for recommending meals that were fine for diabetics, but "fatal to epicures."[1] It wasn't only these ardent reformers who were culpable, it was the average middle-class woman who seemed entranced by gadgets, time-saving products, and inferior-tasting artificiality. Blaming the decline of American cuisine on housewives' blithe enthusiasm for modernity is what led the WPA's "America Eats" planners in 1939 to concentrate on community events rather than individual households.

In fact, women were responding to the contradictory information communicated by magazines. On the one hand, they were warned, husbands wanted wives to be sufficiently free of kitchen tasks to be amusing, lighthearted, and attractive companions, yet they also wanted to be served hearty, traditional meals. A woman could err by giving too little attention to meals pleasing to a husband, but also by being overabsorbed in housework and meal preparation.[2] At least this was the impression given by advertisers who warned of both types of marital alienation and pushed products that appeared to be both delightful and convenient, the convenience not just to relieve the women's labor but to make her a fit companion.

As an expression of domesticity and affection, cooking food was more overt, pleasing, and varied than was simply keeping a house in good order. During the 1960s, Quaker Oats developed the succinct tag "Good hot Quaker Oats for breakfast—because you love them so much!" A more threatening version of this idea is an ad for Fleischmann's yeast from the same period in which a woman is shown offering baked goods to a man reading a newspaper with the legend "Maybe home-baked butterscotch buns never saved a marriage—but they never did one any harm. You bake them *yourself.* Right from scratch. You just add everything, especially lots of love."[3]

One of the best-selling recipe collections of the twentieth century was *The "Settlement" Cook Book*, which bore the subtitle "The Way to a Man's Heart." First published in 1903, it was still being updated as late as the mid-1970s.[4] Not just a form of emotional maintenance, food could be used as "bait" to attract men who were unattached. (Recall Renny Powell, who won second prize in the junior category of the 1953 Pillsbury Bake-Off for her "Blueberry Boy-Bait."[5]) Seduction by food was not limited to teenagers. A recipe for chocolate cake in *The Delineator* magazine in 1935 was labeled "Bachelor Bait."[6] The sexual implications of cooking became even more forceful in recipes and cookbooks after 1960, such as *How to Appeal to a Man's Appetites* (1962), or a *Mademoiselle* article from 1990 for "Refriger-Dating: Putting Guy Food in the Fridge." "Guy Food" meant salsa, nuts, and cold pizza.[7]

The negative corollary is that if a wife does not cook well, she is in danger of losing her husband, a fear marketed as early as 1872 in a cookbook entitled *How to Keep a Husband, or Culinary Tactics.*[8] Advertisers often showed men who were annoyed by their wives' apparent lapses or incompetence in the kitchen. A 1957 ad shows an irritated husband chastising his wife, "Mother *never* ran out of Kellogg's Corn Flakes." Schrafft's recommended its frozen meals in 1966 as a solution to the threat of "why husbands leave home."[9]

At the same time, if women spent too much time and effort in cooking, their husbands would become bored and regard them as competent but not alluring. As the ideal body shape of women became slimmer in the 1920s, the perfect wife was no longer expected to look like the received image of a mother or food provider. This change is sometimes referred to as a shift "from the nursery to the bedroom," but it could also be described as "from the kitchen to the bedroom."[10]

A Jell-O advertisement in 1956 implied that husbands don't care about pastries made from scratch if they require too much of their wives' time:

> *The Queen of Hearts, she made some tarts—*
> *It took her the whole afternoon.*
> *Said the king with a bellow, "I'd rather have Jell-O,*
> *It's* grand *and it's ready so soon."*[11]

The husband may be happy for his wife to have an easier time in preparing dessert, but what he really appreciates is time-saving convenience that takes her out of the kitchen. Over the course of the twentieth century, middle-class women increasingly took up leisure activities like sports, games, reading groups, and other forms of self-improvement. Women had been social reformers and civic activists in the past, but now their free time was more physically oriented. They cultivated health through exercise and diet not just for the care of the self but for the approval of men. Advertisers profited from concerns with slimming by shaming women and offering their product as a solution. The makers of Ry-Krisp crackers were particularly outrageous. A 1940 advertisement shows a man smooching with a slim, busty woman at a fairground kissing booth while a plump woman unhappily observes. An onlooker remarks "Someone should tell her about Ry-Krisp."[12]

A more positive message was that women could be good cooks and still stylish. A recipe booklet from 1950 given to purchasers of the Grand Gas Range shows how to please a husband without undue trouble. The oven door is open and a standing rib roast, accompanied by rolls and a pot of some side dish, are being appreciated by a man, his head bent down to sniff the wonderful aroma.[13] Although the woman has on an apron, she is wearing a low-cut dress and pearls, ready to go out for a night's entertainment once the home-cooked dinner is concluded.

Recipe booklet from Grand Appliance, "Cooking the Grand Manner," 1950. The right appliance promotes marital happiness.

A 1950S RECONSTRUCTION

A meal served by a friend of the author of Can She Bake a Cherry Pie? *to her grown children sometime toward the end of the twentieth century to recall their childhood:*

Cocktails: frozen daiquiris; whisky sours

Appetizers: clam dip
Olde English and Roquefort cheese logs (covered with ground-up nuts)

Salad: Iceberg wedges with (bottled) Russian dressing

Main course: casserole of chicken and noodles with a sauce of canned mushroom soup and Velveeta. Brown-and-serve rolls.

Side dishes: Frozen green beans with canned French-fried onion rings
Lemon Jell-O aspic with tomato juice, celery, olives, canned shrimp, and mayonnaise

Dessert: Betty Crocker Biscuit Tortoni (ice cream with macaroon crumbs, candied cherries, and chopped almonds).

Wine: Almaden rosé

From Mary Drake McFeely, *Can She Bake a Cherry Pie? American Women and the Kitchen in the Twentieth Century* (Amherst: University of Massachusetts Press, 2000), 93.

Female and Male Food Preferences

Women were supposed to manage picky, even irascible husbands or attract skittish prospective boyfriends by sacrificing their own food preferences, reserving those for occasions with other women. What might women choose when they could eat what they wanted? For much of Western history they were thought to have a particular preference for sweets. They were also subject to passionate and often odd food desires in pregnancy. The theme of a late-medieval French satire, *Les quinze joies de mariage* (*The Fifteen Joys of Marriage*), is the haplessness of men dominated by their wives. Special attention is given to a poor husband's expeditions through night and snow to fetch exotic fare (especially out-of-season fruit) for a finicky wife bored with normal food.[14]

In keeping with the idea of women as lovers of sweet delicacies, the nineteenth century saw the rise of ice cream as a particularly female attraction. Ice cream "saloons" were situated near dry goods or department stores to entice female shoppers. Between 1867 and 1877, there was an explosion of soda fountains that sold ice cream drinks. As a contemporary observer noted, "It goes without saying that the major part of the income to the soda water dispenser is the income that is either directly that of woman-kind, or that is influenced by her."[15]

Other than their notorious fondness for sweetness or the peculiar longings caused by pregnancy, women were not credited with tastes much different from those of men. Before the Civil War, large hotels often reserved a separate dining room for women eating alone or in groups in order to avoid their being made uncomfortable by proximity to men. At such "Ladies' Ordinaries," as they were termed, women were served the same sort of dishes as were furnished in the Gentlemen's Ordinary. At the Astor House Hotel in New York, a Gentlemen's Ordinary menu for September 9, 1841, offers seventeen entrées, rendered in French, including mutton cutlets, duck with olives, macaroni à l'Italienne, and fried marinated calf's head.[16] A menu for August 25, 1843, from the Ladies' Ordinary of the same hotel is the oldest in the immense New York Public Library collection. Here the twelve entrées are referred to as "side dishes" and are presented in English, but despite the formatting difference, they are similar to what men were offered: mutton cutlets, duck with olives, macaroni, and calf's head (here served with brain sauce). The rest of the menu is similarly hearty: sautéed kidneys with *fines herbes*, stewed mutton with turnips, and breaded veal cutlets with tomato sauce.[17]

Antebellum cookbooks show a similar lack of gender-based taste distinctions. One might expect that cookbooks, written by women for women, would include some indication of female favorites, but that is not the case, even though the books are addressed to women and offer often chatty, even hectoring, household advice. A woman was not yet expected to direct her culinary efforts toward pleasing her husband. Cookbook writers assumed that the housewife prepared what was appropriate for the entire family and that everyone's tastes naturally aligned. Popular American cookbooks, such as *The Lady's Receipt Book* by Miss Leslie (1847) or Mary Randolph's *The Virginia Housewife* (1824), say nothing about women dining together or their preferences.

Jennie Croly's *American Cookery Book* (1866) and Mary Henderson's *Practical Cooking and Dinner Giving* (1877) are early examples of a new trend to identify ladies' tastes. Croly (or "Jennie June," as she calls herself) tells the reader that the mere fact of women dining out together is not new. It was already fashionable for ladies' groups to engage a private room at a stylish restaurant.[18] Croly goes on to say that although it is convenient to hold fancy lunches at restaurants because this does not tax the domestic routine, ordinary "ladies' lunches" at home are delightful and can be organized on a rotating basis. Entertaining friends allows the hostess to share the simple but elegant food women enjoy, such as chicken salad, omelets, poached eggs with boiled ham, rice cakes with cold ham, and diced tomatoes with tender broiled lamb chops.[19]

Mary Foote Henderson, married to a wealthy Missouri senator and a leader in efforts to beautify Washington, DC, says in *Practical Cooking and Dinner Giving* that ladies are especially fond of lunch and that part of its charm is its informality. It is perfectly acceptable for friends to drop in unannounced, the tablecloth is colorful, and the servant remains in the room only to pass around the first course. Five sample menus served by specific women of Mrs. Henderson's circle differ from regular restaurant or male-directed menus, though not dramatically. There is an inclination toward chicken salad or mayonnaise of chicken, pastry scallops as vehicles for chicken, sweetbreads or oysters, and creamy and chocolaty desserts. The subsequent section about "Gentlemen's Suppers" begins by saying that for a light late-evening meal, men like the same sorts of things that women do, but they expect it to include game and wine.[20]

By the end of the nineteenth century, it was agreed that women were partial to sweets, cakes, ice cream, salads, and generally to "dainty food." This term *dainty* was the most common adjective used to describe women's taste preferences in the period from 1890 until the Second World War. The word could be associated with all manner of feminine things, from lingerie to affect, but with regard to food it meant delicate, colorful, and decorative. *Dainty* is the ancestor of the contemporary term *light*, describing meals that have little or no meat and emphasize salads or vegetables, but it conveyed a sense of delight more than abstemiousness. An article from 1915 with the title "Two Dainty February Festivals" notes that the modern hostess no longer tries to serve excessively complicated food. Lunches for female friends are now smart and sensible, saving time, labor, and expense while promoting health. Simplicity does not mean plainness by any means, but rather "daintiness and perfection of detail." A book of "dainty" recipes from 1907 includes angel food cake and vanilla cake with jelly and decorated with candied cherries. *Dainty Desserts* (1922) offers ginger sponge and tapioca fluff with fruit. The sandwich began its long career as the quintessential dainty dish for ladies' tea parties and other social occasions. *A Book of Dainty Recipes for Special Occasions* (1910) recommends cutting sandwiches into pretty squares and triangles, or even fancier shapes using a cookie cutter.[21]

One of the many significant aspects of Jell-O was that it helped democratize daintiness.[22] No longer was aspic reserved for the wealthy who could hire someone to make time-consuming dishes using it. Jell-O was ridiculously easy to prepare, came in bright colors, and made a neater presentation than traditional desserts or salads. It started to appear at tea parties and ladies' lunches shortly after its introduction at the beginning of the twentieth century and was a standard family dessert, especially for kids, and a medium for salad well into the 1970s.[23] Along with other decorative and colorful dishes that might feature canned pineapple or marshmallows, Jell-O as a salad or aspic medium was dismissed by advocates for male-centered cooking as typically female, "fussy" or "frou-frou." It was widely thought that women's food was characterized by artifice.[24] Between the two world wars, decorative processed foods involving Jell-O, mayonnaise, or bottled maraschino cherries symbolized female dining more than the vol-au-vent or sliced meat of the turn of the century.

Women supposedly liked food that was pretty and insubstantial rather than food in the hearty or satisfying sense men preferred. In 1934 Leone B. Moates,

Mt. Fuji King Crab gelatin salad, 1950. Put out by the Japanese crab export industry, the menu was meant to foster "creativity" and postwar rapprochement.

a (male) writer for *House and Garden*, scolded American housewives for serving men fruit salads or "a bit of fluff like marshmallow-date whip." They were told, "Keep your dainties for women's luncheons but remember that where such delicacies as squab leave a man cold, the very mention of corned beef hash with a poached egg on top will bring a gleam to his eye."[25] The situation was laid out dramatically in a letter to Betty Crocker from a woman who said that normally she didn't bake fudge cake because she preferred white cake, but her neighbor made it all the time. Was this neighbor going to "capture" her husband?[26]

Male food was substantial, flavorful, and spicy. It was simple in the sense that unlike women's cuisine, the actual ingredients were enhanced rather than disguised. An article for *Good Housekeeping* in 1941 was contemptuous of "sissy food" as opposed to what men can "sink their teeth into."[27] A list of man-pleasing dishes mentioned in cookbooks and magazine articles includes steak, spaghetti with meatballs, chili, fried potatoes, mutton chops, sharp or runny cheeses, curry, chocolate cake, Indian pudding, stewed tomatoes, and Roque-

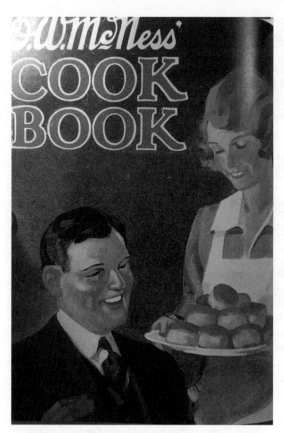

F. W. McNess Cook Book, 1935. Men are depicted as appreciative and easy to please. The Furst-McNess Company is now best known for products for the livestock industry.

fort dressing. These lusty items were presented as antithetical to women's inclination toward processed foods, which were increasingly associated not only with convenience but with a fundamental female aversion to "real" food.

Beginning in the 1920s, two complementary cookbook genres proliferated, one telling women what men like, another directly addressing men as cooks.[28] The former category included books such as *A Thousand Ways to Please a Husband* (1917), *Man-Sized Meals from the Kitchenette* (1928), *333 Ways to a Man's Heart* (1932), *Feeding Father* (1939), *Feeding Peter* (1924), and, a particularly engaging title, *Feed the Brute!* (1925). All acknowledged the sacrifice women make in putting their husband's tastes for strongly flavored but simple food first. According to Eleanor Howe, a noted food and cookbook writer, any woman looking at the word *menu* should know that primacy must go to "men" rather than "u." Women should set aside their preferences, giving priority to what their husbands like. Men's tastes are, after all, easy to identify and satisfy: "The men—bless 'em—ask for nothing better, from time to time, than some simple dessert of pudding to complete the perfect meal."[29]

Women's deference to male tastes was not sufficient, however. Between 1920 and 1970, there was a vogue for publishing men's cookbooks. The compilers acknowledged that men are only occasional cooks, but this allowed them to indulge their innate taste for improvisation. Tied to routine meal preparation day after day, women are conformist and unadventurous. Male inventiveness is presented not as a sociological opinion but as a manifestation of natural culinary superiority. Christine Frederick, introducing her husband's misogynist *Cooking as Men Like It* (1930), said that women don't really enjoy food. They dutifully prepare it all the time, but it does not lift their spirits or excite them. It has no romance—on the contrary women find cooking boring. It is logical that all the great chefs have been male, because, unlike women, men enjoy food and cook with flair and exuberance. An anonymous article in the magazine *American Home* entitled "Men, Meet the Kitchen" (1933) is a distillation of themes found in men's cookbooks. Men approach cooking as a pleasurable hobby. Far from being a "sissy" pursuit, cooking with the panache that men bring to the task is as masculine as expertise in sports or chess. The key difference is not that men have more actual skill, but that they are not rule-bound. Women dutifully follow recipes while men are creative. "What woman would have thought of adding a cupful of chili to that old standard salmon soufflé recipe?" Women just aren't imaginative in the kitchen and, after all, why should they be when getting together

Canned Swedish meatballs ad, 1959. Long before IKEA went global, Sweden was known for hors d'oeuvre–size meatballs. The advertisement is an entry in both the "how to please men" and the processed gourmet foods categories.

Men are slaves to

Spiced Swedish Meat Balls

WHEN IT comes to making hors d'oeuvres, only a true-blue know-nothing would boggle at awarding the Swedes First Prize.

We have imported many of their appetizing little masterpieces for your enjoyment.

Today, we deal happily with Spiced Swedish Meat Balls. Moist, tender morsels so consummately seasoned as to make each bite a promise and a fulfillment.

We know, alas, men who have become enslaved by these tidbits: men who forget their upbringing and bawl vulgarly for whole trayfuls of these appetizers. Enjoy them with restraint, we beg you.

P.S. *This is one of 60 rare foods, picked from the four corners of the world. If your department stores or fine food shops don't carry it yet, write us today for store nearest you.*

GENERAL FOODS

GOURMET FOODS
White Plains, New York

30

three meals every day, thinking about vitamins and other health factors, and staying within a budget leave no room for imagination?[30]

LEN DEIGHTON'S ACTION COOK BOOK

A curious offshoot of the men's cookbook genre is *Len Deighton's Action Cook Book,* published in 1965. Deighton is the author of celebrated novels of espionage and intrigue, notably *The IPCRESS File* and *Funeral in Berlin*. His *Action Cook Book* is not addressed just to men. For the Penguin paperback edition, the front cover shows a man with a gun in a holster ladling pasta while being caressed by a woman—and the back cover has the poses reversed. *Action Cook Book* has the no-nonsense tone of male cookbooks and is by an author whose masculine credentials are reinforced by the ambiguity of the word *action* in the title. He provides detailed directions for shopping, judging food and wine, and evaluating kitchen equipment. The recipes are given by means of comic strip drawings, or "action cook strips," as Deighton terms them. Most recipes serve two except when a dish, such as osso bucco or roast beef, can't be cut down in size.[31]

There is a contradiction in this literature with regard to such nebulous values as "creativity" or "simplicity." Women are associated with a pointless or at best decorative sort of complexity, whereas men like forthright food. Creativity is what women think casseroles, processed ingredients, and peculiar combinations are all about. Yet, according to the men's cookbooks, women are timid cooks who lack verve, while men impose their own ideas on recipes, taming them to their audacious will. The common aspect seems to be that men like strong flavors and women don't, an idea that has persisted long after the male versus

A decoration by Elizabeth Colbourne from *A Thousand Ways to Please a Husband* by Louise Bennet Weaver and Helen Cowles LeCron, published in 1917. The second chapter, entitled "Bettina's First Real Dinner," highlights the pleasures of economical homemaking in the early twentieth century: "'Say, isn't it great to be alive!' exclaimed Bob, as he looked across the rose-decked table at the flushed but happy Bettina. 'And a beefsteak dinner, too!'"

female cookbook category has become obsolete. Women are still identified with vegetarianism and dieting today, while men are described as loving barbecue, craft beer, and hot sauce. Amanda Cohen, chef and owner of the vegetable-forward restaurant Dirt Candy in New York, says in her graphic comic–style cookbook that chefs generally believe that "vegetables are for girls."[32] The notion that women really don't like food, or prefer desserts, is still strong. Women supposedly advocate a renunciatory ethos of giving up things, such as meat or fat, while men are sensual carnivores. In a half-serious article written for the *New York Times* in 2007, Allen Salkin took note of the phenomenon of women on first-date dinners ordering steak to show that they don't have hang-ups about food.[33] The need to appear to be one of the guys is not only about self-presentation, but also a signal that the young woman won't try to get the guy to change his eating habits. This may not be quite the same as the 1950s housewife giving up her preferences and preparing hearty male food, but it is an admission of differing tastes, and it is still the woman who is making the accommodation.

Food of the Future

The apotheosis of modern food—the priority for speed, ease, and efficiency along with a lack of interest in the niceties of taste—occurs in an imagined future when cooking will be transformed, unnecessary, or prohibited. An article entitled "Frozen Foods 2000 A.D.: A Fantasy of the Future" appeared in the August 1962 issue of the trade journal *Quick Frozen Foods*. A frozen food distributor has a vision of the opening of the twenty-first century with air-conditioned cities and flying cars. On the spur of the moment, he is invited to dinner by a friend. The arrival of an unexpected guest provokes no anxiety for Marty's wife, Janet. In a matter of minutes, at the touch of a few buttons, she serves a meal made from frozen ingredients. Joe, the astonished executive from 1962, exclaims, "This is some kitchen!" Janet laughs and says, "That's a word I haven't heard in a long time. There's no such thing as a 'kitchen' nowadays. . . . Just freezer space, automatic cooking, automatic dishwashing. Life's really simple nowadays—science has emancipated women right out of the kitchen."[34]

What's amusing about this prediction is not the food technology, which is not inaccurate (as opposed to the helicopter-cars). After all, today meals are routinely microwaved, and 75 percent of American households have a dishwasher. It is rather the tacit assumption that gender roles as imagined in the early 1960s will not have changed. A classic advertising-generated fear for housewives was the husband inviting someone important to dinner, or showing up unexpectedly with a colleague. Janet's "emancipation" has freed her from cooking, but not from a male-dominated society. In reality, social settings have altered dramatically. The way families eat differs greatly from 1962, but this is not primarily due to new cooking technology.

Swans Down flour ad, *Good Housekeeping*, March 1926. This was supposedly a common anxiety—a wife's cakes are usually perfect, but when company comes, "something always happens."

Forecasting the food of the future begins with one of the grimmest and most famous futurologists, the eighteenth-century cleric Thomas Malthus. His observation that population grew exponentially while agricultural production could only increase arithmetically led him to posit a future demographic disaster in which the number of people would outstrip the supply of food. Malthusianism has a long history and even still may prove itself, but thanks to technology, the growth of agricultural yields has surprised pessimistic experts. Anxiety about population increase has been constant, although taking various forms. Its linkage to popularized Darwinist theories of the struggle for survival led to racialized fears that poor or inferior people would breed more children and so their degraded "stock" would take over the world. The fear of a teeming and impoverished China created the "Yellow Peril" scare of the late nineteenth and early twentieth centuries; concern over teenage pregnancy and family disintegration in late-twentieth-century America was tied to an "underclass" conceived as African American. Mainstream American polemics over immigration are tinged by manufactured threats from inferior countries or peoples.

Not that population growth is benign. The degradation of the natural environment has advanced alarmingly and now clearly threatens our survival, not because of sheer numbers, but because of the consequences of the technology needed to produce all this food, as well as its wasteful and unequal allocation. In 1980, the demographer Paul Ehrlich made a well-publicized bet with an economist, Julian Simon, about the price of five metals in ten years.[35] Ehrlich, the author of a sensational best-seller *The Population Bomb* (1968), believed that at over 3.5 billion, the world's population was severely taxing the earth's ability to feed it. Events of the 1970s, in particular the two great oil supply crises, seemed to indicate a future of chronic and unmanageable shortages. The Club of Rome, an international group of business and policy leaders concerned with contemporary and future challenges to humanity, issued a report in 1972 entitled *The Limits to Growth* that warned that technological and economic growth could not continue to mitigate the effects of population growth. The response of economists like Simon was that markets and innovative adaptation would address the challenge of scarcity no matter what the population increase turned out to be.

The bet used the price of tungsten, copper, chromium, nickel, and tin as indicators of inflationary pressure on vital commodities. As it turned out, by 1990, the ten-year horizon for the wager, the price of these metals had fallen an average of 50 percent. For the nearly forty years since the bet, as the world's population has reached 7.6 billion, Simon turns out to have been right. Famine and acute malnutrition are due more to war and repressive governments than to any global imbalance between people and resources. This has been demonstrated by less quantitative and extrapolative studies of population by scholars like the Nobel laureate Amartya Sen.[36]

What is interesting here is a parallel or oblique version of the same optimistic/pessimistic divide, that between utopian and dystopian expectations about what people will eat at some future date. One observer's utopia of entirely chemical food—nutritious, no fuss, resource conserving—is another's nightmare of humanity degraded, forgetful of pleasure and deprived of the enjoyment of real food. Since the vogue for meat bouillon in eighteenth-century France, futurologists have believed that some essence of healthful food would be sufficient for nourishment by itself, without the bother of elaborate meal preparation. The reduction of meat, vegetables, and other ingredients is the first stage of radical food simplification whose eventual successor was the meal-in-a-pill ideal. In Edward Bellamy's classic *Looking Backward*, the time traveler from the year 1887 visiting the world of 2000 is revived with a miraculously restorative broth. Jules Verne predicted that by 2889, life expectancy would have been extended to age sixty-eight, and nutritious air would allow people to obtain all they needed by way of nutrition simply through breathing. Another scenario presented as favorable was for adjustable feeding tubes that would have a delicious version of liquefied food whose spices or saltiness could be individually controlled.[37]

This future was not to everyone's taste. The postapocalyptic school of science fiction imagined a society dependent on efficient but awful food. In the movie *Soylent Green* (1973), a grossly overpopulated world depends on a mysterious substance that turns out to be made from dead people. Not quite as shocking in its origin, but bad-tasting enough, are the artificial foods on which the people in George Orwell's *1984* survive—a stew that looks like vomit, cheese cubes, artificial coffee, saccharine tablets, and synthetic "Victory gin," which tastes like Chinese rice-wine. In Aldous Huxley's *Brave New World*, people happily eat healthful and abundant vitamin-enriched beef surrogate and carotene sandwiches.

In these fictions, real food as we know it has become the preserve of either the privileged or subversives. Jam made from actual strawberries costs a prohibitive $150 for a small glassful in *Soylent Green*. In *1984*, Julia defies the prohibition on sensual pleasure not only by engaging in sex, but by consuming "proper white bread," sugar, coffee, and jam. On the Indian reservations in *Brave New World*, deprived of the artificial bliss of the "civilized" world, one can hunt rabbits and enjoy them along with tortillas and corn.

The notion that good food is subversive in authoritarian and deprived societies is more a reflection of reality than a particularly imaginative leap. The fact that in the 1970s and 1980s, the ruling cadre of Nicolae Ceausescu's Romania enjoyed oranges and real coffee, unavailable to ordinary citizens, was a cause for pity among foreigners, who could consume these things anytime, and rage among Romanians after secreted stores of luxury food were discovered following the fall of the dictator in late 1989.

Resistance would be the core of the rediscovery of taste beginning in the 1970s. A key aspect of Alice Waters's deceptively revolutionary ideas for Chez Panisse was that far from being merely a bourgeois form of ostentation, seasonal, local, and delicious food was a form of defiance and human affirmation. Her maxim, taken from Gandhi, was "I want to live the change I want to see," expressing in food, thought, and action "the values that are important to my life."[38] Certainly her ambitions were formed in surroundings of apparent plenty rather than in a country such as India, where getting enough to eat has been an urgent problem, but the American experience managed somehow to fuse abundance with declining food quality. The power of scientific progress tended to distract attention from deterioration of taste, and Waters saw part of her task as the recovery of flavor and, equally significantly, memory. Ignorance or deprecation of the past is a key element in making people forget what food should be, and resistance consists of salvaging memory as well as taking action.

Science as the engine of change in the unveiling of food's future was the dominant story in fiction as well as speculative science. Another aspect of speculation, which has ended up being more significant than technology, is about how social changes would completely alter the setting and ritual of dining. This might be a communist utopia in which public dining rooms would replace the inefficient and female-enslaving private kitchen. Rather than each family preparing its own food, thereby effectively tying women to domestic servitude, the state, locality, or factories would take over the business of cooking, serving, and cleaning up. As part of its vision of transforming society, the architects of the Russian Revolution planned for dining commons not only for lunch at work, but for all meals in residential apartment blocks. The preparation of a family's meal would be replaced by canteen-like restaurants, allowing workers more time to do their job and centralizing edible resources. Communal dining would release women from drudgery and subordination, bringing closer the socialist goal of weakening family insularity and private property in favor of state-guided egalitarianism.

Joseph Stalin reversed the idealist, futurist elements of early Soviet social thought and restored petit-bourgeois family life, albeit without property.[39] He even authorized a cookbook addressed to housewives in keeping with the official statement of 1934 that "life has become better, merrier too." This work, recently translated into English as *Book of Tasty and Healthy Food*, appeared first in 1939 and sold eight million copies over subsequent decades.[40]

Communal plans went nowhere in the United States, but other social forces have resulted in the near-extinction of family meals in favor of a regime of snacking, of different meals for different family members at different times, and of a decline in food preparation at home. It is not so much that, as in the socialist vision, meals have become aspects of mass efficiency or utopian small communal solidarity, but rather that they have fragmented. How we consume meals has been influenced by the increasing percentage of women in the workforce, the creation of autonomous youth cultures, fast food chains, and other forms of dining out, and redefinitions of family, gender, and lifestyles.

Resistance to Homogenization

Contrary to common beliefs, there was resistance to culinary modernism even before the 1970s, when environmental activists, alternative lifestyle pioneers, and the organic food movement signaled a new era. Particularly of interest in connection with gender are the different roles ascribed to men and women as dissenters from the general opinion and practice of food and cooking.

In enclaves such as food and wine clubs or among readers of the magazine *Gourmet*, which began in January 1941, the doughty but pathetic veterans of the grand old cuisine of pre-Prohibition, pre-nutritionist America clustered together like the beleaguered remnants of the Resistance in *The Last Jedi*. This culinary resistance was composed not of social reformers critiquing corporate food hegemony, nor of subversives in the manner of the rebels in *1984* and *Brave*

New World, but rather of reactionary, privileged critics who lamented an overall decline of graciousness.

These men blamed women for the debasement of American food. Women had been seduced by science and health on the one hand and fondness for frivolous, artificial food on the other. The guttering flame burning before the altar of gourmandise was protected by societies organized by men, often spinoffs from private clubs in cities like Boston, New York, and San Francisco. The Food and Wine Society, based in London, had six chapters in the United States. Les Amis d'Escoffier was a society for hotel and restaurant chefs and managers, and the Confrèrie des Chevaliers du Tastevin established branches outside of its native Burgundy. These groups had elaborate initiation rituals, and they organized splendid banquets. They were to some extent subsidized or at least encouraged by wine importers as well as amateurs attempting to resuscitate delight in food after the destruction wreaked by Prohibition.

Whatever publicity in favor of fine food these groups were trying to offer was vitiated by their social exclusivity. The whole point of appreciating oases of French cuisine in a desert of cheeseburgers and Reddi-Wip was to separate oneself from the ignorant rather than attempt to convert them. Beginning with the foundation of *Gourmet* magazine in the seemingly inauspicious year 1941, a more concerted effort was made to find and support the isolated but enthusiastic partisans of a brighter culinary world. *Gourmet* regarded its mission as the defense of real food, of pleasure rather than health:

> We are trying to . . . renew interest in cooking and eating as an art, not a penance. We in this country have been enslaved for so long to the ritual of vitamins, calories, cook it quick, get it to the table, get it down, take a pill, that we have lost sight of the obvious fact that it is perfectly simple—cook willing—to plan and prepare a meal that is nutritious and delicious.[41]

For *Gourmet* in its early years, the culprit was still female. America's housewives had succumbed to the complementary attractions of decorative triviality and dreary nutritionism. Since women were mesmerized by the image of healthfulness over pleasure, *Gourmet* in its initial phase addressed itself to men. An advertisement for the magazine in its October 1941 issue states: "*Gourmet* is a man's magazine on food that men enjoy. No vitamins, just good food and, yes, good drinks." The first "*Gourmet* chef" was Louis De Gouy, a Frenchman whose father had cooked for the Austro-Hungarian Emperor Franz Joseph and the Belgian royal family. A disciple of Escoffier, De Gouy had made his career in the United States at grand hotels and in the service of millionaires like J. P. Morgan. The cover of the first issue shows a Christmas boar's head on a decorated platter. De Gouy and others rhapsodized about hunting rabbits and pheasants. As the above-quoted advertisement said: "Shooting's only half the fun," the other half being the pleasure of "cooking and eating what you've bagged."[42]

The assumption that men made up the readership base was mistaken, and fortunately so because the magazine could not have survived as a quirky publication for the rather small number of men with a sustained interest in cooking projects. From the start, the outdoorsy tone notwithstanding, women were

Gourmet, January 1951. Boar's head was a traditional English winter (particularly Christmas) dish. The magazine offered elegant and historical recipes not always geared to suburban convenience.

Gourmet, May 1954. The magazine maintained its male and outdoorsy image, although most of its subscribers were women.

enthusiastic readers of *Gourmet*. De Gouy died in 1947 and was succeeded by the veteran chef Louis Diat, also a Frenchman, who had devoted himself to American institutions like the Ritz-Carlton Hotel in New York, where he is credited with inventing vichyssoise. He was better than his predecessor at guiding amateur cooks. In collaboration with Helen Ridley, a home economics teacher, public relations expert for the food industry, and *Good Housekeeping* contributor, Diat addressed female readers, invoking cooking lessons he had acquired from his mother rather than relying on his authority as a restaurant chef. He balanced his haute-cuisine reputation with friendly and unpretentious reassurance.[43]

David Strauss, author of a thorough and engaging treatment of the early history of *Gourmet*, doubts that many readers actually cooked from the magazine's recipes. Even if Diat was more friendly and informative than De Gouy, many readers "admitted their preference for reading over cooking the recipes."[44] Ingredients like shallots or fresh herbs were impossible to come by for most Americans, few knew how to use the elaborate range of kitchen tools and equipment called for, and the instructions were sketched out by professional chefs who did not point out what seemed to them obvious practices: not overcrowding the pan, distinguishing between when to stir frequently and when not to disturb cooking ingredients, letting meat rest after cooking. The reader might be told to start with a white sauce without knowing how to make it.[45] By comparison, one of the virtues of Julia Child would be that she took nothing for granted. If you followed her admittedly long but not unusually difficult recipes, the soufflé or the *boeuf en daube* would turn out as planned. Such considerate thoroughness had to await her time in the 1960s and 1970s, however.

I would say that in the 1950s and early 1960s, *Gourmet* accomplished more than simply creating a cozy fantasy world for avid readers who still routinely cooked the usual casseroles and canned soups. From the magazine's beginning, a column entitled "Sugar and Spice" allowed readers to send in questions and provide their own tips and recipes. In 1944, the editors added "You Asked for It," which was mostly requests for recipes from restaurants where the diner had enjoyed some special dish. This column too sometimes answered questions from readers who had received unexpected windfalls—a gift of five pounds of sturgeon or a five-foot rattlesnake in the freezer. The two overlapped, so that a general question about what to do with eggplants appeared in "Sugar and Spice" in 1960, while a specific request for an eggplant salad recipe "that I believe is Near Eastern" appears in "You Asked for It" in 1954.[46] In the latter case, in addition to furnishing a recipe, the editors note that the dish is called "Baba Gannoj."

This last example shows a lack of sophistication when it came to many international dishes that are now familiar to Americans. A reader had eaten tapenade in the South of France and could not find a recipe for it. In 1981, there was a request for "a pickled vegetable dish called *kim chee*," popular in Korea.[47] Such naiveté is offset by surprising examples of international knowledge. Many readers had experience abroad either through the military, postwar foreign aid and reconstruction or corporate assignments. Some comments may simply reflect privileged tourism—a request for a chicken dish with truffles served at Al Pappagallo in Bologna, for example.[48] Others demonstrate familiarity with nonobvious items—tripe with pig's feet (a variation on menudo) or recipes for corbina, including one from the Inter-American Women's Club of Panama.[49] Readers asked for esoteric recipes and information: how to cook and serve terrapin, or what exactly is the Majorcan pastry *ensaïmada*?[50] In general, the postwar readers of *Gourmet* had a less extensive repertoire of ingredients and dishes than we possess today. Even when they had heard of what were considered exotica, these were hard to obtain. There are constant inquiries about how to find kumquats or tarragon. On the other hand, familiarity with cooking overall was greater than is the case now, where so much of our time is spent consuming food we do not make. Early *Gourmet* readers were unfazed by messy and ambitious recipes.

A perusal of *Gourmet* issues before 1970 shows cheerful, skilled, and curious correspondents. The publication, though, did pay attention to the preferences of its advertisers, exhibiting a weakness for packaged "gourmet" foods like frozen South African lobster tails or canned turtle soup. The column "Food Flashes" touted mass-market innovations like Sara Lee frozen cakes or Pepperidge Farm European cookies ("the quality is European, but the packaging is American").[51] There is a particular fondness for first-class food on airlines. Although more caviar and foie gras were dished out then than now, airline food was at best pretentious rather than actually pleasant.

Readers showed affection for the magazine. Often recipes were tendered as thank-you notes, while frequent comments appear on the order of "my patients keep stealing issues from the waiting room," or "why didn't anyone tell me about this magazine before?" Some sense of the audience can be derived from two surveys reported by *Gourmet*, not a publication otherwise particularly diligent in soliciting data from its subscribers. In 1954 the editors gave a list of the eight most frequently requested recipes from the "You Asked for It" feature. In order they were:

Lindy's cheesecake (based on the recipe of a famous Broadway show-business hangout)

Caesar salad

Pommes soufflés (puffed potatoes, a specialty of Antoine's in New Orleans and tricky to make)

Cannelloni ripieni (*ripieni* meaning stuffed—what are now known simply as cannelloni)

Sourdough French bread (like the pommes soufflés, requiring a high degree of skill)

Shrimp tempura (deep-fried shrimp, attesting to the popularity of Japanese cooking adopted for Westerners—traditionally, Japanese cooking did not use oil)

Chinese egg rolls

Key West lime pie[52]

For the magazine's fiftieth anniversary, the seven most frequent questions from 1941 to 1991 were listed:

Why is it necessary to proof yeast, and how is proofing accomplished?

What is a caper?

What is the difference between boil and simmer?

What is zest?

What is coriander and how is it different from cilantro and Chinese parsley?

Sometimes when I melt chocolate it becomes tight and grainy. What
    causes this and how can it be avoided?
Why is it necessary to soften unflavored gelatin?[53]

Gourmet intended to serve as a beacon in the darkness, to restore gastronomic pleasure in a world given over to hurried, modern, and mediocre food, in
thrall to nutritionism and efficiency. Postwar prosperity did nothing to dampen
the prevailing belief in progress, faith in scientific expertise, and the food industry's ability to dictate what people bought, where they bought it, how they
cooked at home, and in what places they dined out. Yet predictions that meals
would be replaced by pills or that pleasure in food was an obsolete, lower-order
instinct were wrong.

What is often recalled today as a dismal period in American culinary history appeared to many observers to be experiencing a revival of gourmandise
and joie de vivre. In his regular "Along the Boulevards" column in *Gourmet*
for January 1958, the snobbish bon vivant Lucius Beebe, who owned his own
luxurious railroad car, remarked that "never has so much good food . . . been
consumed by so many grateful gourmets." After the damage inflicted by Prohibition, depression, war, and technology, "good living" had returned.[54] Ten years
later, Nora Ephron, a keen observer of, among many things, food in relation to
social status, considered herself to be experiencing an expansive gourmet craze.
Everyone was serving exotica like curry and rumaki (marinated chicken livers
and water chestnuts wrapped in bacon and sprinkled with soy sauce). All her
friends had learned to mince garlic rather than squashing it in a press.[55]

At the 1964–1965 New York World's Fair, the Populuxe aesthetic that had
been so successful at the 1939–1940 Fair seemed tired, according to Thomas
Hine, who first identified this spiffy ultramodern style. To be sure, General
Motors, General Electric, and other major corporations had displays of under-
water cities, farms with machine workers, and jungles being cleared by lasers,
but the world of tomorrow seemed rather soulless. Corporate visions of the
future were unexciting compared to the Fair's great culinary innovation, the
Belgian waffle, first served at Belgium's medieval village. Among the outstanding restaurants at the exposition was Festival '64 American Restaurant in the

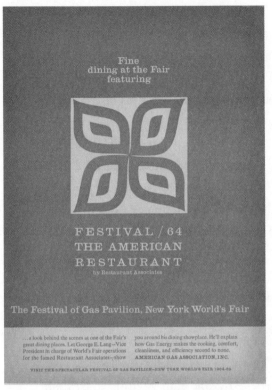

Ad for Festival/64 Restaurant located in the "Festival of Gas" Pavilion at the New York World's Fair of 1964–1965. Festival/64 placed an unusual and precocious emphasis on American food and seasonal dining.

American Gas Association pavilion. Joe Baum, the charismatic idea man for Restaurant Associates, which ran Festival '64, characterized its menu as paying tribute "to the native gourmet cooking of the United States with such dishes as St. Augustine shrimp ramekin, Plantation wedding cake, Shaker herb soup, Green corn pie with shrimp, West Coast lime-broiled chicken, Crackling bread, and California broiled fig on ham."[56] Baum's love of pyrotechnics was on display with mignons of beef in bourbon, set on fire at tableside. Watermelon ice and angel food cake with peanut-brittle sauce were two of the desserts. The *Gourmet* review marvels that fresh vegetables on the menu vary with the time of the year, a testimony to the rarity of this policy even at the luxury end of the restaurant spectrum.[57]

A final example of what appeared to be the accelerating epicureanism of the pre–Chez Panisse era is a 1972 piece for *New York* magazine by the food writer and later *New York Times* restaurant reviewer Mimi Sheraton entitled "I Tasted Everything in Bloomingdale's Food Shop."[58] She didn't describe all 1,961 items that she sampled during a year-long research project, but she did write about her favorites from the cheese and bread departments, and also noted some awful convenience "gourmet" foods such as canned pheasant and cheese soufflé mix.

As Sheraton's report indicates, the apparent postwar passion for fine dining was related to the number of things available. Options and varieties characterize modern American food, whether at Bloomingdale's gourmet food store or in the thousands of items carried by a typical supermarket. The industrial food system created an efficient but boring standardization—the same brand of ketchup, the same McDonald's cheeseburger—but this was accompanied by an explosion in choice. The product might be factory made, but it came in many flavors.

CHAPTER 7

Have Your Cake, Choose from Our Fifteen Fabulous Flavors, and Eat It Too

Linda—Willy, dear, I got a new kind of American-type
cheese today. It's whipped.
Willy— . . . how can they whip cheese?

DEATH OF A SALESMAN, ACT 1

Explosive growth in the variety of consumer products available to the American consumer accompanied the rise of processed food. For most of the twentieth century, members of all economic and ethnic groups ate Oreo cookies and Kraft American cheese, yet hundreds of different brands jostled for position on supermarket shelves, and food companies tried out thousands of new ideas every year.

Another form of bewildering food choice was created by so-called ethnic restaurants. In contrast to most of the rest of the world, so-called ethnic restaurants were successful as far back as the 1880s. They challenged whatever American cuisine was.

The Appeal of Variety

It would seem logical that the industrial food system would reduce the variety of what is offered, but in fact, as anyone who steps inside a supermarket can see, the reverse is true. Its fifty thousand different items are perhaps compensation offered by food companies for the taste deficiencies of their industrial products.

Standardization means that major brands are universally available. Gold Medal flour or Hamburger Helper are the same in every location, but the difference between an old, basic product like flour and a packaged item like Hamburger Helper is that the latter comes in many flavors. General Mills, which owns the brand, developed options such as Bacon Cheeseburger Hamburger Helper and Cheese Lover's Lasagna Hamburger Helper, then expanded beyond beef into seafood featuring several kinds of Tuna Helper.

The basic transaction is that the processed item sells itself on the basis of convenience, health (as with breakfast cereals or yogurt), price, brand recognition—everything but taste. The processed or artificial taste is ameliorated, or at least covered, by an array of flavors. Taste can be enhanced chemically, and people forget the natural version, thus Hellmann's mayonnaise has a fluffy texture and a spreadability that people came to prefer over homemade mayonnaise that is comparatively runny and has a different flavor. Not everyone likes "natural" peanut butter, which might not be sweet enough and has the oil separated from the solids. Americans have become accustomed to blandness in such products as processed cheese or sliced white bread. To overcome insipid tastes, we turn to table condiments—A.1. steak sauce, Tabasco, ketchup, shrimp cocktail sauce, and more recently Sriracha. Presenting industrial food in an appealing way means inventing new flavors (Dannon blueberry-açai yogurt), creative mixtures (Combos cheddar cheese and pretzel snacks), and varieties (Tropicana orange juice with added calcium or "Grovestand" style).

Within standard product categories, the multiplicity of choices is dizzying: olives in a jar or can, black or green, unpitted or stuffed with pimentos or garlic or anchovies, chopped or sliced. The options tend to multiply over time; thus, in the 1950s, tomato sauce and tomato paste came in cans and Del Monte and Hunt's were the largest brands. Later you could buy ready-made tomato sauce in a jar. Ragú, the leader, now comes in Homestyle, Old World Style, and Chunky. The Homestyle line subdivides into tomato-basil, red-pepper and garlic, "traditional tomato," and roasted garlic. Old World includes organic traditional, mushroom, marinara, and meat sauces. Chunky sauces feature mushroom, mushroom and green pepper, "7-herb," and garlic and onion. Ragú also makes cheese sauces and pizza sauces.

The stated reason for having so many kinds of sauces, or yogurt flavors, or orange juice types is to offer options. There is no doubt that Americans love options, but then, one might ask, doesn't everyone? Up to a point, certainly. The originally German Knorr company (now owned by Unilever) makes ten kinds of instant soups in addition to bouillon, gravy mixes, a "Latino flavor" line, and instant meals. A L'Olivier, a French company, sells olive oil infused with herbs (thyme, marjoram, rosemary, basil, lavender) as well as with lemon and espelette peppers. Americans, however, make choice a goal in itself, believing that there are no rules and that anything might appeal to individual mood and the urge to experiment. You should be able to eat what and how you wish, a version of "have your cake and eat it too"—an approach to dining not shared by every nation.

In French and American focus groups, the American preference for choice as opposed to quality was prominent. In response to questions such as "Do you prefer having fifty ice cream flavors or ten to choose from" or "Do you want a restaurant menu to have lots of choices, or a limited number of suggestions from the chef?" Americans were in favor of as many options as possible, while the French preferred a select assortment.[1]

The American view in the aforementioned Moscow "Kitchen Debate" of 1959 between Nixon and Khrushchev saw the advantage for the United States as providing not just a superior standard of living, but freedom of choice. Nixon boasted to the Soviet leader that Americans could decide what sort of washing machine to buy and what sort of house to live in. The exhibition planners focused on freedom, progress, and prosperity. Their internal memorandum stated: "Freedom of choice and expression, and the unimpeded flow of diverse goods and ideas [are] the sources of American cultural and economic achievement."[2] In the 1950s, the president of the US Chamber of Commerce described the deficiencies of the USSR food supply in terms of lack of choice. Soviet premier Khrushchev could produce "more goulash," but it was impossible for communism to furnish "better goulash—not frozen, or dehydrated, or irradiated goulash—not '57 varieties' or '20 delicious flavors.' Just more goulash." Ignoring the fact that goulash is Hungarian and not Russian, this remark shows the bounty and promise of America through providing consumer options, even if some of them do not sound very appealing.[3]

For an American readership, this abundance may not seem worth remark because it is so familiar. The rest of the world, however, does not adhere to the same unexamined priority for choice. It is not that people in France or elsewhere want diminished possibilities, but rather that taste and tradition are more important than changing the subject of mediocre quality by offering variety.

An obvious example of European variety when it comes to food is the hundreds of different pasta shapes and names in Italy. Many are local products, however, and not available to consumers elsewhere. A pasta shaped into an indented disk, called *ladittas*, is found in Sardinia; *pacozze* are rhombuses the size of a palm, a specialty of Castelbottaccio in Molise.[4] The northern Italian city of Bologna is famous throughout Italy for its tortellini, lasagna, and tagliatelle. There, tortellini options are nonexistent—the only way to make tortellini is with meat, a small amount of Parmesan, and spices. Tortellini from Bologna have more mortadella in comparison to those of Reggio Emilia, forty miles away, where fresh rather than cured pork predominates. Modena (where, according to chef Massimo Bottura, tortellini are "a religion") fabricates tortellini with prosciutto. In other regions—in Piedmont, for example—it is common to stuff pasta with chopped vegetables.[5] There are, therefore, different ways to make tortellini, but the variations are within an established and geographically demarcated framework. Unlike America, Italian tortellini centers do not make three-cheese, portabella, spinach and feta, or herb chicken tortellini.

Such examples of rulemaking are found everywhere. In the Banat region of southwestern Romania, there is an approved way of making the vanilla cream cake known as *Kremspitte*. Not only is using vanilla pudding mix not allowed, but mixing the filling requires mastery of technique. *Kremspitte* requires only a few ingredients (basically milk, eggs, flour, and vanilla), but it does not always come out the same and, as with most traditional dishes, there are some people whose special abilities are acknowledged as outstanding.[6]

Culinary rulemaking may seem merely an elite preoccupation. The great French chef Auguste Escoffier codified the garnishes appropriate for main dishes; later, the authoritative reference work, *Larousse Gastronomique*, listed over one hundred edible decorations according to these ordinances. *Nanette*, for example, is a garnish consisting of artichoke hearts cooked in butter and filled with lettuce chiffonade à la crème, along with mushrooms filled with chopped truffles blended with demiglace. This was to be served with lamb or veal cutlets or sweetbreads. *Réjane*—potato nests filled with spinach in butter, quartered artichokes, and slices of poached bone marrow—was suitable for veal sweetbreads alone.[7]

This might seem like laughable upper-class fussiness, but ordinary people too establish community-enforced rules that discourage variation. Such attention to the "right way" to do things can be found here and there in the US. Aficionados of barbecue won't tolerate too much playing around with their culinary tradition—which varies from region to region in the South. People across the country make all sorts of different dishes they call gumbo, but restrictions are still observed in New Orleans such as not using okra and filé together as thickeners, and never mixing seafood and meat. This attitude, however, is not what shaped American cuisine. The common assumption in this country is that you should not be stuck in a single pattern but should try variations.

The advantage of the seemingly repressive traditional system is that it establishes standards to measure quality. People know who makes the best version of a canonical dish, or if they disagree, the discussion is on the basis of an established set of expectations. The reasons Americans prefer experimentation and variation has something to do with the idea of freedom of personal choice. In Italy, one is not supposed to drink cappuccino after ten thirty in the morning; it is also considered barbaric to put Parmesan cheese on pasta with seafood—and Italian friends will tell you so if you try. In Japan, sushi is eaten with the fingers, while sashimi requires chopsticks. When you are not using them, chopsticks should be placed parallel to the side of the table at which you are sitting. There are ten terms to describe the temperature of sake, ranging from snow-cold *(yukihie)* to superhot *(tabikiri-kan)*.[8]

Lax American attitudes reflect the formation of the country out of variegated immigrant waves. Not only did the presence of neighbors from many different places encourage exchanges of culinary knowledge, but the problems in reproducing the ingredients and tastes of home meant that immigrant dishes changed. Italian Americans developed specialties such as spaghetti with meatballs or chicken parmigiana, both unrecognizable in Italy, where American-style pizza was also unknown until well into the 1960s.

Americans have accepted a deal with the food companies, whose homogenization of American taste defined the twentieth-century palate. The methods of processing, preserving, and transporting food nationally from agricultural monocultures, distribution centers, and factories means a loss of flavor and freshness. In return for sacrificing these, the consumer gets the distraction of choice. The ice cream comes from a large industrial facility, but it is available in dozens of flavors; condensed soup has a similarly large array of options, to say nothing of packaged tortellini.

It is easy for food enterprises to offer assorted flavors of jams, Pop-Tarts, or cream cheese spreads—these are manufactured, mass-market products, after all. What is difficult is to mimic the taste of something freshly picked, baked, or cooked. A giant scientific enterprise has elaborated addictive taste sensations, particularly in the snack and fast food sectors, but has trouble imitating simplicity and freshness. Sweet, salty, or otherwise appealing enhancements are distractions—effective distractions, of course, otherwise people would not accept the artificial tastes that have predominated over the past century. Not all people, however. American food pioneers from M. F. K. Fisher to Alice Waters recounted a revelatory moment in their travels to France when they experienced the natural taste of food as if for the first time. The current popularity of farm-to-table is a change in popular perceptions and shows the limitations of science and even of marketing.

"Satisfactory for Most Usages": The Irrelevance of Flavor

Through most of the twentieth century, the ascribed importance of convenience, technology, and functionalism meant that the pleasures of food played a minor role. In the view of corporations, they were merely trying to make their products attractive. In fairness, these companies did not invent flavorless food. As demonstrated by Joel Barlow's 1793 poem in praise of hasty pudding, indifference to taste originated long before the post–Civil War rise of the consolidated

Shopping in a supermarket, 1957. The shelves offer a wide choice of canned meat brands, mostly similar in taste.

food companies. Barlow lauded hasty pudding as the model dish of the new democracy because of its healthful and republican simplicity. Its name shows that it was also relatively convenient to produce given the technologies available at the time. Barlow never says it is tasty, only that when you are hungry it is satisfying, which could be said about cold oatmeal as well.[9]

As they were developed and marketed, processed foods took advantage of the attitude that natural taste is a secondary consideration. Changing the subject away from mediocre taste by offering variety was one tactic. Another was simply to deny that industrial manipulation had any influence on flavor. For decades, the manufacturers of margarine devoted advertising money to assert that it was indistinguishable from butter, coming up with slogans such as "It's not nice to fool Mother Nature." A well-known margarine spread bears as its brand name "I Can't Believe It's Not Butter!" Equally in defiance of reality was an assertion by the president of Campbell's in 1959 that the most important improvement in food production of the past twenty-five years had come from plant breeding to improve flavor, particularly noticeable in tomatoes.[10]

A more nuanced approach to the taste question was based on a calculation of flavor versus convenience. When the University of Wisconsin created a process to make mozzarella in a few minutes, as opposed to the usual four hours, researchers acknowledged that the flavor was "mild" but claimed it was "satisfactory for most usages." Likewise, under the rubric of "why pay more?" the US Department of Agriculture in the 1970s told consumers that freestone peaches taste best, but they are expensive and don't hold their shape as well as newer breeds.[11] The canned food industry claimed not only that their products tasted good, but that they were superior to what was sold as fresh because canned fruit and vegetables, according to a 1930s brochure, were "harvested at their best" and so not subject to deterioration from transport. The same publication circumvented the taste issue by pointing to variety and diversion: "more fun in the kitchen with foods from far and near."[12] This coupled flat-out denial that canned produce is not as good as fresh with a change of subject in favor of variety, which was easy to deliver, over taste, which was not.

What is more disturbing, and not completely attributable to agribusiness manipulation, is the enduring American preference for bland or mild flavor. It's not only that people forgot what a tomato or apple pie was supposed to taste like, but that, like Plato's cave prisoners, they were unaware of what they had lost and uninterested in the restoration of sense perception. The common remark "I don't like fish that tastes too fishy" could be applied to other food, from cheese to lamb to sour cream. Organ meats offend not only because of their textures, but also because of their strong savor; the reign of iceberg lettuce was based on crunch and looks, not on possession of any perceptible flavor. Besides, iceberg lettuce makes a perfect foil for ranch or blue cheese dressing and artificial bacon bits. Meats such as beef and pork have been bred to be "lean," an example of the power of putative health benefits over taste, and they are fine slathered with steak sauce or barbecue sauce. Cottony modern white bread of the Wonder Bread type doesn't actually taste like anything much at all.

The open disdain for taste began with the food reformers of the late nineteenth century. As noted in reference to the New England Kitchen and the food reform movement, the mistrust of "King Palate" was coupled with exalting health and science as criteria for judging what food to consume. In the preface to the first edition (1896) of the *Boston Cooking School Cook Book*, Fannie Farmer looked forward to a time when man no longer lived to eat but rather the reverse. Thanks to scientific principles of diet, people would work more effectively and live longer.[13]

It isn't quite accurate to say that Americans embraced flavorless food enthusiastically or, as in a standard narrative, that until some point in the 1970s or 1980s when the "food revolution" began, the nation cheerfully or obliviously ate food with no taste. Americans love spicy snacks, for example. A cursory survey of a convenience market or gas station store will present you with Cajun-flavored popcorn, barbecued pork rinds, jalapeño potato chips, and the like. Most people order a topping with their pizza and then may add oregano, garlic powder, or crushed red pepper. We also put relish, ketchup, hot sauce, and mustard on our hamburgers, hot dogs, and French fries. Over the course of the twentieth century, people became accustomed to diminished natural taste. As gourmands lamented, chickens no longer tasted the way they were supposed to, and neither did peaches, lettuce, cheese, or almost any basic food, but these could be ornamented in creative form or with a piquant dressing. The industrial product is, therefore, an inexpensive backdrop for staging varied, if somewhat artificial, tastes.

A few exceptional American food companies stayed with one universally recognizable product. For over a century, Hershey's milk chocolate bars came in only two forms: plain and with almonds. There was exactly one kind of Coca-Cola until the 1960s. Cheerios started in 1941 but waited until 1976 to start selling Cinnamon Nut Cheerios. Currently there are over fifteen varieties of Cheerios. Creamy-smooth processed Velveeta was invented in 1918, but only in 1978 was a related product,

Advertisement for Spam, ca. 1944. Suggestions are given for presenting an economical food as modestly elegant.

Velveeta Shells and Cheese, introduced. Velveeta spinoffs now include Queso Blanco, Mexican Mild, and Cheese Sauce. Even Hershey's and Coke eventually diversified—the allure of choice was irresistible, especially as conformity became socially less attractive and consumers arranged themselves in niches such as those who wanted "lite" versions of standard products like beer or cottage cheese.

What the trade calls "line extension" means creating a new variation on a familiar brand and so leveraging that familiarity. It is easier and less expensive to introduce a product by profiting from an already-established reputation than to launch an entirely new item with an unfamiliar name. The downside of line extension is that it risks tarnishing or confusing the image of the iconic product.

Early on, low-calorie cola was sold by a company called Diet Rite, while Coca-Cola ignored the diet category, not wanting to dilute the universal recognition of its brand. In 1963, the company changed its mind, but it was careful not to detract from the Coca-Cola name and image, especially with what might be perceived to be an inferior-tasting product, and so devised the name "Tab." This was a success, primarily with women. Diet Coke was later marketed, in 1982, to appeal to a broader consumer base that included men. Although 885 million cases of Diet Coke were made in 2011 (compared to merely 3 million cases of Tab), it too became identified with women before 2005, when Coca-Cola Zero appeared.[14]

More often, brands diversified from the beginning. Although famous for ketchup and canned baked beans, the H. J. Heinz company, established in 1888, marketed its multiple offerings early in its history: the famous motto "57 Varieties" was introduced in 1896. Already the company produced considerably more than 57 items (it now has about 5,700), but the slogan was sufficiently memorable as to be incorporated in the company's logo. On the facing page is a list of the "canonical" 57 canned and jarred products in the 1930s.

Other enterprises achieved fame with a single product that came in many flavors. Howard Johnson's ice cream was offered in twenty-eight flavors; Baskin-Robbins had thirty-one. Howard Johnson's went from an ice cream company to a restaurant chain with many different specialties, while Baskin-Robbins remained essentially a many-kinds-of-one-product company.

The creation of new flavors and the plethora of options encouraged an attitude of experimentation. If there were no rules and so many sauces or fillings, why not try out new, even radical ideas? The food companies encouraged innovation because restlessness sells things, especially shortcuts and novelties. "Creativity" was what businesses and magazines called this experimentation, and it dominated the women's pages, community cookbooks, and recipe advice columns for most of the twentieth century.

The concentrated period of weird cooking creativity came in the mid-twentieth century. If casseroles and Jell-O salads do not immediately evoke happy memories, their appeal at the time is worth understanding in the context of variety as a goal. Variety here meant guided experimentation unconfined by rules.

HEINZ 57 VARIETIES[15]

1. Oven-Baked Beans with Pork and Tomato Sauce
2. Oven-Baked Beans without Tomato Sauce, with Pork—Boston Style
3. Oven-Baked Beans in Tomato Sauce without Meat—Vegetarian
4. Oven-Baked Red Kidney Beans
5. Cream of Tomato Soup
6. Cream of Green Pea Soup
7. Cream of Celery Soup
8. Cream of Asparagus Soup
9. Cream of Oyster Soup
10. Vegetable Soup
11. Pepper Pot Soup
12. Mock Turtle Soup
13. Beef Broth
14. Mutton Broth
15. Noodle Soup
16. Gumbo Creole
17. Mince Meat
18. Plum Pudding
19. Fig Pudding
20. Peanut Butter
21. Cooked Spaghetti
22. Cooked Macaroni
23. Pure Fruit Preserves
24. Pure Jellies
25. Apple Butter
26. Preserved Sweet Gherkin
27. Mixed Pickles—Sweet or Sour
28. Sour Spiced Gherkins
29. Chow Chow Pickle
30. Sweet Mustard Pickle
31. Dill Pickles
32. Fresh Cucumber Pickle
33. Fresh Cucumber Relish
34. India Relish
35. Sandwich Spread
36. Pickled Onions—Sweet or Sour
37. Spanish Queen Olives
38. Stuffed Spanish Olives
39. Ripe Olives
40. Pure Spanish Olive Oil
41. Tomato Ketchup
42. Chili Sauce
43. Beefsteak Sauce
44. Pepper Sauce—Red or Green
45. Worcestershire Sauce
46. Prepared Mustard
47. Prepared Mustard Sauce
48. Evaporated Horse Radish
49. Salad Cream
50. Mayonnaise Salad Dressing
51. Pure Malt Vinegar
52. Cider Vinegar
53. Distilled White Vinegar
54. Tarragon Vinegar
55. Rice Flakes
56. Breakfast Wheat
57. Tomato Juice

Creativity: Suburban Self-Expression

"Start with Ocean Spray Cranberry Juice Cocktail . . . then go creative"
1964 ADVERTISEMENT

The women who created home economics at the beginning of the twentieth century put into effect "scientific cooking" by which nutrition received priority over taste, and mindfulness about health trumped appetite. Given the austere menus recommended by the Boston Cooking School and like-minded food reformers, it seems surprising that simultaneous with the recommendations to eat plain oatmeal and cod cakes, there developed a fashion for dainty, decorated, and distinctly odd food. Laura Shapiro opens her path-breaking study of this phenomenon, *Perfection Salad*, by quoting a 1923 recommendation in a magazine called *Food Cookery* for serving even baked beans in an attractive way, "in dainty individual ramekins with a garnish of fried apple balls and cress, or toasted marshmallows stuffed with raisins."[16] Perfection salad itself, invented in 1905, exemplifies the use of new ingredients, unexpected juxtapositions, and new technology to create startling effects. It consists of chopped celery, cabbage, and red bell peppers bound in aspic (using Knox instant gelatin) and cut into cubes.[17] Plain aspic soon gave way to tomato-flavored gelatin, and a long-lasting fad for molded Jell-O salads was launched.

What came to be called culinary "creativity" was a way of asserting variety and experimentation over codified rules of cooking. As such, it was another demonstration of the American preference for personal choice over tradition, yet creativity also reflects the irrelevance of taste. What the frivolity of creative dishes shared with the grim simplicity of the New England Kitchen was a desire to control food, to make it less messy and instinctively pleasurable. Taste must give way to health, and dishes of disordered appearance and strong flavors should yield to decorousness.

Food companies encouraged creativity in order to extend the sales of a product that might otherwise have only limited use. A classic example is Lipton's Onion Soup Mix, introduced in 1952. Some consumers no doubt buy it to make soup, but much more frequently it is mixed with sour cream for what the company dubbed "California Dip." As it happens, I love California Dip and bring it up here to show that not every modernist food innovation is hateful. I serve this dip with ruffled potato chips, preferably of some obviously artificial flavor like mesquite barbecue.

Ernest Dichter, a psychologist who worked with advertising companies, first used "creativeness" in the 1950s to describe convenience products marketed to women. These recipes and styles would save time yet provide a feeling that you were cooking original dishes rather than simply combining and heating prepared ingredients.[18] The impetus to identifying this food category was a combination of the perceived need for convenience and the desire to avoid boredom. Dichter offered a simple syllogism:

Thesis: "I'm a housewife."
Antithesis: "I hate drudgery."
Synthesis: "I'm creative."

Rather than just opening a can of beef stew or heating up frozen peas, you could add "personal touches" such as red wine and parsley to the stew or bacon bits to the vegetables. From the housewife's point of view, the result would be attractive and easy; from the food company's perspective, it promoted convenience products that carried a relatively high profit margin.

"Creativeness" solved a somewhat different problem from that dealt with by the nutritionist movement fifty years earlier. Creativity meant frivolity, lack of tradition, and a fondness for unusual (or at least previously unknown) combinations. The genteel form of creative cuisine elaborated before the Second World War included gelatin salads, marshmallows, and decorating with mayonnaise and whipped cream. In the 1930s, the ladies' lunch aesthetic gave way to Depression frugality, but hard times did not in any sense diminish innovation, they just made it inexpensive. The federal government's Bureau of Home Economics recommended recipes using extremely basic ingredients, such as whole wheat or dried prunes, and processed cheap products. "Whole Wheat, Fish, and Tomatoes" was made with canned fish, canned tomatoes, celery, pepper, and cooked whole wheat. Canned beans could be disguised as stuffing for baked onions or cooked and crushed into patties and fried to resemble croquettes.[19] Among the memorable dishes of the Depression is Mock Apple Pie made with Ritz crackers. This endured as a folk memory long after these crackers were no longer cheaper than using apples. In my childhood, the 1950s and 1960s, everyone my age knew what Mock Apple Pie was, and the recipe was still on the back of the package, but no one had ever tasted it and none of my friends was particularly eager to do so.

There are, therefore, three eras of creativity: 1900–1930, when dainty home economists' recipes attempted to make food fun as long as it was bland and healthful; the Depression and World War II, by which time processed foods such as canned meat and fish or powdered mixes were less expensive than fresh ingredients; and finally the postwar era of higher standards of living coupled with a perceived pressure of time for work, family, and active leisure. The forms of creativity had different goals and leaders: diet reform advanced by professional nutritionists in the first period, economic uplift provided by the federal government in the 1930s, and sales growth for food companies in the 1950s and 1960s.

The third wave actually consisted of two parts, one that was called "glamorizing," or making processed ingredients into dishes that passed muster as "gourmet," and a less pretentious but also less traditional form of adding enough "personal" touches so as to render the results unrecognizable. Glamorizing performed homage to high-end specialties: adding wine to prepared meat or liqueur to ready-made desserts, setting things on fire to imitate an imagined French or Continental haute cuisine. Use of a relatively expensive ingredient in convenient form, such as canned crabmeat or frozen shrimp, gave a better impression than an obvious convenience product such as frozen fish sticks. Canned crabmeat featured in a *House Beautiful* recommendation that also involved canned cream of mushroom soup, cream of tomato soup, sherry, and curry powder. "It's as gourmet as anything," the magazine said, "yet it can be put together in about ten minutes."[20]

In a different class were recipes for dishes that were outré, inexpensive, and devoid of reference to any European gourmet tradition. Casseroles made from leftovers with cream of mushroom soup as the binder have maintained their fame, or infamy, across the decades. Canned fruit cocktail with some addition such as coconut flakes is another classic. In fact, however, the border between upper and lower categories often blurred. A 1963 recipe put out by Minute Rice was given the distinctly low-brow name "Chicken à la Can Can" because it called for cans of condensed chicken soup, cream of celery soup, and French-fried onions. The advertisement, however, claimed the dish was "French, fancy, and flavor-filled," thus advancing a quasi-gourmet claim.[21]

The outstanding example of the having-it-both-ways view of gourmet convenience is Poppy Cannon's *The Can-Opener Cook Book* of 1951.[22] On its front cover, the book presents itself as "a guide for gourmet cooking with canned or frozen foods and mixes." In the early 1950s, Cannon was food columnist for *Mademoiselle*, a publication directed to women in their late teens and early twenties.[23] Its target audience was looking for love and marriage, but also independently minded and adventurous. Cannon was an upbeat advocate of modern, processed food products adapted to the life of a young woman who wanted to attract guys without learning very much about cooking. Vivi, one of her made-up heroines, had never considered "whipping around in the kitchen" worthwhile, but after becoming starry-eyed over Tommy, she found out how to put together gourmet meals with the aid of products like Underwood purée mongole (split pea and tomato soup) and La Touraine's canned baba au rhum.[24]

Cannon viewed creative gourmet cuisine as a sensible response to the pressures of time and the "crowding of many varied interests." Just as the French restaurant chef had a battery of kitchen workers to get the food ready and clean up, the modern young woman had a can opener that allowed her to be an "artist-cook, the master, the creative chef."[25] Explicitly rejecting the dreary side of convenience food—

Campbell's, recipe for Tuna Crunch Casserole, 1968. As the ad indicates, the "crunch" could be supplied by potato chips, Goldfish crackers, chow mein noodles, or canned French-fried onions—convenient and creative.

the tuna fish, cream of mushroom soup, and potato chip sort of concoction—Cannon offers "classic" French recipes, but prepared with canned consommé instead of slowly prepared stock, mayonnaise from a jar ("just as a chef would make it"), and frozen chicken à la king instead of terrapin.[26] The key to making these dishes convincing was dressing them up with flourishes to add flavor and to express individual creativity—adding sherry or red wine to canned soup or gravy, for example. Cannon's discourse emphasized seductive alliteration: "a fleck of spice, a flutter of herbs" for meat and "a flurry of fresh coconut" for desserts.[27] The reader is invited to try paella à la Valencianna [*sic*] using canned chicken fricassee and quick-cooking rice or roast duck bigarade made with orange marmalade and heat 'n' serve beef gravy. Poppy Cannon was convincing in her time: gourmet convenience based on frozen king crab legs and rock lobster tails, canned turtle soup or canned new peas, flourished well into the 1970s.

AN UNLIKELY FRIENDSHIP: POPPY CANNON AND ALICE B. TOKLAS

Poppy Cannon was more knowledgeable about cooking and food than she let on, and in the late 1950s, she experienced a conversion in the direction of real food, lamenting remorsefully the ersatz taste of what she had been instrumental in promoting. Her unlikely mentor in this spiritual pilgrimage was an American in Paris, Alice B. Toklas, the lover of Gertrude Stein.

Alice B. Toklas was a passionate and painstaking cook with little to no interest in convenience products or American tastes. Although Toklas and Stein had collaborated on many projects, it had always been Stein who was the genius and Toklas who was the dutiful housewife. Immune from the pressures of wage labor or any eagerness to please men, Toklas had almost nothing in common with Cannon's

Mademoiselle or *House Beautiful* readers. After Stein died, just after the war's end, Toklas was anxious about her economic circumstances. She started to write about food in order to make money and turned out to be an endearing and charming expositor. In 1954, Harper & Brothers published *The Alice B. Toklas Cook Book*. Although a careful cook, Toklas was, it is fair to say, a disorganized, even dotty compiler and used a number of friends' recipes without either testing or perhaps even quite noticing them. This insouciance explains the inclusion of aspic salad that called for Campbell's condensed tomato soup, Philadelphia cream cheese, and Miracle Whip.[28] A famous oversight appropriated painter Brion Gysin's instructions for how to make "Haschich Fudge." Slowly but relentlessly, this recipe (usually remembered as brownies rather than fudge) would make Toklas inadvertently famous. In 1968, the movie *I Love You, Alice B. Toklas* starred Peter Sellers as a square guy who loses his inhibitions after eating cannabis brownies. At the time it was released, the movie title required no explanation.

In the 1950s, however, *The Alice B. Toklas Cook Book* succeeded as an updated exemplar of the French gourmet niche. Poppy Cannon met Toklas at an event in Venice sponsored by *House Beautiful* and the two became close if mismatched companions. Cannon gave Toklas a Waring blender and convinced her to try some modern products such as cake mixes. Toklas, in turn, showed Cannon the satisfactions of real rather than faux French food. Talking and cooking with Toklas gave Cannon a sense that perhaps she had overstated the case for creativity. In a preface to their collaborative book, *Aromas and Flavors of Past and Present*, Cannon describes Toklas's doubts about both "creative cooking" and the benefits of variety. When Cannon exuberantly tells Toklas that in America one could serve in the same meal a Russian soup, an American steak, Chinese vegetables and a French dessert, the response was merely "how incongruous."

From Laura Shapiro, *Something from the Oven: Reinventing Dinner in 1950s America* (New York: Viking Penguin, 2004), 110–20.

Cannon gradually realized that there was some truth in the common French critique of American eclecticism, in her words "exotic and yet at the same time flavorless." "I who wanted to do everything a new way began to catch at least a glimmering of the classical French attitude. . . . It began to dawn on me that certain dishes, like sonnets or odes, cannot be brought into being without obeisance to classic rules and restrictions." Cannon did not completely renounce her past and remained eager to square the circle of gourmet cuisine and American convenience, but she tried, cautiously, to celebrate authenticity and tradition.[29]

The vogue for "Continental" cuisine in the decades after Cannon and Toklas met shows the persistence of a somewhat artificial European elegance, a small step up from can-opener gastronomy.[30] Dishes such as beef Wellington, chicken Kiev, or steak Diane were hard to locate geographically and full of luxury ingredients. Their showy complexity sometimes covered up thawed or inferior ingredients.

All this shows that there was a sociological spectrum of creative cuisine. At the low end were the casseroles made with canned soup, the Jell-O salads, and an increasingly elaborate repertoire of mixes and instant products. At the pretentious, would-be gourmet end of the spectrum were the Continental restaurants and the elegant Poppy Cannon shortcut gourmet home cooking. Both were destined to decline. The near-extinction of "Continental," preceded by its becoming a joke, is indicated by nostalgia publications such as Peter Moruzzi's *Classic Dining*, which catalogues the few remaining restaurants with elegant paneling, curved booths, and tableside service by tuxedoed waiters.[31] The "quick and easy" part of Poppy Cannon's formula has survived and flourished, but the Francophile cook long ago gave up the can opener and the more egregious convenience products. There was a transitional period in the 1960s when dishes such as fondue combined variation, elegance, fun, and continental flair. Julia Child's success revived a more authentically French cuisine. Although certainly not accepting processed foods and Poppy Cannon–level shortcuts, Child was quite happy with what supermarkets offered and resisted criticizing the quality of American meat and produce.

The advent of hybridized international cooking relieved food writers of the burden of trying to replicate French haute cuisine. Italian pasta and sauce, quiche, stir-fry, and curry could be made with frozen, canned, or powdered ingredients, and they did not have to submit to an authenticity test. La Choy had an advertising jingle in the 1960s and 1970s, "La Choy makes Chinese food swing American."[32] In short, the best of both worlds.

✦   ✦   ✦

POPPY CANNON'S progressive internationalism was not all wrong. She saw the variety of American immigrant culinary possibilities as encouragement for new and convenient ingredients and technologies. The sociological diversity of America and its ability to absorb so many foreign cuisines stemmed from the same love of novelty and indifference to tradition that manifested itself in the brave new world of mixes, jars, blenders, and what Cannon referred to as "the ubiquitous can opener."[33] There were so many more choices of what to buy and eat in the mid-twentieth century than at its beginning. This was partly because Americans had more money on average and could benefit from the manufacturing and communications advances that brought an astounding variety of products, if not to their doors, at least to their supermarkets. An ingrained cultural enthusiasm for choices fit a corporate strategy of providing lots of flavor options in order to make up for the intrinsic taste limitations of industrial food production. Fabulous flavors, whether they were 28 kinds of Howard Johnson's ice cream or Heinz's 57 varieties of pickles, provided diversion and novelty as well as distraction from the inability to replicate natural, original taste. Insofar as it was not actually forgotten, that original taste was assumed to be boring—the term "plain vanilla" comes to mind. A revolutionary rediscovery would come to prominence after 1970, that plain bread, peaches, tomatoes, or chicken might be delicious if cultivated or prepared in a way that showed off their natural qualities.

"CREATIVE" DISHES FROM THE 1950S

Pineapple Betty (pineapple, marshmallows, graham cracker crumbs, nuts)

Poppy Cannon's Floating Island (lemon Jell-O hearts dropped into royal custard pudding)

Candle Salad (half a banana standing in a ring of pineapple with a cherry on top—described in a 1954 *Saturday Review* article as "that bridge-club pest of yesteryear")

Red Crest Salad (chopped tomatoes and pickles in strawberry Jell-O)

Rutabaga-Pineapple Salad

Gourmet Crab (canned crabmeat, frozen spinach, cream of mushroom soup, Cheez Whiz)

Seafood Spread (canned crabmeat, canned shrimp, mayonnaise with crushed saltine crackers, and grated Parmesan on top)

Chicken Salad Pie (pie shell filled with chicken salad, shredded cheese, crushed pineapple, and slivered almonds, covered with mayonnaise and whipped cream, decorated with carrot curls—a winner in the Pillsbury Bake-Off, 1954)

Spam Casserole (Spam, canned macaroni and cheese, canned asparagus, grated cheese, bread crumbs)

Tuna Fish Chow Mein (creamed tuna fish and peanuts over canned asparagus)

From Laura Shapiro, *Something from the Oven: Reinventing Dinner in 1950s America* (New York: Viking Penguin, 2004). A source for an almost infinite number of other examples is the website Midcentury Menu, found at www.midcenturymenu.com.

CHAPTER 8

"Ethnic" Restaurants

The same variety of options offered by the galaxy of retail food products characterizes dining out. Just as there are thirty-one flavors of Progresso "traditional" soups (not counting their "light," low-sodium, or gluten-free lines), the average American city has dozens of restaurants serving some version of international food. Even small towns have at least a Chinese or a Mexican place. Ethnic restaurants currently have a better image than processed food choices among critics and observers of American food history, and they are often praised as examples of American cultural diversity. Such restaurants are independent businesses in a world of corporate hegemony; they are inexpensive and infinitely varied yet comfortingly predictable—all Thai restaurants will have pad thai on the menu; all Italian restaurants feature pasta.

The consumer's experience of choice among international restaurants is part of the overall story of American cuisine. As far back as the 1890s, Americans boasted about how many nationalities were represented by our restaurants, offering diners an extraordinary range of choices. The difficulty of defining American cuisine, the starting point for this book, makes it hard to identify a typical American restaurant serving typical American food. Less narrowly, and more plausibly, it is international variety itself that characterizes American food served outside the home. Fajitas and General Tso's chicken are certainly as American as apple pie—and even more so in terms of how frequently they are consumed.

The term "ethnic restaurant" is less than ideal as it assumes that there is a complementary "regular" or "normal" restaurant type. Moreover, "ethnic" can seem casually insulting, implying condescension toward people from other lands and their food.[1] The late Jonathan Gold, who had been the *Los Angeles Times* food expert, was quoted as saying "I hate the word 'ethnic.'" Gold, who won a Pulitzer Prize for his food reporting, preferred "traditional,"[2] yet this neutral formulation, along with others such as "international," "foreign," or "immigrant" restaurant, is either inadequate or retains a taint of stereotype and subordination. The one thing the food of these restaurants is *not* is "traditional," if that means reflecting the country of its origins. The success of foreign restaurants in the United States depends on giving an air of authenticity to food that is adapted to American palates.

I use "ethnic restaurant" here deliberately, precisely because of its uncomfortable connotations.[3] The popularity of these enterprises, after all, comes from ideas of exoticism in the minds of customers who do not form part of the immigrant group. Ethnic restaurants have been popular with generic Americans over the last 150 years because they offer inexpensive culinary novelty. That novelty has to appeal, nonetheless, to the tastes of patrons initially unfamiliar with the cuisine. Safe exoticism is more important than authenticity. The little umbrellas decorating tropical drinks are preferable to chicken feet, beef with broccoli to stinky tofu.

Before about 1960, such restaurants were referred to as "foreign," "exotic," or most often simply by national type. It was easy to assume a patronizing attitude toward foreign cuisines without employing a general descriptive term. In Lawton Mackall's 1948 guide *Knife and Fork in New York*, grand as well as modest restaurants are grouped under cleverly arch headings (or so they were meant to seem), such as "Chummy and Cheery" (festive atmosphere) or "Shelly and Finny Fare" (seafood). Mackall's suave, urbane diction puts Chinese under "Pagoda Provender," Indian as "Curry Quest," Hungarian as "Paprika in the Pink." Russian cuisine is summarized as "Shashliks and Vodka," overlapping with Middle Eastern "Pilaf and Shish Kebab."[4]

The use of "ethnic restaurant" in publications begins with the 1960s. In a 1959 review of "A Bit of Bali," *New York Times* food critic Craig Claiborne remarked: "Because New York is a city of sophistication and with tremendously different ethnic groups, the public here has extraordinary opportunities to dine on the 'exotic' fare of a hundred regions." The formula "ethnic restaurant" henceforth would become established in the *Times* and elsewhere to describe places serving the cuisine of an immigrant group.[5]

French cuisine, on the other hand, was never included in the ethnic category because France set the standard for international culinary prestige. While its food was certainly "foreign," France produced restaurants of grandeur and authority set apart conceptually from the picturesque, inexpensive experience that "ethnic" implies. Members of the American elite, from Thomas Jefferson to Jackie Kennedy Onassis, cultivated a French aesthetic to demonstrate a level of sophistication and savoir faire that most Americans inherently lacked.

The origins of ethnic restaurants lie in serving immigrant communities the foods of home, but early on they were sought out by the larger population outside that community. Restaurants adjusted their cuisine, atmosphere, and ambience in order to attract nonnative customers. The advantage of an "Anglo" or generic American clientele over members of the immigrant community is that nonimmigrants are more numerous and less discriminating, hence more easily guided. While there have always been Chinese restaurants intended for a Chinese public, the vast majority of restaurants identifying themselves as Chinese target non-Chinese patrons. A Mexican restaurant in Los Angeles called El Nayarit, established in 1951, was popular with immigrants from the Mexican state of that name located on the Pacific coast. It advertised in Spanish-language media and served as a neighborhood center and gathering place in Echo Park. El Nayarit attracted famous, and not necessarily Hispanic, notables like Marlon Brando, but didn't make an effort to tailor its food to the prevailing combination-plate (enchilada, taco, tamale, rice and beans) standard.[6] Most ethnic restaurants, however, opted for a less cozy but more profitable public profile and bypassed the direct role of immigrant community resource.

From the customers' point of view, the proliferation of ethnic restaurants exemplifies the American predilection for options. This is peculiarly American

BOMBAY INDIA INN

A LA CARTE SERVICE:

SHORBA (Soup)	10¢	**DESSERTS**	
CHUTNEY	.10		
SALADS	.10	HULWA	10¢
All Curries CHAPPATEE	.25	BAKLAWA	.10
RICE	.10	SOM-BOSA	.10
PILAUF (Fried and		SESAME SEED CAKE	.10
Flavored Rice)	.15	BURFEE	.10
DAL	.10	NAN KHATTAI	.10
BHAJEE (Vegetable)	.10	* JALLAIBEE	10¢
KHOPA (Cocoanut)	.10		
BOMBAY DUCK	15¢		
PAPARDAM	.10	**BEVERAGES**	
* PUREE KACHUREE	.15	INDIA TEA	10¢
* BHALLA (with Curd)	.15	INDIA SHARBAT	.10
* PAKAURA ,, ,,	.15	TAMARIND	.10
* PATTAUR (Fritters)	.15	American COFFEE	5¢
HOT CHUTNEY	.10	Oriental COFFEE	5¢
CHOW-CHOW (achchar)	.10	MILK	5¢
PILAUF (Fried Rice)	.15	BUTTER MILK	5¢
PILAUF (Meat & Rice)	.25	*ALMOND drink (Summer)	10
INDIA MANGO CHUTNEY	.25		

**** Means prepared to order — 24 hours notice.

VISIT OUR GIFT COUNTER

BOMBAY INDIA INN
"The Home of India's Delicacies in America"
TELEPHONE .... LONGACRE 3-0142

150 WEST 45TH STREET   NEW YORK CITY

Menu, Bombay India Inn, 1940s. The postwar period saw the addition of many different ethnic restaurants to a sector dominated by Chinese and Italian establishments.

because international gastronomic choice has not been paramount elsewhere. The common sort of statement we hear all the time in the United States, à la "I don't want to have Thai food tonight; I had it yesterday," is still strange, even senseless in most of the world, and not only in Thailand.

The diversity of the United States restaurant scene is of course enabled by the presence of immigrants, but it's possible to absorb immigrant foodways into the local cuisine without there being many identifiably ethnic restaurants. New Orleans has had successive waves of immigrants from Spain, Germany, and Italy, but their culinary styles have become part of the local Creole cuisine rather than constituting separate enclaves. Farther afield, the food of Java is heavily influenced by generations of Chinese settlement, but there are relatively few explicitly Chinese restaurants.

Success in the restaurant industry is only tangentially related to numbers of immigrants. There are some sixty thousand Filipinos in New York City but only seven or eight Filipino restaurants.[7] Nor is there a direct relation between the restaurant cuisine type and its owner: there are many people from India living in the US, but most "Indian" restaurants are owned by entrepreneurs from Bangladesh and Pakistan. The ethnic restaurant is so integrated into the American culinary landscape that it is easily assumed to be merely the unmediated result of a supply of immigrants and consumer demand for variety in dining out. The array of restaurants and their popularity is a culturally and entrepreneurially managed phenomenon, however, not an impersonal reflection of demography.

Eagerness to try other cuisines has been a feature of American taste for well over a century. The cultural sociologist Donna Gabaccia says that since colonial times, Americans have eaten "Creole"—that is, they have been open to the influence of new arrivals rather than being rooted in local cooking traditions. The ingrained American predilection for mixing categories in order to create excitement can have some odd effects. In Louisville, Kentucky, a restaurant called the New Orleans House already by reason of its name appeared to offer a nonlocal cuisine. A 1961 menu further enriches, or confuses, the restaurant's regional identity by offering a New England clambake. Lobster was appropriately featured, but so was gumbo, not a dish typically found at a clambake, but the American response might be "so what"?[8]

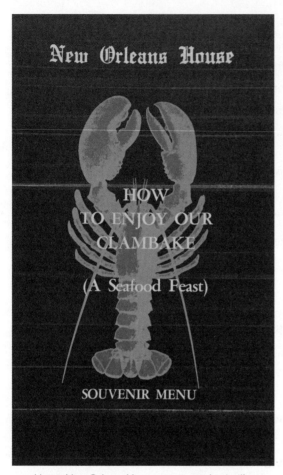

New Orleans House

HOW
TO ENJOY OUR
CLAMBAKE

(A Seafood Feast)

SOUVENIR MENU

Menu, New Orleans House restaurant, Louisville, Kentucky, 1961. Eclecticism or confusion? The New England clambake at this New Orleans–style restaurant in Kentucky includes gumbo.

Another 1961 menu, from the Frascati restaurant in Hollywood, exhibits international rather than regional eclecticism. Frascati is an Italian wine of Roman origin, but this branch of what was a small restaurant chain is described as offering Belgian food. The menu does mention *carbonnades flammandes*, a beef stew made with beer and onions, and filet of sole imported from Belgium, but it also includes a Provençal Bouillabaisse, Wienerschnitzel, "Poitrine de Poulet Hawaienne," and "NY Minute Steak Tyrolienne." If you preferred Italian spaghetti, cannelloni, or ravioli, they too were available.[9]

Examples such as these can be chalked up to charming ignorance or to the same midcentury impulse to "creativity" seen in home-cooked food. Openness to new experiences and lack of strong traditional standards provided the preconditions for the rise of ethnic restaurants beginning in the late nineteenth century.[10] The native population of the United States, not otherwise curious about or impressed by immigrants, enthusiastically embraced a version of their cuisine as far back as the 1880s.

Other countries too have favored foreign restaurant cuisines, but later and more selectively. Before the Second World War, most restaurants in Germany, not surprisingly, served either generic German food, regional specialties, or high-end French cuisine. Starting in the 1960s with the recruitment of "guest

SUPPER SUGGESTIONS

CLAMS, OYSTERS & COCKTAILS
Little Necks 40   Blue Points 50   Cape Cods 55   Cherrystones 45
Crab Flakes 80   Fresh Prawns 75   Lobster 1.10   Sea Food 95
                 Tomato Juice 30   Clam Juice 20

APPETIZERS
Stuffed Celery 40   Olives stuffed with Anchovies 40   Coupe of Fruits au Porto 65
Tomato Surprise 85   Assorted Hors d'Oeuvres 1.00   Imported Beluga Caviar 2.20
Stuffed Prunes, Marguerite 75   Fried Olives and Bacon 75   Sea Food Roosevelt 75
                 Sardine 50   Anchovy 60

SOUPS
Strained Chicken 50   Consomme Julienne 40   Green Turtle 70
French Onion Soup au Gratin 50   Jellied Madrilene, Chicken, Gumbo or Beef Broth 35

SEA FOOD
Fish Mixed Grill, Maison 1.50   Broiled Chicken Lobster 1.75
Lobster Newburgh 1.75   Baked Oysters, Casino 1.00   Brook Trout Saute Belle Meuniere 1.20
Boiled Kennebec Salmon, Mayonnaise 1.25   Grilled Sea Bass, Lemon Butter 1.00

FOREIGN SUGGESTIONS (for two persons)
French - Chicken Marengo - Spring Chicken Saute, Mushrooms, White Wine, Fried Egg, Tomato 3.50
Turkish - Moussaka - Minced Spring Lamb, Eggplant, Mushrooms, Onions, Tomato 3.00
Spanish - Arroz con Pollo - Chicken, Rice, Green Peppers, Peas, Tomato, Mushrooms, Garlic, Safrau 3.50
China - Chicken Chow Mein - Mushrooms, Celery, Fried Noodles, Shredded Eggs 3.00
Chile - Chili con Carne - Red Kidney Beans, Onions, Tomatoes, Garlic and Beef 3.00

COLD DISHES
Coquille of Crab Flakes, Roosevelt 1.20   Virginia Ham, Vegetable Salad 1.35
Terrine of Foie Gras, Truffee 1.25   Half Cold Lobster, String Bean Salad 1.50
Genuine Praguer Ham 1.10   Beech Nut Ham, potato salad 1.25
Sliced chicken and tongue, beet salad 1.50   Sliced Turkey, Waldorf Salad 1.50
Assorted Cold Cuts, Hearts of Lettuce 1.40   Roast Lamb, Pork or Veal, sliced tomato 1.50
                 Stuffed Tomato with Sea Food, Roosevelt 1.25

RAREBITS and SAVOURIES
Welsh Rarebit 75   Long Island Rarebit 80   Golden Buck 85
Melted American Cheese and Bacon 90   Broiled Mushrooms on Toast 1.25
Scotch Wood Cock 85   Tongue, Swiss Cheese, open sandwich, cole slaw, Russian Dressing 1.15

SANDWICHES
Club 90   Lettuce and Tomato 45   Toasted American Cheese and Bacon 65
Tongue 45   Ham 45   Cream Cheese 50   Pimiento, Chopped Olives, or Currant Jelly, cream cheese 60
Swiss Cheese 40   with Ham 75   Cold Chicken or Turkey 75 - Hot 1.00
                 Bacon, Lettuce and Tomato on Toast 75

SALADS
Romaine, Lettuce, Chicory 40   Combination 75   Vegetable 70   Chiffonade 75   Chef Salad 75
Lettuce and Tomato 60   Butterfly, Cream cheese, Pineapple, currant Jelly, lettuce 75
Lobster 1.75   Chicken 1.50   Crabmeat 1.20   Shrimp with Hard Boiled Egg 1.35   Roquefort Cheese Dressing 15

CHEESE
Camembert 45   Roquefort 50   Brie 40   Liederkranz 40
English Stilton 55   Old American 35   Philadelphia Cream 40   Bar-le-Duc 35

DESSERTS
Fresh Fruit, Romanoff 50   Crepe Suzette 1.00   Coupe Carioca 55
Tutti Frutti 50   Assorted Fancy Cakes 25   French Pastry 25
        Strawberry, Burnt Almond, Vanilla, Pistachio, Coffee or Chocolate Ice Cream 40
Cherry-Flambé Jubilee 1.25   Pineapple, Lemon, Orange, Raspberry or Mint Sherbet 35

COFFEE, TEA Etc.
Coffee 20   with Cream 30   Demi-Tasse 15   Sanka 30   Kaffee Haq 30
Hot Chocolate or Cocoa 35   Choice of Tea 20   with Cream 30

Menu, Roosevelt Hotel, New York City, 1935. The "foreign suggestions" section associates chili con carne with Chile and Mexican arroz con pollo with Spain.

workers" from Turkey and other Mediterranean nations, the supply of inexpensive Italian, Greek, and Turkish restaurants increased. As in the United States, the customers for such restaurants quickly comprised mostly "visitors" from outside the migrant group. By 2007, 56 percent of German customers in a survey said they preferred foreign cuisine when dining out. The most popular dishes in restaurants were spaghetti Bolognese (meat sauce), spaghetti with tomato sauce, schnitzel, and pizza.[11]

In Britain, the popularity of Indian curry restaurants goes back to the late nineteenth century, but they really took off only in the decade of the 1950s. As late as 1965, only 8 percent of those who regularly dined out said they had ever tried Indian food (the figure for Chinese was 31 percent).[12] An explosion of interest in curry took place in the 1970s and 1980s, and by 1990 the number of Indian restaurants had reached seven thousand.[13] A sample of 690 people attending the Good Food show in 1995 indicated that over 70 percent of those interviewed were accustomed to dining at an Indian restaurant at least once a month.[14]

Another peculiar example of imperial culinary colonization comes from the Soviet Union. Under Stalin, and long after his death, the food of his native Georgia was shaped as the prestige cuisine, to rival the position of French cuisine in the West. Although Russia ruled the Soviet empire, its food was not considered adaptable to elegant affairs beyond drinks (vodka) and appetizers (caviar). Among his many ascribed accomplishments, Stalin "invented" a spiced lamb stew he named "Aragvi" after a river in Georgia.[15]

Notwithstanding these exceptions, most of Europe expressed little interest in foreign cuisine until quite recently. This is not because of lack of immigrants. Spain has had a substantial population of Latin Americans for centuries, but there has never been a wide market for their cuisine. Also a former colonial power, France has received immigrants from North and Equatorial Africa, the Caribbean, and Indochina, but the culinary novelties of these places were until recently uninteresting to the French majority. In 1965, the *Guide Michelin* listed about 550 restaurants in Paris, of which fewer than 5 percent were foreign—and most of those were Italian.

The United States was different, not just because of its waves of immigration or the absence of a national culinary tradition, but because Americans were eager to experiment with food, both processed and "ethnic." Celebration of New York City's "culinary cosmopolitanism" was under way before the end of the nineteenth century. An article in *Frank Leslie's Popular Monthly* in 1893 admitted that the best restaurants in the world were to be found in Paris but bragged that New York offered superior variety: "On a wager [one] could dine differently four times a day for a week, and have each repast composed of foreign dishes, served by foreign waiters, and eat with foreign-born men and women as his convives."[16] The hypothetical diner being addressed here is, of course "American" rather than "foreign." Boasting about foreign cooking was not confined to New York. In 1922, the *Los Angeles Times*, under a headline "All Nations' Food Served Here," claimed that one could sample the cuisine of "almost every nation of the universe without passing beyond the city limits.[17]

Major Players: Chinese, Italian, and Mexican

Then and now, ethnic restaurants offered good value and food that had vibrant tastes not found in French or Anglo-American standard fare. Given America's expansive immigration history, many foreign cuisines competed for attention. German food was the first successful import, going back to before the Civil War, when German beer gardens and Rathskellers became popular. The beer gardens were among the first restaurants of a type that would now be called "family-friendly." Even though by definition a beer garden was a place to drink, its atmosphere was safe and picnic-like rather than gloomy and threatening as taverns could be. Americans wondered at the presence of children at establishments where drink flowed, but on the whole were favorably impressed. So successful were German restaurants that much of what they served became completely Americanized. German restaurants popularized smoked sausages, ground meat patties, potato salad, and other dishes that soon lost their ethnic associations.

In contrast to the paradoxical success of German food, which was incorporated into the American repertoire, Chinese cuisine remained identifiably for-

Pekin Noodle Parlor, Butte, Montana. The restaurant was established in 1911 and is reputed to be America's oldest Chinese restaurant in continuous operation.

eign. Nevertheless, it surpassed all others in popularity by the first years of the twentieth century, and its rise was not impeded by anti-Chinese feeling and imposition of restrictive immigration laws beginning in the 1880s. The Chinese were singled out for harsh discrimination forty years before Congress reduced to almost nothing immigration from insufficiently Anglo-Saxon or Nordic countries.[18] It is noteworthy that although Germany was America's enemy in two world wars, anti-German sentiment evaporated after the conflicts, its only culinary souvenirs being temporary efforts at new names ("liberty cabbage" instead of sauerkraut). On the other hand, however resilient the image of Germans, their cuisine has become invisible in this country.

Legal restrictions and cultural disdain did not prevent Chinese restaurateurs from expanding the popular appeal of their cuisine. Cultural critics have debated whether dining at ethnic restaurants represents a praiseworthy, typically American openness to diversity or an equally characteristic cultural imperialism. An article in the *Journal of Popular Culture* entitled "I'll Take Chop Suey" argues that dining at ethnic restaurants improves cultural attitudes and racial tolerance.[19] A larger number of experts express dismay that eating ethnic food does not in fact lead to more favorable attitudes toward immigrants or ethnic minorities.[20] It turns out to be eminently feasible to honeymoon in Cancun or eat guacamole while holding intolerant opinions about immigrants from Mexico.

Chinese food came to San Francisco with the Gold Rush of 1849, which attracted Chinese miners, retail entrepreneurs, and subsequently construction workers to build the railroads. However important to the California economy, the Chinese arrivals were punished for their virtues. They were perceived as irritatingly reliable, willing to work for nearly nothing, capable by reason of their race or acceptance of subordination of living on almost nothing and so impossible competition for American-born workers. The first formal act of immigration restriction was the Chinese Exclusion Act of 1882, which prohibited the arrival from China of any persons except for merchants and students. Although the Chinese would find ways around the legislation, the number of immigrants fell from 123,000 between 1870 and 1880 to 63,000 from 1880 to 1890, and 14,800 in the last decade of the century.[21]

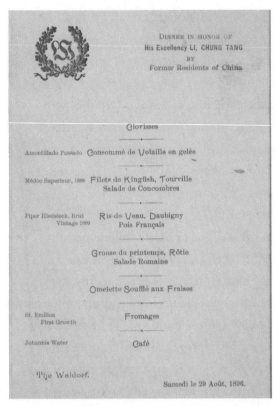

Menu, Waldorf Hotel, New York City, 1896. This dinner, served to the Chinese emissary, features a standard banquet of French dishes without any sign of chop suey.

What came to be known as the Chop Suey Craze began at the height of anti-Chinese sentiment, when fears of the "Yellow Peril" were staples of newspaper scare stories. Viceroy Li Hongzhang (his name was transliterated in different ways), an envoy from the court of the Qing emperor, visited the United States in the late summer of 1896 and created a sensation as the representative of an exotically mysterious realm.[22] Legend has it that chop suey was introduced by the Viceroy Li's chef, or alternatively that it was served for the first time at a reception in the envoy's honor at New York's Waldorf Hotel. A menu for a dinner at the Waldorf given by "former residents of China" (former diplomats) in honor of the Viceroy has no Chinese dishes at all. The menu is in French and consists of jellied chicken consommé, kingfish, sweetbreads, roast grouse, and a strawberry dessert omelet.

American chop suey is based less on a specific Chinese dish than on a cooking style. The southern Chinese term *zasui* denotes odds and ends of organ meats mixed with fungi and bamboo shoots. In Americanized form, the dish was first known as chow chop suey, "chow" derived from the word for stir-fried. Adopted to American palates, beef, pork, or chicken replaced the innards and a thick, gravy-like sauce was substituted for the stir-fried effect. Chop suey attracted an arty avant-garde following, what contemporaries described as "Bohemians." These were young, unattached urban intellectuals and professionals who led mildly unconventional lives and by the 1890s patronized colorful and informal gastronomic novelties like Italian and Chinese restaurants. According to a 1903 article in the *New York Tribune*, "Few Bohemian gatherings are complete without a pail of chop suey, brought fresh and hot, from Chinatown."[23]

Chop suey is a perfect example of culinary adaptation, an inauthentic but successful dish developed deliberately by Chinese restaurateurs. Its Chinese origins, American repackaging, and (at one time) astonishing popularity exemplify the permutations of ethnic foods in the history of American taste. What appealed to Americans were previously unfamiliar ingredients such as soy sauce, ginger, or fermented black beans, but also the particular effect of cooking in a wok very briefly at high heat. So alien was this technique to European or American cooking methods that it took until the 1940s for the term "stir-fry" to be introduced to describe *chow/chau/chao* dishes that are a hallmark of Cantonese cuisine. For most of the twentieth century, Western recipes for chop suey and other Chinese dishes transformed most of these originally stir-fried preparations into stews or ragouts with thick sauces. The inability to grasp the basic principles of Chinese cooking persisted for decades.[24]

Expansion of the Chinese restaurant led to adaptations beyond chop suey. Restaurant owners and chefs made sauces thicker so as to resemble the gravy texture of Western dishes, they substituted boneless meat for innards, and they developed batter-frying (little-known in Cantonese cooking) and sweet sauces (called sweet and sour but effectively without the sour). Chinese-American inventions became Chinese restaurant menu staples: egg rolls, shrimp toast, wonton soup, egg foo yong. Cantonese classics were removed from menus as they did not please American sensibilities: chicken feet, tofu, whole fish, gizzards, and the like.[25]

The second most successful immigrant cuisine was Italian. As with Chinese food, Italian dishes became popular beginning in the 1880s. After the Civil War, large numbers of immigrants arrived from southern Italy and Sicily, and by 1890 there were more than one hundred thousand Italian Americans in New York City alone, and their restaurants as a result proliferated.[26] The Italian restaurant began as a service to the immigrant community. Along with Italian boarding houses in neighborhoods such as East Harlem and Greenwich Village, these restaurants served a predominantly Italian clientele. In the late 1930s,

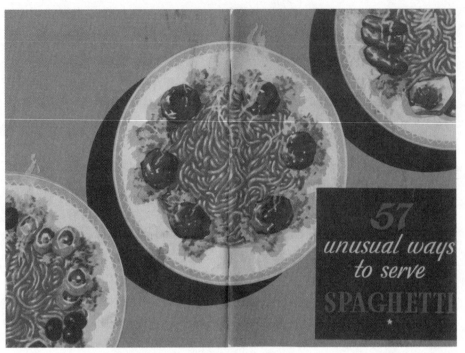

Heinz pamphlet, "57 Unusual Ways to Serve Spaghetti," 1950s. The company's slogan "57 Varieties" applied to spaghetti recipes using Heinz products.

most of the 757 Italian restaurants in New York had an immigrant clientele,[27] but by 1890 they rivaled Chinese establishments in general popularity.[28]

Italian food served in restaurants, especially those catering to American-born customers, bore only oblique resemblance to what was consumed in Italy. Large meatballs accompanied by spaghetti, eggplant Parmesan, marinara sauce (first mentioned in 1930), and ricotta cheesecake are all American inventions.[29] In other cases, as with tiramisù, an Italian innovation that remained obscure in the home country was wildly successful in the United States and then reexported to Italy. The most famous example of the reexport phenomenon is pizza, originally a Neapolitan street food that started to be made in the United States around 1900, and then transformed into an American staple after the Second World War. Until the 1960s, it was unknown in Italy outside of Naples, but subsequently it was adopted all over in its American version for tourists, and then started to be consumed universally.[30] Italian restaurant food in the United States, nevertheless, came closer than what was served at Chinese restaurants to reflecting what immigrant families actually cooked. Such preparations as tomato- and meat-based "Sunday Gravy" or the redundant "shrimp scampi" were Italian American household classics even if they were not familiar to anyone in Italy.[31]

The Bohemian element was especially significant in the acceptance and popularity of Italian food by the nonimmigrant population. In New York's Greenwich Village and San Francisco's North Beach, artists and writers lived alongside Italians and flocked to Italian restaurants for the inexpensive food, copious wine, and an ambience effectively marketed as irrepressible Latin spontaneity. Authenticity was conveyed by "Mamma" in the kitchen, a scratchy rendering of Caruso's voice from a Victrola, gondolas or Mediterranean scenes painted on the walls, a slightly comical staff, and picturesque staging. Renganeschi's and Maria del Prato's in Greenwich Village, and Sanguinetti's and Coppa's in San Francisco, were haunts of Bohemians and soon, of tourists.[32] Italian waiters and owners were often convivial, "colorful" characters. Gonfarone's in Greenwich Village created a plausible Italian gaiety and gustatory hedonism featuring a juggling waiter and a harmonica-playing busboy.[33]

For a time, Chinese restaurants too attempted to project a safe exoticism. The Celestial, a Chinese restaurant in Harlem, advertised in 1912 its "elaborate oriental style," with an orchestra and cabaret.[34] A Chinese night club called Forbidden City, established in 1939, was a San Francisco celebrity hangout; singers, magicians, comedians, and even strippers provided entertainment with an "oriental" flavor.

Eventually Chinese restaurants gave up extraneous entertainment and settled into an austere décor, enlivened only by red and gold dragons, but until just yesterday Italian restaurants preserved a raffish charm and arty nonconformity, complete with checked tablecloths and empty Chianti bottles holding dripping candles. Chinatown, like Greenwich Village, offered what was often considered a lamentable blurring of social boundaries, especially racial mixing. By the 1920s, however, Chinese, Italian and an increasing repertoire of other immigrant nationalities' restaurants attracted a middle-class clientele that followed the trail blazed by Bohemian pioneers, just as over the last forty years lawyers and bankers have succeeded artists in gentrifying urban neighborhoods.

Mexican food is the third member of the trinity responsible together for about 70 percent of all ethnic restaurants currently in the United States.[35] Unlike Chinese or Italian, Mexican food for Americans did not originate in New York or San Francisco. Its modern American inauguration was in San Antonio with mostly female street vendors who, by the 1880s, were known as "chili queens." Their stands were at first considered unhygienic and to be avoided by Anglos, but here the gap in time between Bohemian "discovery" and tourist trap was brief. One reporter wrote that while it would be a mistake to inquire too closely into how tamales were made, they possessed "too rare a deliciousness to be renounced on account of a trifle of dirt."[36] The vogue for chili con carne was unsuccessfully denounced by middle-class Mexicans and Mexican Americans as both inauthentic and unpleasantly sexual in its associations with female hucksters.[37]

Chili became the Mexican equivalent of chop suey or spaghetti with meatballs, but it came to be identified with cowboys and the Southwest generally more than with Mexico. Tacos, burritos, and the like were first Americanized by folkloric restaurants in California that tried to combine a colonial Spanish image with a more contemporary "Mexican" idea. In the 1930s, Olvera Street in downtown Los Angeles was developed by civic leaders as a souvenir of old, Spanish California. Many of the restaurants on and near Olvera Street presented themselves as Spanish, but the most successful, La Golondrina ("the Swallow"), was avowedly Mexican. Consuelo Castillo de Bonzo, an enterprising businesswoman of Mexican origin married to an Italian American, created La Golondrina. Named after a popular sentimental song of the 1880s, the restaurant served Mexican food. A number of features thereafter identified with Mexican restaurants got their start or at least maximum exposure here, notably tacos, enchiladas, and tamales with rice and beans heated together on a plate so as nearly to fuse.[38] After La Golondrina's success, Mexican restaurants became ubiquitous in California, the Southwest, and Texas but had little presence in the rest of the country before 1980 or so.

The first signature dish of what passed for Mexican food was the taco, popularized at fast food establishments, most importantly Taco Bell. This contrasts with Chinese and Italian restaurants which, despite the success of Panda Express and Olive Garden, are even now for the most part independent enter-

Kubla Khan Food Company billboard, 1960s. Company founders were committed to producing authentic fare sold in the US and exported to Asian markets; use of the term Orient in the advertisement reflects the era and the marketing of the time.

prises. Taco Bell was opened in 1952 by fast food entrepreneur Glen Bell in San Bernardino with the name Taco Tia. It based itself on both a Mexican stand and the assembly-line model of the original McDonalds, also in San Bernardino.

Glen Bell didn't actually invent the hard-shell, fast food taco, already developed by Mexican immigrant restaurateurs, but he did tailor it for a mass market. Nor was his the first chain of taco restaurants, an honor that belongs to Taco House, established in Los Angeles in 1946, but Bell certainly put tacos in a prominent place on the ethnic as well as fast food map. Unlike the futuristic golden-arched McDonald's, Taco Bell had a theme-park inspiration, the stands looking like mini-missions with a bell in the building's peaked center. Tacos were already a staple of northern Mexican border cuisine, but Bell and his imitators developed a product with cheddar cheese, sour cream, and other north-of-the-border ingredients, forging their own version of the same compromise between exotic and familiar seen in other ethnic foods.

As Mexican food expanded and split into slightly regional categories (Tex-Mex, New Mexico), other dishes were adopted and denatured for generic Anglo consumption. Burritos were another California contribution. Nachos were the creation of Ignacio "Nacho" Anaya at his Texas border café in the early 1940s. Fajitas first appeared in Tex-Mex restaurants in the late 1960s. The *faja* is a cow's diaphragm and was an ingredient in borderland barbecues. Tough in its normal butchered form, this cut was later labeled skirt steak and is now prized, the word "diaphragm," with its organ-meat implications having been effectively suppressed. The original fajitas were marketed simply as sliced sizzling spiced beef.[39]

Postwar Palates

In the aftermath of the Second World War, other cuisines, in addition to the Chinese-Italian-Mexican trio, became popular. Conventionally it is assumed that during the years between Prohibition and the liberalization of immigration laws in the late 1960s, ethnic restaurants offered laughably inauthentic food. Chinese restaurants served chop suey, chow mein, shrimp toast, and the like; Italian restaurants offered garlic bread in aluminum foil and minestrone soup heated from a can; while Mexican restaurants served combination platters (unknown in Mexico) slathered with sour cream. But in fact a lot changed between 1920 and 1970—the food desert had more oases than might first appear.

New kinds of restaurants were introduced, and as with their Chinese, Italian, and Mexican predecessors, they had to negotiate an unstable identity. A 1930 dining guide identified a New York restaurant called the Rajah as "Turkish (Parsee)" in style. "Upstairs," the guide's author observed, "you will find The Rajah, about as big as a medium-sized clothes-press, and not nearly as sanitary; but you're in Turkey now—and if you were terribly fussy, you wouldn't have gone to Turkey in the first place. Besides, the food is worth the trip." It gets even more peculiar:

> The table d'hote starts with Tamarind—a lemon-colored drink made from
> vegetables—as an appetizer. A watery, albeit true-to-type, native soup follows. Then the real business of the Turkish dinner sets in. Choose lamb,
> chicken, or beef curry—oh, such a fiery curry sauce! . . . You'll enjoy your
> dinner speculating about the other queer-looking diners, and learn, aston-

ishingly enough, that all sheiks don't wear goatees, ride white horses, and brandish swords.

Eventually the category of Indian restaurant was better defined, but this same restaurant, now called the India Rajah, continued to have trouble with outsiders' hazy understanding of tamarind. In his 1948 guidebook *Where to Eat in New York*, Robert Dana describes tamarind juice as "pomegranate nectar . . . a sweet beverage boiled from the tamarind roots that grow on Indian riverbanks."[40] Indian riverbanks or not, learning that there is such a thing as tamarind shows off a certain degree of knowledge.

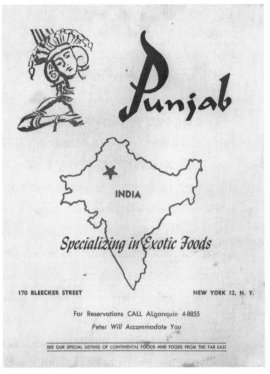

Menu from Punjab restaurant, New York City, 1930s. Here exotic foods include Italian specialties, French onion soup, and ham steak with Hawaiian sauce.

At times ethnic restaurants, including those offering Indian food, contributed to the confusion by venturing into uncertain, even comical globalization. A Greenwich Village spot called Punjab in the 1930s mingled conventional American dishes such as shrimp cocktail and London broil with curries, Chinese pepper steak, "escallop de vin, au Sherry," and "vitello scallopine a la Francaise." The drink suggestion accompanying "foods of the Far East" is "Try a King Size Martini."[41]

Despite a fair amount of comical misapprehension, Americans did become familiar with new cuisines, and much of this was due not to some natural process of osmosis, but the deliberate attempts by restaurateurs and associations to introduce new cuisines and dishes. A basic preparation could move from pariah status (i.e., only natives of the foreign country can appreciate it) to beloved, sushi being a dramatic example. As far back as the Meiji period, the late nineteenth century, Japanese chefs created food to appeal to Westerners, fare like teriyaki and sukiyaki (sliced steak with noodles and vegetables). So popular was sukiyaki that a Japanese hit song of 1960, "Ue O Muite Aruko" ("I Look at the Sky"), was introduced in the United States with the title "Sukiyaki." *Newsweek* remarked that this was like releasing "Moon River" in Japan as "Beef Stew."[42]

As opposed to sukiyaki or tempura, sushi and sashimi remained frighteningly alien. Newspaper columnists advised Americans to stick to sukiyaki and leave the raw fish for the native Japanese. An article in the *Los Angeles Times* in 1934 noted that white Americans often showed up at "Nipponese" restaurants where sushi was available, but "sukiyaki was the favorite." In 1958 a well-known Los Angeles columnist gave a recipe for sushi, which, he had been told, was something that might one day supplant the hot dog, but actually, "On second thought, but with the utmost politeness, I'll take a hot dog."[43]

The *Time-Life* series included a volume on the American "melting pot" of different immigrant cuisines. Published in 1971, its subchapter on "Oriental" restaurants is cautious about sushi. Granted, sushi and sashimi were being eaten by more and more Americans, but the editors noted that tempura and sukiyaki were already "on their way to being as 'American' as herring in sour cream." Nevertheless, at the beginning of the 1970s, sushi still required explanation ("a rice-and-raw-fish delicacy").[44]

By the 1970s, companies such as Japan Airlines had launched campaigns to wean Americans off an exclusive identification of Japanese food with sukiyaki and direct their attention to a wider range of options. One of the key steps in the acceptance of sushi was the discovery that raw tuna was easier to promote in the United States than any other fish. Even more important was the introduction of avocados to make the California roll. It's not as if avocados were ur-American either—they were adopted from Mexico and little known before 1900 or so, but they were an effective, inauthentic bridge toward acceptance of sushi. The invention of California rolls in the 1960s coincided with the opening of the first sushi restaurants catering to non-Japanese Americans. Sushi lends itself to combinations and innovations such as spicy tuna rolls or what the eminent food historian Anne Mendelson calls "multi-vegetable fantasies," fitting in perfectly with the American love of variety.[45]

Unlike most other American culinary fashions such as cupcakes or cronuts, sushi has the advantage of seeming to be nonfattening. In the 1990s, not only was sushi in the mainstream of American food choices, it was a teen favorite, appealing to this supposedly conformist and finicky food demographic. In the 1985 movie *The Breakfast Club*, sushi is embraced by the affluent girl but rejected by her less privileged fellows in detention. In 1995, *Clueless* shows sushi being served at a high school party without evoking any particular comment. A telling if unheralded moment in the culinary history of *The Sopranos* comes in Season 6 when, after years of scenes at home eating pasta, Tony and Carmela are shown dining on take-out sushi.

The example of sushi shows that restaurateurs do more than observe and respond to the whims and preferences of customers. The stories about Viceroy Li's visit and chop suey, for example, were circulated and publicized by Chinese entrepreneurs to promote dining out in Chinatown. The ubiquity of American Chinese restaurants must be due, in the end, to the appeal of the food, however contrived or ersatz it might seem in comparison with authentic Chinese culinary traditions. Granted, Chinese food is one of the world's most subtle and delightful cultural products, but there are historical and practical as well as aesthetic reasons for its global success.[46] That success is based on a different range of dishes depending on the host country—Indian Chinese (no pork, more hot spice), Peruvian Chinese (known as "chifa," incorporating Peruvian potatoes, pineapple and yellow pepper paste), or Indonesian Chinese food (with Dutch colonial elements)—and in each case there is a shaping and accommodation to religious laws, taste preferences, and other aspects of the majority culture.

Some things restaurants cannot readily control, however, among them the class image of a particular cuisine. Americans like variety, but they arrange the available options into different price and prestige categories that are not easy to change. In recent decades, Italian restaurants have been most successful at altering social hierarchical perceptions, breaking through the limitations of their former cheap, red sauce, checked-tablecloth image. Now high-end Italian restaurants are ubiquitous. Perhaps the point of inflection was the invention of pasta primavera in the 1970s at Le Cirque, an elite semi-Italian New York restaurant with a French name, or the opening of Lidia Bastianich's Felidia (also in New York) in 1981—elegant, authentic, Northern Italian, and hearty. As opposed to the cocktails, leather-bound menus, and velvet-flocked wallpaper of the postwar elegant subset, the current fine Italian restaurant offers regional specialization, gondola-free décor, white truffles grated onto your pasta or risotto for an extra $150, wines priced upward of $200, and other accoutrements of international high style.

Japanese restaurants also succeeded in polishing their image and prestige, consequently creating some fabulously expensive restaurants, but other cuisines have found it difficult to follow this path. While there are hundreds of luxury restaurants in China and Hong Kong, the American customer has imposed a low threshold on what prices can be demanded at Chinese restaurants. The effort to establish high-end Chinese restaurants has received new life recently, but La Chine in New York shut its doors after initial success because the Waldorf-Astoria hotel was closed for updating and then tied up in litigation involving its Chinese owners. Eight Tables in San Francisco, with a fixed-price, ten-course dinner for $225, has been accorded less than ecstatic acclaim.[47] In 2018, a Peking duck palace opened in New York by celebrity chef DaDong likewise met with skepticism.[48]

Accomplished chefs are not as tempted now as in the past by a career in America given the opportunities in China and a greater willingness there to spend serious money on food. It may be that travel to Italy has shown American tourists what fine Italian cuisine can be in a way that has not been duplicated for China, which remains more a business and group-tourism destination.[49]

Authenticity: The General Tso Problem

Ethnic restaurant owners in recent decades have been faced with the tricky challenge of balancing authenticity with comfort-zone familiarity; for example, the eventual decline of chop suey reflects gradual disillusionment with a dish long known to be inauthentic. Several factors interact to influence the trajectory of a popular foreign dish: the initial appeal of exotic food, the American desire to neutralize many of the foreign cuisine's distinctive features, and then a reaction against the perceived inauthenticity resulting from that very Americanization.

Pizza has some elements in common with chop suey: it is a poor-people's food so successfully adapted to American taste as to surpass all other forms of cooking imported from its native country. Pizza's growth was slower than that of chop suey, however. Although it was introduced at the beginning of the twentieth century, its mass popularity dates from after the Second World War. Unlike any Chinese dish, pizza has become a phenomenon in itself, with only tenuous connections to its home country, Italy, whereas chop suey was always identified with Chinese restaurants. Finally, pizza seems to be immortal, while chop suey started to die out in the 1950s, just as pizza with its multitude of toppings was spreading across the country.

Ethnic restaurateurs do not simply cook what they grew up with and wait for the cognoscenti to discover them. What informed diners want, however, is exactly that impression. They want to think that they are participating in something not for tourists. The central paradox of sophisticated tourism is that it has to appear not to be tourism at all but rather a creative form of exploration. The ambition to surpass the crowd means that discourses about hidden treasures of authenticity on the one hand and corruption of innocence on the other are intrinsic to restaurant reviews, now especially for online chatter on sites such as Yelp, Serious Eats, or Chowhound. The person making the post boasts about being the only outsider ("everyone else was Asian"; "no one spoke English") or declares a former shrine to be spoiled by crowds of foodies (here meaning people who follow culinary fashions).[50] "Spoiled" or "ruined" might mean that there are too many tourists or that the food isn't spicy anymore. Marks of authenticity might include the *absence* of inauthentic clichés on the menu. According to a Yelp post, if no drunken noodles appear on a Thai menu, it is worth trekking out to Queens to visit it.[51]

Culinary explorers may be unaware that the paths were discreetly cleared and made enticing before their "discoveries." Once a nonnative clientele becomes important, the food will inevitably be altered. The women who run Central American food trucks in Brooklyn's Red Hook neighborhood have added vegetables to Salvadorian pupusas because, as one of them told an interviewer, "That's what *blanquitos* [white people] expect." For decades, when Red Hook was impoverished and isolated, these women prepared meals on the edge of soccer fields where their friends and relatives were playing. Once an IKEA store was constructed in Red Hook and a ferry from Manhattan started running, the customer base changed—and so did the food.[52]

Customers and restaurateurs undergo a process of mutual adjustment. The former must recognize a cuisine as interesting or worth cultivating and then learn rudimentary vocabulary and customs: how to eat spaghetti, how to put wasabi on sushi, or the difference between naan and chapatis. Restaurant owners and chefs have to inform clients about what is, at the start, a strange cuisine and balance the clients' desires for new sensations with the undertow of familiarity—spicy but not too spicy; mu shu pork but not chicken feet; vegetables in the pupusas.

The equilibrium between easy to understand and inauthentic can break down or be transformed. At some point in postwar America, even suburban, middle-class Americans became disillusioned with chop suey, and it began to disappear in the 1960s. It had been long suspected that chop suey was unknown in China, at least in its American form, but for a long time, no one apart from a few sophisticates minded.[53] As early as 1924, the *Los Angeles Times* reported that chop suey was not Chinese, a finding repeated four years later in two *New York Times* articles.[54] By 1948, Lawton Mitchell, a self-described "veteran gourmet," praised Lee's on Pell Street for its "Cantonese traditionals, such as are feasted on in China, where chop suey (San Francisco invention) is unknown."[55] In the 1950s, when the celebrated newspaper columnist Herb Caen asked for chop suey at an elegant restaurant in San Francisco, the owner, Johnny Kan, told him, "We only serve Chinese food here."[56]

Yesterday's savoir faire becomes today's comical ignorance. In the 1970s, everyone knew that chop suey was inauthentic, but General Tso's chicken rode the wave of enthusiasm for Sichuan and Hunan food to become iconic, and then gradually it too lost prestige as the fact that it is unknown in China became clear to Americans. By 2000, General Tso's chicken was the butt of as many jokes as chop suey before it.[57] Its current status resembles that of chop suey for much of the mid-twentieth century: acknowledged as inauthentic, but, as we've already had occasion to ask, so what?

"So what" for some, but for urban sophisticates, hipsters, chowhounds, millennials, or whatever category this identifiable group falls into, the suspicion that one is not maximizing authenticity is a persistent anxiety. Rather than just providing a place of culinary entertainment, ethnic restaurants are a challenge to customers no longer content with popular clichés such as General Tso's chicken or clams casino. The well-informed seek out authentic cuisine, which may require access to an often mysterious code. Calvin Trillin wrote a typically hilarious essay in 1983 about trying to decipher the (to him) baffling signs posted in Chinese on the walls of restaurants that promise delicious and authentic dishes. The frustration increases when the waiter's response to a request to translate is a dismissive "you no like."[58] New York restaurant directories in the 1990s, such as Robert Sietsema's *Good & Cheap Ethnic Eats,* offered solutions to such problems, showing the diner how to order authentic dishes in unfamiliar surroundings.[59]

Even when hunted down, authenticity is fragile. Right from the beginning of the popularity of international restaurants, there was concern that they tend to become spoiled and so rendered less authentic. At first this was more a question of ambiance than cuisine. In *Bohemian San Francisco*, Clarence Edwards recalled the scene before the great earthquake of 1906 when Italian restaurants such as Buon Gusto and Fior d'Italia "appealed to the Bohemian spirit through their good cooking, absence of conventionality, together with the inexpensiveness of the dinners." He laments that Sanguinetti's, once a delightful place of Bohemian festivity, was now patronized by tourists sent there by hotel guides.[60] This sense that spontaneity has been smothered by the masses is a constant preoccupation of ethnic restaurant patrons. Edwards was not worried about the food as much as the atmosphere, but the two would be linked: fake food coincided with staged gaiety.

Signs of authenticity, on the other hand, are all over websites such as Yelp or Chowhound. As already noted, "there were no other Americans there" is a favorite. Another indication of innocent sincerity is that the menu had errors in English or, better yet, there was no English menu. Restaurant owners are aware of these sentiments and sometimes cater to them. Jason Wang, the owner of the small chain Xi'an Famous Foods, at one time deliberately hired cashiers who don't know English, because "that's more authentic."[61]

The price of authenticity is that you can no longer order spaghetti with meatballs on the side if your main course is risotto. The cultivated customer respects the rules of cuisine, an unfamiliar act in a society that values choice above all else. Of course, the truly successful enterprise is one that provides authenticity but variation as well. The high end of the gourmet hierarchy has some of this: David Chang's Momofuku Noodle Bar in New York and his other restaurants offer variations on noodle dishes, soups, fried chicken, and other preparations that partake of a hyperauthentic Korean or Chinese aesthetic, but his creations would be unfamiliar in those countries.

The array of American ethnic restaurants reflects changes in economics, politics, patterns of migration, and the leisure side of globalization. This is not a passive process but rather involves "managed hybridity"—the creation of certain kinds of options, combinations, and adjustments between the attractive exotic and the easily saleable and scalable. In 2008, for example, Michael Solomonov and Steven Cook created the Israeli restaurant Zahav in Philadelphia, offering a lively, high-quality take on Middle Eastern food, but they had to throw out their first hyperauthentic model. The food was confusing to American diners, both in taste combinations and in vocabulary. Without sacrificing the flavors and origins of what is already an eclectic cuisine drawn from many parts of the world, Solomonov and Cook tweaked dishes in ways reminiscent of the earlier observation that *blanquitos* expect vegetables in pupusas. They prepared beet tahini without yogurt or goat cheese mixed in, but added lemon juice and garlic; haloumi cheese was served with dates and walnuts to provide a sweet and salty combination that Americans like.[62]

✦   ✦   ✦

UP TO THIS POINT, we've tracked three long-term trends: the eclipse of regional food, the rise of an industrial system, and the notion that variety livens up an otherwise boring culinary landscape. All these firmly entrenched developments started to face challenges in the 1970s and 1980s, which witnessed a rediscovery of natural taste and of seasonal, local, and heirloom products.

We will next look at what happened after the high point of the standardized, brand-name, supermarket, and fast-food universe. The zenith coincides with the 1970s, a decade that also saw the start of a transformation and revival of American tastes and older traditions.

FOOD FADS AND FASHIONS FROM THE LATE NINETEENTH TO EARLY TWENTY-FIRST CENTURIES

1880s

Angel food cake
Boston cream pie
Gumbo (not just in New Orleans)

1890s

Devil's food cake
Waldorf salad
Croquettes
Deviled eggs
Club sandwich (first mentioned at the Union Club, New York, in 1889
    and the clubhouse of the Saratoga racetrack in 1894)
Chafing dish preparations
Chili con carne

1900s

Chop suey, chow mein
Hot dogs
Lady Baltimore cake (made popular by Owen Wister's 1906 novel,
    Lady Baltimore, in which the protagonist has cake in a tearoom in
    Charleston, South Carolina)

1910s

Welsh rarebit

Spaghetti (moves from Italian to mainstream—canned spaghetti widely
available)

Turkey Tetrazzini

1920s

Green goddess salad dressing (created at Palace Hotel, San Francisco,
and named after a play starring George Arliss that opened in New
York in 1921)

Cobb salad (first served at the Brown Derby in Hollywood)

Ice box cake

Pecan pie (rather surprisingly, no recipe exists before the 1920s according
to McLean, *Cooking in America*, 167)

Congealed salads (and other aspics made from gelatin)

Caesar salad (invented by Caesar Cardini at his restaurant, Caesar's, in
Tijuana)

S'mores (first made popular by a section of recipes entitled "Some More"
in *Tramping and Trailing with the Girl Scouts*, 1927)

Pineapple upside-down cake

Marshmallows (in salads, on sweet potato casseroles, in desserts)

French dip sandwich (supposedly invented by Philippe Mathieu at his
restaurant Philippe's in Los Angeles in 1918)

1930s

Creamed chipped beef

Tiki restaurants (made famous by Don the Beachcomber; Trader Vic's)

Sukiyaki

1940s

Chiffon cakes

Carrot cake

Crêpes suzette

Vichyssoise (invented by Louis Diat, chef of the Ritz-Carlton Hotel in
New York)

1950s

Garlic bread

Key lime pie

Three-bean salad

Cooking on an outdoor grill (called a "barbecue" outside the South)

Red velvet cake

Fondue

Chicken divan

Smorgasbord (especially Swedish meatballs)

Moussaka

1960s

Beef Wellington

Cheese balls (especially port wine–flavored cheddar spread, rolled in
    chopped nuts)

Rumaki

Teriyaki

1970s

Crêpes

Quiche Lorraine

Pasta primavera (invented by Sirio Maccioni of Le Cirque)

Lemon bars

Baked goat cheese salad

Freshly ground pepper offered at restaurants for salad, pasta, anything

Salad bars

Introduction of the term *pasta* to replace *spaghetti* and *macaroni*

Szechwan restaurants

Hunan restaurants

1980s

Squid ink linguini

Ranch dressing (invented by Steve Henson, who marketed it as "Hidden
    Valley Ranch Dressing." Cool Ranch Doritos were introduced in
    1986, extending ranch dressing flavor beyond salad.)

Arugula

Gourmet pizza
Blackened redfish
Sushi
Salsa
Kiwi fruit
Raspberry vinegar
Angel hair pasta
Red peppercorns
Pasta salad
Sun-dried tomatoes
White-chocolate mousse
Tiramisù

1990s

Asian fusion
Bruschetta
Balsamic vinegar
Molten chocolate cake (invented by Jean-Georges Vongerichten)
Vertical (i.e., stacked) food
Focaccia

2000s

Farm-to-table/locavore becomes the general rule
Craft beer
Revival (in higher-quality guise) of hamburgers, pork, barbecue

2010s

Quinoa
Kale
Sriracha
Kimchi
Cronut (invented by Dominique Ansel Bakery in New York)
Craft whiskey

Sylvia Lovegren, *Fashionable Food: Seven Decades of Food Fads* (Chicago: University of Chicago Press, 1995); Alice L. McLean, *Cooking in America, 1840–1945* (Westport, CT: Greenwood, 2006); Stella Parks, *BraveTart: Iconic American Desserts* (New York: W. W. Norton, 2017); Tony Hendra, "The 1970s: A Dynamite *Spy* Boogie-Down Celebration of the Most Embarrassing Decade of the Twentieth Century," *Spy*, Dec. 1988, 82–93; Megan J. Elias, *Food on the Page: Cookbooks and American Culture* (Philadelphia: University of Pennsylvania Press, 2017); *Gourmet* 51, no. 1 (January 1991), the fiftieth anniversary issue.

PART III:

THE GREAT TRANSFORMATION?

CHAPTER 9

The Magical 1970s

Unbeknownst at the time, the decade of the 1970s was the turning point in the modern history of American cuisine. Perhaps this era of paisley and polyester, of shag carpets and avocado-colored kitchen appliances, deserves *Spy* magazine's dismissive epithet "the stupid decade."[1] It certainly has a lot to answer for as yuppie self-absorption and free spending replaced youthful 1960s idealism. Not for nothing did Tom Wolfe dub the 1970s the "Me Decade."[2] Despite its ill-advised popular-culture innovations and virulent narcissism, the decade is crucially important for initiating the women's liberation and gay rights movements. The 1970s also witnessed dramatically unfunny events, such as the American defeat in Vietnam, the Watergate scandal, two energy crises, and the first modern terrorist attack at the Munich Olympics. Political upheaval, economic limits, and a looming sense of a grim ecological future crushed the naïve ebullience of the 1960s.

In culinary terms, the 1970s marked the nadir of American cuisine but also saw an incremental but persistent upturn, the beginning of reconstruction after the devastation created by processed food and national standardization. Tentative rehabilitation centered on the rediscovery of basic, natural ingredients. The current farm-to-table movement, with its emphasis on seasonal and local products, is based on ideas of taste and freshness that surfaced in the 1970s, going against the homogenization of American food consumption. A few rebels led significant but at first barely visible shifts toward a rediscovery of flavor instead of preoccupation with health, convenience, modernity, efficiency, and other extraneous concerns that had dominated the previous decades of the twentieth century.

Magical or Stupid?

With the triumph of standardized, processed food, the 1970s mark the total eclipse of regional cuisine. New conveniences such as the microwave oven perpetuated even further a pattern of food consumption based on sameness and efficiency. However, there was also a widely diffused countercultural indictment of the food industry. A critique of American food gained strength based not just on health or environmental anxieties, but on a radically new aesthetic of pleasure: food ought to be judged by how it tastes, not just according to dubious health criteria. Making sensuality a priority was revolutionary because it broke with a century of misleading guidance about food reform and created a positive resistance to the food industry rather than negative ecological abstemiousness.

The significance of the 1970s might seem counterintuitive because it was experienced at the time as a disappointing period by political activists after the high expectations of the revolutionary late 1960s. The optimism of the Civil Rights Movement and giddiness of the Age of Aquarius were over, but African American political and cultural agitation was not suppressed, while alternative lifestyle practices, from waterbeds to long hair for men, became common beyond the confines of Haight-Ashbury and the East Village. The Watergate crisis, the failure of Lyndon Johnson's Great Society programs to relieve poverty and end discrimination, and the Vietnam debacle eroded trust in political authorities and experts. Perhaps more than anything, the failure of grand political and social transformations in the 1960s meant a turn toward the personal: "the personal is political," as one slogan had it or, in the words of the Beatles' song "Revolution," "You better free your mind instead."

Changes in food consumption resulted from channeling revolutionary idealism in new, safer directions. If the world was not going to be immediately transformed, one could at least lead a more authentic life. The effects of what seemed in the early 1970s like fringe ideas such as organic agriculture or vegetarianism are still unfolding today, with questions like where does food come from, why it is wasted, and how can we cultivate it sustainably? Most significantly, the "stupid decade" belies this contemptuous nickname when it comes to rediscovering the importance of taste.

A Sense of Loss

The vivid but obsolete take of the *Time-Life* cookbook series on American culinary bounty was succeeded by the neoregionalism of Jane and Michael Stern, who acknowledged the overall decline while still picking out oases of resistance. From this point on, regional cuisine was no longer celebrated as a vibrant tradition but rather portrayed as endangered, or already extinct. For example, Edna Lewis's *The Taste of Country Cooking* (1976) interwove with its stories a gentle lament for the lost flavors of locally cultivated and foraged products of fields, woods, and smokehouses. Lewis evoked a time not so long ago when food was part of the community, neighbors borrowing setting hens (those ready to brood over eggs) if their own were late, or helping with hog butchering.[3] By 1976, the Freetown of her memories was a vanished civilization. The past was definitively past, but the book was influential, asserting as it did that ingredients matter, that local ingredients are best, and that cooking is an expression of affection and neighborliness. In tone the book is partly mournful, partly inspirational.

For the time being, saving or cataloguing a threatened heritage was paramount. Under the title *Fading Feast*, the *New York Times* reporter Raymond Sokolov recounted stories of endangered redoubts of traditional foods, places where real Key limes grow and people learned in childhood how to prepare terrapin, squirrel, or whitefish.[4] In 1978, when the Sterns published the first version of *Roadfood*, traditional regional food could be described as flourishing only if you defined grilled cheese sandwiches as charmingly authentic.[5] The guardians of American folkways were no longer farmers or mountaineers, but salvage experts trained in the liberal arts, like the Sterns. American traditions were under siege in their original form but taken up by newcomers. By the 1970s, bluegrass music was no longer played by Appalachian folk sitting on their front porches but by college graduates at festivals.

The mediocrity of American food was evidenced by the decline of regionalism and the encroachment of McDonald's, but also at the pseudo-sophisticated end by the popularity of Continental cuisine, mass-market food served in elegant surroundings with snobbish ostentation. Fancy dishes such as steak Diane, chicken Kiev (when you pierced the breaded crust, butter—or, more likely, margarine—spilled out), and shrimp scampi were prepared from frozen ingredients. In *American Fried* (1974), Calvin Trillin memorably ridiculed Continental restaurants and the idea that fine European food could be found outside of New York, San Francisco, and maybe one or two other places. For the rest of the country, he preferred Kansas City barbecue and other specialties of the American interior, a revolutionary and paradoxical attitude, but he made no effort to show that these represented old-fashioned home cooking.[6]

Trillin preferred to look on the positive side, but others were angry at the hegemony of the processed food industry and the connivance of "gourmets" who pretended that frozen food was wonderful or that America was teeming with great restaurants. An uncompromising denunciation of the state of American food came from John and Karen Hess with the publication in 1977 of *The Taste of America*, the food-world equivalent of Allen Ginsberg's 1956 poem *Howl*. As with Ginsberg's passionate attack on American conformity and obliviousness, *The Taste of America* blamed corporations and an all-too-willing population of zombies who accepted the life-denying tenets of what was touted as modernity. The authors sounded a tocsin about the state of American cooking comparable to Rachel Carson's *Silent Spring* with regard to environmental Armageddon.

For the Hesses, the pathetic state of American food was the result of a food industry conspiracy bolstered by soi-disant gourmet experts. The corporate imperatives for economy of scale, durability, and color had destroyed the flavor of meat, fruit, and vegetables. People had forgotten what these things were supposed to taste like, and the lullaby that had put them into gastronomic lassitude was sung by a chorus of women's magazines, their advertisers, and elite arbiters of taste. Kraft, Heinz, McDonald's, and other usual suspects were denounced, but the Hesses were even angrier at the "gourmet plague" spread by chefs and food writers who cheerfully colluded with the degradation of American tastes.[7]

Portrayed as vain and easily flattered, Craig Claiborne was infatuated with French food and ignored the actual mediocrity of what passed for haute cuisine in the United States. The Hesses also ridiculed James Beard for profiting handsomely from food industry advertising. His endorsements for Shasta soft drinks, Adolph's meat tenderizer and other meretricious items discredited his self-appointed role as defender of American gusto and authenticity

The Taste of America called attention to the precipitous decline in the quality of basic products and exposed as comical the claims of expensive restaurants and high-end cookbooks that presented inferior ingredients dressed up with fancy names. The book was a jeremiad against the state of the American palate, blaming not historical imprints like our alleged Puritan heritage, but rather mass ignorance about what food should be and once had been.

According to the Hesses, America's natural riches had created a refined and sensuous cuisine that reached its peak around 1850. The country was sufficiently developed at that time for New Yorkers to enjoy game from forests and prairies or terrapin from the Chesapeake, but not yet oriented toward standard brands and bland predictability. The authors encapsulated the current (1977) situation with the example of President Gerald Ford, who regarded both eating and sleeping as "a waste of time." Calling attention to what he regarded as his virtuous Midwestern austerity, the president boasted of his unvarying lunch of cottage cheese with a sliced onion or quartered tomato, sprinkled with A.1. Sauce and followed by a scoop of butter-pecan ice cream.[8]

We now realize that while the Hesses despaired, there were encouraging new developments. These are not easily described, for it is not as if on one day chefs and food leaders woke up and spontaneously and simultaneously discovered local, seasonal dining. Something like this, however, is the standard historical narrative.[9] In *Provence, 1970*, for example, Luke Barr argues that during this specific summer, American chefs and writers turned from simply embracing France as a gastronomic model, *tout court,* to drawing lessons that could be applied to the American culinary school. M. F. K. Fisher, James Beard, and Julia Child had been inspired by the French ethos and practice regarding the delights of food. All were in Provence that summer of 1970, and their interlocking experiences supposedly convinced them to mobilize a "reinvention of American taste" emphasizing freshness, simplicity, and sensuousness."[10] This is a little too neat, as if cuisine reform was a type of Manhattan Project developed in the painter Richard Olney's Provence kitchen. In fact, these chefs and food writers had different agendas in 1970 and after.

Another narrative credits Alice Waters and Chez Panisse with bringing about a "delicious revolution" by which taste was returned to the center, but now allied with simplicity, health, and terroir. No one can say that Alice Waters has lacked attention or been underappreciated. That attention, however, is merited, for she, more than the older gourmands of *Provence, 1970*, really did appropriate a French food aesthetic to change American cuisine. Inspired by her French experiences, Waters launched Chez Panisse in 1971 as yet another reiteration of French cuisine, a refuge from American mediocrity. Unlike other restaurateurs, however, she cared passionately about the quality and flavor of primary ingredients. The restaurant changed in the late 1970s and early 1980s, leading to a reinvention of American cuisine on the basis of seasonality, high-quality ingredients, and locavore dining.

The food revolution that commenced in the 1970s has multiple origins. The decade was in many ways harsh and disappointing, a period of political conflict, economic stagnation, and cultural disillusionment that gave rise to trends that progressives, including locavore chefs, do not approve of, from Reaganomics to Pop-Tarts. Rather than picking out those new developments that meet our approval while discarding the rest, it is worth looking at both the good and bad aspects to see how a rejuvenated American taste emerged from the bleak reality of fast and frozen food. What follows begins with a key shift that seemed, at first, to be happening off-stage, a crisis in French cuisine that would end its centuries-old authority over defining fine food. Two American social trends also emerged at this time, the women's movement and the assertion of gay rights. Two other major developments are the diffusion of the microwave oven and the rapid expansion of fast food chains. The microwave took over the American kitchen and fast food controlled the highway off-ramps. The final section then considers culinary movements that combated standardization. What was derisively dismissed as hippie food turns out to have exerted an outsize influence, as would the experiments undertaken by restaurants such as Chez Panisse, the

Quilted Giraffe, or K-Paul's, all of which sought to rediscover primary ingredients, seasons, sensuality, and, above all, taste.

The Waning of French Authority

At the beginning of the 1970s, France still defined international haute cuisine, much as it had since the eighteenth century, when it developed a new style dubbed "the art of cooking foods delicately." A lighter approach emphasizing the taste of primary ingredients triumphed over a complicated medieval style based on spices, vivid colors, and ostentation. With the French innovators of the seventeenth century, European herbs replaced imported Asian spices; rich, buttery sauces drove out acidic or sweet and spicy ones; sugar was reserved for the last course. The reform movement in ancien régime France aimed to simplify cuisine and to intensify the natural taste of ingredients. Statements such as "a cabbage soup should taste entirely of cabbage" or "each food in its natural taste is more agreeable" signaled a return to vivid primary tastes rather than multiple sensations. The birth of what became modern French cuisine was an attempt to restore the authentic flavor and natural beauty of ingredients.[11]

If this sounds a lot like the "nouvelle cuisine" of the 1970s, it is no accident. France has experienced cycles alternating radical culinary simplification and increasing complexity. By the mid-eighteenth century, observers of the food scene already complained that clear, simple tastes were being overlaid by elaborate sauces and showy and unnecessary rare ingredients. In the 1740s, a chef and food writer named François Marin exalted his "modern cuisine" as "less fussy, simpler, more hygienic and perhaps more scientific."[12] This is exactly the program of the progressive French chefs 130 years later. The "Ten Commandments of La Nouvelle Cuisine" by the food journalists Henri Gault and Christian Millau, issued from Mount Sinai in 1973, included dicta such as:

Thou shall use fresh, quality products.
Thou shall lighten thy menu.
Thou shall seek out what the new techniques can bring you.
Thou shall not ignore dietetics.[13]

Something New — For You!

"LES HORS D'OEUVRES COMME EN FRANCE"

Hors d'oeuvre tray service in your room . . . you may now enjoy freshly prepared appetizers in your room . . . and then visit our beautiful dining car for the finest meal service — anywhere!

The following tray will serve one or two . . . check below number of trays desired and give this to your Pullman Porter—he will see that service is arranged:

Shrimp with Special Sauce
Celery stuffed with Roquefort Cheese
Olives stuffed with Pimentos
Kaukauna Club Cheese
Cocktail Franks
Deviled Egg, halved
Rye Rounds

ILLINOIS CENTRAL RAILROAD
A SIGN OF SERVICE

Number of trays desired .... ($2.50 per tray).

Illinois Central train card, "Les hors d'oeuvres comme en France," early 1960s. Illinois Central Pullman (sleeping compartment) passengers could order typically 1960s American hors d'oeuvres, just as in France.

If 1970s nouvelle cuisine had been merely another historical turn of the wheel of French culinary revolutions, it would have no place in this narrative. Its global importance is that it undermined France's centuries-long culinary authority, and then its program was exported to receptive countries such as the United States. Paradoxically, a French reform destroyed French domination, a little bit similar to the effect of attempts by Mikhail Gorbachev to update the Soviet regime. An additional paradox is that despite the short career of the original French movement, nouvelle cuisine in its basic principles fundamentally changed how people eat everywhere.[14]

By the time of the late-1960s social upheavals, French gastronomy seemed stagnant, immured in an orthodoxy of fancy sauces, foie gras, and truffles, with inferior ingredients passed off on uninformed diners lulled into submission by the appearance of luxury and the unthinking worship of tradition. Gault and Millau and the chefs they promoted proposed food that was lighter. This meant sauces made without butter, reduced cooking times, and a Japanese-inspired minimalism. Plating in the kitchen emphasized color instead of elaborate tableside carving and serving of complicated dishes and sauces. Rather than trying to emulate the models set down by the great chefs of the past such as Antonin Carême in the nineteenth and Auguste Escoffier in the twentieth centuries, the modern chef, according to Gault and Millau, must be inventive. In nouvelle cuisine the chef was an *auteur*, a master of surprise, change, and artistry.[15]

Of course, great chefs had never been mere slaves to tradition. At the Ritz, Escoffier had served what would now be called a signature dish of "duckling en cocotte." At his restaurant La Pyramide in Vienne, the greatest chef of the mid-twentieth century, Fernand Point, was famous for a gratin of crayfish tails and *poularde de Bresse en vessie* (Bresse guinea hen cooked with truffles in a pig's bladder). Stars of the new cuisine in the 1970s created renowned dishes like salmon in sorrel sauce (the brothers Troisgros) and truffle soup Élysée Palace (Paul Bocuse), but the real novelty was the cult of innovation itself, because with that, the chef was no longer a master craftsman but an unpredictable, creative genius.

The most influential exponent of nouvelle cuisine was Paul Bocuse. This is ironic since before 1980, Bocuse, sensing the waning of a fashion, had already ridiculed the excesses of its followers.[16] His importance was in his fame, not in what he actually cooked. In August 1975, Bocuse was the first chef ever to appear on the cover of *Newsweek*. He was born and died in the same house in Collonges-au-Mont-d'Or in Lyon, where his namesake restaurant was located, but during the height of his long career, Bocuse traveled constantly and created a global restaurant empire. He expertly used the media to promote himself. Defending his avidity for publicity, he remarked that after all, "God is already famous, but that doesn't stop the priest from ringing the church bells every morning."[17] Bocuse's overweening self-confidence was the expression not merely of a master technician, but of a personality, a brand, and this has become the basis of modern celebrity in the food world. The irony is that the French native

Paul Bocuse, 1926–2018, the first modern celebrity chef.

blazed a publicity trail followed by American chefs—who then abandoned French cuisine.

The most elegant restaurants in the United States in the 1970s were French, and this went back a long way.[18] The first real restaurant in America was Julien's Restorator in Boston, established by a French chef in 1790; Thomas Jefferson demanded that his slave chef, James Hemmings, cook French food. The first nationally famous restaurant, Delmonico's, opened in 1830 as a French restaurant, and it set an example for all high-end establishments throughout the nineteenth century. In the mid-twentieth century, Le Pavillon in New York was universally regarded as the leading restaurant in the country.[19]

The prestige of French cuisine was hardly confined to the United States. In Mexico City, the Maison Dorée was the fanciest restaurant during the late nineteenth century, at a time when the Hermitage was the leading restaurant in Moscow and the Union Hotel served the best (French) food in Melbourne.[20]

At the 1861 coronation dinner for King Wilhelm I of Prussia, the menu was entirely French and included "Poulardes de Mans à la Toulouse," "Timbales à la Talleyrand," and "Foie Gras en Bellevue."[21] A century later, the finest restaurants in London were Mirabelle, Le Caprice, and La Gavroche, while elegant hotels like the Savoy, the Ritz, and the Connaught served French food as well.

French cuisine was oddly but distinctly important in colonial capitals as a symbol of European civilization, contrasting with what Europeans regarded as colorful but inferior "native" food. A typical meal served in 1910 at the grand Hotel des Indes in Batavia, Dutch East Indies (now Jakarta, Indonesia), reveals no concession to the cuisine or climate of Java: "Consommé Montmorency," "Filet de Boeuf Garni à la Châtelaine," "Filet de Soles à l'Amiral," and "Escalopes de Ris de Veau à la Villeroy."[22]

At first, nouvelle cuisine did not change anything very obvious in the United States. Although American high-end restaurants embraced the beautiful plates and high prices model and even a few of the commandments that encouraged artistry and innovation, nouvelle cuisine's impact was only tangentially related to the discovery of American ingredients and a revivified American cuisine. Indirectly, the movement's teachings about preparing the best ingredients available conformed with the rediscovery of seasonal and local food. Its judicious breaking with traditions of rich sauces or complicated, fussed-over food was in keeping with the innovations of American chefs.

Los Angeles, where lightness and beauty of presentation have always been de rigueur, was a pioneer in the American adaptation of French nouvelle cuisine. In particular, Jean Bertranou's L'Ermitage in West Hollywood embraced the new culinary movement in the mid-1970s. Bertranou may have been the first chef in the United States to insist on delicate, real haricots verts instead of the woody domestic string beans and, like Alice Waters and Jeremiah Tower at Chez Panisse, he had to go to great lengths to find duck that didn't taste like tough, overcooked chicken. At Ma Maison in LA, Patrick Terrail and his Austrian-born chef, Wolfgang Puck, were creating what Terrail described in 1975 as "California nouvelle cuisine."[23]

The significant effects of nouvelle cuisine, however, were indirect. It destabilized the reputation of French cuisine, undermining the long-standing power of

MENU

Hors d'Oeuvres Varié.

Consommé Montmorency.

Filet de Soles
à l'Amiral.

Filet de Boeuf Garni
à la Chatelaine.

Escalopes de Ris de Veau
à la Villeroy.

Sorbets Sicilienne.

Chaud-Froid de Volaille
„en Bellevue"

Salade.

Gâteau Fantasie.

Glace Nesselrode.

Fruits—Dessert—Café.

HOTEL „DES INDES."

BATAVIA, 19 Mars 1910.

Menu from the Hotel des Indes, Batavia, 1910. As the premier hotel of the Dutch East Indies, the Hotel des Indes offered international French cuisine. A similar menu could be found in any great city of the world at the time.

France to define and enforce culinary codes. Up to the 1970s, chefs had to follow French ordinances if they wanted to be taken seriously as creators of high-end food. Additionally, the eclecticism of French nouvelle cuisine, which gingerly allowed for Asian flavors and new ingredients such as vanilla or maple syrup, was a cue for Americans to indulge an already strong impulse toward experimentation, rule-breaking, and an anything-goes attitude about food.

But before pursuing these implications for New American cuisine, we must consider social developments in the United States that created spaces for all manner of lifestyle experimentation, including those related to food.

The Women's Movement and the Suburban Awakening

The culinary fashions of the 1970s are not directly related to changes in gender attitudes and sexuality—sushi and squid-ink linguine have hardly anything to do with agitation for the Equal Rights Amendment—but discussions of the place of cooking in women's new awareness meant changes in cuisine that long outlasted the fad for white chocolate mousse.

The food consumed in the 1950s and early, prerevolutionary 1960s may not have conformed to current tastes, but most of it was cooked at home and by women. The television image of the average family presented by advertising was never sociologically accurate. Many more women worked for pay than one would have guessed from watching the domestic television idylls portrayed by advertisers, mini-dramas in which housewives confronted crises like ring around the collar or children sulking over pot roast. In 1963, the same year that Julia Child's cooking show debuted, Betty Friedan in *The Feminine Mystique* identified what she called "the problem that has no name," the fatigue and discontent felt by women trapped in a domestic and subordinate role.[24] Advertisements presented a cheery, ultra-modern kitchen, promising personal fulfillment through subordination to male domestic ideals, but Friedan argued that an inner voice told women they needed and deserved more than tending a home, husband, and children. Not only was *The Feminine Mystique* a best seller, it was surprisingly well received by the media, partly because Friedan was not the first to describe the dark side of middle-class women's lives.[25] Friedan's success was also

Betty Friedan, 1921–2006. Friedan wrote *The Feminine Mystique*, 1963, a critique of female subordination and suburban life.

aided by fortuitous good timing, coinciding as it did with the dynamism of the Civil Rights Movement. Her work was appealing for its lively, first-person style of writing that owed much to the author's journalism background.

Friedan analyzed the false promises of technologically aided housework. Married middle-class women were imprisoned in lonely, boring, suburban domesticity, performing repetitive tasks that advertisers portrayed as creative accomplishments or as contests, as in "Whose linoleum floor is the cleanest?" Friedan demonstrated the manipulation of housewives in order to sell them dubious conveniences that did not, in fact, save them time, along with denatured, high-profit food such as instant coffee and precooked meals. Most women inadvertently created more work for themselves, moving from compact apartments to cavernous suburban houses, undertaking new kinds of drudgery in which their days were busy with decorating and cleaning a larger space, driving kids and husband to school and the train, waiting for the plumber, and other mindless tasks. As one of Friedan's chapter titles has it, "Housewifery Expands to Fill the Time Available."[26]

Friedan's final chapter offered a way out. Entitled "A New Life Plan for Women," it laid out a better world in which women would assert themselves as fully equal human beings, not as petty rulers of an impoverished, female realm. At a personal level, the logical lesson taken from this was for women to leave domesticity in favor of paid labor. The numbing routine of cooking, cleaning, errand-running, childcare, and suburban socializing was to be replaced by accomplishments in the public space of work. The opposition between feminist and housewife was the core of the second-wave feminist program that got going in the 1970s.[27]

To the extent that more women were entering the workforce, many taking on demanding professional jobs with unpredictable hours, cooking had to change. The change, however, was not in a revolutionary direction that freed women from housework, but rather in accentuating already-existing trends pioneered by the food industry. Convenience was marketed less as a sign of push-button modernity and more as a defense for the time-besieged working woman. Instead of the happy housewife gliding down the piano keys with Lemon Pledge or gossiping with friends over canned fruit salad, serious and stressed women were being rescued from chaos by products like Hamburger Helper.[28] It was still women who did the work, but now under a different and more managerial pressure than pleasing a finicky husband.

Rather than downgrading or abolishing meal preparation, two other approaches sought to make cooking an appropriately fulfilling activity for women. One, most conspicuously represented by Julia Child, was to present creating fine meals as a pleasure separate from housework rather than, as with Friedan, a mere distraction, a walk in the prison's exercise yard. For Child, cooking was not inevitably a lonely affair, and her intended audience was not exclusively *la ménagère* (which sounds better than "housewife"), but anyone, male or female, who enjoys cooking. Newspapers were adequate to provide quick and easy ideas for harassed housewives or instruct them how to brighten routine dishes with colored Jell-O or shredded coconut; Child's mission was to teach the mastery of French cooking and was undertaken with a comforting and cheerful approach to kitchen labor.[29]

Some observers of feminist history have condemned the movement's "willful ignorance of the ordinary and mundane,"[30] but while this tendency at times surfaced in mainstream feminism, there were also women who proudly asserted their traditional competence, not for the benefit of men, but rather in female couples or communities. In 1977, Selma Miriam and Noel Furie converted a former machine shop in Bridgeport, Connecticut, into Bloodroot, a bookstore and vegetarian restaurant. Feminist bookstores were becoming ubiquitous, but the founders of this one wanted a gathering place fueled by more than coffee. Food expressed what Miriam and Furie considered "full-time feminism," conducting life as a woman according to principles that included animal rights and pleasure in cooking and sharing food.[31]

Still a going concern, Bloodroot represents one response to the problems of gender and cooking as well as pioneering vegetarian, and later vegan, cuisine. The major influence of the women's movement of the 1970s, however, was in slowly changing expectations of cooking and gender roles. If today women still do most of the cooking, it is no longer remarkable when men share responsibility for meal preparation, which remains more fun and hence more saleable than housecleaning, which few men have good-naturedly embraced. Not all the choices of gender roles and responsibilities are fair or favorable for women, but the fact that different households have made their own arrangements and that the official culture has nothing to say against any of them is indication of a vast, if disappointingly slow, change.

"America, Your Food Is So Gay"

This is the title of an article by John Birdsall about James Beard, Craig Claiborne, and Richard Olney, three gay men of paramount importance during the 1960s and 1970s for the elaboration of something worth calling American cuisine. Although Birdsall offers a few autobiographical vignettes about gay men and their appreciation for food, the emphasis is on famous chefs and food writers.

Ordinary gay domesticity is less easily delineated. The men's cookbooks discussed earlier were insistently heterosexual in order to disprove the association of cooking with what was typified as the "pansy" or "fairy" segment of homosexuality. Up to a point, knowledge of fine food and drink was unexceptional from the heteronormative perspective. Ian Fleming's James Bond, for example, was quite particular about mixed drinks ("shaken not stirred"). Fleming was a connoisseur, and his hero, struggling to live it up in decrepit postwar Britain, has a taste for gourmet meals that doesn't come through in the movies.[32] As a rule, however, men with fussy gastronomic standards were vulnerable to sexual suspicion. It was all right to patronize expensive restaurants, whose attractions were service, socializing, and status rather than food, but to take a serious interest in dining, let alone cooking, was coded as gay. Certain attributes, such as concern with décor and clothes, an "effeminate" kind of good looks, lisping, and mincing gestures, were signals of gay sexuality, used especially in movies when it was forbidden to bring it up openly.

Near the end of the novel *Portnoy's Complaint* (1967), Philip Roth has his narrator complain, not for the first time, that notwithstanding all his sexual escapades, his mother had instilled in him a repressive, guilty response to pleasure. Having constantly chided him to be a "perfect little gentleman," would his mother have been happy had he turned out to be like those "nice young men I see strolling hand in hand in Bloomingdale's"? Or like those nice Jewish boys on the beach in Fire Island? Given his upbringing, the fact that Alexander Portnoy ended up heterosexual is remarkable, for it could so easily have been different:

> I see myself sharing a house at Ocean Beach with somebody in eye make-up named Sheldon. "Oh, fuck you, Shelly, they're *your* friends, *you* make the garlic bread." . . . And *oy Gut*, one is calling out—to me! "Alex? Alexander the King? Baby, did you see where I put my tarragon?" There he is, Ma, your little gentleman, kissing someone named Sheldon on the lips! Because of his herb dressing![33]

As Roth via Portnoy sees it, bitchiness and gourmet food are amusingly effective emblems of being gay. A mass-market version of this outlook came some years later with *Real Men Don't Eat Quiche*, a 1982 humorous treatment of masculinity that chose a popular 1970s dish (and French, at that) to typify something liked by women and men who weren't real men.[34]

There were a few restaurants that were well known, if in a semi-clandestine way, as places of gay sociability. One that offered serious food was Café Nicholson near the Queensboro Bridge in New York, which has become retrospectively famous because of the involvement of Edna Lewis and her importance for American cuisine.[35] Lewis was Johnny Nicholson's business partner and chef from 1948 until the late 1950s. Nicholson was more interested in antiques and interior decoration than food and had intended to open a European café serving only pastry. Lewis' talents induced him to aim for something more gastronomically ambitious.

The restaurant was full of exuberant and unsorted antique furniture, decorated in what Nicholson described as "fin de siècle Caribbean of Cuba style ca. 1944." It featured slowly revolving fans, nude statues, gilt mirrors, and a marble and oak bar—a cross, as one observer said, between a Singapore Grand Hotel and a Balkan Intrigue Palace.[36] There was a talking parrot named Lolita. Nicholson and his intimate partner, the photographer Karl Bissinger, created a nonconformist, spontaneous place with a quirky gay vibe. It was listed in a 1969 gay guide to New York as "high drag" in its style.[37] Craig Claiborne in the *New York Times* guide of 1964 described Café Nicholson under the ambiguous heading of "offbeat."[38]

Under Lewis's direction, the Café became famous not only for its ambience but for its food, which was as simple as the décor was ornate. There was no menu, but the cognoscenti knew to order roast chicken with herbs, steak with béarnaise sauce, and bittersweet chocolate soufflé. The food was carefully made and delicious, but for many regulars, the scene was more important. The Café was a gathering place for Southern writers like Truman Capote and his best friend Harper Lee, William Faulkner, and Tennessee Williams. Gore Vidal was often there, but so was the rather aggressively heterosexual Henry Miller. Café Nicholson was thus more a postwar Bohemian and literary outpost than a gay restaurant, and its French and American food was not unusual, although its emphasis on gracious simplicity was.

A more explicit example of gay gourmandise, but one that still does not identify an actual gay cuisine, is *The Gay Cookbook* from 1965.[39] The author was a former merchant marine chef writing under the name Lou Rand Hogan. The stated reason to put this collection together was that every other group had its own cookbook, so "Oh hell, May, why don't you people have a cookbook?"[40] The chatty recipes and "campy cartoons" were exuberant, especially within the pre-Stonewall context. The cover shows a trim young man wearing a flowery apron, posing contrapposto in front of a grill, a steak held limply in his hand. The tone is comically naughty. A recipe for what the chapter preface refers to as Swiss Steak is actually "Swish Steak." Apropos an extensive discussion of French fries, Chef Hogan proposes "a brief word about sizes (potato!)." Asides are offered to "you girls" or "silly boy," and the reader is exhorted with old-fashioned female names like Maude or Gertie (1960s suburban diminutives like Patti or Tammy never appear).[41]

The recipes are serious if not particularly innovative, items from the prevailing vaguely international eclectic category such as Wienerschnitzel, beef bourguignon, chili, and the like. Hearty dishes such as goulash and corned beef hash are accompanied by comments straight (as it were) from the

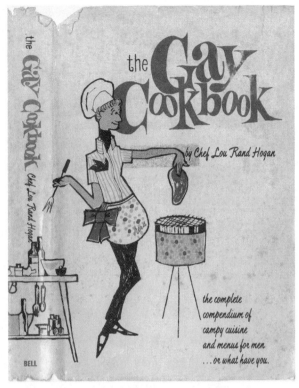

Cover of *The Gay Cookbook*, 1965. The book was a camp portrayal of gay domesticity more than of a distinctively gay cuisine.

cooking-for-men genre: "Men adore real, genuine honest to Gawd Corned Beef Hash. Let's make 'em happy."[42]

However arch the tone, it's a serious cookbook: the actual techniques and information are carefully presented, and the book is full of useful advice. Unfashionable ingredients like tripe are included; there are at least eighty sauce recipes. A well-informed discussion of Mexican sauces regretfully concludes that they are too hard to make at home and that even Mexican people living in the United States "seldom do it the old and hard way. (For sauce, you understand)." While paella makes a magnificent show, no recipe is given because it is too complicated and saffron is expensive.[43] As if to anticipate Philip Roth's observation, there are twenty-six kinds of salad dressing, although none with tarragon.

We are not yet at the point where gay culture would be identified with gourmet food or fine cooking. The 1960s and 1970s did, however, popularize an image of gay men as fun-loving, stylish, witty, and easily capable of a version of American home life with all its pleasures and discontents. The established stereotype of furtive deviance was being replaced, or at least supplemented, by one of affectionate domesticity.

The male gay movement and the women's movement, both 1970s phenomena with permanent effects, did not have a clear-cut or reciprocal relationship. Women's emancipation from the kitchen was not directly joined to gay men's increasing enthusiasm for elaborate cooking. The outcome of the decade was that people could try on or perform different sexual and social roles through food.

Saffron Rice

In the Orient, where *Ryjstafel* is most often served in all its glory—(yes, Winnie Mae, that's what our Curry buffet dinner is called in international culinary circles)—it is customary to serve more than one kind of rice; most often a second will be pungent Saffron Rice. For this we use the same cooking method, with one minor addition. After we have washed our rice, or while we are doing this, we bring a cup or so of water to a boil. Into it we stir a rounded teaspoon of MSG (as most of you know by now, this is mono-sodium glutamate), ⅓ teaspoon salt and one lightly rounded teaspoon of powdered or shredded saffron.

Let this boil up, reduce the fire to almost nothing and simmer 3 to 5 minutes until the water is a violent yellow. Pour this yellow water through a hair-strainer or through the corner of a cloth into a cup. When your rice is washed and drained for the last time, pour this yellow water onto it, quickly adding enough clear cold water to bring the level an inch over the rice. Cover tightly and proceed as with plain rice. . . . Saffron rice tastes altogether different and many people like it a lot.

When finally dishing out the cooked rice—and we don't serve it until the last moment—as all Oriental cooks do, we dish it out of the pot and into the bowls, with a wooden spoon or fork. They say metal makes cooked rice soggy.

Why? Oh hell girl. I don't know why, it just does. . . . So there's our two bowls of rice. (Easy, wasn't it?). Now for the curry. . . .

From Chef Lou Rand Hogan, *The Gay Cookbook* (Los Angeles: Sherbourne Press, 1965), 41–42.

The Microwave and the Slow Cooker: Dumbing Down or Saving Lives?

Leaving the field of gender and lifestyle performance to take up convenience and technology once again, we can posit that the most obvious change for home cooking in the 1970s was the introduction of the microwave oven as a household appliance. The microwave is another convenience following on those described in previous chapters, but one with a dramatic impact.

Microwave ovens had been used in industrial and institutional settings as far back as 1947, but it took twenty years for the first home-kitchen countertop model, the Amana "Radarange," to become available. At $500 (the equivalent today of $3,600) this was not yet a routine household item, but the price declined until by 1986, 25 percent of American households owned a microwave, and that number became close to 100 percent by the opening of the twenty-first century.[44]

As with 1950s TV dinners, the microwave was envisaged by its promotors as revolutionizing how people cooked their meals but ended up filling only a limited set of niches. Early microwave cookbooks included recipes for preparing "roasted" chicken, "barbecued" baby back ribs, bread, and other unlikely items. In practice, microwaves were rarely employed as substitute ovens but rather used to reheat foods (coffee, leftovers), make popcorn, and prepare packaged meals. The adaptation of Lean Cuisine, Pop-Tarts, and other heat-and-serve products to the microwave expanded the influence of the still relatively new technology.

Neither glamorous nor even particularly comforting, the microwave is a vital appliance in the everyday food world. There aren't a lot of Instagram photos of microwave creations out there, and a dreary aura surrounds the microwave, but recent phenomena, like so-called mug meals, indicate the continuing adaptability of the fifty-year-old appliance. The microwave is especially useful when cooking for one, in which case convenience almost always beats taste and creativity. A substantial percentage of the population lives alone, and once the desire to please others is removed as a consideration, actual meals eaten at home remain defined by convenience. Unlike urban cowboys or mood rings, the microwave continued to grow in importance after the 1970s.

The slow cooker is another 1970s phenomenon, although its origins go back thirty years earlier, with the invention of the Crock-Pot.[45] It cooks so slowly that you can mix the ingredients in the morning, leave for work, and have something ready for dinner when you return. The slow cooker was invented as a way of accommodating Jewish Sabbath regulations that forbid any kind of work, including cooking or even turning on or off a heat source, from Friday at sundown to Saturday at sundown. The early "beanpot," as it was known, could be turned on before the Sabbath began and go off automatically with a timer. In 1971, a patent was applied to a device that was basically a pot, heating element, and glass lid. The limitations in terms of taste are that if you are away all day, you can't add things at different times. Slow cookers are best for beans, stews made with cheap cuts of meat, and other dishes that don't have delicate ingredients.

Slow cookers went out of fashion in the 1980s because microwaves were considerably more convenient, and the slow cooker produced rather mushy results. They have come back as one of a number of compromises by which it is possible to home cook a meal and work somewhere else, compromises that now include such innovations as the Instant Pot (a programmable pressure cooker) and meal "kits" from companies such as Blue Apron that deliver pre-measured and pre-sliced ingredients.

Fast Food at Its Peak

The 1970s saw not only the introduction of the home microwave but also the apparent triumph of fast food chains. The stories of their founders are well known: elderly Colonel Sanders driving around the country selling his recipe and pressure-cooker method of frying chicken or Ray Kroc's appropriation of the McDonald brothers' high-speed and low-cost hamburger stand.[46] Glen Bell made tacos an American fast food staple. Even Burger King, less celebrated in the annals of entrepreneurship, depended on its founder CEO Dave Egerton to save it from ruin in the mid-1950s when he smashed a broiler used to make the prevailing mediocre burgers and developed the Whopper.[47]

It was in the 1970s that these businesses came to control the highways, malls, and suburbs. By 1983, there were 122,500 fast food places in the country, triple the figure in 1963, and they accounted for 40 percent of all the money spent on dining outside the home.[48] In recent years, fast food has varied its menus in order to escape the image of providing boring items for unhealthy sad sacks. In the early 1970s, however, the options were strictly limited, and the customers were happy because the small menu enhanced predictability. The typical McDonald's offered a hamburger, cheeseburger, Quarter Pounder, Quarter Pounder with cheese, Big Mac, Filet-O-Fish, French fries, apple pie, and beverages—that was it.[49] The introduction of breakfast items, notably the Egg McMuffin, was among the 1970s innovations.

Another 1970s invention was the clown, Ronald McDonald, emblem of the aggressive courtship of families with children. While Howard Johnson's had catered to kids by providing paper and crayons, large lollipops, and a friendly staff, McDonald's and other fast food companies abandoned the idea of merely accommodating children and instead turned many of their branches into "fun" environments of entertainment and militant informality. In some ways, this is ironic, since the 1970s also saw a crisis in traditional family dining as even preteens started to have separate and busy schedules, and a rise in solitary dining related to more people living alone. The typical McDonald's now serves a variety of demographic and sociological groups: elderly cronies at breakfast, moms with kids later in the day, teens after school, and, in another of the great inventions of the era, the drive-thru lane designed for people alone, on the way to work, on break, or simply accustomed to eating in their car. The first McDonald's with a drive-thru lane was opened in Arizona in 1975.

In the 1950s, Ray Kroc had deliberately targeted families. He abhorred rowdy teens—greasers, surfers, and the like—and was afraid they would adopt McDonald's as a place to hang out and intimidate grown-up customers. Nevertheless, in its first decades, McDonald's was a place of sleek, youthful, jet-age optimism. It was fast, fun, efficient, and—Kroc notwithstanding—very popular with teenagers. During the 1970s, the first signs of a more utilitarian ambience took shape as McDonald's became routine rather than iconic. The drive-thru was one such sign, as was the saturation of McDonald's and the growth of social segmentation and inequality so that the upper-middle class became more concerned about health and graciousness and less concerned with full participation in majority culture. In the 1970s and 1980s, affluent taste veered toward potted plants, Tiffany glass décor, and salads rather than burgers and golden arches.

Hippie Food[50]

While fast food belonged to those Vice President Spiro Agnew called "the silent majority," a vocal, entertaining, and much-maligned youth demographic challenged the hegemony of the suburban shopping center, patio, and two-car garage. The culinary agenda of the 1960s flower children anticipated the 1970s in both its beneficial and dubious aspects, ephemeral fads like the macrobiotic diet alongside durable innovations like tofu and whole grains. Beginning with 1967 and the Summer of Love in San Francisco, the agenda of an alternative life style became universally known and, although derided, increasingly imitated. Denunciation of the Vietnam War spilled over into critiques of technology and dehumanization. Demonstrations and civil disobedience were accompanied and then supplanted by communal and back-to-the-land movements. Self-sufficiency and stepping away from American consumerism came to be seen as not just a conversion experience ("Turn on, tune in, drop out"), but as a change requiring a freer and healthier lifestyle than the anesthetized suburban norm.

The hippies of the 1960s were distinguished from their seeming progenitors, the beatniks, by their more ecstatic, less downtrodden ("beat") affect, a distinction visible in comparing the cool jazz of the beatniks with the lush psychedelic music of the late 1960s. To escape conformist America, beatniks lived like hobos, meditated at Zen retreats, or embarked on frantic cross-country drives through the wide-open if blighted landscape, the scenery evoked by Jack Kerouac's 1950s classic *On the Road*. Beatnik drugs of choice courted oblivion—alcohol or heroin.

Hippies were looking for fun in anticipation of a dawning new age. Products of the same postwar optimism and opulence that they rebelled against, hippies envisioned a world in which alienated labor would yield to leisure or craft. At the heart of the hippie ideology, such as it was, there was a love of nature rather than alleys, of ecstatic religious experience rather than Zen, of acid (LSD) and peyote rather than downers. The redwoods of California were more spiritually comforting than skid rows.

Neither movement initially was particularly interested in food, but from the start of the hippie era there was a need for at least marijuana-related snacks and, in keeping with communal optimism, meals promoting revolutionary self-sufficiency. In 1966, a San Francisco group calling themselves the "Diggers" fed all who showed up at their soup kitchens in the Haight-Ashbury Panhandle Park. Emmett Grogan, an actor with a guerilla theater group, conceived events that would make political statements. Taking their name from the radical egalitarian movement formed during the seventeenth-century English Civil War, the San Francisco Diggers attempted to bridge the growing gap between political activists and flower children, between the movements spawned during the Civil Rights era and opposition to the Vietnam War on the one hand and the psychedelic heightened awareness of the hippies on the other. Among their many manifestos was one describing the horrific ecological consequences of "winning breakfast at the cost of smog and insanity." The Diggers predicted an imminent apocalypse of industrial collapse brought about by both ecological and social factors.[51]

There were no menus for the free food that the Diggers provided. One flyer promised "good hot stew, ripe tomatoes, and fresh fruit."[52] This was hardly the formula for any particular cuisine, and what they served depended on what was being thrown or given away at the city's wholesale produce depot. The Diggers did have standards, however, refusing to accept processed white bread and developing instead their own whole-wheat bread made in coffee cans.

The Diggers reflected an embryonic culinary expression of the general hippie critique of the American mainstream. The prevailing greed and status seeking were based on wasteful mistreatment of the Earth, and the alternative lifestyle emphasized sexual, musical, and pharmacological high spirits. Youth culture generally, certainly from 1967 to the late 1990s, embraced aspects of this agenda but preferred musical and sexual pleasure to anything having to do with

Diggers providing food in San Francisco, 1966 or 1967. The Diggers scavenged food, baked bread, and served all comers at their open-air soup kitchens.

food. Yet as the radical remaking of the entire society faded as a practical goal, the hippie critique of the unhealthful sameness of the American diet became more compelling, particularly as alternative lifestyle seekers moved out of cities to rural communes. The agenda of one of these utopian encampments is typical: "Our intentions are to raise our own food, our animals' food, and our states of consciousness, using hand, animal, and solar powered tools." More than two thousand rural communes were set up between 1966 and 1970.[53]

The first Earth Day took place on April 22, 1970. It was organized by the environmentalist US Senator Gaylord Nelson and timed to come after college students' spring break and before their final exams. That first year, millions of people took to the streets and parks to promote environmental responsibility and celebrate nature. The event, which has since been repeated every year, is an example of the wide institutionalization in the 1970s of what had been fringe ideas just a few years earlier.

A new organic food movement traced its roots to this environmental concern as well as to a long-standing but previously marginal critique of unhealthful American food. Health advocates like Adelle Davis had preached against processed food and chemical additives to a limited group of converts for more than a decade before the Summer of Love. Davis was not particularly interested in nature and the outdoors, preferring vitamin supplements to herbal remedies. Foraging for plants was a more eco-friendly form of alternative dietary practice. Euell Gibbons was, as it were, the Johnny Appleseed of plant gathering in the wild. Davis's revised *Let's Cook It Right* and Gibbons's *Stalking the Wild Asparagus* appeared in 1962, the same year as Rachel Carson's *Silent Spring*.[54] From being considered a peculiar cult idea, natural foods teachings achieved mainstream success in the 1970s and formerly niche books like those of Davis and Gibbons became long-term best sellers.

Natural food was supposed to be free of artificial ingredients or chemicals, used in either production or packaging. It also had two positive implications: a look backward to a time of cooking as craft, and a state of mind that rejected standardization in favor of individuality and skill. The term "artisanal" was not yet widely used, but much of today's infatuation with "small-batch," "handmade," and "free-range" comes from the 1970s natural food outlook.[55]

Food Additives—
What They Are,
Where They Come From

Food additives can be derived
from foods such as corn— or can be created by
food scientists in answer to special problems.

Farm, lab, and home. "Food Additives—What They Are, Where They Come From" was a booklet put out in 1961 by the Manufacturing Chemists' Association as a defense of the food industry's use of chemicals for color, preservation, texture, and flavoring.

For the time being, the most influential natural foods idea was a health-conscious style of cooking, which amounted to modified vegetarianism not dependent on wild greens. While there was never an effective, legal definition of "organic" or "natural" as applied to food products, the terms were associated with an increasingly mainstream cooking style: unprocessed ingredients, fish rather than meat, whole grains rather than white rice or bread, and vegetables everywhere. Between 1940 and 1970, there were only fifteen cookbooks oriented to organic food; over three hundred were published in the 1970s.[56]

Beginning in the 1970s, personal health was linked to ecological preservation. Among the most important publications in this regard was Frances Moore Lappé's *Diet for a Small Planet* in 1971.[57] The trouble with the alternative diets that Lappé advocated as lifesaving and environmentally friendly was that they didn't taste particularly good. Lappé anticipated criticism that her proposals would make food simultaneously dull and complicated, but she just dismissed such carping and recommended experimenting with permitted ingredients. Euell Gibbons extolled the interesting textures and taste sensations of wild plants, but generally health food popularizers eschewed pleasure in favor of a restricted and unattractive list of approved foods. Health food advocates were often vegetarian, thus allying themselves to what a majority of the public considered a no-fun ideology, just as their alleged fondness for flannel shirts and Birkenstock footwear gave them a fashion-resistant image.

The counterculture movement shared the food activists' disdain for corporate America's food system and started effectively to challenge mainstream tastes. *The Tassajara Bread Book* (1970) and *Tassajara Cooking* (1973), produced by a meditation community in Big Sur, are early examples of well-thought-out alternative lifestyle cooking. The emphasis was on a return to basics, in both method and content, beginning with bread. The second book, *Tassajara Cooking*, was vegetarian, with plenty of tofu and alfalfa sprouts, but not all that renunciatory or unfamiliar. Its coffee cake, cinnamon rolls, popovers, date-nut bread, and the like would have been at home in any of the mass-market women's magazines of the time.[58] Most communal cookbooks from the 1970s are what Stephanie Hartman calls "earthy-crunchy," with wheat berries, soybeans, and sprouts prominent, and cheese, sesame and sunflower seeds, lemon, curry, and tamari supplying the flavor.[59] The hippie communes developed methods and ingredients now taken for granted, from stir-frying applied to non-Chinese dishes to reviving obscure plants such as farro, amaranth, and millet.

ALFALFA SPROUTS

Very popular in salad and sandwiches, these make an excellent side dish with beans as well. Lemon juice sweetened with honey dresses them adequately. For a more substantial side dish or salad, how about:

Alfalfa-Banana Sprouts with Nuts

alfalfa sprouts

bananas

walnuts

Mash the banana to make a dressing for the alfalfa sprouts. Thin and season with lemon juice if necessary, then mix it with the sprouts and walnut pieces.

Sliced apples and raisins could also be added to this dish.

Fenugreek sprouts could be used in place of alfalfa sprouts. Other nuts or seeds could be used.

From Edward Espe Brown, *Tassajara Cooking* (Berkeley and London: Shambhala, 1973), 42–43.

An experiment exemplifying a "back to the land" utopian ideal was the Farm, a commune in Lewis County, Tennessee, organized in 1971 by Stephen Gaskin, leader of a group of three hundred Bay Area refugees. Gaskin considered his followers to be "voluntary peasants"; the media called them "technicolor Amish." The success of the community was such that no less than the *Wall Street Journal* referred to the Farm as the "General Motors of communes."[60] Its program was in certain ways ultra-traditional, not only in its rural aspirations but in prohibiting birth control and abortion. Gaskin and his followers revived lapsed Southern farm practices such as growing and grinding sorghum. The diet was vegan before that term came to be used, and the community believed that no animal should be killed or exploited. No artificial stimulants or drugs were allowed, but (natural) marijuana was regarded with reverence. The Farm was economically and demographically viable for a long time, and among its innovations and adaptations were products now found everywhere such as soy ice cream and tempeh.[61]

The late 1970s and 1980s also witnessed experiments to introduce healthier, vegetarian food to a larger market, based not only on virtue but on taste. Among the most prominent was *Moosewood Cookbook*, which was first published in 1977 and has gone through several editions and sold three and a half million copies.[62] The vegetarian Moosewood Restaurant in Ithaca, New York, is still flourishing and is among the best-preserved culinary survivals of the 1970s. Mollie Katzen established Moosewood in 1972 as a community project where workers did everything on an equal basis. The menu drew from traditional recipes, especially those of Katzen's grandmother, as well as healthy versions of conventional dishes

Moosewood restaurant. The pioneering vegetarian restaurant in Ithaca, New York, opened in 1973.

such as a casserole of broccoli, cheese, and brown rice instead of tuna and noodles.[63] Katzen adopted international dishes featuring ingredients such as tamari, hummus, and tortillas, items familiar to hippie kitchens but not then to be found in supermarkets or restaurants.[64] Nothing in the *Moosewood Cookbook*, spun off from the restaurant, is very spicy, and the foreign-inspired food is eclectic more than authentic. The Moosewood dishes actually resemble, in a slightly more health-conscious and of course vegetarian fashion, what *Sunset* magazine had been publishing for decades, a West Coast cuisine of mild, neo-Mexican, "Oriental," and Middle Eastern preparations. Through the Moosewood publications, nevertheless, an internationally varied, health-oriented cuisine escaped its former California limits and spread nationally.

There were many different health-food agendas. Some African American groups advanced a vegetarian diet to combat the deleterious physical effects of Southern rural traditional food, what was becoming identified as "soul food." Originally typified simply as "Southern" or "down-home," soul food was now part of a black identity. Not everybody was pleased with this form of cultural expression, however. The Nation of Islam denounced soul food as a diet imposed on Southern slaves by their masters to undermine their health. Reliance on pork (forbidden to Muslims) was especially criticized, but so were black-eyed peas and cornbread. In *How to Eat to Live* (1967) and *How to Eat to Live, Book 2* (1972), Elijah Muhammad promoted whole grains, brown rice, and vegetables. Sweet bean pie was one of the leader's favorites and a feature of the Black Muslim bakeries that proliferated in the 1970s.[65]

The African American comedian Dick Gregory embraced vegetarianism in 1963, claiming that black people needed to make a radical change in diet. Beginning in 1967, Gregory promoted the idea of "soul food with a mission." He collaborated with the nutritionist Alvenia M. Fulton on *Dick Gregory's Natural Diet for Folks Who Eat: Cookin' with Mother Nature*, which appeared in 1973. According to this book, traditional soul food is responsible for the symptoms of ill health suffered by the black community. Gregory claimed that black leaders who promoted soul food as a treasured cultural expression were guilty of undermining, even murdering, their own people.[66]

The Mediterranean Diet

It would have been impossible to impose Dick Gregory's diet or the Tassajara diet on the general population of the United States. Americans want to eat healthy, whatever that means at any particular time, but are not willing to give up familiar comforts like fat, sugar, salt, and meat, at least not completely. Successful diet reforms have been compromises (don't eat so much meat) or addressed one element (calories, carbohydrates, proteins), but even these lack a positive, sensuous element, and that tends to discourage long-term commitment. Perhaps the most important and long-lasting shift has been effected by the so-called Mediterranean diet, which features interesting and varied foods and flavors but is perceived as healthful. Rather than preaching vegetarianism, the Mediterranean diet emphasizes how delicious vegetables can be when they are grilled, served with herbs and olive oil, or part of a pasta sauce. Without cutting out meat altogether, fish and veal substitute for thick steaks and roast beef. Olive oil rather than butter, fruit for dessert, yogurt, eggs, wine in moderation—these components created something attractive, the opposite of what was regarded as a dull health-food regime.

The Mediterranean diet was not exactly invented in the 1970s, but it attained sudden and, as it turned out, long-lasting fame then. Under this rubric many California innovations were spread throughout the country—serving salads as main courses, grilling vegetables, cooking with olive oil. The Mediterranean diet also influenced fashions not directly related to health, such as pasta other than spaghetti and macaroni, or niçoise salad. The main accomplishment of the new cuisine or diet was that it presented what was considered light food (opinion on pasta has changed several times) but also delicious and flavorful food: healthful but attractive, chic but not abstemious.

In 1959, physiologist Ancel Keys and his wife, Margaret Keys, noted in *Eat Well and Stay Well* that people in Mediterranean European countries followed a diet associated with a low rate of heart disease and other diet-related illnesses. Olive oil, fruit, fish, and vegetables differentiated this food regime from northern European or American reliance on meat, butter, dairy products, cookies, and cake.[67] During the 1960s, this book had a certain currency among health-food advocates but little popular resonance. In 1974, in a different cultural climate, the Keyses published what proved to be a wildly popular version of their earlier work, now entitled *How to Eat Well and Stay Well the Mediterranean Way.*[68] The vogue for this diet was advanced by an article published in the *American Journal of Clinical Nutrition* entitled "Health Implications of Mediterranean Diets in Light of Contemporary Knowledge."[69]

There is some question as to who in the Mediterranean ever consumed such consistently light food. In what country did people eat Balkan yogurt and Italian pasta? Far from rejecting meat, Europeans living on or close to the Mediterranean are fond of game, lamb, sausage, organ meat, pork, and other non-California foods. The Mediterranean region does not have anything approaching a unified cuisine. Supposedly all Mediterranean food involves "the trinity" of olive oil, bread, and wine. This might have been true when the Roman Empire controlled the Mediterranean, but wine is not permitted by Islam, practiced by more than half the Mediterranean shoreline's population. Neither is olive oil universal, as sheep fat is preferred in parts of the Middle East, while butter and lard are essential to the cooking of Lombardy and Emilia-Romagna. In North Africa, the food is quite spicy, and skill at mixing spices is a key attribute of culinary prestige, but just across the Straits of Gibraltar in Spain, there are few spices, and even garlic and saffron are used very selectively. Given such diversity, where did this idea of "light" Mediterranean cuisine come from? Two eminent historians of food only half-jokingly remarked that the so-called Mediterranean diet is essentially the summer food served at Italian beach resorts in the 1960s marketed to Americans.[70]

And yet, despite its absurdity from a strictly factual point of view, the Mediterranean diet has been enshrined by UNESCO as part of the world's intangible cultural heritage, apportioned among Italy, Portugal (most of which faces the Atlantic), Spain, Morocco, Greece, Cyprus, and Croatia.[71] More significantly, for our purpose, the term "Mediterranean diet" effectively denotes a satisfying but light form of healthy dining. Unlike many of the other fads of the 1970s, the Mediterranean diet has increased in its influence, extending beyond its original nutritional orientation to encompass an entire, global culinary aesthetic that presents itself as light but flavorful, healthful but sensuous and satisfying. No other 1970s innovation is so important today. Institutions, notably college dining halls, have deliberately cultivated a Mediterranean diet and had success in reducing the amount of meat served and convincing students to consider vegetables as main courses.[72]

The California Food Revolution Begins

The Mediterranean diet is part wishful thinking, part successful reworking of the way people actually eat. To the extent that Americans actually do consume less meat, more vegetables, and fresher produce and buy more olive oil and wine than in the past, this comes from a food reform more plausible than anything recommended by diet books or produced by hippie nirvana cuisine. California was not only the site of most of the social and gastronomic experiments of the 1970s, but also the place where the Mediterranean diet combined with a local and seasonal ethos to create a change in dining, a development that merits the overworked term "revolution."

The California food revolution that began in the early 1970s reoriented American restaurant and home cooking toward seasonal and local ingredients. Joined to a Mediterranean aesthetic (mostly Italian and Greek, but including tapas borrowed from Spain) and the blurring of the boundaries between high and low (gourmet pizza), these taste preferences have permanently affected how we eat. Its most important aspect is that the California food revolution emphasized the quality of primary ingredients. Instead of mass-produced products with no season or clear point of origin, the pioneering restaurateurs of the 1970s offered a fresh, local set of dishes. Rather than obscuring mediocre, industrialized taste with choice and variety, this movement advocated simplicity and the vivid flavor of meat, fish, and produce whose quality meant they needed little ornamentation.

Alice Waters and her restaurant Chez Panisse cannot be credited with the entire revolution, but they are the best places to begin.[73] Waters's accomplishment was to combine the hippie, countercultural critique of mainstream food consumption with a quest for the most pleasurable tastes, a blending of social healing with gastronomic distinction.[74] Instead of eating brown rice and seaweed because they are virtuous, one should experience healthful *and* sensuous enjoyment. Waters, who had exemplary activist credentials, vigorously denied that taking pleasure in food is linked to wasteful consumerism, nor should advocating culinary enjoyment be dismissed as a reactionary movement of elderly snobs: it is an act of defiance against a functionalist age that sets the machine above the human being.

Alice Waters was a product of the 1960s political movements and lifestyle changes in Berkeley. She disdained both her mother's flavorless health food cooking and the priorities of her conformist sorority sisters at the University of California, Santa Barbara. Her time in France changed her, as did the leftist politics of the late 1960s. Waters rejected the established order, but not the aesthetic pleasure of food that her radical colleagues dismissed as part of the decadent prevailing ethos.

Chez Panisse began in 1971 as an effort to recreate a rustic French auberge, where what was offered would change weekly, or even daily, depending on what was in season or available locally.[75] This was a different kind of French cuisine from that offered by famous fancy restaurants like La Bourgogne in San Francisco or La Côte Basque in New York. Considerable effort would go into obtaining the best possible primary ingredients rather than to creating showy effects with truffles, rich sauces, or tableside flambéing. From the start, Chez Panisse sought out ducks raised locally and not frozen, wild foraged mushrooms, and fresh herbs. Its chefs used older, tastier, if more fragile varieties of fruit and obtained butter and cheese from small Marin and Sonoma County farms.

Chez Panisse was not the first restaurant to emphasize seasonal or American ingredients. The Four Seasons in New York, established in 1959, was a resplendent, classic restaurant whose fanatical and exuberant chefs grew their own herbs and encouraged mushroom foragers. As its name implies, the menu changed with the seasons, but "seasonal" did not necessarily mean local. The cuisine was international rather than American, and featured air-freighted luxuries such as Dover sole and European truffles.

The focus on ingredients was not, therefore, something Alice Waters magically pulled out of a hat, but it was not how elegant food was usually prepared in the United States. This was even the case with French cuisine, which equaled high-end dining. Waters forthrightly rejected the dynamic of efficiency, convenience, and faux elegance that had defined American cuisine during the previous century. To say that you must start from excellent primary products and that no amount of professional training or ingenuity can compensate for flavorless chicken or tomatoes bred for transport was to break with what had been happening since the Civil War. The American food system could deliver vast quantities of food cheaply and with great variety, but it could not reproduce the intense and fresh tastes of the past on the scale demanded by the retail system. Everything follows from making taste a priority. Seasonality, eating locally, and the revival of older breeds might be environmentally or aesthetically desirable, but to get these ideas accepted beyond a cult following required a shift in fundamental American attitudes.

Alice Waters opposed the hippie indifference to the pleasures of cuisine and presented to her friends and customers game, goat cheese, unusual salad greens, and a French repertoire bearing no resemblance to commune food. She did, however, adopt hippie informality, egalitarian disorganization, and sexual liberation. The restaurant was inspired by a Berkeley ethos rather than by the kitchen hierarchy codified by Escoffier. Collective decision-making, a nonprofessional staff (the first chef, Victoria Kroyer, had been a Ph.D. student in philosophy at Berkeley), and a dislike of conventional management distinguished Chez Panisse, as did the extraordinary quality of its otherwise familiar food. Early patrons reported that they had eaten duck à l'orange many times but that the version served at Chez Panisse was a revelation or Platonic ideal. Within a few years after it opened, Chez Panisse was nationally recognized. In 1975, *Gourmet* anointed it one of the best restaurants in the United States.

Success did not diminish the passion to transform society by the seemingly unlikely means of food. Food as the agent of social change was always central to Alice Waters's agenda, but it is only in the past twenty years or so that it has come to be shared by other restaurateurs. Some of these chefs have been urged to use their star status to influence policies; others, like René Redzepi at Noma in Denmark, want to influence matters that chefs touch but do not control—food waste, fisheries, and globalization, for example. The idea that what we eat expresses an embrace of nature and human community owes a great deal to Waters and Chez Panisse.

With all this attention to context and social implications, the actual nature of the food making up the shifting tastes of the 1970s revolution should not be ignored. In the standard, celebratory narrative about Chez Panisse and the invention of New American cuisine, October 7, 1976, is the moment when a previously French restaurant transformed itself. A "Northern California Dinner" broke with the restaurant's French orientation to create an actual local cuisine. The menu stated that the oysters were from Tomales Bay, the trout was from Garrapata Creek near Big Sur, and it was steamed over California bay leaves. There followed Monterey Bay prawns, duck from the Hand Ranch in Sebastopol, and a dry Monterey Jack cheese from Vella Cheese Company, also in Sonoma County. Patric Kuh, in *The Last Days of Haute Cuisine,* wrote, "The switch had been thrown, one should now treat California with the same seriousness as Alsace or Brittany."[76]

Alice Waters later said the menu for that dinner could easily have been from thirty years later.[77] Initially, Jeremiah Tower, chef at Chez Panisse at the time, recollected the event as merely one among many enjoyable experiments he put together on his way out. Later, however, it became the proof text for his claim to have invented New American Cuisine and for which he asserts he has received insufficient credit.[78] The identification of this meal as a discovery on the order of penicillin or semiconductors is overstated. The next week in October 1976, Chez Panisse reverted to French cuisine.

Chez Panisse followed through haltingly on the New American agenda. Other Bay Area places in the 1980s, such as Zuni Café and Fourth Street Grill, were more consistently and deliberately American in their inspiration. Chez Panisse continued its French orientation until the mid-1980s, when it started to feature a combination of Italian, Provençal, and American menus.[79] An emblem of this transition and eclecticism is baked goat cheese salad, which became a cliché of California cuisine, first served at Chez Panisse on February 13, 1982. Based on Provençal ingredients but resulting in a dish unknown in Provence, this epitomized the new American cuisine that emerged from the Mediterranean-inspired California food revolution.

Because of the long-term success of what was started in the 1970s, it is easy to ignore the fragility and vicissitudes of what was sometimes regarded as essentially a fad.[80] In the 1980s, it was feared that California cuisine was degenerating into a series of gimmicks such as mesquite grilling or weird salads. In reaction to the distortions of excessive popularity, Joyce Goldstein, later to be an authoritative chronicler of the food revolution, said that most Bay Area chefs in the mid-1980s would utter "agonized groans and swift denials" when asked about their loyalty to "California cuisine."[81]

Alice Waters is important not because she alone invented farm-to-table, but because of her commitment to a wider social and cultural agenda. Left to themselves, other chefs could have opened up opportunities for a seasonal and locally sourced cuisine. The accomplishment of Waters was to create an audience, beginning with activists and what would later be called "foodies," then joined by a wider public for a combination of health concerns, regional pride, and rediscovery of taste.

The Year 1979

Granted, 1979 may not seem like a memorable year, comparable to, say, 1989 (the fall of the Berlin Wall) or 2001. It was burdened by the Three Mile Island nuclear reactor disaster. The Iranian revolution's hostage-taking of American embassy personnel in Tehran led to an oil supply panic and the price of a gallon of gas approached a dollar. The first Victoria's Secret boutique opened. Etan Patz, a young boy, disappeared in New York and only recently has his murderer been found and judged. Unremarked, several restaurants opened in 1979, consolidating and extending what Chez Panisse was accomplishing. Restaurateurs on the East and West coasts opened establishments of varying degrees of elegance, ranging from Barry Wine's Quilted Giraffe (New York) on the high end to Mark Miller's Fourth Street Grill (Berkeley) in the rustic category. Other restaurants that appeared in 1979 were Chanterelle in New York, Michael's in Santa Monica, and K-Paul's in New Orleans.

The Quilted Giraffe, established in upstate New Paltz in 1975, moved to New York City in 1979. It developed an expensive cuisine that included beggar's purses (crêpes stuffed with caviar and crème fraîche) and poached eggs with chocolate, and it attracted a new kind of customer, described by a restaurant reviewer for *Gourmet* as typically "an optometrist who was willing to shell out two hundred dollars on white truffles—nobody knew such a creature existed."[82] People had paid a lot of money in restaurants before, but not for mere gustatory pleasure unrelated to social status. Now flavor and expense were being divorced from ostentatious atmosphere. At Paul Prudhomme's resolutely informal K-Paul's, there were no reservations and long lines and the furniture, plates and cutlery were mismatched and cheap, but the food was intense and remarkably new.[83]

What these different places had in common was a fixation on the best primary ingredients and an enthusiasm for flavor sensations, from the seafood sausage of Chanterelle to the then-novel blue corn tortillas at Fourth Street Grill. The new tastes were the creations of American chefs or, at least, as in the case of the Austrian Wolfgang Puck, non-French chefs. Probably Caroline Bates, another *Gourmet* writer, invented the term "California cuisine," but even in the late 1970s, the innovations Alice Waters would later describe as "a delicious revolution" were not limited to one state.[84]

Paul Prudhomme was the only one of these 1979 luminaries who began with a traditional cuisine based on the land. The others were eclectic and invented elements that would define the new aesthetic: beautiful colors, Mediterranean dishes, mesquite-grilled meat, salads as a main course, everything just slightly undercooked, sophisticated pizzas, and high-end American California wines. Michael McCarty's Santa Monica restaurant Michael's was a pioneer in service by friendly, casually dressed waiters. Wolfgang Puck's Spago in Los Angeles made pizza a high-end and creatively varied item. Elevation of popular style is characteristic of contemporary American food, the gourmet hamburger being its most widely diffused example. High and low began to mix and merge in the 1970s. Patrons of the same restaurant might arrive in denim or evening wear; burgers and pizza appeared on the menu along with caviar and white truffles. Star architects and lighting specialists designed expensive and breathtaking settings in which waiters wore lumberjack shirts.

Regional labels proliferated in the late 1970s and early 1980s: "new Texan," "new Southern," and some previously unknown designations like Hudson River cuisine or Willamette Valley cuisine. Sometimes this just meant adding local ingredients to dishes you could find anywhere, so, for example, pizza made with goat cheese to which hot peppers might be added in Tucson, andouille sausage in New Orleans, or fiddlehead ferns in Vermont. Larry Forgione's New York restaurant, An American Place, began the practice of routinely listing the provenance of local ingredients by specific farms, followed by Jasper White's restaurant Jasper's in Boston, Marcel Desaulniers's Trellis in Williamsburg, the American Restaurant in Kansas City under Chef Bradley Ogden, and Mark Miller's two Berkeley restaurants, Fourth Street Grill and Coyote.

Finally, 1979 marks a development in the history of home cooking, the publication of *The Silver Palate Cookbook*, epitomizing an accessible gourmet outlook.[85] The authors, Julee Rosso and Sheila Lukins, ran a gourmet shop in Manhattan but pitched their recipes to cooks who might not have access to esoteric ingredients or ethereal seasonal items. No lemongrass, ramps, or white truffle oil here. Balsamic vinegar, fresh produce, and all manner of pasta were more along the lines of this cookbook. In the last issue of the food magazine *Lucky Peach*, dedicated to the suburbs, *The Silver Palate Cookbook* is credited with popularizing ratatouille, tapenade, and stuffed grape leaves: "Sheila Lukins is why there still is raspberry vinaigrette pooling on salad plates all over America."[86] The cookbook represents a middle ground between the high-end pretensions of New American restaurants and suburban reality.

✦   ✦   ✦

THE POWER OF THE NEW AMERICAN STYLE as the prevailing cuisine would grow in the more prosperous 1980s. At the close of the 1970s, developments such as a new aesthetic based on primary products and high quality might be dismissed as a passing fashion, but what came after would prove that the revolution was real and that the shift in American taste was enduring.

CHAPTER 10

The Food Revolution Grows Up

New American Cuisine became popular in the 1970s, and far from going the way of other fads of that era like urban cowboys or disco, it continues to expand forty years after the end of the Me/Stupid/Magical decade. No longer exactly new, to be sure, American cuisine evolved into the farm-to-table movement, which extends to concern with the natural and social environment surrounding food. It has taken over serious dining everywhere, not just the Bay Area or Northeast coast, and now every part of America has restaurants that boast about their local, seasonal, and artisanal approach. Concerns about where food comes from, sustainability, and treatment of animals, all aspects of the social program of the culinary revolution, have gone well beyond health-food co-ops to influence Walmart and Target. When Mimi Sheraton wrote an article for *Time* magazine in 1984 entitled simply "Eat American!," she effectively summarized a change in fine dining trends that would grow in the future.[1] The 1980s and subsequent decades represent the consolidation and elaboration of the revolutionary turn toward freshness, flavor, seasonality, and the rediscovery of American flavors and origins.

A key factor explaining why what would become identified as farm-to-table flourished in the 1980s is its promotion by a newly identified class of affluent cultural experimenters, the yuppies. These descendants of the early-twentieth-century Bohemians pursued progressive lifestyle ambitions but, unlike the anti-materialist hippies, did so while getting and spending money. A comfortable way of life was not the enemy, as it had been for the hippies, but a creative form of self-expression and self-actualization. Far from contradicting enlightened behavior, affluence, it was believed, made it possible.

The word "yuppie" is derived as an acronym for Young Urban Professional and dates precisely from 1980, when it was first used in opposition to Yippie (Youth International Party), a group of 1960s theatrically anarchist agitators.[2] Rather than dividing the world into impoverished hip versus dull bourgeoisie, the yuppies and their successors (e.g., hipsters) monetized alternative lifestyles. Instead of jogging in a pair of ordinary old sneakers, why not buy Nike running shoes for hundreds of dollars? What has been called the Bohemian Bourgeoisie (or "Bobos") is now so numerous that the very concept of "square" or "bourgeois" has ceased to have any meaning.[3] Starbucks coffee, yoga gear, aromatherapy, and eating locally began as the property of a self-described enlightened elite. Now these are mass-market accoutrements that retain, to one degree or other, a cool, progressive image.

A hip lifestyle requires a considerable investment. The bicycle is no longer a cheap ecological vehicle but an opportunity to spend thousands on equipment, clothing, and measuring devices. Machu Picchu, Big Sur, ashrams in India, and wellness centers in the Arizona desert are patronized by people with money, not the glorified hitchhikers of the hippie era. Hitchhiking itself has gone the way of hopping freight trains. Yuppie disposable income had many effects, some favorable (such as the revitalization of cities that seemed moribund in the 1970s), some not (for example, income inequality that separates those who routinely buy expensive meals along with exotic vacations from those who are struggling economically).

For all the disapproval of yuppies in the 1980s and 1990s and the hand-wringing over the disappearing middle class, fine restaurants could not exist without a substantial upper class that wants to show off its sophisticated tastes. This applies to ordinary expensive restaurants like steakhouses, but also the hand-crafted, zero-carbon-footprint international temples of gastronomy.

American food has been transformed since the 1980s, and restaurants serve better food than they did before, but this is part of a larger story of social ferment that here we leave offstage.

Not Just a Fad

The term "farm to table" emphasizes primary products, flavor, and seasonality. Although it did not have that name at first, this ingredients-focused outgrowth of New American Cuisine challenged the paradigm of standardization that held nearly undisputed sway until the 1970s. Farm-to-table was a revolutionary development because it represented a reversal of what well-off people expect. For centuries the whole point of being wealthy from a culinary perspective was to be free from constraints of season and locality, to be able to eat things not available to ordinary people. While the average peasant relied on seasonal pro-

Union Square Greenmarket. Established in 1976, the Greenmarket helped farmers bring their seasonal products to consumers and began the rescue of Union Square Park from crime and neglect.

duce, the mark of privilege was to consume exotic products from far away, like birds' nests from Borneo caves, or things out of season, like hot-house plums in winter. In the Middle Ages, all chickens were "free range" and ordinary people were locavores. On the other hand, prestigious and high-priced spices such as cloves, cinnamon, pepper, or the African spice known as "grains of Paradise" had to be imported from lands so distant that Europeans didn't really know where they were located.[4] Distance, rarity, and expense defined luxury cuisine.

In *The Count of Monte Cristo*, which was serialized in 1844–1845 and became one of the most popular novels ever written, Alexandre Dumas has his protagonist host a meal that exemplifies the age-old taste of the wealthy for the exotic. The Count, who possesses inexhaustible wealth, serves extraordinary fruit, birds, and fish "from the four corners of the globe," but the two sensations of this "oriental feast" are an immense lamprey (resembling an overgrown eel with lots of teeth) from Lake Fusaro in Southern Italy and a sturgeon from the Volga. Given their particular habitats, Italian lamprey and Russian sturgeon have never before been served at the same meal, the Count informs his guests. Both have been kept alive across vast distances in casks with water and appropriate food, and two of each were transported in case one died en route. As an amusing anticlimax, the Count acknowledges that very likely the rare creatures taste wonderful only because of the seeming impossibility of obtaining them together; intrinsically they are no better than readily available salmon or perch.[5]

Like the Count, the elegantly dressed patrons of mid-twentieth-century temples of haute cuisine such as Le Pavillon in New York or Ernie's in San Francisco would have looked down with derision at mere "local" food. Caviar from the Caspian Sea was the way to start a meal, which moved on to Maine lobster on the West Coast or Columbia River salmon on the East.

Focused on proximity, taste, and environmental sustainability, farm-to-table runs contrary to the love of exoticism and distant sources for food, yet it has been the dominant tendency of American dining over the past two decades. The origins of farm-to-table lie in the 1970s, but the emphasis on primary ingredients and defining their quality in terms of seasons and locale became generalized in the 1980s and 1990s among restaurants with a claim to excellence.

Notwithstanding a certain amount of understandable mockery, it is not a movement limited to complacently enlightened coastal communities but is found throughout the United States.[6] In a geographic-cultural trend that would have shocked *soigné* diners in the 1950s, Columbus, San Diego, and Austin are now gastrotourism destinations, and the focus on ingredients and terroir has revived moribund regional cuisines, especially in the South and Southwest.

The "farm" in farm-to-table refers to an ideally small, environmentally responsible enterprise as opposed to the large-scale processors of meat, dairy, and produce. There is both an aesthetic and an environmental side to the program. The aesthetic emphasizes taste enhanced by seasonality and nearby location. Rather than Peruvian asparagus available the entire year, farm-to-table asparagus is limited in its season and origin. The environmental component is that plants and animals should be nurtured with little or no chemical, bio-engineered, or fertilizer inputs and that water use and the carbon footprint of transport need to be considered in deciding what to buy and eat. Ultimately this ties in to concerns with the degradation of the global environment by industrialized agriculture as manifested, for example, by the extension of cattle-grazing in the Amazon or the deforestation of Sumatra to grow palm oil trees. Restaurants following a farm-to-table ethos pay attention to where they obtain their ingredients and how those are produced. They try to make "in-house" much of what they serve, such as pasta, pickles, charcuterie, and the like. Many restaurants contract with local farms, specifying on their menus, sometimes in excruciating detail, what their food sources are. Aesthetic advantages of taste and craft combine with the environmental virtue of local production.

There is a relationship between the American farm-to-table trend and campaigns to rescue the food heritage of other countries, as with the Slow Food organization founded in Italy. The European movements, however, tend to be targeted at globalization, reflecting the fear that fast food chains, sushi, bubble tea, or pizza are undermining regional traditions. A result of this concern is that long-established regional products are now protected by certification of origin defined by the European Community to identify zones outside of which products cannot use special designations, like San Daniele prosciutto or Roquefort cheese. This adaptation of the French wine industry's *appellation contrôlée* has no juridical parallel in the United States. An industrial trademark can be protected, but a Vidalia onion does not have to be from Vidalia.

Another difference between the United States and Europe is that American small farms and artisanal products had become nearly extinct by the last third of the twentieth century and so had to be reinvented rather than merely defended. While Italy, France, and Spain have experienced migration from the land, the rise of an integrated and globalized food industry, and other woes of the current era, their small-scale local agriculture never died, nor did the memory of the countryside and its products decline to the degree that it did in the United States.

Restaurants and the Food Revolution

The innovations of restaurants serving New American Cuisine were paralleled by developments in how people regarded the food they prepared or obtained from takeout and other intermediaries, even fast-food. We concentrate here on restaurants, however, because they led the way toward a new attitude and because one of the large shifts of the last forty years has been that people go out to eat much more than they used to. Affluence of the yuppie, bobo, or hipster type has made restaurant dining a fashion, lifestyle, and competitive status item.

Alice Waters herself always rejected the term "California Cuisine" as a way of describing what came out of the food revolution, because there is no tradition of California regional food that could be revived. The idea that California innovations spread to the rest of the country does have some merit, however. An early identification of distinction was a book from 1983 entitled *The Cuisine of California*.[7] The state's chefs, according to the author, Diane Worthington, had broken with classical culinary rules and rich sauces. Simple styles of cooking such as grilling and fresh, ethnic, and indigenous ingredients were paramount. Already shiitake mushrooms, poblano chilies, lemongrass, and baked goat cheese appear in the book as well-established California adaptations.

CHEZ PANISSE MENUS, 1980–1984

These menus from the early 1980s show the transition and coexistence of traditional French dishes with what was to become the prevailing style, a combination of Italian, Provençal, and California. Some menus are presented in French, some in English.

December 8, 1980: A Northern California Regional Dinner

Pigeon Point oysters grilled and served with butter and caviar
Pasta with Monterey shrimp and garden vegetables
Roast leg of suckling pig from Dal Porto Ranch with wild mushrooms
Garden salad with Sonoma goat cheese
Kiwi, persimmon, pomegranate, and pear sorbets

December 31, 1980: New Year's Eve Dinner

Soufflé d'huîtres au caviar
Foie gras en gelée de poivre
Timbale de fruits de mer
Rôti d'oie aux truffes
Salade de mâche
Les fromages
Bavarois rubané

May 20, 1981

Petite salé aux lentilles en salade
Pasta in brodo
Saumon grillé, beurre aux poireaux
Soufflé au pêche

February 13, 1982

Seafood brodettes aioli
Grilled pork loin with apples, potato, and leek gratin
Baked goat cheese salad
Nuptial Bavarian cream
Almond tart

May 5, 1982

Green beans and aioli
Bouillabaisse
Salad from the garden
Meyer lemon soufflé

September 13, 1983

Pizza with fresh black and yellow chanterelles
Pimento soup
Veal scaloppini with olive paste and garden green beans
Salad
Drowned figs in honey and framboise

February 10, 1984

Grilled Baja shrimp, sautéed sea scallops, roasted peppers, grilled fennel,
    and warm aioli
Risotto with braised chicken, shallots, greens, and Parmesan
Sautéed sweetbreads with Sauternes sauce and truffles
Garden salad
Blood orange compote

From a collection of menus kept at Chez Panisse, entitled "Way Beyond Tears: The Next Twelve Years,"
edited by Linda Parker Guenzel and Joyce McGillis.[8]

Despite its fame, Chez Panisse was regarded as too much wedded to France as well as to a modest, Berkeley self-image for many chefs who wanted something either more clearly American-earthy or who sought to create a new high-end food and celebrity aesthetic. As can be seen from its menus, Chez Panisse was not advancing the revolution at a rapid pace. Some of its staff wanted to forget about the French auberge in favor of attention to New American Cuisine. Credit for the nascent food revolution must, therefore, be apportioned among many inventive and experimental chefs. Judy Rodgers, a Chez Panisse veteran, devised an ambitious New American menu at the Union Hotel in Benicia, California, in 1981. In 1987, she became the chef at Zuni Café in San Francisco. Rodgers was not a purely California-oriented chef. The Union Hotel had a New England–inflected menu and Zuni, despite its name, was heavily influenced by Italy, showing that distinctions such as Italian or Mediterranean versus a more "pure" American are not clear. A Zuni menu from August 1, 1989, includes polenta, antipasto, and *arista* (stuffed pork roast).[9] Nevertheless, Rodgers was more decisive in leaving behind French influence than Alice Waters.

Other chefs and restaurateurs bypassed Mediterranean detours on the road to new American cuisine. Mark Miller and Susie Nelson, for example, brought Southwestern cooking to Fourth Street Grill in Berkeley beginning in 1979. The restaurant was creative but paid attention to traditionally prepared ingredients like handmade tortillas that were new to coastal sophisticates. Arizona 206 was a New York version of new Southwestern cuisine that opened in 1985, perhaps the first place where blue-corn tortillas were popularized on the East Coast.

Paul Prudhomme of Louisiana was the most successful regional, New American chef of the 1980s. He mixed things up at his K-Paul's restaurant, bringing rural Cajun dishes and ingredients such as andouille sausage to Creole New Orleans. He also served his own inventions such as blackened redfish and Cajun popcorn. This regional style was built not so much on precedent but was rather the creation of an innovative chef with a compelling personality. Prudhomme epitomized the winning combination of heartiness and spontaneity (i.e., fun) that was to have a bright future, especially for chefs who benefited from the growth of the Food Network in the 1990s.[10]

Pricey Farm-to-Table

Not all 1980s New American restaurants were as deliberately simple and funky as the Fourth Street Grill or K-Paul's. Yuppies created an audience for restaurants that offered carefully crafted, ecologically impeccable food but at strikingly high prices. In 1984, Alice Waters's erstwhile collaborator, Jeremiah Tower, opened Stars in San Francisco, a place that celebrated celebrities. Chez Panisse was never very expensive and tried as much as possible to ignore its growing fame and serve everyone equally. Once freed from what must have been an irritating egalitarianism, Tower welcomed the glitterati of Hollywood, couture, New York, and Paris. He liked both the imperial and the revolutionary part of his designation by the magazine *Focus* as "the new Napoleon spreading the revolution." That food revolution included traditions on overdrive (caviar and Champagne everywhere) and farm-to-table standbys like heirloom vegetables, braised and grilled meat, high-end pizza, and gourmet hamburgers.[11]

Another high-end but innovative new restaurant was Jonathan Waxman's Jams, a sensation when it opened in 1984, bringing California cuisine to backward New York City.[12] Looking back, Waxman's partner, Melvyn Master, marvels that California requisites like mesquite grilling, open kitchens, and baby vegetables were unknown in New York before Jams. Waxman fits the model of American bowled over by France and determined to remake United States restaurant food according to French methods and aesthetics, but without imitating French ingredients or dishes. Waxman asked himself, "What if we took all the sort of classic regional foods of America and did what they did in France . . . lighten them up, make them more accessible?" At Jams he interpreted this agenda as meaning perfect ingredients and lots of grilling. Instead of tired coq au vin, he served free-range chicken grilled over wood and then lightly brushed with rosemary oil. The menu changed constantly and at whim, and previously unknown ingredients like purslane were introduced.

All this spontaneity was expensive. Grilled chicken with French fries (daringly informal at the time) went for twenty dollars, the equivalent of fifty dollars today. In what became a not-uncommon pattern in the restaurant stratosphere, Waxman overreached at Jams, imposing his mercurial personality on the restau-

rant but often not showing up, or opening a restaurant in London without sufficient planning, and giving away free meals to a star-studded clientele. Waxman
and Master were on the cover of *Esquire* and Waxman posed in his silk pajamas
for the *New York Daily News*. Jams closed in 1989, a victim of management
problems and the neglect of the actual business resulting from Waxman's celebrity status.[13]

A similar but more restrained restaurant was Hubert's in New York's Gramercy Park area, opened in 1979 by Len Allison and Karen Hubert. They brought
an intellectual sensibility and presented updated American classics such as turkey pot pie or pork loin braised with bourbon. This restaurant lasted until 1991,
when it closed because of the economic downturn that year.[14]

These restaurants shared an extension or intensification of the seasonal, local
agenda of the 1970s. They had varying price points and levels of formality, but
all were experimental and anti-traditional, run by American chefs, many with
little professional training. Their owners were willing, even eager to break rules
and to try out non-French culinary ideas via Mexico or Japan, for example. They
all provided a personal and informal setting and a menu that was curated (to use
an overworked later term).

MENU FOR "AN AMERICAN CELEBRATION" IN HONOR OF JAMES BEARD'S EIGHTIETH BIRTHDAY

A key moment of recognition for New American Cuisine came with
James Beard's eightieth birthday party on May 4, 1983. The occa-
sion was marked by what was called "An American Celebration" at
San Francisco's Stanford Court Hotel. Leading chefs and friends of
Beard's brought out quintessentially American dishes, not in their
folkloric form, but using regional ingredients for original creations.[15]

Three kinds of West Coast oysters: Olympia (Puget Sound), Belon (Tomales Bay), and Portuguese (Vancouver Island, BC)

Terrine of three American smoked fish with their respective caviars (Larry Forgione, River Café, Brooklyn)

Red pepper pasta with grilled scallops (Jonathan Waxman, Michael's, Santa Monica)

Garden salad (Alice Waters, Chez Panisse, Berkeley)

Blackened red fish (Paul Prudhomme, K-Paul's Louisiana Kitchen, New Orleans)

Marinated grilled quail with poblano chili, cilantro, and lime sauce (Mark Miller, Fourth Street Grill, Berkeley)

Roasted rack of lamb stuffed with Missouri greens and hazelnuts and gratin of wild root vegetables, fiddlehead ferns, and cattail sprouts (Bradley Ogden, American Café, Kansas City, and Jimmy Schmidt, London Chop House, Detroit)

American cheese selections

Pecan pastry with chocolate sabayon sauce (Jeremiah Tower, Santa Fe Bar and Grill, Berkeley, and Balboa Café, San Francisco)

For the after-party, Wolfgang Puck supplied Spago pizza and the lone female chef, Barbara Kafka (Star Spangled Foods, New York), made tripe gumbo.

The 1983 dinner encapsulates the accomplishments of a decade of experimentation that reoriented American cuisine toward high-quality and seasonal primary products. In this meal, however, we can also see a program for the future.

In the 1980s, an ingredients-based cuisine took over the best and newest restaurants. Their chefs used French cooking techniques and traditions but cooked American products according to personal creativity or revived American recipes. So effective was this expansion and so trendy that the editors of *Spy* magazine in 1988 felt compelled to map endangered "regular guy" places in New York such as Irish bars and grills (preferably with the word "Blarney" in the title), along with steak places and Greek-owned coffee shops.[16] Away from metropolitan centers, restaurants might absorb sophisticated fashions for sun-dried tomatoes or pasta with seafood, but only at the end of the twentieth century did the new food aesthetic start to take over everywhere. Rather than simply adding fashionable ingredients to uninspired formulae, the source of products and their actual flavor came to matter in the twenty-first century.

The prominent chefs and restaurants of the 1980s created the American cuisine that still dominates medium- to high-end dining. With Chez Panisse, the path to a new American culinary approach was by way of Italy and Provence,

Chef Michael Romano and owner Danny Meyer at Union Square Cafe, ca. 1988. Taking advantage of the Greenmarket, Union Square Cafe opened in 1985 with seasonal and Italian-inflected food.

but it was not unique in this regard. At Wolfgang Puck's Spago, established in Los Angeles in 1982, the famous dish was pizza in exotic, never-before-seen flavors such as barbecued chicken or potato and egg. In 1985, Danny Meyer opened the Union Square Café in New York, inspired by three key trends: the informal joy in the cuisine of the Italian trattoria, the Californian respect for ingredients, and attentive French notions of attentive service.[17]

SOME "FIRSTS"

Gourmet hamburgers: Jeremiah Tower's Balboa Café, San Francisco, 1983, though anticipated by Judy Rodgers at the Union Hotel, Benicia, California, and, long before, at Twenty-One Club, New York, which started serving expensive hamburgers in 1950.

Comfort food: The term was first used by M.F.K. Fisher in *Bon Appétit*, 1978.

Foodie: *The Official Foodie Handbook* by Ann Barr and Paul Levy was published in 1985. The word began as a comic takeoff of the 1980 bestseller *The Official Preppy Handbook* by Lisa Birnbach.

Free Range: The term was invented by Larry Forgione, chef and owner of An American Place, New York, 1980. See also "day-boat" (scallops); "line-caught" (fish), and "grass-fed" (beef).

Pop-up restaurants: Paul Prudhomme's temporary restaurants in San Francisco and New York, early 1980s.

Restaurant or chef raising their own produce: Deborah Madison at Greens, San Francisco, 1979.

Use of the bar as a dining space: El Internacional, New York, 1984, and Union Square Café, New York, 1985. Anticipated by the Colony, New York, during the 1950s (not exactly eating *at* the bar, but small tables set up next to the bar).

Pasta in fancy, non-Italian restaurants: If not literally the first example, the invention and popularity of Pasta Primavera at Le Cirque (a French restaurant), New York, 1977, was a milestone.

Open kitchen for reasons other than proof of hygienic conditions (as had been the case at the Chinese restaurant Kan's, San Francisco, 1950s) or as spectacle (e.g., Fourneau's Ovens, San Francisco, 1960s): Depuy Canal House, High Falls, New York, 1974. The trend took off with wood-burning pizza ovens at Chez Panisse Café, Berkeley, 1983, and Spago, Los Angeles, 1982, and was introduced in New York by Jonathan Waxman at Jams, 1984.

Kitchen "chef's table": Charlie Trotter's, Chicago, 1987.

Small plates: Charlie Trotter's, Chicago, 1987, and popularized particularly by Thomas Keller at the French Laundry, Yountville, California, 1994. Anticipated by Spanish tapas, first popularized by El Internacional, New York, 1984.

Vertical (stacked) food on small plates: Alfred Portale, Gotham Bar and Grill, New York, late 1980s. Perfected by Charlie Trotter's, Chicago.

"Fusion": The term was introduced at a culinary conference by Florida restaurateur Norman Van Aken, 1988. The style was anticipated by a number of chefs, notably Wolfgang Puck at Le Chinois, Santa Monica, 1983.

From Alison Pearlman, *Smart Casual: The Transformation of Gourmet Restaurant Style in America* (Chicago: University of Chicago Press, 2013); Andrew Friedman, *Chefs, Drugs and Rock and Roll* (New York: HarperCollins, 2018); and Michael Ruhlman, *The Soul of a Chef: The Journey toward Perfection* (New York: Viking Penguin, 2000).

Modernist Cuisine: Admired but Not Imitated

All the pieces of New American cuisine—farm-to-table, seasonal, and local—were in place by the end of the 1980s. What has occurred in the subsequent three decades is the intensification of the prevailing aesthetic. The program has also been defined by negative precepts: no food from outside the region, no food deemed unhealthy, less meat, no ecologically suspect seafood. Concentrating on flavor means that instead of orienting food around renunciation, contemporary trends emphasize positive simplicity and innovation. Vegetables are moved to the center of the meal because they can be made deliciously, not just because they are more environmentally responsible than meat. New primary ingredients (or new to fine dining) are "discovered" or at least newly appreciated. Pork belly, for example, found its way onto menus like that of David Chang's Momofuku Noodle Bar that mixed up high and low, but also at uncompromisingly elegant Eleven Madison Park. High and low are combined, not just with hamburgers and pizza, but ramen and barbecue as well. The basis for innovation is taste, not exotic origins or novelty for its own sake.

Amidst all of this innovation, modernist cuisine, also known for a time as "molecular gastronomy," has been surprisingly weak in the United States. Surprising, because it continues to be the dominant trend among the most famous restaurants in the world and because America would seem to be fertile territory for novelty. A longing to restore the hazily recollected family farm and its produce may explain why the United States has been almost indifferent to modernism in food. While sharing with farm-to-table an antipathy to mass-market food, modernist cuisine focuses on transformations, pushing extremes of texture, ingredients, and flavor combination rather than the literally conservative efforts to preserve rustic heartiness, simplicity, and authenticity.

Beetroot and yogurt meringue, one of the 1,846 dishes invented by Ferran Adrià at elBulli in Catalonia before it closed in 2011, has a different philosophical as well as gustatory attraction than hoppin' John made with heirloom golden rice from Low Country South Carolina. The hoppin' John case exemplifies American preoccupations and our recent rediscovery of neglected but delicious primary products. Sean Brock, the former chef and owner of Husk, which started in Charleston, South Carolina, described his realization that ingredients matter when he made a properly cooked plate of this simple local specialty of rice and beans and it tasted of cardboard and paste. The problem was the mediocrity of supermarket-quality basic ingredients. Preparing the dish using what were once almost forgotten breeds, Carolina Gold rice and Sea Island red cowpeas, revealed why hoppin' John is delicious, even lucky to eat.[18]

This heart-warming vignette shows Americans' longing for authenticity and a distant rural past. In other countries, farm life, even though damaged by globalization, urban opportunities, and the long-term depopulation of the countryside, is not as remote as in the United States. Today it is illegal in the European Community to kill pigs except in a slaughterhouse, but in Catalonia, for example, almost anyone above the age of forty remembers attending festivities associated with a late-fall pig-killing. By contrast, only an exceptional, and probably elderly American, one who perhaps grew up on an Appalachian or Amish farm, will have such a memory.[19]

In Catalonia or the Basque Country, where molecular gastronomy was invented, the rural eclipse is a recent phenomenon and still not total: there are small farms, markets, hyperlocal specialties, and at least the vivid memory of how previous generations lived. Modernist experimentation is more successful in Europe therefore, because its traditions do not require reinvention to the degree that is the case in the United States.

Some of Ferran Adrià's creations at elBulli from 1992 to 2011 showed transformations of dishes that everyone still eats at home: pa amb tomàquet—a liquid version of the Catalan favorite, grilled bread smeared with tomato and olive oil, or "melon with ham," Iberian ham consommé with spherical melon "caviar," served in a glass. Others played off familiar dishes but appropriating foreign ingredients: "Cantonese musico"—a Chinese inflected version of the traditional Spanish after-dinner mixture of nuts and raisins that here includes star anise and Sichuan pepper. The majority, however, were completely original creations whose titles give only mysterious or deceptive information about what they might be: "3Ds al ras-el-hanout and lemon basil shoots" turns out to be a cone-shaped potato chip stuffed with basil cream and sprinkled with a Moroccan spice mixture.[20] "Ajo blanco" on a Spanish menu normally means a white gazpacho, but in the elBulli version the cold soup was made into ice cream with additional almonds and garlic. "Japanese ravioli" was actually spherified miso soup with tofu; "pond," a flat, circular layering of flavored ice and water.[21]

ElBulli, originally a French restaurant, was founded by a German couple in 1964 and named after their bulldog. It was located in an isolated cove on the mostly overtouristed Costa Brava north of Barcelona. Ferran Adrià took over in 1987, and his first change was to make the food more Catalan. By the mid-1990s, he was in the process of creating dishes and techniques no one had ever heard of before, in Catalonia or anywhere else, and became known as a master alchemist of cuisine. He made foam famous, beginning in 1994 with "white-bean foam with sea urchins." By the late 1990s, foam was both celebrated and satirized. Although he later became a fan, the late Anthony Bourdain in *Kitchen Confidential* approvingly quoted an interlocutor who said, "That foam guy is bogus."[22] Adrià, aka "that foam guy," reiterated foam not merely as a sauce style but as a dish on its own with "smoke foam" and went on to develop "airs," even lighter, almost floating reinventions of products such as Mandarin oranges or carrots.

Adrià has received accolades and adoration as a genius, artist, and philosopher, acclaim that has proven hard to live up to. He closed elBulli at the height of its fame, in 2011, and it's not clear how much attention his opinions would have received without the basis of an actual restaurant. Other intellectual or at least articulate chefs have succeeded him—René Redzepi in Denmark, Thomas Keller in the United States—but Adrià remains undoubtedly the most internationally influential chef of the twenty-first century so far. That influence includes the United States, but exerted indirectly. He stands behind innovative cooking styles using advanced technology and the vogue, even here, for odd combinations and unexpected textures.

It is not as if there is no modernist presence in the United States: Nathan Myhrvold, formerly chief technology officer for Microsoft, is perhaps the leading American modernist advocate and expert. His *Modernist Cuisine* is a definitive, six-volume encyclopedia of techniques and preparations. The American food community also reveres Harold McGee and Hervé This, experts in the chemistry of food and flavor.[23]

"The Thaw," a dessert from elBulli in Catalonia, Spain, the most famous restaurant in the first decade of the twenty-first century.

ELBULLI:
A FEW INNOVATIONS FROM THE YEAR 2000

The restaurant was open only six months of the year. The other half was spent in experiments, and new dishes were chronicled until elBulli closed in 2011. Here is a list of the categories of experimentation chosen for research in 2000 and a sample dish from each category. Jellies were big that year.

Water and infusions (using water strained off from cooking): textured pumpkin with deconstituted grapefruit

Juices, extracts, and nectars: melon jelly with aromatic young almond meringues (after a melon is baked, its juice has a jellied texture)

Consommés and soups: hot baked potato jellied consommé

Purées: sweet vanilla potato purée (an example of what Adrià referred to as the symbiosis between sweet and savory)

Cold agar-agar-based jellies: beetroot soup with solid oil and frozen yogurt powder (agar-agar, a seaweed derivative, allows for changes in texture, making possible the unexpected forms of this combination)

Hot jellies: aubergine (eggplant) with hot jellied tuna, apricot, and yogurt consommé (agar-agar makes it possible for a substance to keep its gelatinous texture while hot)

Other jellies: transparent saffroned fruit paste

From *elBulli 1998–2002* (Roses, Spain: elBulli Books, 2003), 320–41.

The elegantly minimalist restaurant Alinea in Chicago offers a modernist combination of mystery, surprise, and wit. Chef Grant Achatz has created dishes with concise elBulli-like names that belie their complexity: "ice" is a combination of liquid beet, hibiscus, and licorice served in a hollowed-out block of ice and drunk with a straw. Or the name itself is provocative: "wooly pig" combines fennel, orange, and squid in a way that looks, maybe, like a wooly pig; "winter in New Hampshire" turns out to be sour cherry pudding, blood orange, gingerbread marshmallow, and jelled honey resting on a bed of peppermint-flavored snow and served with a mug of clear hot chocolate.[24]

Eleven Madison Park in New York ascended to the top of the world's best rankings in 2017 by coming up with new inventions that, in typical modernist fashion, combine seemingly clashing ingredients and concepts, such as sea urchin cappuccino, or are mysterious—"winter in Provence" is a combination of liquefied goat cheese, celery root, potato, and black truffles.[25]

Not every modernist development in America flowed from the elBulli example. Thomas Keller at The French Laundry, in California's Napa Valley, anticipated Ferran Adrià with his invention of cornets made from tuile cones filled with salmon and red onion crème fraîche. He conceived this idea in 1990 while ordering an ice cream cone at Baskin-Robbins. Another classic Keller item is "coffee and doughnuts," the coffee presented as a semifreddo with foam.[26] Vespertine, a sensational restaurant in Los Angeles, serves enigmatic food with dishes called kelp, almond, endive, hirme, and crystalline ice plant that, suffice it to say, are not what one expects. But then again, the whole point of this extreme surprise establishment is that you can't have any expectations. A dish called "pickled scallops" is presented in a bowl that looks puzzlingly empty, but underneath a blackened crust that seems part of the ceramic are the scallops. The restaurant building looks like a spaceship, and chef Jordan Kahn has plausibly claimed that it was built by moon-worshipping extraterrestrials many years (or moons) ago.[27]

1 SEPTEMBER 2018
WANING GIBBOUS 67% ILLUMINATION

MR. TOM BARTON

GIANT KELP SEA LETTUCE

BURNT ONION BLACK CURRANT

MILK BREAD ABALONE MUSHROOMS

FAVA BEANS HORSERADISH GRILLED RASPBERRY

WHITE ASPARAGUS OSETRA CAVIAR ELDERFLOWER

SCALLOP BONE MARROW SALTED PLUM

BLACK THROAT PERCH PEAR VINEGAR

SPOT PRAWN ROSE BEGONIA

CRAB CARAMELIZED YEAST

ROCK GAME HEN BLACK CURRANT HYSSOP

HALIBUT BLACK TRUMPET STRAWBERRY

BLACK RASPBERRY MEADOWSWEET BLACK CARROT

ALMOND CUCUMBER REDWOOD

BIODYNAMIC BLACKBERRIES

ORGANIC PLUMS

Menu from Vespertine, Los Angeles, 2018. The restaurant takes the elements of invention and surprise to a new level.

PRINCIPLES OF MODERNIST CUISINE

1.   Cuisine is a creative act in which the chef and diner are in dialogue.
2.   Culinary rules, conventions, and traditions must be understood, but they should not be allowed to hinder the development of creative new dishes.
3.   Creatively breaking ordinary rules and traditions is a powerful way to engage diners and make them think about the dining experience.
4.   Surprising them [diners] with food that defies their expectations is another way to engage them intellectually.
5.   In addition to surprise, many other emotions, reactions, feelings and thoughts can be elicited by cuisine. Those include humor, whimsy, satire, and nostalgia. . . .
6.   Creativity, novelty, and invention are intrinsic to the chef's role.
7.   Science and technology are sources that can be tapped to enable new culinary inventions, but they are a means to an end rather than the final goal.
8.   First-rate ingredients are the foundation on which cuisine is built. . . .
9.   Ingredients originating in food science and technology, such as hydrocolloids, enzymes, and emulsions are powerful tools in helping to produce dishes that would otherwise be impossible.
10. Diners and chefs should be sensitive to the conditions under which food is harvested and grown. . . .

Items 8 and 10 seem like pro forma gestures to the importance of primary materials and concern over the human and environmental costs of how food gets to the diner. It's not that the sentiments are insincere, but they are not central tenets of molecular gastronomy. The core set of ideas is summarized in the repetition of the word *creativity* and the assumption that the intellectualization of food is a good thing for all concerned. Novelty, surprise, and creativity are more important than sensuous delight.

From Nathan Myhrvold, *Modernist Cuisine: The Art and Science of Gastronomy*, vol. 1 (Bellevue, WA: Cooking Lab, 2011).

EIGHT FUNDAMENTAL NEW COOKING
TECHNOLOGIES AND TECHNIQUES

Agar-agar: Derived from seaweed. Allows gelled food to be served hot and textures to be manipulated, as in "fettucine consommé."

Alginate and calcium chloride: Makes it possible to encapsulate liquid without a solid cover. A famous example is the "liquid olives" invented by elBulli.

Sous-vide cooking

Foams

Sugar tuile technique: To enclose a soft preparation such as foie gras in a fine, crisp layer.

Aggressive use of aromas, such as hay, smoke, or apples

Unconventional serving devices

Unconventional temperatures, such as hot gelatin or frozen foie gras

From Michael Ruhlman, *The Soul of a Chef: The Journey toward Perfection* (New York: Viking Penguin, 2000), 145–46.

Sous-vide has become an established method of restaurant cooking. Foam, sugar tuile, and alginate are common at the high or daring level, but the others remain unusual and are not required for a notable restaurant to succeed.

All these exceptional examples notwithstanding, the prevailing American trend is against modernism, at least in its globally sophisticated form. Americans are, after all, already overfamiliar with alchemical transformations thanks to decades of food industry innovation. Americans were eating Cheez Doodles and Froot Loops when Catalans still attended pig-killings and made their own sausages. Wylie Dufresne, one of the most creative modernist chefs, said that food manufacturers taught him how to use gelling and thickening agents and various tricks to manipulate hot and cold so that he could produce effects such as fried mayonnaise.[28]

Farm-to-Table Plus Modernism: Thomas Keller

The most successful modernist innovations in this country have come in tandem with respect for tradition and taste, blending an ingredient-focused farm-to-table ethos with originality and technology. More than any other chef, Thomas Keller at the French Laundry and Per Se has combined purity of ingredients with the unexpected and amusing elements of culinary innovation.[29] He has done this within a consistent French tradition and orientation, reflecting his training at half a dozen distinguished Parisian restaurants. The "French" in French Laundry is not a vestigial term but a constant inspiration, as opposed to the French name of Chez Panisse, which no longer accurately refers to what the restaurant serves.[30] Few chefs share Keller's obsession with detail and willingness to take pains. He stores fish in the same position that it swims so as to avoid stressing its flesh, and peels fava beans before cooking for better color and removes the tiny germ on the side, which can be bitter. You can't make stock by simply simmering bones and vegetables for a long time, according to Keller. The quantities have to be exactly measured and the proper level of boiling followed consistently.[31]

Corey Lee at Benu and Grant Achatz at Alinea both served for years with Thomas Keller at the French Laundry and share his fanatical attention to beauty and perfection. Such practices are possible only at the very highest and most expensive level of restaurant service and are not the favored style of American cuisine at the moment. More influential on prevailing trends is Keller's insistence on combining the best ingredients, many from the restaurant's garden, with creative transformation.

The French Laundry opened in 1978 in what had been a steam laundry building in the Napa Valley town of Yountville. Built in 1900, its idyllic setting attracted Keller, at that time a great but underrecognized chef seeking refuge from both New York and Los Angeles. He took over in 1994 and by 1996 was making a profit. In 1999, Keller published *The French Laundry Cookbook*, a lavishly produced combination of aspirational recipes (from the point of view of the amateur cook), autobiography, an evocation of the restaurant's rhythm and practices, and stunning photography. As with many aspects of Keller's world-view, this at first seemed overproduced, but it has set the standard for a celebrity cookbook that is both a coffee table book and a culinary philosophical treatise, with pictures.

Dishes like "oyster and pearls"—caviar, tapioca, and oyster in a custard of crème fraîche and whipped cream—demonstrate original and alluring flavor combinations. A few of the dishes in Keller's cookbook, like the gazpacho, are simple; others are quite elaborate. "Head to Toe" is braised and stuffed pig's head with pig's feet on a green lentil ragout.[32] Over time, the experimental variations have tended to increase. Always within a recognizable French tradition, dishes are transformations and rendered in quotes. On a sixteen-course tasting menu for December 29, 2017, half the courses have something in quotation marks: Beef "rouelle" or "vichyssoise" are not too far from the original braised round cut of beef and potato-leek soup, but "piña colada" is a complicated pineapple coconut dessert for which the coconut "mousse" base is itself in quotes.

At Keller's New York restaurant, Per Se, there is less emphasis on sourcing and certainly no hint of a rural or outdoor ambience. In contrast to bucolic Yountville, this expression of Keller's art is located in a skyscraper complex with glitzy stores for neighbors. It does display, however, a recognizably Thomas Keller approach combining simplicity, perfect ingredients, effort, and solemnity. The four- or five-hour meal has its *longueurs* but is relieved by extraordinary creations like radish pie, a small tart with delicious and thinly sliced radishes on top, unexpected combinations like dried tomatoes and fresh milk curd or sea urchin and cabbage, and unexpected techniques—moss cooked in chocolate; grilled rose ice cream.[33]

This cuisine is ironic, referential, creative, and technically extraordinary. It is not "molecular" in the sense that the basic constituents are recognizable, and the intent is to focus and reveal taste possibilities, not to bring news from another planet. Modernist gastronomy may not have taken hold of the American imagination, but its international renown has encouraged ambitious (but not necessarily hyperexpensive) restaurants to try out new techniques.

Smart Casual

Although modernist cuisine has been around for over twenty-five years, the governing fashion for both American restaurants and home cooking has taken a different, heartier, and more artisanal path. American food has expanded at both the high and low ends: barbecue as well as foie gras; old-format but high-quality hamburgers as at the Shake Shack chain. Or, as *New York* magazine restaurant reviewer Adam Platt put it, "During the aughts, the crackpots and kitchen slaves in the back of the house stormed the barricades and brought a new brand of informed, high-end comfort food to the masses."[34] His examples are bad-boy Italian chef Mario Batali and thought-leader chef Tom Colicchio, different personalities but both purveyors of intense flavor. Chefs in Platt's pantheon share an indifference to reverent atmosphere and a love for previously unlikely animal parts. The "crackpot" chefs have come out of the kitchen and taken over the front of the house. If this means minimalist furniture, loud music, no-choice menus, and in-your-face attitude in place of the svelte maître d'hôtel, oversize leather-bound menus, velvet banquettes, and soft lighting of the past, just go for it.

In 2006, the irreverent David Kamp published *The United States of Arugula,* whose subtitle is *The Sun-Dried, Cold-Pressed, Dark-Roasted, Extra Virgin Story of the American Food Revolution.* This list of specific, mostly Italian, features perfectly summarized the mega-trends of the 1980s and 1990s, but if one were going to update this list it might now be a "wood-burning, double smoked, fermented, vegetable-forward" story. Or maybe, given the rising Asian influence, a "mala-infused, nuoc cham–marinated, sambal-flavored, tamarind-scented story."

The current restaurant fashion can be defined as what Alison Pearlman calls "smart casual."[35] This expression takes into account the coexistence of high- and low-end aesthetics and presentations. Some of the restaurants where it is hardest to obtain reservations offer modest décor with customers dressed in every possible fashion, and a personal take on atmosphere and service ranging from family-like to intimidating, but always informal. A nonexhaustive checklist of smart casual attributes might include open kitchens and open fires; informal service styles; unusual industrial or improvised space; noise; artisanal beer and whiskey lists; comfort food; eclectic and even meta-cultural food (i.e., riffs on rather than imitations of foreign cuisine); tasting menus; small plates (based perhaps on a combination of low-end Spanish tapas and high-end Japanese *kaiseki*); the inclusion of popular favorites like burgers or fried chicken alongside forgotten ingredients like salsify or ramps.

Smart casual style complements farm-to-table because both are expressions of a desire for a stylish authenticity as opposed to European-derived pretension. The restaurant category that is least easy to fit in with the smart casual, seasonal, locavore ethos is the ethnic restaurant. The popularity of ethnic cuisine is that it is inexpensive and collectively offers a tremendous variety of tastes. Authenticity, seasonality, and searching out the best ingredients are not demanded by customers at Chinese, Indian, Ethiopian, or other foreign restaurants. What is necessary to succeed is an assertive set of tastes offered inexpensively. Rather than the blandness associated with traditional American comfort foods like meatloaf or chicken pot pie, the new idea is an intense form of flavor, something international and farm-to-table restaurants have in common.

Many of the most dramatic twenty-first-century changes appear less in actual dishes—avocado toast and kale do not constitute a new revolution—but in the media, particularly the role of chefs and, through social media, the role of customers and the making of opinion. The current food frenzy started with the invention of food television in the 1990s and the cult of the celebrity chefs that television has enabled. The food served at restaurants today is based on innovations of the 1970s and 1980s, but the position of food in the world of popular culture has been completely transformed.

Out of the Kitchen: Celebrity Chefs

Although the media-savvy celebrity chef dates only from the 1970s, when Paul Bocuse rocketed to fame, outstanding cooks have been praised for centuries. In the Western world, perhaps the first celebrity chef was Guillaume Tirel, known as "Taillevent," who lived from about 1310 to 1395.[36] Taillevent served King Charles V of France, who was so impressed with his *maître de cuisine* that he bestowed on him a knighthood. His coat of arms displays three stewpots or

Wolfgang Puck, the Austrian-born chef of Spago in Los Angeles, created widely imitated restaurants, dishes, and concepts.

Tomb effigy of Taillevent (ca. 1310–1395), chef for the kings of France, Hennemont (Lorraine). Guillaume Tirel, known as "Taillevent," was among the most famous chefs of the Middle Ages.

marmites along the center of the field. Cooking vessels are hardly typical chivalric emblems, but Taillevent himself was proud to display this heraldic device. At his sculpted tomb in Lorraine, he is shown with his shield bearing the stewpots, clothed in armor and with a sword by his side rather than a ladle. In accord with aristocratic example, he is accompanied by effigies of his two wives (the first died) and a dog at his feet.

Taillevent was credited with writing *Le Viandier*, the most renowned in its time among the approximately 150 cookbooks that survive from the thirteenth through fifteenth centuries. The *Viandier* was started before Taillevent was born, but he seems to have added to it, and his fame was such that the whole collection became identified with him.

MEDIEVAL SAUCE RECIPE FROM *LE VIANDIER,*
ATTRIBUTED TO TAILLEVENT

Cameline Sauce
(so-called because its light brown color
resembled that of a camel)

A favorite medieval sauce with many spices, among which cinnamon predominates, served with meat or fish.

1–2 slices white bread

9 oz white wine

1–2 Tbsp wine vinegar

1 tsp cinnamon

½ tsp ground ginger

½ tsp ground cloves

⅛ tsp ground nutmeg

¼ tsp black pepper

pinch of ground saffron

2 Tbsp brown sugar

salt

Toast the bread until brown, cut it into pieces, and put to soak in the wine and vinegar. Press the softened mixture through a sieve or mix it with a hand mixer until smooth. Add the spices and, if you wish, the brown sugar and a tiny amount of salt. Taste. The flavor of cinnamon should be dominant. Serve the sauce either cold or heated in a saucepan.

From Hannele Klemettilä, *The Medieval Kitchen: A Social History with Recipes* (London: Reaktion, 2012), 182.

The renowned chefs of the Middle Ages, Renaissance, and Baroque were in the employ of great noblemen or rulers. They put on elaborate banquets and seldom worried about any sort of financial bottom line. Master Chiquart, chef for the Duke of Savoy in the 1430s, envisages a banquet for about five hundred guests lasting two days. We know little about Chiquart's personality or biography, but he seems to be a businesslike and undaunted chef. He calmly notes that it might require as much as two months to prepare this meal, mostly involving gathering sufficient game. Purveyors with forty horses are to set out to acquire all manner of birds and mammals. Several hundred pounds of spices will be needed, as well as at least twelve thousand eggs. Twelve pounds of gold leaf will be required for decoration of the dishes to be presented at the meals, including an edible castle with four towers and a courtyard with a fountain. Atop each castle tower is a different virtuoso dish: a pike cooked three ways and three colors without being cut into pieces before serving (tricky), a skinned and redressed swan (i.e., cooked but sewn back into its original skin and feathers), a glazed piglet, and a glazed boar's head. Each animal is breathing fire by means of a camphor-soaked wick in its mouth.[37]

Another example of the ostentatious and entertaining tastes of premodern Europe is a dinner in 1524 during Lent at the court of Alfonso d'Este, Duke of Ferrara, that was served to twenty-four guests in three courses, each with forty-five dishes. Lent meant no meat, but apparently not abstemiousness. Thirty dishes were made with sturgeon: sturgeon head cooked in a white sauce with pomegranate seeds, sturgeon meatballs in sauce served on bread, sturgeon slices in pistachio sauce, sturgeon pies, sturgeon with cherries and dates, sturgeon caviar, sturgeon pasta fried with oranges, sturgeon tripe on bread, and so forth. Giovanni Battista Rossetti, the chef for this meal, was greatly admired in his time.[38]

Then and now, there was plenty of stress in the life of a celebrity chef. In 1671, François Vatel, chef for the Prince de Condé, killed himself when the fish failed to arrive at the Chateau of Chantilly for a banquet celebrating the visit of King Louis XIV. It's unclear whose wrath the hapless Vatel feared more, that of his employer the count or the notoriously hard-to-please monarch. Vatel's fate has become a legend, emblematic of the pressures under which chefs operate.

These chefs were regarded as masters of a demanding, if somewhat lowly

The Marvelous Sauce, ca. 1890, by Jehan Georges Vibert (1840–1902), a French painter known for his depictions of luxury-loving clerics.

craft, but they did more than merely follow precedent. The Italian Bartolomeo Scappi in the sixteenth century and the French chefs François de la Varenne in the seventeenth, Antonin Carême in the nineteenth, and Auguste Escoffier in the nineteenth and twentieth were all culinary stars who introduced fundamental changes to haute cuisine. They replaced one authoritative system with another, but always within a set of practices that from our vantage point seems incredibly elaborate and rule-bound. They were not creative artists who broke with tradition.

Perhaps the most significant divide in the history of chefs and their fame occurred before and after the invention of the restaurant. Until the late eighteenth century, when restaurants were first established in Paris, great chefs cooked for ecclesiastical, aristocratic, or princely employers. The leading chef of the early nineteenth century, Carême, followed this older career mode, running the kitchens of a series of powerful men: the astute diplomat and gourmet Prince Talleyrand, the corpulent and corrupt Prince Regent of England (the future George IV), and the great banker, the Baron de Rothschild. Carême, whose name ironically means "Lent" in French, was even offered a job in Saint Petersburg by the Russian tsar, but he declined.[39]

Carême was a prince among celebrity chefs, and he was also the last to spend his entire career in the employ of private individuals. He was famous because of his books of recipes, which influenced chefs everywhere, but few people ever had an opportunity to sample his cooking. Contrast this with the life of the other authoritative French chef, Escoffier, whose career closes the nineteenth century and begins the twentieth.[40] Escoffier collaborated with Caesar Ritz, manager of the Savoy in London and the Ritz in Paris, and then, after Ritz had a nervous crisis, Escoffier returned to London as chef at the Carlton Hotel. On one occasion Escoffier prepared a dinner for Kaiser Wilhelm II featuring a new creation, veal Orloff, veal roasted, sliced, and layered with *soubise* (an onion mixture) and *duxelles* (a mushroom mixture) and then reassembled. The German ruler told the chef that while he, Wilhelm II, was emperor of Germany, Escoffier was "the emperor of chefs." Escoffier cooked this magnificent one-off meal for the kaiser, but unlike Carême, Escoffier had affluent restaurant clients who could partake of elegant dishes like veal Orloff whenever they wished.

Restaurants allowed chefs a large audience, hence considerable fame, but until the 1970s, a chef, no matter how revered, operated within a tradition and was not an iconoclastic artist who could simply do away with inherited techniques and training. As long as the chef was a species of master craftsman, he or she fit a formula enunciated recently by Alex Atala of the restaurant D.O.M. in São Paulo, who said, "Creativity isn't doing something that nobody has ever done before. It's doing the same thing that everybody does, but doing it better."[41] Piety toward one's ancestors notwithstanding, Atala is not, in fact, a traditional chef but rather a radically innovative force who has, among other things, incorporated the products of the Amazon and the insights of indigenous people into his cooking.

To return to the United States, the path to celebrity status in recent decades has been less focused on a drive to invent new dishes, but rather through ability to present a memorable personality to the media. Instead of haughty Paul Bocuse in his impeccable and ultra-traditional white outfit, American chefs portray themselves as fun-loving outlaws in jeans and tee shirts. Anthony Bourdain bears some responsibility for popularizing the hard-living, tattooed male chef with an unerring eye for authenticity. The American male chef might be just as temperamental and authoritarian as Bocuse, but more likely to be found investigating the secrets of remote places than exchanging pleasantries with European royalty. American celebrity chefs had no problem, however, bantering with television hosts and other media stars. Mario Batali's collaboration with Gwyneth Paltrow in the Spain road trip series comes to mind; on the one hand an unlikely pairing of the rambunctious and earthy chef with the svelte movie star and on the other, a perfect complementary attraction.

Food Television

There are, in fact, two phases of culinary stardom in recent American history. The first involved chef-restaurateurs such as the "free spirits" of the 1980s, people like Paul Prudhomme in Louisiana or David and Karen Waltuck at Chanterelle in New York, who fit the Andrew Friedman typology of wanderers and misfits.[42] Even in the twenty-first century, it is possible to be a world-famous chef without a constant visual media presence. Ferran Adrià, creator of modernist gastronomy, is not a particularly charismatic speaker in either Spanish or Catalan, and he does not speak English. David Chang, René Redzepi, and Alex Atala, enshrined as "the gods of food" on the cover of the November 18, 2013, *Time* magazine, did not owe their divinity to television. Nevertheless, most celebrity chefs require the visual and virtual media to launch their careers.

The founding of the Television Food Network (TVFN) in 1993, known as the Food Network after 1995, was not appreciated at the time for the cataclysmic series of events it actually set in motion. Television turns out to be crucial for making food a form of entertainment and the subject of passionate interest and conversation.[43] Food TV has attracted a seemingly unlikely audience of people who seldom cook, creating a large constituency for food and food fashions beyond the self-described sophisticates of the big cities.

In the mid-1990s, the idea was simply to build on the long-standing popularity of cooking broadcasts like *The Galloping Gourmet* (Graham Kerr) or *The French Chef* (Julia Child). As far back as the 1950s, daytime TV had relied on instructional programing such as cooking shows, along with cartoons, quiz shows, and soap operas. Cooking on television had to be fun and easy to follow, and the personality of the chef had to be compelling, although there were a surprising number of ways to achieve this—friendly, authoritative, intimidating, even nebbishy all worked. The format, however, always involved a kitchen and an instructional process of preparing a dish or meal. The original Food Network innovation was the seemingly crazy idea of broadcasting cooking and food-related programs all the time. There was considerable doubt about whether an audience for this much food programming existed, but after all, CNN had demonstrated that it was possible to make money on a twenty-four-hour news format.

The model initially was, in fact, CNN, and TVFN was even derisively called "CNN with stoves." TVFN brought back earlier stars like Julia Child and created traditional-format shows about how to cook. Marion Cunningham, author of a number of cookbooks including the delightful *Cooking with Children*, hosted a show whose sixty-five episodes included guest chefs, food writers, and others who discussed food topics and cooked. The show was sophisticated and heartwarming, just the thing for a cultivated PBS or NPR kind of audience.

TVFN aimed at a wider set of viewers. Its first stand-out personality was Emeril Lagasse, who was born and raised in Massachusetts and became chef at the storied New Orleans restaurant Commander's Palace in 1990. He got his start in 1993 on a show called *How to Boil Water*, but beginning with *Essence of Emeril*,

Emeril Lagasse, the New England–born chef who made his career in New Orleans and was the first breakaway success for the Food Network.

he projected his own dynamic brand of expertise and inventiveness. Perhaps more rugged than handsome, Lagasse invented taglines like "Let's kick it up a notch" and projected an insouciant assertiveness that appealed to men and even kids, way beyond the usual female cooking-show audience. In the late 1990s, Emeril carried the network, which went through several owners, managers, staff, and programs. The Food Network still was unable to broadcast in enough markets to be profitable, and as late as 2000, its upward trajectory was still not assured.

TVFN SHOWS, FALL 1994, A TYPICAL WEEKDAY

How to Boil Water
7-Day Workout
Food News and Views (Donna Hanover and David Rosengarten)
Getting Healthy
Meals without Meat
Feeding Your Family on $99 a Week
The Dessert Show
Café Olé
Taste (David Rosengarten)
Essence of Emeril
TV Dinners (Nina Griscom—restaurant reviews)
Robin Leach Talking Food
Cooking Classics

From Allan Salkin, *From Scratch: Inside the Food Network* (New York: G. P. Putnam's Sons, 2013), 92.

The turning point came the moment chefs were taken out of the studio kitchen and put into all manner of places and situations. Contests, travel, drama, and the inspiration of reality TV transformed the Food Network from an information source into a major form of entertainment. The new owner as of 1997 was media giant E. W. Scripps, which set out to make what one executive referred to as "Food TV Lite," with programming that would be diverting rather than educational. Scripps adhered to so-called family values, limiting just how edgy the new shows would be, but with the seemingly unlikely introduction of *Iron Chef*, the transformation accelerated. Kids especially, already attracted to the network by Emeril, were enthusiastic for the chefs' contests, whose stylized Japanese ritual and ceremony translated as mock solemn, riveting yet hilarious. The seeming disadvantage of the cultural gap between Japan and the United States, including dubbing into English, was actually a draw. *Iron Chef* made Americans famous, beginning with Bobby Flay, one of the chefs who brought Southwestern cuisine to New York with his Mesa Grill in 1991. Typically, the way to fame was not victory. Notoriously, Flay not only lost to *Iron Chef* master Masaharu Morimoto but, anticipating victory, he jumped up onto his cutting board in a victory gesture, an offense to Japanese meticulousness about tools. Flay's antics, arrogance, and energy might not be appropriate for Japan, but American audiences loved it.

Iron Chef spun off many imitators. Bravo cable network built on the contest model to create *Top Chef*, but rather than looking like a sports arena event, it came with reality TV features such as chefs bad-mouthing each other, "behind the scenes" preparations, money, surprises, and unpredictability.

What all cooking shows absorbed after 2000 was something they also aided: the chef as media celebrity. Celebrity chefs had been thought to be on the verge of extinction in the early 1990s, but in fact their cult was only beginning. The older model of fame had featured men (mostly) who were first and foremost restaurant chefs (mostly French), shown in their kitchen or not far away. The new model was the chef as fun-loving hipster, a tough but lovable guy who could be found in all sorts of dangerous or at least unexpected places. The celebrity chef today may be a morally serious world-changer like Alex Atala or an edgy character like Guy

Fieri. As the long history of ignoring women in professional cooking unravels, female celebrity chefs too have permission to express their personalities.

The constituents and causes of celebrity are related to the rise of food television. Such status is likely to survive the eclipse of syndicated television as well. As streaming replaces cable, the viewers' control and ability to find information and entertainment in bite-size pieces will mean a shift in whom they watch. A 2018 article about Rachael Ray noted that in order to adapt to an environment of Instagram influencers and ninety-second cooking videos, Ray is making digitally streamed programs that deemphasize cooking in favor of lifestyle.[44]

✦　　✦　　✦

RECENT DECADES HAVE MADE IT CLEAR that the progressive culinary innovations of the 1970s are permanent. Organic products, seasonality, and a preference for artisanal over industrial are not merely yesterday's ephemeral fashions like vertical food or red peppercorns, but represent real social and cultural change. This is obvious in the popularity of restaurants that emphasize seasonal and local ingredients, but also in the less visible infrastructure of small farms, provisioners, and suppliers who have created an artisanal revolution affecting beer, cheese, bacon, and dozens of other products that used to be exclusively produced by large companies in industrial quantities and with all-too-industrial quality. Beginning in the 1970s and accelerating with each succeeding decade, farms that grew heirloom breeds multiplied, while cheesemakers, such as Upland in Wisconsin or Grafton in Vermont, created cheeses that can compete with those of Europe for sensuous and complex flavor. The hippie, back-to-the-land movement did not work as a subsistence economy, but it was the inspiration for specialized agriculture incorporating older methods to supply a demand for authenticity and taste.[45]

There are many turning points posited in accounts of recent culinary history, moments when a shift in priorities became too obvious to ignore. The *New York Times*' style magazine identified the three years from the beginning of 1981 to the end of 1983 as "thirty-six months that changed the culture." These developments in food were focused on global ingredients. Kiwi was the "gateway drug" to a new set of choices such as falafel, souvlaki, and tiramisù.[46] The discovery of new international ingredients was not in itself new, even if the pace increased in the 1980s, nor did the rest of the world follow immediately. Some exceptional cities like Tokyo, London, and São Paulo already had an eclectic set of restaurants by the end of the 1980s, but dining in Barcelona, Rome, or Helsinki changed in this direction only recently, well into the twenty-first century.

Then there is 2004, "the year that changed how we dine," according to the *New York Times* food journalist Jeff Gordinier.[47] His article is about New York restaurants, but changes would take place everywhere in 2004. Per Se and Masa started at the high end, and David Chang created Momofuku Noodle Bar at the high-low end. Buying fresh ingredients was no longer enough for Dan and David Barber who in that fateful year 2004 opened Blue Hill at Stone Barns on the Rockefeller estate in Westchester County. They started growing their own produce and scouring upstate farms for knowledge, old breeds, and soil conservation techniques. Danny Meyer established Shake Shack that same year in Madison Square, bringing high-end sourcing and craft to a fast food setting. For *New York Magazine*'s restaurant reviewer Adam Platt, the whole first decade of the new century is crucial, bringing fresh ingredients to the forefront (again), but even more significantly, it marked the ascent of American-born chefs cooking according to an American tradition, and the closing of the French gastronomic temples such as Lutèce.[48]

American Cuisine: And How It Got This Way is a history, not a prognostication. Nevertheless, the title implies there is a "this way" currently, so we will now offer some speculation about where things stand and how they might progress.

Food in the Year 2020 and Beyond

Having arrived at this point, we can say that there really is such a thing as American cuisine. Among world cuisines it is unusual because the United States does not rely on a repertoire of recognized dishes such as coq au vin or blanquette de veau for France, ackee and saltfish for Jamaica, or roast beef and Yorkshire pudding for England. Food in the United States is about variety, eclecticism, and choice. This is apparent in the proliferation of foreign cuisines, the innovations of the processed food industry, and the tendency to mix things up. Pizza began as a distinctly foreign import and has become as American as hamburgers, themselves based on another (German) import. They both come with dozens of toppings and flavors.

Americans have been enthusiastic consumers of modern products. It is not just that historically the United States was technologically precocious or that its citizens value convenience, although these are true. The key factor is a peculiar attitude toward food. Americans have attempted to apply ideas about health and efficiency to diet. Obsessed with technological progress, anxious about time-saving, and worried about physical well-being, Americans for well over a hundred years have embraced scientific nutrition, industrial food, and convenience. They have been willing to sacrifice tradition and regional variation in favor of standard brands and *their* array of flavor and style. Infatuation with science, convenience, and variety require giving up the natural taste of food in favor of texture, color, multiplicity, and simplicity of preparation. Quick, easy, and healthful have been more important than flavor.

The result is a cuisine that loosens the ties of food to time and place. Seasons and regions no longer matter if food can be shipped cheaply from distant climates. Assuring the reliability of those shipments means a decrease in quality in favor of a cheap, efficient, good-enough norm.

This pattern started to change in the 1970s. New American Cuisine and farm-to-table mean renewal of flavor, terroir, seasonality, and even regional character such as that of the South or, in their own ways, California and Vermont. This does not mean that Americans have abandoned long-term preferences and attitudes favoring homogenization and blandness. In 2020, the revolution hasn't quite been accomplished.

Entrenched ways of dining do not shift immediately or totally. The old and new are side by side, but in sociologically separated compartments. A fascinating 2004 description of dining out in New Martinsville, West Virginia, contrasts a downtown, creative, independently owned restaurant called Baristas with a branch of the national casual-dining chain Bob Evans, located outside town alongside the usual gas stations and fast food outlets.[1] Bob Evans patrons perceive Baristas as too fancy, or believe it pushes health food ("sprout sandwiches"), when in fact it offers nothing more exotic than fried green tomatoes, handcrafted burgers, and steaks. Baristas customers, in turn, scorn Bob Evans for its mediocre, thawed-out, and predictable food. The writer of the article tried and failed to get regulars at either place to sample the other, showing that cultural divisions had already hardened in 2004. The conclusion was politically prescient:

> Bob Evans people and Baristas people live together all over the United States. They often go to the same stores and send their kids to the same school, but try as they might, they simply can't understand why anyone in his right mind wouldn't eat the way they do, think the way they do and vote the way they do. Unfortunately, I'm not sure a burger can change that, not even a really, really good one.

A brilliant analysis of America's cultural gaps, this article may be too pessimistic as regards food—Baristas is still open in New Martinsville fifteen years later, and so for that matter is Bob Evans. Unlike politics, there remain hopeful possibilities for a culinary middle ground. Although Hell's Backbone Grill in remote Boulder, Utah, is described as a "Buddhist-based restaurant," its conservative, largely Mormon neighbors patronize it. Hell's Backbone serves meat and is literally conservative enough to operate according to the principle ("compass") "What would great-great-grandmother do?"[2] This adaptation of Michael Pollan's famous dictum means that the restaurant rejects processed food, factory-produced meat, dairy, and eggs, beet sugar, and hydrogenated oils. Since 2000, owners Blake Spalding and Jen Castle have offered the bounty of a harsh desert climate and have become fixtures of a closely knit ranching community. It helps that there is no Bob Evans–style alternative in a town that lacks a bank, grocery store, or traffic light, so people can't be too choosy. Nevertheless, a common bond to a special landscape has ensured not only the restaurant's success, but its local credibility.[3]

Far from Boulder, Utah, recent years have seen the revival of opulent dining and stratospheric prices. It may be hard to believe that anyone could regularly consume the fourteen-course meals outlined by the menus from Delmonico's or other fine restaurants of the first Gilded Age, but the high-end tasting menu of today returns us to a style of excess, even without as much meat and with an environmentally aware orientation. It is all too easy to spend over three hundred dollars per person at restaurants that will offer you no choice, multiple small courses, and a lecture on sustainability.

Elite food practices were not invented in the United States. The avant garde restaurant elBulli in Catalonia can take credit (or bear responsibility) for first serving a cascade of small, unique dishes with no choice. Among its most conspicuous Catalan successors, El Celler de Can Roca, in the northern city of Girona, offers at least ten dishes in its prix fixe tasting menu, and often one presentation contains several different preparations. A first course, for example, entitled "The World: Mexico, Peru, Thailand, Morocco, and Japan" consists of caramelized olives, truffled bonbons, calamari rings, Campari bonbons, marinated mussels, and truffled brioche.⁴ Equally ambitious is a menu from Restaurant Sant Pau in Sant Pol de Mar, northeast of Barcelona along the coast. In the summer of 2017, its menu, "inspired by the universe," lists fifteen courses with names like "Blue Planet" (prawn, lemon pulp, fennel) and "Taurus Constellation" (stewed Wagyu beef with three kinds of miso). Dessert consists of nine kinds of petit fours, each named after a different planet, the sun, and the Earth.⁵

American fine dining is not far behind. Alinea, the French Laundry, Per Se, Eleven Madison Park, Benu, and other leading restaurants present between twelve and twenty courses. None of this closely resembles the heavy, bejeweled ostentation of dining in the nineteenth century, but it is harder to get a reservation at Noma or even simple places such as the Lost Kitchen in Freedom, Maine, than it ever was at Rector's or Delmonico's. The social cachet of restaurant dining has never been greater, reflecting the gastronomic aspirations of a competitive upper class as well as of young people more eager to spend money on experiences than on the durable trappings of suburban life such as houses, cars, kids, and the like.

The most obvious changes in attitudes toward food come from popular culture. The varieties of food-based entertainment range from the reverentially serious (*Chef's Table* on Netflix) to the more out-there corners of Food Network. In a 2015 TEDx presentation, the entrepreneur and restaurant owner Kimbal Musk said, "Food is the new internet."⁶ Of course, food is a biological necessity, which the internet is not, or not yet at least. The pithy comparison is plausible, however, because of the upsurge in attention paid to food as the object of reviews, tourism, social media posts, and cultural positioning. While Musk was describing innovation and investment in sustainable agriculture, his statement fits the intensity of food conversations, especially through social media.

Instagram, Twitter, and Facebook have changed how restaurants are evaluated. As newspapers and magazines have declined, the authority of experts in restaurant reviewing has waned, although the few left standing are more powerful than ever. The collective opinion of ordinary diners, manifest in websites like Yelp or Open Table, promises a more democratic form of rating, but as with many social media discussions, comments lurch between adulatory and hateful and the process is susceptible to manipulation. Restaurants both profit from social media opinion and are fearful of it. Inundated by praise one week, they are then attacked for small missteps, or the public gets bored and moves on.

The internet has expanded the reach of chefs and their reputation-building opportunities. In 1990 there were a limited number of mostly French-trained chef celebrities, but since then the bar has been set lower. There are hundreds of chefs described as celebrities by the media. At the same time, simply because of media exposure, fame is more fragile than before.

Much is changing with the sudden if overdue impact of the #MeToo movement. It turns out that a number of chefs, such as Mario Batali and John Besh, were, at best, careless about their reputations. It might seem slightly hypocritical for the same media outlet to gush over strutting, assertive, bad-ass chefs and later affect shock at their behavior, but there is no doubt that some food celebrities used their fame and power abusively. Perhaps in the future chefs will have to be nicer and more sensitive, something still hard to picture. It also may mean more attention to female chefs, who, among other things, don't have the same inappropriate baggage. With regard to that prospect, however, a remark by Amanda Cohen of the vegetable-forward restaurant Dirt Candy in New York is worth keeping in mind: "I've worked in food for twenty years. Now you finally care about female chefs?"[7]

Beyond elite restaurant kitchens, a significant recent development is that large food companies face threats to their sway and business model. The consolidated national food industry has figured in every aspect of the story told here since the Civil War. By 1990, there were frequent complaints about these companies: their manipulation of government dietary recommendations, their devious inclusion of sugar in almost everything, their marketing of unhealthful snacks, cereals, and soda to kids, and their attachment to fat. Many of these attacks carried over to the fast food industry, and McDonald's became an international symbol of American addiction to an unhealthful regime. What has changed recently is that such questioning now has a massive and long-term impact. Cereal without artificial color, organic baby food, meat raised without

Table of contents from Amanda Cohen and Ryan Dunlavey, *Dirt Candy: A Cookbook*, 2012. The recipes come from Cohen's New York restaurant with an autobiography, meditations, and advice presented in graphic comic style.

antibiotics, and eggs from cage-free hens, are not just small niches for ageing hippies or bicoastal liberals, but represent permanent, mass-market shifts.[8] More Chobani yogurt (without artificial preservatives) is sold at Walmart or Kroger than at Whole Foods.[9]

The top twenty food and beverage corporations lost approximately eighteen billion dollars in market share to small companies from 2011 to 2017. Soda consumption declined 25 percent from 1998 to 2015. Processed orange juice, once considered a healthful breakfast drink, is now recognized as a vehicle for sugar. Cereal sales have declined more than 25 percent since 2000. Even in stable categories, what is perceived as a healthier and less corporate alternative has negatively affected familiar brands: Lean Cuisine, owned by Nestlé, has lost ground to Amy's Kitchen organic products; Mars bars are challenged by Kind bars.[10]

McDonald's and its competitors may have lost their ability to dominate the fast food market, but the interstate highway environs remain as crowded as ever with quick-service chains. More than ever, in fact: There are now 620,000 places to eat and drink in the United States, and the number of restaurants is growing at twice the rate of population increase. The result is pressure on profitability and a decline in sales.[11]

There are several ways companies are dealing with the situation. One is cutting costs, a strategy pursued by Kraft Heinz, which is owned by the Brazilian investment firm 3G Capital, renowned for running companies efficiently—i.e., closing plants and firing workers. Kraft Heinz now has a high operating profit margin but is faced by sales declines in products like Oscar Mayer packaged meats, declines so extensive that no savings through efficiency will offset them in the long term. At a time when the overall stock market rose (June 2017 to June 2018), Kraft Heinz lost 40 percent of its value.[12]

A more forward-looking strategy is to simplify the ingredients list and create a more natural product with fewer texturizing, stabilizing, coloring, or preservative agents. Hershey's has dropped emulsifier chemicals and now emphasizes simple, easily understood ingredients such as fresh milk, almonds, cocoa beans, and sugar. Kraft Heinz no longer enhances the color of its macaroni and cheese with dye substances. Campbell's too has reduced coloring agents, along with chemical flavor enhancers, and is replacing high-fructose corn syrup with sugar. Its advertising slogan "Made for Real, Real Life," plays to concerns about health and quality.[13]

Corporations recognize that the millennial demographic thinks differently from their parents. Forty-two percent of millennial consumers (ages twenty to thirty-seven) in a recent survey said they mistrusted large companies, compared with 18 percent for other age groups.[14] They prefer smaller companies whose products have simple, organic ingredients, and they are shopping for a different kind of family from the one advertisers are most familiar with, one that could be multicultural, multigenerational, single or same-sex parents.

The well-attested current crisis of the middle aisles of the supermarket— the eclipse of Miracle Whip, frozen vegetables, and canned fruit—is a consequence of wider public acceptance of basic farm-to-table principles.[15] This is not to argue that a figurative millennium has arrived. "Americans Still Packing on the Pounds" reads a *New York Times* headline, and the conclusion of a *Wall Street Journal* item entitled "No, Americans Aren't Finally Ready to Cook" is that while Americans "talk a good game" about home cooking and healthful food, they still put convenience ahead of everything else.[16]

We remain in a recognizable world whose boundaries and landscape were established between 1890 and 1950. The three major characteristics dating back at least as far as the nineteenth century and still with us are the usual discourses over whether or not specific foods are healthful, the importance of convenience, and the search for novelty and variety rather than quality and simplicity.

Throughout its history, the United States offers a dynamic, entertaining, if not always enlightening culinary scene. The succession of trends has diversified and accelerated in the twenty-first century. Korean cuisine has taken over some of the Asian territory, and West African and Filipino food may be up and coming. Things that seemed at first like isolated fads, such as the gluten-free diet, have become objects of constant conversation. Trying to set aside the distracting spectacle of constantly changing food products, we can identify trends that seem likely to grow in the near future. These include vegetarianism or its more flavor-oriented alternative "vegetable-forward," emphasizing the positive over the negative virtues of eating vegetables. Rather than simply being not-meat, vegetables can be presented as wonderful in themselves. Another shift is in the "ethnic food" category. In keeping with uneasiness about this terminology is a view that does not separate conceptually supposedly "normal" from "foreign" foods, and encourages incorporation of ingredients such as kimchee, lemongrass, or chipotle peppers into everyday dining. Parallel to this is a new twist to eclecticism so that the contemporary descendants of New American restaurants define "American" in a more international way. There is even a tentative rediscovery of regional food, not simply in revived ingredients or breeds but in dishes as well. This is likely to expand from the South and Southwest to regions with a lesser-known culinary legacy—the Midwest or Northwest, for example.

A riskier prediction is that dining out may have peaked, at least at restaurants and fast food establishments. There are hot sectors like food trucks, but it may be that the millennial generation as it matures will restore cooking at home. Its cohort's concern with health, economic incentives, and a desire for control over personal life choices would seem to encourage making one's own meals. Yet, for the first time, Americans have come to spend more money dining out than eating at home, something our ancestors would have greeted with shock.[17] Food has become a lifestyle marker, but less cooking is taking place at home. The rise of restaurants, fast food, takeout, and now delivery constitutes a long-term trend, stunning as a sign of both enthusiasm for dining out and unwillingness to engage directly with one of the fundamental attributes of home in the first place: preparing meals.

Dining out at trendy restaurants has been identified with millennial behavior and has something to do with young adults' preference for cities and willingness to spend disposable income on sociable if ephemeral pleasures such as food. Millennials are not the only group driving the high rate of consumption outside the home, however. Obvious other factors include working couples, the pace of life, the perceived convenience and availability of alternatives to home cooking, and the love of variety, particularly with someone else making the effort. The attraction of lifestyle fantasies connects with a fascination with cookbooks, food television, blogs, photos of meals on Instagram, and a variety of other indices of the popularity of food.

If the creation of the Food Network and its transformation from information to entertainment represents the start of the popular-culture enthusiasm for food, discourse about it was kicked into high gear by the internet, social media, and the smartphone. Collectively they enable wide participation in debates and the formation of opinions, not just about awesome restaurants but about sustainability, health, gender, the food industry, and the ways in which food defines class, privilege, and cultural capital. It remains to be seen if all the talk will lead to a rediscovery of cooking one's own food. There are various experiments in trying to make this easier or more appealing. One idea is the meal kit, offered by companies such as Blue Apron, Green Chef, and Purple Carrot. The company delivers all the ingredients and instructions to make various meals. You are given some choice and relieved of the burden of figuring out what to make, buying the ingredients, peeling and slicing them, and dealing with what to do with the rest of the herbs, zucchini, ground meat, or whatever else you bought too much of. At the same time, these services are not panaceas; they are not cheap, sometimes there are mix-ups with the orders, sometimes the food doesn't arrive in time, and there is inevitably a degree of blandness resulting from the need to cater to a common set of tastes.

Meal kits are among the innovations designed to take advantage of discontent with unhealthful, boring, or repetitive aspects of dining out and desire to control what you eat and to experience the mildly creative feeling that cooking is supposed to produce. Another embryonic possibility is a communal sharing exchange. Some people in one neighborhood may be ambitious cooks or used to cooking for a large family, and they can obtain licenses to sell food to others. Especially in areas with different immigrant groups, this could result in a wide range of choice for customers and the advantages of takeout, but with a home-cooked taste and a personal connection. The quest for the near-term future is to marry current lifestyles with the real, rather than exclusively virtual, pleasures of food.

The two most important developments of this century that affect food, directly and indirectly, are the disastrous present reality and future danger of climate change and the growth of economic inequality. Human-generated rises in temperature are already creating havoc. The most immediate threats are an intensification of drought and desertification in many parts of the world and the rising ocean levels that, along with increasingly powerful storms, create catastrophic flooding. The effect on agriculture means that many crops will no longer be feasible to grow in their traditional locations, although warming means that certain things such as wine will extend their range into latitudes previously deemed too cold.

Nonagricultural products are migrating as well. Lobsters are at the moment very plentiful in Maine as Long Island Sound and other formerly hospitable waters have become too warm. In time, and probably soon, the migration will move further north and then the Maine industry will be decimated.[18] The consequences of climate change will be more severe than just where lobsters come and other shifting sources. It is likely to overturn many assumptions about the future of food, particularly the optimistic ones.

With regard to inequality, this too has global resonance, but within the United States, it has meant falling out of the middle class and into a just-barely-coping or impoverished condition. Just as before, experts are inclined to consider the underprivileged as irresponsible. Poor nutrition, obesity, and drug addiction are no longer identified with the "inner cities," a code for African Americans and Hispanics. Instead, such adversities have become typified as white, rural crises. The effect of increasing population at both the low and high ends of the income scale has meant the erosion of the middle class, visible not only in economic statistics but in the decline of middle-market stores such as Sears, and of once-standard consumer brands.

The swelling upper class, not just the proverbial 1 percent but the top 10 percent, has fueled the growth of restaurants and of many aspects of food enthusiasm such as international gastrotourism. Whatever the visibility of chefs and restaurateurs as advocates for environmental responsibility, better labor conditions, or making food a way of bringing people together, the business thrives on the increasing wealth and ostentation of a professional, technical, and managerial elite.

Concerns over the diet of poor people have been around for a long time.

For almost 150 years, nutrition professionals have scolded the lower classes for their supposedly wasteful and unhealthful ways of eating. In the late nineteenth century, workers and immigrants were said to like food that was too spicy, or too fancy and uneconomical, or they were too fond of alcohol. In the twenty-first century, poor people are depicted as ignorant about nutrition and inclined recklessly to give their children soda, snacks, McDonald's burgers, and other junk food. This is not to say that there isn't a public health food crisis visible in problems like rates of obesity, but it is the propensity of the well-fed to assume that poor nutrition can be solved by education or willpower rather than being the accompaniment of real-life poverty.

Obesity and other nutritional ills are not experienced by the poor alone: A considerably larger percentage of Americans are now overweight than the number living at what is defined as the poverty level. This decline in the level of public health exists simultaneously with the acceleration of interest in food visible through the media, contests, festivals, expenditure at restaurants, and the proliferation of food writing—of which, after all, this book is an example.

✦   ✦   ✦

AMERICAN FOOD is recognizably different from that of the rest of the world. It has a distinctive set of tastes that can be called American cuisine. The American model of variety and change has spread internationally, but foreign visitors remain struck by the galaxy of offerings, the casualness of dining (including eating on the street), the American need for speed, and the mediocre quality of basic products such as bread. All these have their origins in the past two centuries, which the recent cult of innovation and disruption has not completely undermined. The great aspect about the United States generally is the exuberance of its people and, despite the many negative peculiarities of food in this country, that high-spirited approach is a saving grace.

WHAT'S IN AND WHAT'S OUT

According to an article in the *Wall Street Journal,* food fashion cycles have become so short that yesterday's must-have item is today's eye-rolling cliché.

In

Brisket of beef (and smoked meat in general)

Crudo (thinly sliced raw fish)

Pakora (South Asian vegetable or chicken fritters)

Duck

Japanese seasonings such as furikake (bonito flakes, sesame seeds, dried fish) and karashi mustard

Japchae (Korean stir-fried noodles)

Out

Avocado toast (so 2017)

Tuna tartare (expensive—see crudo, above)

Kale (too popular—even fast food chains now serve kale salads)

Veal (part of the decline of meats usually prepared with sauce)

Microgreens (it has been discovered that they have no flavor)

Alina Dizik, "On—and Off—Menus in 2018," *Wall Street Journal,* January 4, 2018, A13.

ACKNOWLEDGMENTS

I am glad to have an opportunity to thank the people and institutions who helped me with this project, an outgrowth and expansion of my previous work on American restaurants. With regard to the present book as well as *Ten Restaurants That Changed America*, I am especially grateful to Bob Weil, editor-in-chief and publishing director of Liveright, who has been a constant source of encouragement for undertaking food-related projects. At Liveright I have been greatly helped by Gabe Kachuck and Marie Pantojan, who saw the chapters into publication; Julia Druskin, the production manager; and Peter Miller and Cordelia Calvert in the publicity department. My agent Lynn Nesbit not only represented me but is also a wonderful informant for the intersection of food, history, and culture in New York. I am immensely grateful to Holly Watson, who handled a considerable amount of the publicity for this book as well as *Ten Restaurants*.

Many food studies scholars shared their knowledge and advice with me. I have noted in the footnotes some specific debts, but here I would like to thank those who read large parts of the manuscript or whose work has consistently inspired me and often changed my uninformed or insufficiently considered opinions: Stephen Schmidt, Laura Shapiro, Andy Smith, Anne Mendelson, Cara De Silva, Anne McBride, Fred Kaufman, Andrew Friedman, John T. Edge, and Krishnendu Ray. I have occasionally taught an undergraduate class on the history of food and cuisine and learned a lot, especially about contemporary trends, from my Yale University students.

I thank David Cole, director of the Hagley Library and Museum in Wilmington, Delaware, not only for showing me the gastronomic items in the collection but also for arranging an event at the Wilmington Club, a source of particular information about terrapin, at one time the great delicacy of the mid-Atlantic region and famous throughout the United States. Mark B. Letzer and the Maryland Historical Society, of which he is the executive director, helped me immensely both with terrapin history and the overall culinary accomplishments of the Chesapeake Bay area. Nathaniel Welch of Boston introduced me to the history of Le Club des Arts Gastronomiques, which was among the institutions that conserved culinary knowledge and enjoyment in the dark years of Prohibition and the Depression. His grandfather, E. Sohier Welch, was the head of that club for many years. Arthur Spector, Rick Wheeler, and Jay Stiefel, wonderful dining companions, helped me with the history of food in Philadelphia.

Within and outside the United States, many chefs and restaurateurs have directly and indirectly offered me points of comparison, advice, and general orientation about food in history and in the present. I would particularly like to thank Amanda Cohen and Grady Hendrix (Dirt Candy); Cecilia Chiang (The Mandarin); Dan and David Barber (Blue Hill at Stone Barns); René Redzepi (Noma); Corey Lee (Benu); Alex von Bidder (The Four Seasons); Danny Meyer (Union Square Hospitality Group); Billy Oliva, Dennis Turcinovic, Milan Licul, and Carin Sarafian (Delmonico's); Jaume Biarnès (formerly of elBulli and now at Yondu Co., USA); and Toni Massanés (Fundació Alicia).

Rebecca Federman at the New York Public Library guided me to sources for culinary history. For information about the Texas Panhandle, I received help from Warren Stricker, research center director of the Panhandle-Plains Historical Museum and Library in Canyon, Texas. Professor Bruce Brasington, a fellow medievalist, hosted me at West Texas A&M and introduced me to the Panhandle-Plains Library. Barbara Hand, who studied with me at Vanderbilt University beginning in 1979, my first year of full-time college teaching, introduced me to her mother, Shirley Rich, and to a community of neighbors and friends in Byrdstown, Tennessee. Among other accomplishments, they put together *Not By Bread Alone*, a cookbook to benefit the Moodyville Missionary Baptist Church, which I refer to toward the end of Chapter 3.

Victoria Presser, my indefatigable classmate from second grade through high school, gave me her invaluable collection of *Gourmet* magazines from the 1950s and 1960s and has always, since the days when we used to dine at the Maharajah restaurant on New York's West Side, been a source of support and encouragement. George Chauncey, formerly my colleague at Yale and now at Columbia, gave me good advice about gay history and New York. As always, I owe a lot to Henry Voigt, the great menu collector and historian of restaurants, some of whose phenomenal collection will soon be exhibited at the Grolier Club in New York.

Larry Carty, a man of many talents and considerable wisdom, affected the shape and tone of this book more than he perhaps realizes, as did John Del Giudice and Joan Fisher. My former doctoral student Tom Barton, professor of history at the University of San Diego, discussed his gastronomic adventures, took me to the one meal I had at Alinea in Chicago, and provided the Vespertine menu pictured on page 348.

My wife, Bonnie Roe, to whom this book is dedicated, has shared memorable as well as ordinary meals with me. She has always given me good advice, and reminded me to have fun and to say what I mean.

NOTES

INTRODUCTION—WHAT IS AMERICAN CUISINE?

1. Sidney Mintz, *Tasting Food, Tasting Freedom: Excursions into Eating, Culture, and the Past* (Boston: Beacon, 1996), 96.
2. Lee A. Farrow, *Alexis in America: A Russian Grand Duke's Tour, 1871–1872* (Baton Rouge: Louisiana State University Press, 2014), 91–92.
3. This account by British visitor Robert Burford is accompanied by other examples of American haste in Michael Batterbury and Ariane Batterbury, *On the Town in New York: The Landmark History of Eating, Drinking and Entertainment from the American Revolution to the Food Revolution* (New York and London: Routledge, 1999), 46–47.
4. Claude Fischler and Estelle Masson, *Manger: Français, Européens et Américains face à l'alimentation* (Paris: Odile Jacob, 2008), 11.
5. Quoted in an invaluable work for both reference and creative time wasting, *The Food Lovers' Anthology* (Oxford: Bodleian Library, 2014), 245–46, a reprint of *Eating and Drinking: An Anthology for Epicures*, compiled by Peter Hunt (London: Ebury Press, 1961).
6. *Food Lover's Anthology*, 117.
7. Fischler and Masson, *Manger*, 50–51.
8. Amelia Simmons, *American Cookery or the Art of Dressing Viands, Fish, Poultry and Vegetables . . .* (Hartford, CT: Hudson & Goodwin, 1796). In the same year, another edition appeared in Albany and the book was reprinted by a different publisher in Hartford in 1798. In 1804, a third edition was printed in Salem, NY.
9. The definitive treatment is Keith Stavely and Kathleen Fitzgerald, *United Tastes: The Making of the First American Cookbook* (Amherst and Boston: University of Massachusetts Press, 2017). The origins of the recipes are on 21–22.
10. Phillip Stephen Schulz, *As American as Apple Pie* (New York: Simon & Schuster, 1990).
11. Schulz, *As American as Apple Pie*, 11 acknowledges this: "American food is free form. Unlike classic French and Chinese cuisines, our fare has no basic set of rules."
12. "What Is the Most Popular Food in the United States?" Reference.com, https://www.reference.com/food/popular-food-united-states-8d878ebfd6b00f09#, accessed November 2, 2018.
13. Paul Freedman, *Ten Restaurants That Changed America* (New York: Liveright, 2016), 299.

CHAPTER 1—FLOWERING AND FADING: AMERICAN REGIONAL FOOD

1. Steven Raichlen, "A Borderline for Barbecue," *New York Times,* October 24, 2018, D1, D8.

2. Crosby Gaige, *New York World's Fair Cook Book: The American Kitchen* (New York: Doubleday Doran, 1939).

3. Jane Stern and Michael Stern, *Roadfood*, 10th ed. (New York: Clarkson Potter, 2017).

4. Lou Sackett and David Haynes, *American Regional Cuisines: Food Culture and Cooking* (Upper Saddle River, NJ: Pearson, 2012), 9.

5. Betty Fussell, *I Hear America Cooking: A Journey of Discovery from Alaska to Florida—the Cooks, the Recipes, and the Unique Flavors of Our National Cuisine* (New York: Viking, 1986).

6. James P. Shenton et al., *American Cooking: The Melting Pot* (New York: Time-Life, 1971). The immigrant cuisines considered are Italian, Jewish, Hungarian, Czech, Yugoslav, Polish, Lithuanian, Romanian, Ukrainian, Basque, Armenian, German (in Texas), Portuguese (in California), Greek (in Florida), and "Oriental restaurants." Chinese and Mexican cuisine in the US are dealt with in other volumes.

7. Rhona Richman Kenneally, "'There *Is* a Canadian Cuisine, and It Is Unique in All the World': Crafting National Food Culture During the Long 1960s," in *What's to Eat? Entrées in Canadian Food History*, ed. Nathalie Cooke (Montreal and Kingston: McGill-Queen's University Press, 2009), 167–96, esp. 180–82. For Québec and its regional culinary specialties, see Hélène-Andrée Bizier et al., *Cuisine traditionelle des régions du Québec* (Montreal: Gouvernement du Québec, 1999).

8. *American Regional Cuisine* (New York: John Wiley and Sons, 2002), 4.

9. An apt metaphor devised by Richard Pillsbury, *No Foreign Food: The American Diet in Time and Place* (Boulder, CO: Westview, 1998), 211.

10. Alice L. McLean, *Cooking in America, 1840–1945* (Westport, CT: Greenwood Press, 2006), 158. The eminent writer Reynolds Price in 1981 said that the pimento cheese sandwich must have been invented by a Southerner, and that he had seldom met a non-Southerner who even knew what it was, quoted in John Egerton, *Southern Food: At Home, on the Road, in History* (Chapel Hill: University of North Carolina Press, 1987), 199–200. Gayden Metcalfe and Charlotte Hays, *Being Dead Is No Excuse: The Official Southern Guide to Hosting the Perfect Funeral* (New York: Hyperion, 2005), 83, suggest that pimento cheese might just be "the most Southern dish on earth."

11. I am grateful to the cookbook expert Stephen Schmidt for this information.

12. The thesis of James E. McWilliams, *A Revolution in Eating: How the Quest for Food Shaped America* (New York: Columbia University Press, 2005).

13. Sidney Mintz, *Sweetness and Power: The Place of Sugar in Modern History* (New York: Penguin, 1985), 67; Elizabeth Abbott, "Sugar," in *The Routledge History of American Foodways*, ed. Michael D. Wise and Jennifer Jensen Wallach (New York and Abingdon: Routledge, 2016), 137.

14. McWilliams, *A Revolution in Eating.* See also Frederick Douglass Opie, "Influences, Sources, and African Diaspora Foodways," in *Food in Time and Place: The American Historical Association Companion to Food History*, ed. Paul Freedman, Ken Albala, and Joyce E. Chaplin (Berkeley: University of California Press, 2014), 192–95; Judith A. Carney and Richard Nicholas Rosomoff, *In the Shadow of Slavery: Africa's Botanical Legacy in the Atlantic World* (Berkeley: University of California Press, 2010), 100–08.

15. Michael W. Twitty, *The Cooking Gene: A Journey through African-American Culinary History in the Old South* (New York: HarperCollins, 2017), 147.

16. On the importance of slavery in this region, Wendy Warren, *New England Bound: Slavery and Colonization in Early America* (New York: Liveright, 2016).

17. Kelly J. Sisson Lessens, "Grains," in *The Routledge History of American Foodways*, 83.

18. Joyce Chaplin, *Subject Matter: Technology, the Body and Science on the Anglo-American Frontier, 1500–1676* (Cambridge, MA: Harvard University Press, 2001).

19. For details on these and other foods and how they would have been prepared, see Keith Stavely and Kath-

erine Fitzgerald, *America's Founding Food: The Story of New England Cooking* (Chapel Hill: University of North Carolina Press, 2004).

20. Bruce Kraig, *A Rich and Fertile Land: A History of Food in America* (London: Reaktion, 2017), 66–67.

21. Stavely and Fitzgerald, *America's Founding Food*, 9, 88.

22. McWilliams, *A Revolution in Eating*, 263–70, 284.

23. McWilliams, *A Revolution in Eating*, 201–38.

24. David S. Shields, *The Culinarians: Lives and Careers from the First Age of American Fine Dining* (Chicago: University of Chicago Press, 2017), 71–75.

25. Katharina Vester, *A Taste of Power: Food and American Identities* (Berkeley: University of California Press, 2015), 25–29.

26. Amelia Simmons, *American Cookery* (Hartford, CT: Hudson and Goodwin, 1796); Lucy Emerson, *The New-England Cookery* (Montpelier, VT: Parks, 1808).

27. McWilliams, *A Revolution in Eating*, 313.

28. [Ms. E. A. Howland], *The New England Economical Housekeeper and Family Receipt Book* (Worcester, MA: S. A. Howland, 1844).

29. Harvey Levenstein, *Revolution at the Table: The Transformation of the American Diet* (Berkeley and Los Angeles: University of California Press, 2003), 47–55.

30. Fannie Merritt Farmer and Wilma Lord Perkins, *The Boston Cooking-School Cook Book* (Boston: Little, Brown & Co., 1896).

31. Chris Kimball, *Fannie's Last Supper: Re-Creating One Amazing Meal from Fannie Farmer's 1896 Cookbook* (New York: Hyperion, 2010), 25–27.

32. Particularly evident in the second edition, published in 1906.

33. Stephen Schmidt, "Seeing Cooking in Its Time: How Manuscript Cookbooks Help Us to Unravel 'Sampler' Food Histories," unpublished paper given at the Manuscript Cookbook Conference, New York University, May 12–13, 2016. I am grateful to Stephen Schmidt for sharing this important paper with me.

34. Stavely and Fitzgerald, *America's Founding Food*, 36–39.

35. Thomas Robinson Hazard, *The Jonny-Cake Papers of "Shepherd Tom"* (Boston: Merrymount Press, 1915).

36. Although in Maine, it has to be acknowledged, it is still common to serve baked beans on Saturdays. Robert Karl Skoglund, who as "The Humble Farmer" writes a popular column for the *Portland Press Herald*, asked readers in August 2017 about this custom and got back a number of responses, many on the order of "we used to have beans every Saturday" or "we now have canned beans with franks." I am grateful to Mr. Skoglund who posed this question at my request, http://www.pressherald.com/2017/08/19/the-humble -farmer-vegan-power-are-these-skinny-americans-too-healthy-to-die/, accessed August 25, 2017.

37. Jasper White, *Jasper White's Cooking from New England* (New York: Harper Row, 1989. Reprinted Newton, MA: Biscuit Books, 1998), xiii (introduction to the reprint).

38. White, *Jasper White's Cooking from New England*, xii, 24, 33, 166, 168, 229, 237, 261–63, 270, 275–76.

39. Beth A. Latshaw, "The Soul of the South: Race, Food, and Identity in the American South," in *The Larder: Food Studies Methods from the American South*, ed. John T. Edge, Elizabeth S. D. Engelhardt, Ted Ownby (Athens, GA: University of Georgia Press, 2017), 115–19.

40. This article is discussed by Jane Lear, "What Is Southern? The Annotated Edna Lewis," in *Edna Lewis: At the Table with an American Original*, ed. Sara B. Franklin (Chapel Hill: University of North Carolina Press, 2018), 17–26.

41. Sackett and Haynes, *American Regional Cuisines*, 9.

42. Frederick Douglass Opie says that what unites Southern cuisines is the trio of pork, greens, and cornmeal, *Hog and Hominy: Soul Food from Africa to America* (New York: Columbia University Press, 2008), 33.

43. Quoted in Latshaw, "The Soul of the South," 122.

44. Cited in James C. Cobb, "From 'Cracklins' to 'Gourmet Bacon Puffs': The Complex Origin and Shifting Shape of Southern Foodways," in *Citizen Scholar: Essays in Honor of Walter Edgar*, ed. Robert H. Brinkmeyer, Jr. (Columbia: University of South Carolina Press, 2016), 166.

45. Sorghum became popular in the Midwest for the same reason. On sorghum, see David S. Shields, *Southern Provisions: The Creation and Revival of a Cuisine* (Chicago: University of Chicago Press, 2015), 271–85.

46. *The Foxfire Book of Appalachian Cookery: Regional Memorabilia and Recipes*, ed. Linda Garland Page and Eliot Wigginton (New York: E. P. Dutton, 1984), 139. It is likely that what she said was "squirrel *and* dumplings," a well-known mountain dish, but she was misheard by her interviewer.

47. Twitty, *The Cooking Gene*, 151.

48. Shields, *Southern Provisions*, 148, has a more favorable estimation of the balance and variety of the African American diet in the Deep South.

49. Marcie Cohen Ferris, *The Edible South: The Power of Food and the Making of an American Region* (Chapel Hill: University of North Carolina Press, 2014), 126–44.

50. Julia Moskin, "Soul, Yes, and Heart: Two Southern Cooks Chew Over Culture, Cuisine and Identity," *New York Times*, August 8, 2018, D1, D5.

51. Quoted in Twitty, *The Cooking Gene*, 232–33. See also Shields, *Southern Provisions*, 148–51.

52. Mary Randolph, *The Virginia Housewife or Methodical Cook* (Washington, DC: Way and Gideon, 1824). Here "Virginia" might refer simply to the author's origins and residence, not necessarily to something equivalent to "the way we cook in Virginia."

53. Twitty, *The Cooking Gene*, 235–36.

54. Stephen Schmidt, "When Did Southern Begin?" in Manuscript Cookbooks Survey, posted November 2015, http://www.manuscriptcookbookssurvey.com/when-did-southern-begin, accessed August 30, 2017.

55. *Visitors Guide to the Centennial Exhibition and Philadelphia 1876* (Philadelphia: J. B. Lippincott and Co., 1876), 19.

56. C. Vann Woodward, *The Strange Career of Jim Crow* (New York: Oxford University Press, 1957).

57. https://www.encyclopediavirginia.org/Colonial_Williamsburg, accessed, September 14, 2017.

58. Ferris, *The Edible South*, 214–15. In fact, from the opening of Colonial Williamsburg in 1937 until 1971, its restaurant had an African American chef, Frederick D. Crawford, author of a Christmas cookbook based on dishes he had served for holiday celebrations. Nelda N. Knemeyer, "Frederick D. Crawford, 91, Longtime Chef," *Daily Press* (Williamsburg, VA), September 3, 1993, http://www.dailypress.com/news/dp-xpm-19930903–1993–09–03–9309030157-story.html, accessed October 4, 2018. The cookbook is *A Christmas Cookbook from Williamsburg: Recipes by Chef Fred D. Crawford* (Williamsburg, VA: Williamsburg Publishing, 1980).

59. Gretchen L. Hoffman, "What's the Difference Between Soul Food and Southern Cooking? The Classification of Cookbooks in American Libraries," in *Dethroning the Deceitful Pork Chop. Rethinking African America Foodways from Slavery to Obama*, ed. Jennifer Jensen Wallach (Fayetteville: University of Arkansas Press, 2015), 61–75.

60. In general, see Jessica B. Harris, *Iron Pots and Wooden Spoons: Africa's Gifts to New World Cooking* (New York: Athenaeum, 1989).

61. Eugene D. Genovese, *The Sweetness of Life: Southern Planters at Home* (Cambridge, UK: Cambridge University Press, 2017), 59–60.

62. Charles Gayarré in *Harper's Magazine*, cited by Scott Alves Barton, "Eu Tenho um Pé na Cozinha: Put(ting) Your Foot in It," in *Edna Lewis: At the Table with an American Original*, 92.

63. Ferris, *The Edible South*, 205. My copy of this pamphlet was printed in 1939 for Meridian, Mississippi. They were given different covers for different places: *The Southern Cook Book: 322 Old Dixie Recipes* (Reading, PA: Culinary Arts Press, 1939), 5.

64. Genovese, *The Sweetness of Life*, 61.

65. Toni Tipton-Martin, *The Jemima Code: Two Centuries of African American Cookbooks* (Austin: University of Texas Press, 2015), 23–64, esp. 40–41.

66. Ferris, *The Edible South*, 217.

67. Tipton-Martin, *The Jemima Code*, 46.

68. Angela Jill Cooley, *To Live and Dine in Dixie: The Evolution of Urban Food Culture in the Jim Crow South* (Athens: University of Georgia Press, 2015), 19–42. This title plays off a line from the song "Dixie": "To live and die in Dixie." For the history of domestic work in the South, Rebecca Sharpless, *Cooking in Other Women's Kitchens: Domestic Workers in the South, 1865–1960* (Chapel Hill: University of North Carolina Press, 2010).

69. Anne Mendelson, "Glossy South: *Gourmet*'s Long-Running Romance with Southern Cuisine and Clichés," *Oxford American* 49 (Spring 2005), 128–29.

70. John T. Edge, *The Potlikker Papers* (New York: Penguin, 2017), 42–47.

71. Edge, *Potlikker Papers*, 129–44. On these shows and their appeal, Sara K. Eskridge, *Rube Tube: CBS and Rural Comedy in the Sixties* (Columbia: University of Missouri Press, 2018).

72. Metcalfe and Hays, *Being Dead Is No Excuse,* 145. The authors note that in the Mississippi Delta, everyone knows that when the church bell starts ringing because someone has died, it tolls for all, but its more immediate message is "open a can of Campbell's cream of mushroom soup and get busy," 143.

73. Important treatments of soul food in both reality and representation include Adrian Miller, *Soul Food: The Surprising Story of an American Cuisine One Plate at a Time* (Chapel Hill: University of North Carolina Press, 2013); and Opie, *Hog and Hominy*, 121–153.

74. Katherina Vester, "*A Date with a Dish*: Revisiting Freda DeKnight's African American Cuisine," in *Dethroning the Deceitful Pork Chop*, 47–60. In the new edition, put out in 1962 as *The Ebony Cookbook: A Date with a Dish*, the "Collector's Corner" was excised in order to present a less Southern, more mainstream image (Vester, 60).

75. Bob Jeffries, *Soul Food Cookbook* (Indianapolis: Bobbs-Merrill, 1969), 1–2.

76. Vertamae Smart-Grosvenor, *Vibration Cooking, or Travels of a Geechee Girl* (New York: Doubleday, 1970).

77. On this and other aspects of the history of chitterlings, see Miller, *Soul Food*, 91–110.

78. Cited by Francis Lam, "Edna Lewis and the Black Roots of American Cooking," in *Edna Lewis: At the Table with an American Original*, 67.

79. Edge, *Potlikker Papers*, 193, 241, 245.

80. Ferris, *Edible South*, 322–28; Edge, *Potlikker Papers*, 235–53; Shields, *Southern Provisions*. Husk also has restaurants in Nashville, Savannah, and Greenville, SC.

81. Edge, *Potlikker Papers*, 220, 308.

82. On Creole versus Cajun cuisine, John D. Folse, *The Evolution of Cajun and Creole Cuisine* (Donaldsville, LA: Chef John Folse and Co., 1989) (mostly recipes); Peter S. Feibleman and the editors of Time-Life Books, *American Cooking: Creole and Acadian* (New York: Time-Life, 1971). Paul Prudhomme disliked like the term "Cajun" applied to his cooking, preferring simply "Louisianan" or "American," Edge, *The Potlikker Papers*, 171.

83. See Lawrence N. Powell, *The Accidental City: Improvising New Orleans* (Cambridge, MA: Harvard University Press, 2012).

84. A locution used in Shields, *Southern Provisions*, 78–91.

85. *The Creole Cookery Book, Edited by the Christian Women's Exchange of New Orleans, La.* (New Orleans: T. H. Thomason, 1883); Lafcadio Hearn, *La Cuisine Creole, A Collection of Culinary Recipes from Leading Chefs and Noted Creole House-Wives, Who Have Made New Orleans Famous for Its Cuisine*, 2nd ed. (New Orleans: F. F. Hansell & Bro., Ltd., 1885).

86. Rien Fertel, *Imagining the Creole City: The Rise of Literary Culture in Nineteenth-Century New Orleans* (Baton Rouge: Louisiana State University Press, 2014).

87. On the cultural as well as socioeconomic situation of New Orleans at the time of the Fair, see *The New Orleans of George Washington Cable: The 1887 Census Office Report*, ed. Lawrence N. Powell (Baton Rouge: Louisiana State University Press, 2008).

88. Anthony J. Stanonis, "The Triumph of Epicure: A Global History of New Orleans Culinary Tourism," *Southern Quarterly* 46 (2009), 145–61.

89. The presence of generic dishes is evident from looking at the two cookbooks. The particular borrowings were described in an unpublished paper by Rien Fertel, "Creole Cookbook, Creole Cookery, Creole Identity in 1885 New Orleans," presented at "Words in Food Symposium," New Orleans, October 2009.

90. *Picayune* means "trivial" or "of no value" and takes it name from small coins that circulated in Southern France and Spain. The New Orleans newspaper established in 1830 adopted the name both as a gesture to the French setting and an indication of cheap price, not unimportant content.

91. For what follows, Rien Fertel, "'Everybody Seemed Willing to Help': *The Picayune Creole Cook Book* as Battleground, 1900–2008," in *The Larder,* 10–31.

92. Lady Helen Henriques Hardy and Raymond J. Martinez, *Louisiana's Fabulous Foods and How to Cook Them* (Jefferson, LA: Hope Publications, ca. 1939), 3. Datable by references to studies concerning molasses. The sugar and rice industries appear to have sponsored the publication.

93. Tipton-Martin, *The Jemima Code,* 52.

94. Lena Richard, *New Orleans Cook Book* (Boston: Houghton Mifflin, 1940), unpaginated preface. See also Paul Freedman, *Ten Restaurants That Changed America* (New York: Liveright, 2016), 65.

95. Feibleman et al., *American Cooking: Creole and Acadian*, 108–09. Nathanial Burton and Rudy Lombard, *Creole Feast: 15 Master Chefs of New Orleans Reveal Their Secrets* (New York: Random House, 1978), xv.

96. See the discussion of the "flurry of fine dining" after the 1984 World's Exposition in Tom Fitzmorris and Peggy Scott Laborde, *Lost Restaurants of New Orleans and the Recipes That Made Them Famous* (Gretna, LA: Pelican Publishing, 2012), 255–61.

97. Tom Fitzmorris, *Hungry Town: A Culinary History of New Orleans: A City Where Food Is Almost Everything* (New York: Stewart, Tabori and Chang, 2010), 44–54.

98. Fitzmorris and Laborde, *Lost Restaurants of New Orleans.*

99. Susan Tucker et al., "Setting the Table in New Orleans," in *New Orleans Cuisine: Fourteen Signature Dishes and Their Histories*, ed. Susan Tucker (Jackson: University Press of Mississippi, 2007), 8.

CHAPTER 2—CULINARY NOSTALGIA

1. Richard J. Hooker, *Food and Drink in America: A History* (Indianapolis and New York: Bobbs-Merrill, 1981), 168.

2. Quoted in Betty Fussell, *I Hear America Cooking: A Journey of Discovery from Alaska to Florida—the Cooks, the Recipes, and the Unique Flavors of Our National Cuisine* (New York: Viking, 1986), xxviii.

3. *The Invention of Tradition*, ed. Eric Hobsbawm and Terence Ranger (Cambridge, UK: Cambridge University Press, 1983). On food and imagined regions, David Bell and Gil Valentine, *Consuming Geographies: We Are What We Eat* (London and New York: Routledge, 1997), 149–61.

4. Pierre Nora, "Between Memory and History," *Representations* 26 (Spring 1989), 7–25.

5. On Howard Johnson's clams, see Paul Freedman, *Ten Restaurants That Changed America* (New York: Liveright, 2016), 152–53; Key lime pie, Stella Parks, *BraveTart: Iconic American Desserts* (New York: W. W. Norton, 2016), 171–72; chili, Timothy C. Lloyd, "The Cincinnati Chili Culinary Complex," in *The Taste of American Place: A Reader on Regional and Ethnic Foods*, ed. Barbara G. Shortridge and James R. Shortridge (Lanham, MD: Rowman and Littlefield, 1998), 45–56.

6. Paul Freedman, "Die schwäbische Küche" (Swabian Cuisine) in *Was ist schwäbisch?* ed. Sigrid Hirbodian and Tjark Wegner (Ostfildern: Jan Thorbecke, 2016), 145. Other false traditions are mentioned by Rachel Laudan, "A Plea for Culinary Modernism: Why We Should Love New, Fast, Processed Food," *Gastronomica* 1, 1 (2001), 36–44.

7. Simon Johnson, "Haggis Was Invented by the English, Not the Scottish Says Historian," *Daily Telegraph*, August 2, 2009, http://www.telegraph.co.uk/foodanddrink/foodanddrinknews/5960237/Haggis-was -invented-by-the-English, accessed August 2, 2017.

8. On his trip, see Lee A. Farrow, *Alexis in America: A Russian Grand Duke's Tour, 1871–1872* (Baton Rouge: Louisiana State University Press, 2014), especially 91–92 for his remark about food in America.

9. Charles Ranhofer, *The Epicurean* (New York: Charles Ranhofer, 1893), 1092.

10. *The New York Times Guide to Dining Out in New York*, ed. Craig Claiborne (New York: Athenaeum, 1964). The exception (page 137) was the Coach House in Greenwich Village, which served a few American dishes such as its signature black bean soup and pecan pie, but most of its offerings were "continental" specialties like veal piccate à la Française or South African rock lobster tails. Claiborne remarks "If there is such a thing as a distinguished American restaurant in New York, this is it," but a menu from the mid-1960s at the library of the Culinary Institute of America in Hyde Park shows only lukewarm enthusiasm for American tradition. In 1976, Seymour Britchky said that most of the dishes were foreign and the rest were merely plain rather than American, *Seymour Britchky's New Revised Guide to the Restaurants of New York* (New York: Random House, 1976), 16–17. In 1964, the food columnist Clementine Paddleford listed six restaurants in answer to being asked whether such a thing as American cuisine could be found in New York. One was a New Orleans–style place, another Southern, a third New England. There was a tearoom and a somewhat generic "continental" restaurant that served apple pie. Only one, Zoe Chase, seems to have offered non-regionally identified American food. Clementine Paddleford, "Gourmet's Choice," in Tom Wolfe et al., *New York Herald Tribune Presents New York, New York* (New York: Delta, 1974), 171–73.

11. A story told in Becky Libourel Diamond, *The Thousand Dollar Dinner: America's First Great Cookery Challenge* (Westholme, PA: Yardley, 2015).

12. A point made by David S. Shields, *Southern Provisions: The Creation and Revival of a Cuisine* (Chicago: University of Chicago Press, 2015), 133.

13. James W. Parkinson, *American Dishes at the Centennial* (Philadelphia: King and Baird, 1874), 2–17.

14. Mark Twain, *A Tramp Abroad* (Hartford, CT: American Publishing Co., 1880), part II, Chapter 19.

15. Andrew Beahrs, *Twain's Feast: Searching for America's Lost Foods in the Footsteps of Samuel Clemens* (New York: Penguin, 2011), 6.

16. Beahrs, *Twain's Feast*, 69.

17. Harvey Levenstein, *Revolution at the Table: The Transformation of the American Diet* (Berkeley and Los Angeles: University of California Press, 2003).

18. On his life see Louis Hatchett, *Duncan Hines: How a Traveling Salesman Became the Most Trusted Name in Food*, 2nd ed. (Lexington: University Press of Kentucky, 2014); Damon Talbott, "Senses of Taste: Duncan Hines and American Gastronomy, 1931–1962," Doctoral Dissertation, American Studies, University of Kansas, 2013.

19. David Schwartz, "Duncan Hines: He Made Gastronomes Out of Motorists," *Smithsonian* 15 (November 1984), 86–97.

20. Duncan Hines, *Duncan Hines' Food Odyssey* (New York: Thomas Y. Crowell, 1955), 71, 95, 186–90.

21. Talbott, "Senses of Taste," 33–43.

22. On Duncan Hines and automotive travel, Talbott, "Senses of Taste," 69–115; Schwartz, "Duncan Hines."

23. Hines, *Food Odyssey*, 40–42.

24. Hines, *Food Odyssey*, 70–71, 105.

25. Damon Talbott, "Recommended by Duncan Hines: Automobility, Authority, and American Gastronomy," Master's Thesis, American Studies, University of Kansas, 2008, 118–20.

26. Phyllis Larsh, "Duncan Hines," *Life*, July 8, 1946, 17.

27. Hines, *Food Odyssey*, 28–29.

28. Talbott, "Senses of Taste," 95–96, 209.

29. Hines, *Food Odyssey*, 245.

30. *The Negro Motorist Green-Book* (and slight variations in title such as *The Negro Travelers' Green Book*), issued annually 1936–1966 (New York: Victor H. Green). The last book covered the years 1963-1966. Available digitally from the New York Public Library, https://digitalcollections.nypl.org/collections/the-green-book#/?tab=about&scroll=18, accessed July 23, 2017.

31. On Rex Stout and the Nero Wolfe mysteries, see John McAleer, *Rex Stout, A Biography* (Boston and Toronto: Little, Brown, 1977), especially 242–77; 409–508.

32. Oddly enough, Wolfe also extolls "Chicken Marengo," a French dish named in honor of one of Napoleon's great battles. *The Nero Wolfe Cookbook* does not mention it.

33. Rex Stout, *Too Many Cooks* (New York: Farrar and Rinehart, 1938).

34. Anne Mendelson, "Food Writing Lives: Sheila Hibben," cookNscribble 2013, www.onebigtable .com?cooknscribble/2013/06/06/food-writing-lives-sheila-hibben, accessed July 30, 2017.

35. One might assume that the absence of wine in the Wolfe series was because the author was uninterested in it, but this is not the case—Stout was a wine enthusiast, McAleer, *Rex Stout*, 250.

36. Rex Stout and the Editors of Viking Press, *The Nero Wolfe Cookbook* (New York: Viking, 1973). Burn is credited in the preface.

37. Camille Bégin, *Taste of the Nation: The New Deal Search for American Food* (Urbana, IL: University of Illinois Press, 2016), 5–6, 26, 33.

38. Mark Kurlansky, *The Food of a Younger Land* (New York: Riverhead, 2009); Bégin, *Taste of the Nation*.

39. On the impact of the Great Depression on American food, see Andrew Coe and Jane Ziegelman, *A Square Meal: A Culinary History of the Great Depression* (New York: HarperCollins, 2016).

40. Bégin, *Taste of the Nation*, 23.

41. Bégin, *Taste of the Nation*, 74–153.

42. Bégin, *Taste of the Nation*, 33, 38–39.

43. Kurlansky, *Food of a Younger Land*, 35–39

44. Published in the 1990s as Nelson Algren, *America Eats* (Iowa City: University of Iowa Press, 1992).

45. Bégin, *Taste of the Nation*, 24, cautions that the Midwestern section is probably not by Algren. On the basis of careful examination of the project materials in the Library of Congress, noted food history expert Anne Mendelson wrote a letter to me with convincing reasons for doubting that Algren ever wrote this.

46. Algren, *America Eats*, 84–85, where it appears as an African dish called "Charchouka."

47. Crosby Gaige, *New York World's Fair Cook Book: The American Kitchen* (New York: Doubleday Doran, 1939).

48. Gaige also wrote *Food at the Fair: A Gastronomic Tour of the World, New York World's Fair 1939* (New York: Exposition Press, 1939), a survey of international cooking from the foreign pavilions at the Fair.

49. Levenstein, *Revolution at the Table*, 72–96, 156–58; Laura Shapiro, *Perfection Salad: Women and Cooking at the Turn of the Century* (New York: Northpoint, 1986), 7–9, 176–90; Angela Jill Cooley, *To Live and Dine in Dixie: The Evolution of Urban Food Culture in the Jim Crow South* (Athens, GA: University of Georgia Press, 2016), 17–42.

50. Gaige, *New York World's Fair Cook Book*, 30, 31, 35. There are two other apple pandowdy recipes, from Rhode Island and Massachusetts, 222, 263.

51. Paul Freedman, *Ten Restaurants That Changed America* (New York: Liveright, 2016).

52. *The Second Ford Treasury of Favorite Recipes from Famous Eating Places* (New York: Golden Press, 1954), 206 and 210; *The New Ford Treasury of Favorite Recipes from Famous Restaurants* (New York: Golden Press, 1963), 95.

53. *The Ford Treasury of Favorite Recipes from Famous Eating Places*, [vol. 1,] 2nd ed. (New York: Simon & Schuster, 1955), 20, 71, 163.

54. *Ford Treasury* [1], 27, 193, 216.

55. *The Ford Treasury* [1], 152; *The Ford Times Cookbook: A Traveler's Guide to Good Eating at Home and on the Road* (New York: Simon & Schuster, 1968), 29; *The Second Ford Treasury*, 211; *The New Ford Treasury*, 114.

56. *Ford Treasury* [1], 53, 63, 82, 189.

57. *Ford Times Cookbook*, 74, 91, 173. The same volume contains twelve other crab or crabmeat recipes.

58. *Ford Treasury of Favorite Recipes from Famous Eating Places*, vol. 3 (New York: Golden Press, 1959), 167.

59. Green-bean casserole was supposedly invented in 1955 by Dorcas Reilly, who worked for Campbell's. It took off when Campbell's began putting the recipe on the label of its cans of cream of mushroom soup,

Karen Zraick, "Dorcas Reilly, Creator of the Classic American Green-Bean Casserole, Dies at 92," *New York Times*, October 24, 2018, http://www.nytimes.com/2018/10/24/obituaries/dorcas-reilly-dead.green-bean-casserole, accessed November 3, 2018. This version is made without condensed soup and takes longer.

60. On her life, times and travels, see Kelly Alexander and Cynthia Harris, *Hometown Appetites: The Story of Clementine Paddleford, the Forgotten Food Writer Who Chronicled How America Ate* (New York: Gotham House, 2008).

61. Alexander and Harris, *Hometown Appetites*, p. 83.

62. In 1948, early in her cross-country journeys, Paddleford wrote up ten recipes from Antoine's for *This Week*. It was published separately as a "service booklet," *Recipes from Antoine's Kitchen,* with the author credit (Paddleford appearing as "editor") appended as a small endnote.

63. Harris, *Hometown Appetites*, 175.

64. Harris, *Hometown Appetites*, 222.

65. Clementine Paddleford, *How America Eats* (New York: Scribner's, 1960), 165.

66. Paddleford, *How America Eats*, 3.

67. Paddleford, *How America Eats*, 121.

68. As noted in Marcie Cohen Ferris, *The Edible South: The Power of Food and the Making of an American Region* (Chapel Hill: University of North Carolina Press, 2014), 225–26. In another column, reviewing New York's Café Nicholson, Paddleford singled out its African American chef Edna Lewis for a somewhat patronizing encomium, Caroline Randall Williams, "How to Talk about Miss Lewis? Home Cook, Writer, Icon. One Young Black Woman's Act of Remembering," in *Edna Lewis: At the Table with an American Original*, ed. Sara B. Franklin (Chapel Hill: University of North Carolina Press, 2018), 82.

69. Noted in a column by R. W. Apple, Jr., "A Life in the Culinary Front Lines," *New York Times*, November 30, 2005, D1, D10.

70. Paddleford, *How America Eats*, 97.

71. Paddleford, *How America Eats,* Foreword, iii.

72. Dale Brown, *American Cooking* (New York: Time-Life, 1968), 67–105.

73. Reprinted in *The Most of Nora Ephron* (New York: Random House, 2013), 420.

74. Gerald Sussman, "Welcome to the Cooking of Provincial New Jersey," *National Lampoon* 51 (June 1974), 57–63.

75. José Wilson, *American Cooking: The Eastern Heartland* (New York: Time-Life, 1971), 83, 108–09, 126–27.

76. Jonathan Norton Leonard, *American Cooking: New England* (New York: Time-Life, 1970), 156–57; Paddleford, *How America Eats*, 9.

77. There would be later regional culinary descriptions and recipe collections, but they portrayed the hidden survival of diversity as a private, household phenomenon rather than public gathering (the WPA project) or restaurants. Betty Fussell, *I Hear America Cooking*, is a search for authentic, regional American food based on cooking in homes more than restaurants (although not entirely excluding the latter, especially for German traditions in Wisconsin, 327–405). Fussell acknowledges that American cooking is *not* regional in the European sense of local products native to a place with strong traditions, xviii–xix. She seeks to "hear America's silent cooks," who are busy at home.

78. Harvey Levenstein, *Paradox of Plenty: A Social History of Eating in Modern America* (Berkeley and Los Angeles: University of California Press, 2003), 233.

79. Jane Stern and Michael Stern, *Roadfood* (New York: Random House, 1977).

80. Jane Stern and Michael Stern, *Chili Nation* (New York: Clarkson Potter, 1999); *Eat Your Way across the USA* (New York: Broadway Books, 1997).

81. Stern and Stern *Eat Your Way*, 35, 93, 171, 213, 220.

82. Stern and Stern, *Roadfood*, 4th ed. (New York: Broadway Books, 2002), xi.

83. Stern and Stern, *Roadfood,* 10th ed. (New York: Clarkson Potter, 2017), 11.

84. Jane Stern and Michael Stern, *Blue Plate Specials and Blue Ribbon Chefs* (New York: Lebhar-Friedman, 2001) is a selection of restaurants and is organized alphabetically. These are therefore noteworthy restaurants, not just attractive stops along a journey.

85. Stern and Stern, *Roadfood*, 2nd ed. (New York: Random House, 1980), 208: "Always on the lookout for regional specialties, we had just about given up on persimmon pudding, a Midwestern and Kentucky dish. . . ."

86. Jane and Michael Stern, *500 Things to Eat Before It's Too Late and the Very Best Places to Eat Them* (New York: Houghton Mifflin Harcourt, 2009).

87. Calvin Trillin, *American Fried: Adventures of a Happy Eater* (New York: Vintage, 1979), 5

88. See Yvonne R. Lockwood and William G. Lookwood, "Pasties in Michigan's Upper Peninsula: Foodways, Interethnic Relations, and Regionalism," in *The Taste of American Place*, 21–36.

89. Matthew Gavin Frank, *The Mad Feast: An Ecstatic Tour through America's Food* (New York: W. W. Norton, 2017). The recipes are contributed by various local authorities.

90. Gabrielle Langholtz, *America: The Cookbook: A Culinary Road Trip through the 50 States* (London and New York: Phaidon, 2017).

91. Amy Bentley, "From Culinary Other to Mainstream America: Meanings and Uses of Southwestern Cuisine," in *Culinary Tourism*, ed. Lucy M. Longi (Lexington: University Press of Kentucky, 2004), 209–25.

CHAPTER 3—COMMUNITY COOKBOOKS

1. Marion Brown, *Marion Brown's Southern Cookbook*, 2nd. ed. (Chapel Hill: University of North Carolina Press, 1968), originally published by the University of North Carolina in 1951 as *The Southern Cook Book*.

2. John T. Edge, *A Gracious Plenty: Recipes and Recollections from the American South* (New York: HP Books, 1999).

3. Ella B. Meyers, *The Centennial Cook Book and General Guide* (Philadelphia: J. B. Meters, 1876).

4. Mary Randolph, *The Virginia House-Wife, or Methodical Cook* (Washington, DC: Davis and Force, 1824); Lettice Bryan, *The Kentucky Housewife* (Cincinnati: Shepard and Stearns, 1839); [Sarah Rutledge], *The Carolina Housewife, or House and Home: By a Lady of Charleston* (Charleston, SC: W. R. Babcock, 1847).

5. Estelle Woods Wilcox, *Buckeye Cookery and Practical Housekeeping: Compiled from Original Receipts* (Minneapolis: Buckeye Publishing, 1877).

6. The text of the original edition and contextual information are available through the Michigan State University "Feeding America" site, http://digital.lib.msu.edu/projects/cookbooks/html/books/book_33.cfm, accessed July 13, 2017.

7. Marion Fontaine Cabelle Tyree, *Housekeeping in Old Virginia, Containing Contributions from Two Hundred and Fifty Ladies in Virginia and Her Sister States, Distinguished for Their Skill in the Culinary Art, and Other Branches of Domestic Economy* (Richmond, VA: J. W. Randolph & English, 1878).

8. *Housekeeping in Old Virginia*, 253–54:

    RESIPEE FOR CUKIN KON-FEEL PEES.

    Gether your pees 'bout sun-down. The folrin day, 'bout leven o'clock, gowge out your pees with your thum nale, like gowgin out a man's eye-ball at a kote house. Rense your pees, parbile them, then fry 'em with som several slices uv streekt middlin, incouragin uv the gravy to seep out and intermarry with your pees. When modritly brown, but not scorcht, empty intoo a dish. Mash 'em gently with a spune, mix with raw tomarters sprinkled with a little brown shugar and the immortal dish ar quite ready. Eat a hepe. Eat mo and mo. It is good for your genral helth uv mind and body. It fattens you up, makes you sassy, goes throo and throo your very soul. But why don't you eat? Eat on. By Jings. Eat. *Stop!* Never, while thar is a pee in the dish.

    Mozis Addums.

9. Megan J. Elias, *Food on the Page: Cookbooks and American Culture* (Philadelphia: University of Pennsylvania Press, 2017), 25–26.

10. Minnie L. Fox, *The Bluegrass Cook Book* (New York: Duffield and Co., 1904). See http://digital.lib.msu.edu/projects/cookbooks/html/books/book_57.cfm, accessed, July 15, 2017.

11. Stephen Schmidt, "Seeing Cooking in Its Time: How Manuscript Cookbooks Help Us to Unravel 'Sampler' Food Histories," unpublished paper given at the Manuscript Cookbook Conference, New York University, May 12–13, 2016, 8–9.

12. Schmidt, "Seeing Cooking in Its Time," 6.

13. Lynne Ireland, "The Compiled Cookbook as Foodways Autobiography," in *The Taste of American Place: A Reader on Regional and Ethnic Food*, ed. Barbara G. Shortridge and James R. Shortridge (Lanham, MD: Rowman and Littlefield, 1998), 111–17; Janice Bluestein Longone, "'Tried Receipts': An Overview of America's Charitable Cookbooks," in *Recipes for Reading: Community Cookbooks, Stories, Histories*, ed. Anne L. Bower (Amherst: University of Massachusetts Press, 1997), 21. On these cookbooks, see also Don Lindgren and Mark Germer eds., *UnXld: American Cookbooks of Community and Place*, vol. 1 (Biddeford, ME: Rabelais, 2018), 5–19.

14. *The Home Cook Book, Compiled by the Ladies of Toronto and Chief Cities and Towns of Canada* (Toronto: Rose Publishing, 1877). On this cookbook see Emily Weiskopf-Ball, "'Tried! Tested! Proven!': *The Canadian Home Cook Book Compiled by: Ladies of Toronto and Chief Cities and Towns in Canada*, 1877, 384 Pages," *Cuizine* 6, number 1 (2015), www.erudit.org/en/journals/cuizine/2015-v6-n1-cuizine01991/1032258ar/, accessed July 19, 2017. For local Canadian community cookbooks see Elizabeth Driver, *Culinary Landmarks: A Bibliography of Canadian Cookbooks, 1825–1949* (Toronto: University of Toronto Press, 2009). Driver is also the author of an article that considers the degree to which community cookbooks reflect regional distinctions, "Regional Differences in the Canadian Daily Meal? Cookbooks Answer the Question," in *What's to Eat? Entrées in Canadian Food History*, ed. Nathalie Cooke (Montreal and Kingston: McGill-Queen's University Press, 2009), 197–212. See also Elizabeth Driver, "Home Cooks, Book Makers and Community Builders in Canada," *Moving Worlds: A Journal of Transcultural Writings* 6:2 (2006), 41–60.

15. Margaret Cook, *America's Charitable Cooks: A Bibliography of Fund-Raising Cook Books Published in the United States (1861–1915)* (Kent, OH: Kent State University Press, 1971). Longone, "'Tried Receipts,'" 20–21, says that her own research suggests probably twice that number were printed in the same period.

16. Eleanor Brown and Bob Brown, *Culinary America: 100 Years of Cookbooks Published in the United States from 1860 through 1960* (New York: Roving Eye Press, 1961).

17. Cook, *America's Charitable Cooks*.

18. The rarity of such African American compilations may be related to the largely oral rather than written nature of recipe invention and diffusion in the black community, as Frederick Douglass Opie suggested to me.

19. Bertha L. Turner, *The Federation Cook Book: A Collection of Tested Recipes Contributed by the Colored Women of the State of California* (Pasadena, CA: Applewood Books 2007, original edition 1910); Toni Tipton-Martin, *The Jemima Code: Two Centuries of African-American Cookbooks* (Austin: University of Texas Press, 2015), describes this on 26–27 and discusses these community cookbooks: *Cooking with Soul: Favorite Recipes of Negro Homemakers*, *West Oakland Soul Food Cook Book*, and the *Penn School and Sea Island Heritage Cookbook* on 90–91, 98–99, 136.

20. *Tort Pleasers: Lincoln Attorneys' Wives* (Lincoln, NB: no publisher listed, 1976), cited in Ireland, "The Compiled Cookbook as Foodways Autobiography" 111. In common law, a tort is a civil wrong (typically negligence or trespass) and the offender is a "tortfeasor."

21. *Church Suppers: 722 Favorite Recipes from Our Church Communities*, ed. Barbara Greenman (New York: Black Dog & Leventhal, 2005), vii.

22. Rebecca Sharpless, "The Women of St. Paul's Episcopal Church Were Worried: Transforming Domestic Skills into Saleable Commodities in Texas," in *The Larder: Food Studies Methods from the American South*, ed. John T. Edge, Elizabeth S. D. Engelhardt, Ted Ownby (Athens: University of Georgia Press, 2017), 36.

23. *The Art of Cooking in Emporia* (Emporia: Boston Grange, no date). Datable from an advertisement between pp. 23 and 24 for the General Electric P7 oven, introduced in 1963. Publication cannot have been much

later than 1963, because local advertisers give telephone numbers using both letters and numerals, a system phased out in the 1960s.

24. For resistance to cake mixes in the 1950s, see Laura Shapiro, *Something from the Oven: Reinventing Dinner in 1950s America* (New York: Penguin, 2004), 72–79.

25. Ireland, "The Compiled Cookbook," p. 109.

26. *Our Favorite Recipes: Ladies of the Upper Keys* (Kansas City, KS: Bev-Ron Publishing, 1974).

27. *C. P. Workers Cookbook* (Canyon City, TX: Canyon City News Print, 1903).

28. An 1888 book from St. Paul's Episcopal Church in Waco, Texas, includes a scalloped oysters recipe given by a self-described young housewife who said the dish is neither novel nor extravagant. The oysters allowed her "to some extent, to maintain the good humor of my very particular husband," Sharpless, "The Women of St. Paul's Episcopal Were Worried," p. 48.

29. *The Canyon City Cookbook* (Canyon City, TX: no publisher listed, 1909).

30. *Amarillo Cookbook* (Amarillo: no publisher listed, 1909).

31. *Favorite Recipes of the Women of Randall County* (Amarillo, TX: Canyon News, no date but 1942–1945).

32. Arthur and Bobbie Coleman, *The Texas Cookbook* (New York: A. A. Wyn, 1949).

33. *Favorite Recipes of Texas* (Montgomery, AL: Favorite Recipe Press, 1964).

34. *The Three Hundredth Anniversary Cook Book*, 2nd ed. (East Hampton, NY: Ladies' Village Improvement Society, 1948).

35. *The East Hampton Cookbook of Menus and Recipes*, ed. Ruth A. Spear (Bridgehampton, NY: Dan's Papers, 1975).

36. *American-Pakistani Cook Book, Published by the Army Wives of Rawalpindi—Pakistan* (Rawalpindi: Red Star Press, ca. 1955).

37. *Island Born and Bred: A Collection of Harkers Island Food, Fun, Fact and Fiction Compiled by the Harkers Island United Methodist Women* (Atlantic Beach, NC: Weathers Printing Company, 1987). Karen Willis Amspacher is mentioned as the editor on p. vi. The Down East way of life and its food have been evocatively described by David Cecelski, *The Art of Making Oyster Fritters* (Durham, 2012). I am grateful to him for telling me about food in this region. Nancy Davis and Kathy Hart, *Coastal Carolina Cooking* (Chapel Hill: University of North Carolina Press, 1986) encompasses a larger part of the inner coast and includes diverse cooking customs.

38. *Island Born and Bred*, pp. 304–05. Mullet roe is not unknown elsewhere—the Sterns list smoked mullet roe as a specialty of the Florida Panhandle and Tampa Bay, Jane Stern and Michael Stern, *500 Things to Eat Before It's Too Late and the Very Best Places to Eat Them* (New York: Houghton Mifflin Harcourt, 2009), 198–99.

39. Davis and Hart, *Coastal Carolina Cooking*, 6, 7, 89, 95, 132, 138, 155, 156 (the book is organized by contributor, not by type of dish); Cecelski, *The Art of Making Oyster Fritters*, 2–3.

40. Information kindly supplied by David Cecelski in a message to me, May 9, 2012.

41. *The Jackson Cookbook* (Jackson MS: Symphony League of Jackson, 1971). I am grateful to my old friend Ann S. Holmes, who gave me this cookbook, autographed by Eudora Welty, many years ago.

42. Ernest Matthew Mickler, *White Trash Cooking* (Berkeley: Ten Speed Press, 1986). The term "white trash" is offensive for a number of obvious reasons. Apart from its frank pejorative import, it implies that "trash" is a default setting for black people but a special case for whites. As a putative sociological label, "white trash" has a long history, as does the category of poor, rural people it includes, for which see Nancy Isenberg, *White Trash: The 400-Year History of Class in America* (New York: Viking, 2016).

43. All these are in an unpaginated preface.

44. The Scripture cake recipe appears on p. 85 in this book.

45. *White Trash Cooking*, 69 (here the fruit consists of mandarin oranges and Libby's fruit cocktail): *Jackson Cookbook*, 39 (canned mandarin oranges, canned pineapple tidbits, canned spiced grapes).

46. John T. Edge, *The Potlikker Papers: A Food History of the Modern South* (New York: Penguin, 2017), 240.

47. *Cabbagetown Families, Cabbagetown Food* (Atlanta: Patch Press, 1976). No author is given, but Pam Durban Porter is the "editor" on the copyright page.

48. https://www.youtube.com/watch?v=oLgmk323H6k, accessed July 26, 2018.

49. Ronni Lundy, *Victuals: An Appalachian Journey, with Recipes* (New York: Clarkson Potter, 2016).

50. Lundy, *Victuals*, 88.

51. Lundy, *Victuals*, 33.

52. I am grateful to my friend Barbara Hand and to her mother, Shirley Rich, who was involved in putting together this cookbook. I also want to thank their friends and neighbors in Pickett County, Tennessee.

53. Jon Michaud, "Sheila Hibben," *The New Yorker*, November 16, 2010, https://www.newyorker.com/books/double-take/sheila-hibben, accessed November 3, 2018.

54. Sheila Hibben, *The National Cookbook: A Kitchen Americana* (New York and London: Harper Brothers, 1932). On Hibben and this cookbook, see Jane Ziegelman and Andrew Coe, *A Square Meal: A Culinary History of the Great Depression* (New York: HarperCollins, 2016), 269–73.

55. Hibben, *The National Cookbook*, x–xvi.

56. On Eleanor Roosevelt's tastes and those of her White House chef Henrietta Nesbitt, "the most reviled cook in presidential history," see Laura Shapiro, *What She Ate: Six Remarkable Women and the Food That Tells Their Stories* (New York: Viking, 2017), 91–130, esp. 117.

57. Sheila Hibben, *American Regional Cookery* (New York: Crown, 1946).

58. Hibben, *American Regional Cookery*, ii–iii.

CHAPTER 4—THE GOLDEN AGE OF FOOD PROCESSING, 1880–1970

1. The full title of chapter 7 (101–18) in Harvey Levenstein, *Paradox of Plenty: A Social History of Eating in Modern America* (Berkeley and Los Angeles: University of California Press, 2003), is "The Golden Age of Food Processing: Miracle Whip Über Alles."

2. On modern food, Jack Goody, "Industrial Food: Towards the Development of a World Cuisine," in *Cooking, Cuisine and Class: A Study in Comparative Sociology* (Cambridge, UK: Cambridge University Press, 1982), 154–74; Harvey Levenstein, *Revolution at the Table: The Transformation of the American Diet* (Berkeley and Los Angeles: University of California Press, 2003); Levenstein, *Paradox of Plenty*; Gabriella M. Petrick, "Industrial Food," in *The Oxford Handbook of Food History*, ed. Jeffrey M. Pilcher (Oxford, UK: Oxford University Press, 2012), 258–78; Richard Pillsbury, *No Foreign Food: The American Diet in Time and Place* (Boulder, CO: Westview, 1998), 52–117.

3. Robert H. Hadow, *Pavilions of Plenty: Exhibiting American Culture Abroad in the 1950s* (Washington, DC: Smithsonian Institution, 1997), 65–68; Shane Hamilton, *Supermarket USA: Food and Power in the Cold War Farms Race* (New Haven: Yale University Press, 2018), 97–110.

4. Cristina Carbone, "Staging the Kitchen Debate: How Splitnik Got Normalized in the United States," in *Cold War Kitchen: Americanization, Technology, and European Users*, ed. Ruth Oldenziel and Karin Zachmann (Cambridge, MA: MIT Press, 2009), 59–81; Susan E. Reid, "'Our Kitchen Is Just as Good:' Soviet Responses to the American Kitchen," in the same collection, 83–112. The model house was nicknamed "Splitnik," a jocular but competitive reference to the postwar fashion for split-level houses and the Soviet Union's stunning Sputnik space satellite launch in 1957.

5. A recent defense of industrial food is Rachal Laudan, "A Plea for Culinary Modernism" in *Food Fights: How the Past Matters to Contemporary Food Debates*, ed. Charles C. Ludington and Matthew M. Booker (Chapel Hill: University of North Carolina Press, in press).

6. US Department of Agriculture, https://www.ers.usda.gov/data-products/chart-gallery/gallery/chart-detail/?chartId=83033, accessed November 23, 2017; Derek Thompson. "How America Spends Money: 100 Years in the Life of the Family Budget," *The Atlantic*, April 5, 2012, https://www.theatlantic

.com/business/archive/2012/04/how-america-spends-money-100-years-in-the-life-of-the-family
-budget/255475/, accessed November 19, 2017. Since so much of what we spend now goes to meals eaten
away from home (just over 50 percent), this data distorts household food expenditures for meals cooked at
home, formerly a better representation of basic needs.

7. Detailed figures categorized according to race and gender are given by the Centers for Disease Control
and Prevention, https://www.cdc.gov/nchs/data/nvsr/nvsr54/nvsr54_14.pdf, accessed December 24, 2017.

8. For what follows, I rely on a short paper written in 2017 by Christina Stankey, a Yale undergraduate stu-
dent, "The Honeycrisp: An American Story." See also Michael Pollan, *The Botany of Desire: A Plant's Eye
View of the World* (New York: Random House, 2001), 12–58; John Seabrook, "Crunch," *The New Yorker*,
November 21, 2011, 54–64.

9. Tim Hensley, "A Curious Tale: The Apple in North America," Brooklyn Botanic Garden, June 2, 2005,
http://www.bbg.org/gardening/article/the_apple_in_north_america, accessed November 21, 2017.

10. David S. Shields, *Southern Provisions: The Creation and Revival of a Cuisine* (Chicago: University of Chicago
Press, 2015), 41–43.

11. A useful introduction to technological change, particularly in Germany, is Hans J. Teuteberg, "The Birth
of the Modern Consumer Age," in *Food: The History of Taste*, ed. Paul Freedman (London: Thames and
Hudson, 2007), 233–61.

12. https://www.statista.com/statistics/575229/brewery-groups-market-share-germany/; https://www.marketwatch
.com/story/these-11-brewers-make-over-90-of-all-us-beer-2015-07-27, accessed November 20, 2017.

13. John F. Love, *McDonald's: Behind the Golden Arches* (New York: Bantam Books, 1995).

14. Paul Freedman, *Ten Restaurants That Changed America* (New York: Liveright, 2016), 160–62.

15. Pillsbury, *No Foreign Food*, 66–67.

16. Levenstein, *Revolution at the Table*, 35.

17. Levenstein, *Revolution at the Table*, 32.

18. Howard Markel, *The Kelloggs: The Battling Brothers of Battle Creek* (New York: Pantheon, 2017).

19. The Bing Crosby song of 1968, "What's More American?"

20. Much of this section relies on Deborah Fitzgerald, *Every Farm a Factory: The Industrial Ideal in American
Agriculture* (New Haven: Yale University Press, 2003).

21. Harry Slattery, *Rural America Lights Up: The Story of Rural Electrification* (Washington DC: National
Home Library Foundation, 1940); *Rural Electric Fact Book* (Washington, DC: National Rural Electric
Cooperative Association, 1960).

22. Michael J. McDonald and John Muldowney, *TVA and the Dispossessed: The Resettlement of Population in the
Norris Dam Area* (Knoxville: University of Tennessee Press, 1982).

23. Walter L. Creese, *TVA's Public Planning: The Vision, the Reality* (Knoxville: University of Tennessee Press,
1990); David Lilienthal, *TVA: Democracy on the March* (New York: Harper and Brother, 1944); *TVA:
Fifty Years of Grass-Roots Bureaucracy*, ed. Erwin F. Hargrove and Paul H. Conkin (Urbana: University of
Illinois Press, 1983).

24. Keith Stewart, *It's a Long Road to a Tomato: Tale of an Organic Farmer Who Quit the Big City for the (Not
So) Simple Life* (New York: Marlowe and Company, 2006).

25. Donald Davidson et al., *I'll Take My Stand: The South and the Agrarian Tradition, by Twelve Southerners*
(New York: Harper & Brother, 1930). See also Allan Carlson, *The New Agrarian Mind: The Movement
toward Decentralist Thought in Twentieth-Century America* (New Brunswick, NJ: Transaction, 2000).

26. Although some of the members of this movement considered the TVA preferable to Northern business
intrusion, Edward Shapiro, "The Southern Agrarians and the Tennessee Valley Authority," *American Quarterly* 22 (1970), 791–806. In general, see Emily Bingham and Thomas Underwood, *The Southern Agrarians
and the New Deal: Essays after I'll Take My Stand* (Charlottesville: University of Virginia Press, 2001).

27. Fitzgerald, *Every Farm a Factory*, 157–83.

28. James McWilliams, "Contemporary Issues," in *The Routledge History of American Foodways*, ed. Michael D.
Wise and Jennifer Jensen Wallach (New York: Routledge, 2016), 59.

29. Jim Hightower, *Hard Tomatoes, Hard Times: The Failure of the Land Grant College Complex* (Washington, DC: Agribusiness Accountability Project, 1972).

30. McWilliams, "Contemporary Issues," 61–62.

31. On shopping in the suburbs, Alex Marshall, *How Cities Work: Suburbs, Sprawl and the Roads Not Taken* (Austin: University of Texas Press, 2000), 88–92, 105–09.

32. A point made by Tracey Deutsch, "Untangling Alliances: Social Tensions Surrounding Independent Grocery Stores and the Rise of Mass Retailing," in *Food Nations: Selling Taste in Consumer Societies*, ed. Warren Belasco and Philip Scranton (New York and London: Routledge, 2002), 156–74.

33. Marc Levinson, *The Great A&P and the Struggle for Small Business in America* (New York: Hill & Wang, 2011); Marc Levinson, *The Box: How the Shipping Container Made the World Smaller and the World Economy Bigger*, 2nd ed. (Princeton, NJ: Princeton University Press, 2016).

34. Michael Ruhlman, *Grocery: The Buying and Selling of Food in America* (New York: Abrams, 2017), 38.

35. Ruhlman, *Grocery*, 39–41; Andrew F. Smith, *Eating History: Thirty Turning Points in the Making of American Cuisine* (New York: Columbia University Press, 2009), 176–83.

36. Smith, *Eating History*, pp. 177–78; Levenstein, *Paradox of Plenty*, 113–15.

37. Stephanie Strom, "Is the Supermarket Done For?," *New York Times*, May 16, 2016, published online under the title "What's New in the Supermarket? A Lot, and Not All of It Good," https://www.nytimes.com/2017/05/16/dining/grocery-book-michael-ruhlman-supermarket-shopping.html?_r=0, accessed January 14, 2018.

38. On Harvey, see Stephen Fried, *Appetite for America: Fred Harvey and the Business of Civilizing the Wild West One Meal at a Time* (New York: Bantam Books, 2010).

39. James D. Porterfield, *Dining by Rail: The History and the Recipes of America's Golden Age of Railroad Cuisine* (New York: St. Martin's, 1993), 24–48; Katie Rawson and Elliott Shore, *Dining Out: A Global History of Restaurants* (London: Reaktion, 2019), 138–48.

40. Freedman, *Ten Restaurants That Changed America*, 129–70.

41. Josh Ozersky, *The Hamburger* (New Haven: Yale University Press, 2008), 57–59.

42. "McDonald's Real Estate: How They Really Make Their Money," *Wall Street Survivor*, October 15, 2015 (authorship credited to "Team Wall Street Survivor"), blog.wallstreetsurvivor.com/2015/10/08/mcdonalds-beyond-the-burger/, accessed December 26, 2017.

43. Eric Schlosser, *Fast Food Nation: The Dark Side of the All-American Meal*, 2nd ed. (New York: HarperCollins, 2002).

44. Although even McDonald's can benefit from popular food fashions. Some McDonald's branches occasionally serve a "McRib sandwich," but it's hard to find. Online groups exchange tracking information about this specialty, Anthony J. Stanonis, "Food Tourism," in *The Routledge History of American Foodways* (New York and Abingdon: Routledge, 2016), 241.

CHAPTER 5—WHY AMERICANS WELCOMED INDUSTRIAL FOOD

1. On consumers and acceptance of canned food in particular, see Anna Zeide, *Canned: The Rise and Fall of Consumer Confidence in the American Food Industry* (Oakland: University of California Press, 2018).

2. On Wonder Bread, Carolyn Wyman, *Better Than Homemade: Amazing Foods That Changed the Way We Eat* (San Francisco: Chronicle Books, 2004), 72–74.

3. Rhodri Marsden, "Rhodri Marsden's Interesting Objects: The Sliced Loaf," *The Independent* (UK), July 5, 2014, https://www.independent.co.uk/life-style/food-and-drink/features/rhodri-marsdens-interesting-objects-the-sliced-loaf-9579661.html, accessed September 29, 2018.

4. Kim, Sylvie, "The End of Spam Shame: On Class, Colonialism and Canned Meat," https://hyphenmagazine.com/blog/2011/6/3/end-spam-shame-class-colonialism-and-canned-meat.

5. A point made by John L. Hess and Karen Hess, *The Taste of America* (New York: Grossman, 1977), 26–29.

6. On nineteenth-century food reform, see Adam D. Shprintzen, "The Nineteenth Century," in *The Routledge History of American Foodways,* ed. Michael D. Wise and Jennifer Jensen Wallach (New York and Abingdon: Routledge, 2016), 37–47.

7. Charlotte Biltekoff, *Eating Right in America: The Cultural Politics of Food and Health* (Durham, NC: Duke University Press, 2013), 17–20.

8. Harvey Levenstein, *Revolution at the Table: The Transformation of the American Diet* (Berkeley and Los Angeles: University of California Press, 2003), 90.

9. Biltekoff, *Eating Right in America*, 23–24.

10. Helen Zoe Veit, *Modern Food, Moral Food: Self-Control, Science and the Rise of Modern American Eating* (Chapel Hill: University of North Carolina Press, 2013), 157–80.

11. On the New England Kitchen, Laura Shapiro, *Perfection Salad: Women and Cooking at the Turn of the Century* (New York: North Point Press, 1986), 145–61; Biltekoff, *Eating Right in America,* 24–36; Megan J. Elias, *Food on the Page: Cookbooks and American Culture* (Philadelphia: University of Pennsylvania Press, 2017), 32–42.

12. Harvey Levenstein, "The American Response to Italian Food, 1880–1930," in *Food in the U.S.A.: A Reader,* ed. Carole M. Counihan (New York: Routledge, 2002, first published 1985), 82.

13. Shapiro, *Perfection Salad*, 145.

14. Biltekoff, *Eating Right in America*, 33–35.

15. Levenstein, *Revolution at the Table*, 151–52.

16. Examples in Levenstein, *Revolution at the Table*, 153.

17. On "fortifying" food with added vitamins and minerals, see Marion Nestle, *Food Politics: How the Food Industry Influences Nutrition and Health*, 2nd ed. (Berkeley and Los Angles: University of California Press, 2007), 298–314.

18. David Strauss, *Setting the Table for Julia Child: Gourmet Dining in America, 1934–1961* (Baltimore: Johns Hopkins University Press, 2011), 21–29; Levenstein, *Revolution at the Table*, 158–59.

19. Katherine J. Parkin, *Food Is Love: Advertising and Gender Roles in Modern America* (Philadelphia: University of Pennsylvania Press, 2006), 162–63.

20. Parkin, *Food Is Love*, 166.

21. Nestle, *Food Politics*, 104–10.

22. Many examples in Nestle, *Food Politics*, and also see Warren Belasco, *Appetite for Change: How the Counterculture Took On the Food Industry, 1966–1988* (New York: Pantheon, 1989), 39–43, 69–70, 220–25, 245–46.

23. Mary Beth Quirk, "Capri Sun Replacing High Fructose Corn Syrup with Sugar in Original Drinks," Consumerist, February 10, 2015, https://consumerist.com/2015/02/10/capri-sun-replacing-high-fructose-corn -syrup-with-sugar-in-original-drinks/, accessed December 27, 2018.

24. Shapiro, *Perfection Salad*, 145.

25. Levenstein, *Revolution at the Table,* 83; Angela Jill Cooley, *To Live and Dine in Dixie: The Evolution of Urban Food Culture in the Jim Crow South* (Athens: University of Georgia Press, 2015), 30.

26. Levenstein, *Revolution at the Table*, 93.

27. Jennifer Jensen Wallach, "Dethroning the Deceitful Pork Chop: Food Reform at the Tuskegee Institute," in *Dethroning the Deceitful Pork Chop: Rethinking African American Foodways from Slavery to Obama*, ed. Jennifer Jensen Wallach (Fayetteville: University of Arkansas Press, 2017), 168–69.

28. James E. McWilliams, *A Revolution in Eating: How the Quest for Food Shaped America* (New York: Columbia University Press, 2005), 1–5.

29. The latter is a Poppy Cannon recipe from Laura Shapiro, *Something from the Oven: Reinventing Dinner in 1950s America* (New York: Penguin, 2004), 96.

30. Steven Laurence Kaplan, *Good Bread Is Back: A Contemporary History of French Bread, the Way It Is Made and the People Who Make It*, trans. Catherine Porter (Durham, NC: Duke University Press, 2006).

31. Shapiro, *Something from the Oven*, 133–34.

32. Levenstein, *Revolution at the Table*, 163.

33. Pierre Franey, *The New York Times 60-Minute Gourmet* (New York: Fawcett Columbine, 1979). For a mass-market audience, Rachael Ray set a standard in the late 1990s beginning with her 30-minute meals on the Food Network, Allen Salkin, *From Scratch: Inside the Food Network* (New York: Putnam, 2013), 268–74.

34. Parkin, *Food Is Love*, 61.

35. Jessamyn Neuhaus, *Manly Meals and Mom's Home Cooking: Cookbooks and Gender in Modern America* (Baltimore: Johns Hopkins University Press, 2003), 47–56; Sherrie Inness, *Dinner Roles: American Women and Culinary Culture* (Iowa City: University of Iowa Press, 2001), 73–75; Levenstein, *Revolution at the Table*, 60–71.

36. Inness, *Dinner Roles*, 74–75.

37. Peg Bracken, *The I Hate to Cook Book* (New York: Harcourt, Brace and World, 1960).

38. Poppy Cannon, *The Can-Opener Cook Book: A Guide for Gourmet Cooking with Canned or Frozen Food and Mixes* (New York: Thomas Y. Crowell and Co., 1951); Justin Spring, *The Gourmands' Way: Six Americans in Paris and the Birth of a New Gastronomy* (New York: Farrar, Straus and Giroux, 2017), 224–25; Shapiro, *Something from the Oven*, 103–07.

39. *Campbell's Great Restaurants Cookbook, U.S.A.* (New York: Rutledge, 1969), 9. I am grateful to my friend William David Burns for giving me a copy of this fascinating book.

40. *Campbell's Great Restaurants Cookbook*, 46, 67.

41. Thomas Hine, *Populuxe: From Tailfins and TV Dinners to Barbie Dolls and Fallout Shelters* (New York: Alfred A. Knopf, 1984).

42. Noted by Betty Friedan in *The Feminine Mystique* (New York: W. W. Norton, 1997), 305–14.

43. Shapiro, *Something from the Oven*, 41–84.

44. Shapiro, *Something from the Oven,* 34–37.

45. https://www.pillsbury.com/bake-off-contest/rules, accessed October 6, 2018.

46. Shapiro, *Something from the Oven*, 9–15.

CHAPTER 6—WOMEN AND FOOD IN THE TWENTIETH CENTURY

1. David Strauss, *Setting the Table for Julia Child: Gourmet Dining in America, 1934–1961* (Baltimore: Johns Hopkins University Press, 2011), 30.

2. As in the Cal Smith country song "Between Lust and Watching TV" from 1974:

   My wife's a good cook,
   But a man can't exist just on bread
   What I'm longing for
   Is the one thing I ain't being fed.

3. Katherine Parkin, *Food Is Love: Advertising and Gender Roles in Modern America* (Philadelphia: University of Pennsylvania Press, 2006), 32–33.

4. Mrs. Simon Kander (Lizzie Black Kander), *The "Settlement" Cook Book: The Way to a Man's Heart* (New York: Gramercy Publishing, 1903). A second edition appeared in 1949 and a third in 1976, and there were at least forty printings. *The New Settlement Cookbook* (New York: Simon & Schuster, 1954) reflected the cuisines of immigrants who were the beneficiaries of the original Settlement House movement.

5. *From Pillsbury's 5th $100,000 Recipe and Baking Contest, 100 Grand National Recipes* (Minneapolis: Pillsbury Mills, 1954), 46–47.

6. Harvey Levenstein, *Paradox of Plenty: A Social History of Eating in Modern America* (Berkeley and Los Angeles: University of California Press, 2003), 36.

7. Sherrie Inness, *Dinner Roles: American Women and Culinary Culture* (Iowa City: University of Iowa Press, 2001), 33–35.

8. *How to Keep a Husband, or Culinary Tactics* (San Francisco: Cubery and Co., 1872).

9. Parkin, *Food Is Love*, 136–39.

10. Harvey Levenstein, *Revolution at the Table: The Transformation of the American Diet* (Berkeley and Los Angeles: University of California Press, 2003), 164.

11. Parkin, *Food Is Love*, 143.

12. Parkin, *Food Is Love*, 176.

13. *Cooking in the Grand Manner* (Cleveland: Grand Home Appliance Company, 1950).

14. *The Fifteen Joys of Marriage: Les XV joies de mariage*, trans. Brent A. Pitts (New York: P. Lang, 1985), 21, 93.

15. Wendy A. Woloson, *Refined Tastes: Sugar, Confectionery, and Consumers in Nineteenth-Century America* (Baltimore: Johns Hopkins University Press, 2002), 90. See also Paul Freedman, *Ten Restaurants That Changed America* (New York: Liveright, 2016), 101–06.

16. Wilmington, Delaware, Henry Voigt Collection of American Menus.

17. New York Public Library, Rare Books Room, Buttolph Menu Collection.

18. J. C. Croly, *Jennie June's American Cookery Book* (New York: American News Company, 1866), 306.

19. Croly, *Jennie June's American Cookery Book*, 307.

20. Mary F. Henderson, *Practical Cooking and Dinner Giving* (New York: Harper and Brother, 1877), 36–39.

21. Inness, *Dinner Roles*, 52–63.

22. Inness, *Dinner Roles*, 63. On the history of Jell-O, Carolyn Wyman, *Jell-O: A Biography* (San Diego: Harcourt, 2001).

23. On Jell-O salads, Wyman, *Jell-O: A Biography*, 44–56, 141; Sarah Grey, "A Social History of Jell-O Salad: The Rise and Fall of an American Icon," Serious Eats 2015, http://www.seriouseats.com/2015/08/history-of-jell-o-salad.html, accessed January 29, 2018.

24. Laura Shapiro, *Something from the Oven: Reinventing Dinner in 1950s America* (New York: Viking Penguin, 2004), 174.

25. Jessamyn Neuhaus, *Manly Meals and Mom's Home Cooking: Cookbooks and Gender in Modern America* (Baltimore: Johns Hopkins University Press, 2003), 77.

26. Levenstein, *Paradox of Plenty*, 36.

27. Bryan McFadden, "Give a Man Man's Food," as described in Inness, *Dinner Roles*, 24.

28. Neuhaus, *Manly Meals and Mom's Home Cooking*, 73–97; Inness, *Dinner Roles*, 17–36; Katharina Vester, *A Taste of Power: Food and American Identities* (Berkeley and Los Angeles: University of California Press, 2015), 66–136; Megan J. Elias, *Food on the Page: Cookbooks and American Culture* (Philadelphia: University of Pennsylvania Press, 2017), 73–106.

29. Neuhaus, *Manly Meals*, 80–81.

30. Neuhaus, *Manly Meals*, 85–86.

31. Len Deighton, *Len Deighton's Action Cook Book* (Harmondsworth, UK: Penguin, 1967). Originally published 1965 by Jonathan Cape in London.

32. Amanda Cohen and Ryan Dunlavey, *Dirt Candy: A Cookbook. Flavor-Forward Food from the Upstart New York City Vegetarian Restaurant* (New York: Clarkson Potter, 2012), 93.

33. Allen Salkin, "Be Yourselves, Girls, Order the Rib-Eye," *New York Times*, August 9, 2007, http://www.nytimes.com/2007/08/09/fashion/09STEAK.html, accessed January 12, 2018.

34. Shapiro, *Something from the Oven*, 7.

35. Paul Sabin, *The Bet: Paul Ehrlich, Julian Simon and Our Gamble over Earth's Future* (New Haven: Yale University Press, 2013).

36. Amartya Sen, *Poverty and Famines: An Essay on Entitlement and Deprivation* (New York: Oxford University Press, 1982).

37. On these prospects, Warren Belasco, *Meals to Come: A History of the Future of Food* (Berkeley and Los Angeles: University of California Press, 2006), 113–18.

38. Thomas McNamee, *Alice Waters and Chez Panisse: The Romantic, Impractical, Often Eccentric, Ultimately Brilliant Making of a Food Revolutionary* (New York: Penguin, 2007), 308–09.

39. Sheila Fitzpatrick, *Everyday Stalinism: Ordinary Life in Extraordinary Times. Soviet Russia in the 1930s* (Oxford, UK: Oxford University Press, 2000).

40. *Book of Tasty and Healthy Food*, trans. Boris Ushumirsky (Middletown, DE: Skylark Publishing, 2017).

41. Elias, *Food on the Page*, 93–94.

42. Strauss, *Setting the Table*, 201–02.

43. Louis Diat, *Louis Diat's French Cooking for Americans: La cuisine de ma Mère* (Philadelphia and New York: J. B. Lippincott, 1946). Rex Stout wrote the foreword.

44. Strauss, *Setting the Table*, 193.

45. Strauss, *Setting the Table*, 210–19.

46. *Gourmet* 20, no. 1 (January 1960), 2; *Gourmet* 14, no. 9 (September 1954), 52.

47. *Gourmet* 44, no. 10 (October 1964), 84; *Gourmet* 49, no. 7 (July 1981), 83.

48. *Gourmet* 19, no. 8 (August 1959), 46.

49. *Gourmet* 24, no. 8 (August 1964), 4; *Gourmet* 26, no. 11 (November 1966), 2.

50. *Gourmet* 16, no. 11 (November 1957), 90; *Gourmet* 18, no. 10 (October 1958), 71.

51. *Gourmet* 16, no. 6 (June 1956), 40.

52. *Gourmet* 14, no. 1 (January 1954), 52–53.

53. *Gourmet* 51, no. 1 (January 1991), 212.

54. Lucius Beebe, "Along the Boulevards," *Gourmet* 18, no. 1 (January 1958), 8.

55. Nora Ephron, "The Food Establishment: Life in the Land of the Rising Soufflé," in *The Most of Nora Ephron* (New York: Alfred A. Knopf, 2013), 408–11.

56. Belasco, *Meals to Come*, 224–25.

57. Anonymous review in *Gourmet* 25, no. 6 (June 1965), 11.

58. Mimi Sheraton, "I Tasted Everything in Bloomingdale's Food Shop," *New York*, October 16, 1972, 51–75.

CHAPTER 7—HAVE YOUR CAKE, CHOOSE FROM OUR FIFTEEN FABULOUS FLAVORS, AND EAT IT TOO

1. *Manger: Français, Européens et Américains face à l'alimentation*, ed. Claude Fischler and Estelle Masson (Paris: Odile Jacob, 2008), especially 84–87.

2. Cristina Carbone, "Staging the Kitchen Debate: How Splitnik Got Normalized in the United States," in *Cold War Kitchen: Americanization, Technology, and European Users*, ed. Ruth Oldenziel and Karin Zachmann (Cambridge, MA: MIT Press, 2009), 59–62.

3. Shane Hamilton, *Supermarket USA: Food and Power in the Cold War Farms Race* (New Haven: Yale University Press, 2018), 118–19.

4. Oretta Zanini de Vita, *Encyclopedia of Pasta*, trans. Maureen B. Fant (Berkeley and Los Angeles: University of California Press, 2000), 144–45, 191.

5. Massimo Bottura, *Never Trust a Skinny Italian Chef* (London and New York: Phaidon, 2014), 36.

6. Doina Harsanyi and Nicolae Harsanyi, "On the Fringes of History: Food and Eating Habits in the Banat," *Petits Propos Culinaires* 47 (1994), 28–29.

7. Prosper Montagné, *Larousse Gastronomique: The Encyclopedia of Food, Wine and Cookery* (New York: Crown, 1961), 454–55.

8. Hiriko Shimbo, *The Sushi Experience* (New York: Alfred A. Knopf, 2006), 19–20, 42.

9. Katharina Vester, *A Taste of Power: Food and American Identities* (Berkeley: University of California Press, 2015), 25–29.

10. Harvey Levenstein, *Paradox of Plenty: A Social History of Eating in Modern America* (Berkeley and Los Angeles: University of California Press, 2003), 110.

11. Examples from John L. Hess and Karen Hess, *The Taste of America* (New York: Grossman, 1977), 42, 48.

12. *So Fast Recipes and So Good Too* (Washington, DC: National Canners Association, nd, 1930s), 1.

13. Harvey Levenstein, *Revolution at the Table: The Transformation of the American Diet* (Berkeley and Los Angeles: University of California Press, 2003), 84.

14. Laura M. Holson, "Where's My Tab? A Shortage Panics Fans," *The New York Times*, October 21, 2018, BU 3.

15. The components would change periodically, but they are taken here from a 1930s brochure of recipes using Heinz Cooked Spaghetti, *57 Unusual Ways to Serve Spaghetti*. The booklet is undated but contains a preface by Josephine Gibson, the director of the Home Economics Department at Heinz; she was the first person to hold this office, from 1927 until 1937. Some items were already out of fashion—mock turtle soup, for example. Others, such as rice flakes or breakfast wheat, haven't been made by the company within living memory.

16. Laura Shapiro *Perfection Salad: Women and Cooking at the Turn of the Century* (New York: HarperCollins, 1986), 3–4.

17. Bunny Crumpacker, *The Old-Time Brand-Name Cookbook: Recipes, Illustrations and Advice from the Early Kitchens of America's Most Trusted Food Makers* (New York: Smithmark, 2011), 26–27.

18. Laura Shapiro, *Something from the Oven: Reinventing Dinner in 1950s America* (New York: Viking Penguin, 2004), 64.

19. Jane Ziegelman and Andrew Coe, *A Square Meal: A Culinary History of the Great Depression* (New York: HarperCollins, 2016), 196–97.

20. Shapiro, *Something from the Oven*, 66.

21. From the website "Hey, My Mom Used to Make That!" http://pzrservices.typepad.com/vintagerecipes/2012/08/chicken-a-la-can-can-ready-in-12-minutes.html, accessed March 22, 2018.

22. Poppy Cannon, *The Can-Opener Cook Book* (New York: Thomas Y. Crowell, 1951).

23. On Cannon's career, Shapiro, *Something from the Oven*, 87–127.

24. Shapiro, *Something from the Oven*, 97.

25. Cannon, *Can-Opener Cook Book*, 1.

26. Cannon, *Can-Opener Cook Book*, 2, 3, 130.

27. Shapiro, *Something from the Oven*, 97–98.

28. Justin Spring, *The Gourmands' Way: Six Americans in Paris and the Birth of a New Gastronomy* (New York: Farrar, Straus and Giroux, 2017), 182–83.

29. Alice B. Toklas, *Aromas and Flavors of Past and Present: A Book of Exquisite Cookery* (New York: Harper & Bros, 1958), xvii–xix. Poppy Cannon wrote the introduction and the comments placed before the recipes.

30. Jane Stern and Michael Stern, *American Gourmet: Classic Recipes, Deluxe Delights, Flamboyant Favorites, and Swank "Company" Food from the '50s and '60s* (New York: HarperCollins, 1991), 147–55.

31. Peter Moruzzi, *Classic Dining: Discovering America's Finest Mid-Century Restaurants* (Layton, UT: Gibbs Smith, 2012).

32. http://www.youtube.com/watch?v=jN-9XUzg1DM

33. Spring, *The Gourmands' Way*, 227.

CHAPTER 8—"ETHNIC" RESTAURANTS

1. Lavanya Ramanatha, "Why Everyone Should Stop Calling Immigrant Food 'Ethnic,'" *Washington Post*, July 20, 2015, https://www.pinterest.com/pin/145452262936424918/, accessed March 12, 2018.

2. Dana Goodyear, "The Scavenger: Pig's Ears, Octopus and Fish-Kidney Curry with L.A.'s Most Adventurous Eater," *New Yorker*, November 9, 2009, 40.

3. Thus following Krishnendu Ray, *The Ethnic Restaurateur* (London and New York: Bloomsbury, 2016). Ray, a leading authority on immigrants and food in America, deliberately uses the word *ethnic* in the title of this book, which is concerned with the apparent subordination as well as agency and strategies of his protagonists.

4. Lawton Mackall, *Knife and Fork in New York* (Garden City, NY: Doubleday, 1948).

5. Ray, *The Ethnic Restaurateur,* 73.

6. Natalia Molina, "Beyond the Enclave: Echo Park and Its Ethnic Mexican Place-Makers in Mid-Twentieth Century LA," talk given at Yale University, April 11, 2018.

7. I am grateful to Krishnendu Ray for this information. This underrepresentation may be changing, Ligaya Mishan, "The Spread of Filipino Cuisine," *New York Times*, March 14, 2018, D1, D7.

8. Hyde Park, NY, Culinary Institute of America Library, menu collection, unnumbered.

9. University of California, Los Angeles, Special Collections, Restaurant Menus, Box 7.

10. Donna R. Gabaccia, *We Are What We Eat: Ethnic Foods and the Making of Americans* (Cambridge, MA: Harvard University Press, 1998), 10–35.

11. Maren Möhring, *Fremdes Essen: Die Geschichte der ausländischen Gastronomie in der Bundesrepublik Deutschland* (Munich: Oldenbourg, 2012).

12. Panikos Panayi, *Spicing Up Britain: The Multicultural History of British Food* (London: Reaktion, 2008), 172.

13. "Curry Statistics," in *The Cobra Indian Lager Good Curry Restaurant Guide,* ed. Pat Chapman (London: Piatkus, 1991), 18.

14. Panayi, *Spicing Up Britain*, 479.

15. Erik R. Scott, "Edible Ethnicity: How Georgian Cuisine Conquered the Soviet Table," *Kritika: Explorations in Russian and Eurasian History* 13 (2012), 831–58. On ethnic food in the Soviet Union, Anton Masterovoy, "Eating Soviet: Food and Culture in the USSR, 1917–1991," doctoral thesis, City University of New York, 2013, 125–86.

16. Andrew P. Haley, *Turning the Tables: Restaurants and the Rise of the American Middle Class, 1880–1920* (Chapel Hill: University of North Carolina Press, 2011), 111.

17. Josh Kun, *To Live and Dine in L.A.: Menus and the Making of the Modern City* (Los Angeles: Angel City Press, 2015), 72–73.

18. On Chinese responses to formal and informal oppression and discrimination, see Heather Lee, "Entrepreneurs in the Age of Chinese Exclusion: Transnational Capital, Migrant Labor, and Chinese Restaurants in New York City, 1850–1943," Doctoral Dissertation, Brown University, 2014; Anne Mendelson, *Chow Chop Suey: Food and the Chinese American Journey* (New York: Columbia University Press, 2016), 54–96.

19. Samantha Barbas, " 'I'll Take Chop Suey:' Restaurants as Agents of Culinary and Cultural Change," *Journal of Popular Culture* 26 (2003), 669–86.

20. E.g., Vicki I. Ruiz, "Citizen Restaurant: American Imaginaries, American Communities," *American Quarterly* 60 (2008), 1–21.

21. Mendelson, *Chow Chop Suey*, 84.

22. On the envoy's visit and the ensuing publicity for chop suey, see Andrew Coe, *Chop Suey: A Cultural History of Chinese Food in the United States* (New York: Oxford University Press, 2009), 161–67; Sarah Lohman, *Eight Flavors: The Untold Story of American Cuisine* (New York: Simon & Schuster, 2016), 97–103.

23. Michael Lesy and Lisa Stoffer, *Repast: Dining Out at the Dawn of the New American Century, 1900–1910* (New York: W. W. Norton, 2013), 150–56; Lohman, *Eight Flavors*, 134.

24. Mendelson, *Chow Chop Suey*, 100–16.

25. Mendelson, *Chow Chop Suey*, 116–27.

26. Cindy R. Lobel, *Urban Appetites: Food and Culture in Nineteenth-Century New York* (Chicago: University of Chicago Press, 2014), 181–82.

27. *The Italians of New York: A Survey* (New York: Random House, 1938), 171. This study was undertaken as part of the WPA's Federal Writers Project.

28. Haley, *Turning the Tables*, 100–01.

29. John F. Mariani, *How Italian Food Conquered the World* (New York: Palgrave Macmillan, 2011), 43–52.

30. Carole Helstoski, *Pizza: A Global History* (London: Reaktion, 2008).

31. See Simone Cinotto, *The Italian American Table: Food, Family and Community in New York City* (Urbana: University of Illinois Press, 2013).

32. Paul Freedman, *Ten Restaurants That Changed America* (New York: Liveright, 2016), 182–86.

33. Maria Sermolino, *Papa's Table d'Hôte* (Philadelphia: Lippincott, 1952), 15–16.

34. The advertisement is reproduced in Lee, "Entrepreneurs in the Age of Chinese Exclusion," 1.

35. Walter Zelinsky, "You Are Where You Eat," in *The Taste of American Place: A Reader on Regional and Ethnic Foods*, ed. Barbara G. Shortridge and James R. Shortridge (Lanham, MD: Rowman and Littlefield, 2008), 244.

36. Donna R. Gabaccia and Jeffrey M. Pilcher, "'Chili Queens' and Checkered Tablecloths: Public Dining Cultures of Italians in New York City and Mexicans in San Antonio, Texas, 1870s–1940s," *Radical History Review* 110 (2011), 116–17.

37. Jennifer Jensen Wallach, *How America Eats: A Social History of U.S. Food and Culture* (Lanham, MD: Rowman and Littlefield, 2013), 182.

38. Jeffrey M. Pilcher, *Planet Taco: A Global History of Mexican Food* (New York: Oxford University Press, 2012), 132–36.

39. Pilcher, *Planet Taco*, 147–50.

40. Ray, *The Ethnic Restaurateur*, 41–42. A menu of 1940 from the Rajah is in the Henry Voigt Collection of American Menus, Wilmington, Delaware. Its motto is "Dine in India."

41. Menu in the Henry Voigt Collection of American Menus, Wilmington, Delaware.

42. Jane Stern and Michael Stern, *American Gourmet: Classic Recipes, Deluxe Delights, Flamboyant Favorites, and Swank Company Food from the '50s and '60s* (New York: HarperCollins, 1991), 82.

43. B. M. Little, "What You Can Eat in Los Angeles," *Los Angeles Times,* September 23, 1934. Cited by Esther Hahn, "The Acceptance and Assimilation of Sushi in Post–World War II White America," Senior Essay, Yale University, April 2008, 15, 27. See also Anne Mendelson, "A Fish Story," *Gourmet* (October 2002), 176–83.

44. *American Cooking: The Melting Pot*, ed. James Shenton et al. (New York: Time-Life, 1971), 168–71.

45. Hahn, "The Acceptance and Assimilation of Sushi," 32–35.

46. Chinese food has been exported around the world. For its impact on rural Canada, Lily Cho, *Eating Chinese: Culture on the Menu in Small Town Canada* (Toronto: University of Toronto Press, 2010). For its different Asian manifestations, *The Globalization of Chinese Food*, ed. David Y. H. Wu, Sidney C. H. Cheung (Honolulu: University of Hawaii Press, 2002).

47. Michael Bauer, "At $225, Food Needs to Dazzle, Too," *San Francisco Chronicle*, January 31, 2018, L4. Bauer applauds the idea of a four-star Chinese restaurant and is eager for the restaurant to succeed but finds the food does not measure up to the implicit claims of the atmosphere and service.

48. Adam Platt, "At Midtown's New, Glitzy DaDong, the Signature Dish Is Overwhelmed by the Spectacle," Grub Street, June 15, 2018, http://www.grubstreet.com/2018/01/dadong-nyc-restaurant-review.html, accessed November 9, 2018.

49. A possible explanation for the differentiation mentioned to me by Michael Tong, owner of the two Shun Lee restaurants in New York, interview November 24, 2014.

50. This is changing as the presence of more bloggers and the spread of taste-making means that the lag between first discovery and widespread knowledge has shrunk.

51. Barbara Fang, "From Bangkok to Brooklyn: The Role of Authenticity in Thai Gastrodiplomacy and Thai Cuisine in New York City," paper given at conference "When Foods Travel," Asia Dynamics Initiative Conference, Copenhagen, 2015. On Mexican cuisine and Yelp-related authenticity, Dylan Gottlieb, "'Dirty . . . Authentic . . . Delicious': Yelp, Mexican Restaurants, and the Appetites of Philadelphia's New Middle Class," *Gastronomica* 15, no. 2 (2015), 39–48.

52. Sharon Zukin, *Naked City: The Death and Life of Authentic Urban Places* (New York: Oxford University Press, 2010), 159–92.

53. Arthur Bonner, *"Alas! What Brought Thee Hither?" The Chinese in New York, 1800–1950* (Madison and Teaneck: Rowman and Littlefield, 2005), 97–105; Coe, *Chop Suey*, 161–68, 176–77; Liu, "Chop Suey as Imagined Authentic Chinese Food."

54. Haiming Liu, *From Canton Restaurant to Panda Express: A History of Chinese Food in the United States* (New Brunswick, NJ: Rutgers University Press, 2015), 66.

55. Mitchell, *Knife and Fork in New York,* 207.

56. Mentioned in a eulogy for Johnny Kan by Herb Caen, quoted by Hsu, "From Chop Suey to Mandarin Cuisine," 180.

57. On the history of General Tso's Chicken, see Jennifer 8 Lee, *The Fortune Cookie Chronicles: Adventures in the World of Chinese Food* (New York: Twelve, 2008), 66–83, and the film "The Search for General Tso" (2014), directed by Ian Cheney.

58. Calvin Trillin, *Third Helpings* (New Haven and New York: Ticknor and Fields, 1983), 26–39.

59. Robert Sietsema, *Good & Cheap Ethnic Eats in New York City*, revised ed. (New York: City and Co., 1997). Contrast this with the 1970s, Milton Glaser and Jerome Snyder, *The Underground Gourmet,* 3rd ed. (New York: Simon & Schuster, 1977), whose entries are based exclusively on price and include American and "Continental" cuisine.

60. Clarence E. Edwards, *Bohemian San Francisco* (San Francisco: Paul Elder & Co., 1914), 25.

61. Steven Stern, "Based on an Old Family Recipe," *New York Times*, June 8, 2011, D1.

62. Paul Freedman, *Ten Restaurants That Changed America*, revised edition (New York: Liveright, 2018), 451.

CHAPTER 9—THE MAGICAL 1970S

1. *Spy*, August 1988.

2. Tom Wolfe, "The Me Decade or the Third Great Awakening," *New York Magazine*, August 23, 1976, http://nymag.com/news/features/45938/, accessed November 19, 2018.

3. Edna Lewis, *The Taste of Country Cooking* (New York: Alfred A. Knopf, 1976). See essays in the collection *Edna Lewis: At the Table with an American Original*, ed. Sara B. Franklin (Chapel Hill: University of North Carolina Press, 2018), especially those by Jane Lear, Megan Elias, and Lily Kelting.

4. Raymond Sokolov, *Fading Feast: A Compendium of Disappearing American Regional Foods* (New York: Farrar, Straus & Giroux, 1981).

5. Jane Stern and Michael Stern, *Roadfood* (New York: Random House, 1978).

6. Calvin Trillin, *American Fried: Adventures of a Happy Eater* (New York: Vintage, 1979), 5–14.

7. John L. Hess and Karen Hess, *The Taste of America* (New York: Grossman, 1977), especially 87–93, 152–72.

8. Hess and Hess, *The Taste of America*, 9.

9. An example of this consensus point of view is David Kamp, *The United States of Arugula: The Sun-Dried, Cold-Pressed, Dark-Roasted, Extra Virgin Story of the American Food Revolution* (New York: Broadway, 2006).

10. Luke Barr, *Provence, 1970: M. F. K. Fisher, Julia Child, James Beard, and the Reinvention of American Taste* (New York: Clarkson Potter, 2013). A less awe-struck account of the same phenomenon is Justin Spring, *The Gourmands' Way: Six Americans in Paris and the Birth of a New Gastronomy* (New York: Farrar, Straus & Giroux, 2017).

11. On the invention of modern French cuisine, Susan Pinkard, *A Revolution in Taste: The Rise of French Cuisine* (Cambridge, UK: Cambridge University Press, 2009); Priscilla Parkhurst Ferguson, *Accounting for Taste: The Triumph of French Cuisine* (Chicago: University of Chicago Press, 2004).

12. The similarities between the culinary reform movements and what was being proposed by 1970s nouvelle

cuisine was noticed at the time, Bénédict Beaugé, *Plats du jour. Sur l'idée de nouveauté en cuisine* (Paris: Métaillié, 2013), 39–51.

13. Michael Steinberger, *Au Revoir to All That: The Rise and Fall of French Cuisine* (London and New York: Bloomsbury, 2009), 31–34.

14. On nouvelle cuisine, see Jean El Gammal, *Tables en vue: trois âges de la gastronomie des années 1950 à nos jours* (Paris: Les Belles Lettres, 2018), 81–104.

15. Patrick Rambourg, *Histoire de la cuisine et la gastronomie française* (Paris: Perrin, 2010), 283–99.

16. Steinberger, *Au Revoir to All That*, 34, who quotes Bocuse as telling him retrospectively that nouvelle cuisine was little more than minimalist food served on large plates at a high price, "nothing on the plate and everything on the check."

17. William Grimes, "Paul Bocuse, Celebrated French Chef, Dies at 91," *New York Times*, January 20, 2018, https://www.nytimes.com/2018/01/20/obituaries/paul-bocuse-dead.html, accessed July 5, 2018.

18. On French culinary authority, Amy Trubek, *Haute Cuisine: How the French Invented the Culinary Profession* (Philadelphia: University of Pennsylvania Press, 2018).

19. On Julien's Restorator, David S. Shields, *The Culinarians: Lives and Careers from the First Age of American Fine Dining* (Chicago: University of Chicago Press, 2017), 25–29, 102–06; James O'Connell, *Dining Out in Boston: A Culinary History* (Hanover, NH: University Press of New England, 2016), 11–13. For Delmonico's, Lately Thomas, *Delmonico's: A Century of Splendor* (Boston: Houghton Mifflin, 1967). For Le Pavillon, Paul Freedman, *Ten Restaurants That Changed America* (New York: Liveright, 2016), 288–322.

20. Rachel Laudan, *Cuisine and Empire: Cooking in World History* (Berkeley: University of California Press, 2013), 282–83.

21. I am grateful to Professor John Van Engen of the University of Notre Dame for this menu from the Prussian State Archives in Berlin.

22. New York Public Library, Rare Books Division, Buttolph Menu Collection.

23. Andrew Friedman, *Chefs, Drugs and Rock and Roll: How Food Lovers, Free Spirits, Misfits and Wanderers Created a New American Profession* (New York: HarperCollins, 2018), 64, 71–72.

24. Betty Friedan, *The Feminine Mystique* (New York: W. W. Norton, 1963).

25. A point made by Laura Shapiro, *Something from the Oven: Reinventing Dinner in 1950s America* (New York: Viking Penguin, 2004), 240–41.

26. Friedan, *Feminine Mystique*, 298–317; 333–61.

27. Charlotte Brunsdon, *The Feminist, the Housewife and the Soap Opera* (Oxford, UK: Oxford University Press, 2000), 216.

28. A point made by Michael Pollan, *Cooked: A Natural History of Transformation* (New York: Penguin, 2014), 187.

29. Joanne Hollows, "The Feminist and the Cook: Julia Child, Betty Friedan and Domestic Femininity," in *Gender and Consumption: Domestic Cultures and the Commercialisation of Everyday Life*, ed. Emma Casey and Lydia Martens (Aldershot, UK: Ashgate, 2007), 33–48.

30. Leslie Johnson and Justine Lloyd, *Sentenced to Everyday Life: Feminism and the Housewife* (Oxford: Berg, 2004), 112.

31. Tejal Rao, "Bloodroot Is 40 and Still Cooking," *New York Times*, March 14, 2017. https://www.nytimes.com/2017/03/14/dining/bloodroot-feminist-restaurant.html, accessed June 12, 2018.

32. Charlotte McDonald-Gibson, "No Mr. Bond, I Expect You to Dine," *Independent*, May 18, 2012, https://www.independent.co.uk/life-style/food-and-drink/features/no-mr-bond-i-expect-you-to-dine-7763921.html, accessed June 12, 2018.

33. Philip Roth, *Portnoy's Complaint* (New York: Vintage, 1994), 127.

34. Bruce Feirstein, *Real Men Don't Eat Quiche: A Guide to All That Is Truly Masculine* (New York: Pocket Books, 1982).

35. On Café Nicholson, see William Grimes, *Appetite City: A Culinary History of New York* (New York: North

Point, 1999), 263–65. On Edna Lewis and Café Nicholson, Toni Tipton-Martin, "A Message from My Muse," in *Edna Lewis: At the Table with an American Original*, 49–51.

36. Michael and Ariane Batterberry, *On the Town in New York: The Landmark History of Eating, Drinking and Entertainment from the American Revolution to the Food Revolution* (New York and London: Routledge, 1999), 294.

37. *New York Gay Guide 1969*, 53. I am grateful to George Chauncey at Columbia University for this reference.

38. *The New York Times Guide to Dining Out in New York*, ed. Craig Claiborne (New York: Atheneum, 1964), 21. He gave Café Nicholson two stars out of a possible four. Clementine Paddleford also uses "offbeat" in reference to Café Nicholson, Clementine Paddleford, "Gourmet's Choice," in Tom Wolfe et al., *New York Herald Tribune Presents New York, New York* (New York: Delta, 1964), 185–86.

39. Lou Rand Hogan, *The Gay Cookbook* (Los Angeles: Sherbourne Press, 1965). The book is discussed in Stephen Vider, "'Oh Hell, May, Why Don't You People Have a Cookbook?': Camp Humor and Gay Domesticity," *American Quarterly* 65 (2013), 877–904. On gay camp attitudes, see George Chauncey, *Gay New York: Gender, Urban Culture, and the Makings of the Gay Male World, 1890–1940* (New York: Basic Books, 1994), 47–63, 286–329.

40. Hogan, *The Gay Cookbook*, vii.

41. Hogan, *The Gay Cookbook*, 126, 129, 218.

42. Hogan, *The Gay Cookbook*, 114. Goulash, 124, "Most men like 'em" (i.e., various kinds of goulash).

43. Hogan, *The Gay Cookbook*, 138, 177.

44. What follows is based on Emily Contois, "Microwave Cookbooks: Technology, Convenience and Dining Alone," on the website "Nursing Clio," October 24, 2014, https://nursingclio.org/2017/10/24/microwave -cookbooks-technology-convenience-dining-alone/, accessed November 4, 2017.

45. Alison Spiegel, "A Brief History of the Crock Pot, the Original Slow Cooker," Huffington Post, January 12, 2015, https://www.huffingtonpost.com/2015/01/12/what-is-a-crock-pot_n_6443398.html, accessed July 6, 2018.

46. Josh Ozersky, *Colonel Sanders and the American Dream* (Austin: University of Texas Press, 2012); Ray Kroc, *Grinding It Out: The Making of McDonald's* (Chicago: Contemporary Books, 1977); John F. Love, *McDonald's: Behind the Arches* (Toronto: Bantam Books, 1986). The 2016 film *The Founder* is a lightly fictionalized portrayal of Kroc.

47. James R. Hagerty, "Founder's Angry Outburst Saved Burger King," [obituary] *Wall Street Journal*, April 21–22, 2018, A9.

48. Harvey Levenstein, *Paradox of Plenty: A Social History of Eating in Modern America* (Berkeley and Los Angeles: University of California Press, 2003), 233.

49. Joe Roberts, answer to the question "What Was McDonald's Like in the 1970s?" on the website Quora, https://www.quora.com/What-was-McDonalds-like-in-the-1970s, accessed April 20, 2018.

50. The pioneering account of food in the alternative lifestyle movements is Warren Belasco, *Appetite for Change: How the Counterculture Took On the Food Industry, 1966–1988* (New York: Pantheon, 1989). The food innovations of the hippies are the subject of Jonathan Kauffman, *Hippie Food: How Back-to-the-Landers, Longhairs, and Revolutionaries Changed the Way We Eat* (New York: William Morrow, 2017). See also Stephanie Hartman, "The Political Palate: Reading Commune Cookbooks," *Gastronomica* 3 (Spring 2003), 29–40.

51. Belasco, *Appetite for Change*, 17–18. According to Belasco, the name also referred to the Digger Indians of California, whom the anthropologist Ruth Benedict in the 1930s described as rejecting all food from modern sources and living off what the desert provided.

52. Kauffman, *Hippie Food*, 99–105.

53. Hartman, "The Political Palate," 29.

54. Adelle Davis, *Let's Cook It Right* (New York: Signet, 1962); Euell Gibbons, *Stalking the Wild Asparagus* (New York: Alan C. Hood, 1962). On the organic food movement and its long-term effects, Mary Drake

McFeely, *Can She Bake a Cherry Pie? American Women and the Kitchen in the Twentieth Century* (Amherst: University of Massachusetts Press, 2000), 130–48.

55. Belasco, *Appetite for Change*, 40–42.
56. Megan J. Elias, *Food on the Page: Cookbooks and American Culture* (Philadelphia: University of Pennsylvania Press, 2017), 155.
57. Frances Moore Lappé, *Diet for a Small Planet* (New York: Ballantine, 1971). See Belasco, *Appetite for Change*, 56–59
58. Edward Espe Brown, *The Tassajara Bread Book* (Berkeley: Shambhala, 1970); Edward Espe Brown, *Tassajara Cooking* (Berkeley: Shambhala, 1973).
59. Hartman, "The Political Palate," 33.
60. John T. Edge, *The Potlikker Papers: A Food History of the Modern South* (New York: Penguin, 2017), 94–95.
61. Edge, *Potlikker Papers*, 87–106. On the communal farms movement generally, Ryan Edington, "'Be Receptive to the Good Earth': Health, Labor and Nature in Countercultural Back-to-the-Land Settlements," *Agricultural History* 82 (2008), 279–308.
62. Mollie Katzen, *Moosewood Cookbook: Recipes from Moosewood Restaurant, Ithaca, New York* (Berkeley: Ten Speed Press, 1977).
63. Hartman, "The Political Palate," 32.
64. A point made by Elias, *Food on the Page*, 171.
65. Frederick Douglass Opie, *Hog and Hominy: Soul Food from Africa to America* (New York: Columbia University Press, 2008), 159–65; Jessica B. Harris, *High on the Hog: A Culinary Journey from Africa to America* (New York: Bloomsbury, 2011), 209–11; Jennifer Jensen Wallach, *Every Nation Has Its Dish: Black Bodies and Black Food in Twentieth-Century America* (Chapel Hill: University of North Carolina Press), 178–83.
66. Opie, *Hog and Hominy*, 165–68.
67. Ancel Keys and Margaret Keys, *Eat Well and Stay Well* (New York: Doubleday, 1959).
68. Ancel Keys and Margaret Keys, *How to Eat Well and Stay Well the Mediterranean Way* (New York: Doubleday, 1974).
69. B. Haber, "The Mediterranean Diet: A View from History," *American Journal of Clinical Nutrition* 66 (4), (1997), 1053–58.
70. Alberto Capatti and Massimo Montanari, *Italian Cuisine: A Cultural History* (New York: Columbia University Press, 2003), 32–33.
71. On the designation and its cultural context, Gisela Welz, "Taste the Mediterranean: Food, Culture and Heritagization," in *New Horizons: Mediterranean Research in the 21st Century*, ed. Mihran Dabag et al. (Paderborn, Germany: Verlag Ferdinand Schöningh, 2016), 407–26.
72. Conversations with Rafi Taherian, Associate Vice President of Yale Hospitality, Yale University.
73. One of the points central to the account of Joyce Goldstein, *Inside the California Food Revolution: Thirty Years That Changed Our Culinary Consciousness* (Berkeley and Los Angeles: University of California Press, 2013).
74. Elias, *Food on the Page*, 177–79.
75. On the history of Chez Panisse, Thomas McNamee, *Alice Waters and Chez Panisse: The Romantic, Impractical, Often Eccentric, Ultimately Brilliant Making of a Food Revolution* (New York: Penguin, 2007); Paul Freedman, *Ten Restaurants That Changed America* (New York: Liveright, 2016), 369–406.
76. Patric Kuh, *The Last Days of Haute Cuisine: The Coming of Age of American Restaurants* (New York: Viking, 2001), 147
77. McNamee, *Alice Waters and Chez Panisse*, 127.
78. Jeremiah Tower, *California Dish: What I Saw (and Cooked) at the American Culinary Revolution* (New York: Free Press, 2003), 111: Tower, *Start the Fire: How I Began a Food Revolution in America* (New York: Anthony Bourdain/Ecco, 2017), 126–27.
79. Freedman, *Ten Restaurants That Changed America*, 394–402.
80. See the menus from the early 1980s mentioned below, Chapter 10.

81. Cited in Bertram M. Gordon, "Shifting Tastes and Terms: The Rise of California Cuisine," *Revue Française d'études Américaines* 27–28 (1986), 116. The article (pages 109–26) is a fascinating early scholarly evolution of a culinary change then in progress.

82. Friedman, *Chefs, Drugs and Rock and Roll*, 158–61.

83. Michael Ruhlman, *The Reach of a Chef: Professional Cooks in the Age of Celebrity* (New York: Penguin, 2006), 47.

84. Friedman, *Chefs, Drugs and Rock and Roll*, 299.

85. Julee Rosso and Sheila Lukins, *The Silver Palate Cookbook* (New York: Workman, 1982).

86. Peter Meehan, "Sheila Lukins," *Lucky Peach*, Summer 2017, 49.

CHAPTER 10—THE FOOD REVOLUTION GROWS UP

1. As noted in Andrew Friedman, *Chefs, Drugs and Rock and Roll: How Food Lovers, Free Spirits, Misfits and Wanderers Created a New American Profession* (New York: HarperCollins, 2018), 320.

2. Article on "Yuppies," https://www.investopedia.com/terms/y/yuppie.asp, accessed October 21, 2018.

3. David Brooks, *Bobos in Paradise: The New Upper Class and How They Got There* (New York: Simon & Schuster, 2000).

4. Paul Freedman, *Out of the East: Spices and the Medieval Imagination* (New Haven: Yale University Press, 2008). On the prestige accorded in the Middle Ages to foods of distant origins, Antoni Riera i Melis, "Jerarquía social y desigualdad alimentaria en el Mediterráneo noroccidental en la Baja Edad Media. La cocina y la mesa de los estamentos privilegiados," *Acta Mediaevalia* 16 (1996), 181–205.

5. Alexandre Dumas, *The Count of Monte-Cristo*, vol. 2 (New York: Thomas Y. Crowell Company, 1901), 95–97.

6. Though see the "Colin, the Free-Range Chicken" episode of *Portlandia*, https://www.youtube.com/watch?v=G__PVLB8Nm4, accessed July 26, 2018.

7. Diane Rossen Worthington, *The Cuisine of California* (Los Angeles: J. O. Tarcher, 1983), 6–7, 32–33.

8. My thanks to Alice Waters for allowing me to consult this collection.

9. Joyce Goldstein, *Inside the California Food Revolution: Thirty Years That Changed Our Culinary Consciousness* (Berkeley: University of California Press, 2013), 98–102.

10. John F. Mariani, *America Eats Out* (New York: William Morrow, 1991), 247–48; David Kamp, *United States of Arugula: The Sun-Dried, Cold-Pressed, Dark-Roasted, Extra-Virgin Story of the American Food Revolution* (New York: Broadway Books, 2006), 298–99.

11. Jeremiah Tower, *Start the Fire: How I Began a Food Revolution in America* (New York: Anthony Bourdain/Ecco, 2017), 227–266. Tower had pioneered the dressed-up hamburger at his Balboa Café shortly before Stars opened.

12. Friedman, *Chefs, Drugs and Rock and Roll*, 283–301, 338–46.

13. Friedman, *Chefs, Drugs and Rock and Roll*, 338–46. Jams reopened in 2015.

14. Friedman, *Chefs, Drugs and Rock and Roll*, 146–49.

15. The menu is given in Friedman, *Chefs, Drugs and Rock and Roll*, 272–74.

16. John Brodie, "A Map of Regular Guy Manhattan," *Spy* (October 1988), 106–07.

17. Danny Meyer, *Setting the Table: The Transforming Power of Hospitality in Business* (New York: HarperCollins, 2006), 61.

18. Burkhard Bilger, "True Grits: In Charleston, a Quest to Revive Authentic Southern Cooking," *New Yorker*, October 31, 2011, http://www.newyorker.com/magazine/2011/10/31/true-grits, accessed July 14, 2018.

19. In *The Taste of Country Cooking* (1976), Edna Lewis ends her recollection of hog-killing with these lines: "The following morning my brothers and sisters and I would rush out before breakfast to see the hogs hanging from the scaffold like giant statues. The hogs looked so beautiful. They were glistening white inside with their lining of fat, and their skin was almost translucent." Quoted in Francis Lam, "Edna Lewis and

the Black Roots of American Cooking," in *Edna Lewis: At the Table with an American Original*, ed. Sara B. Franklin (Chapel Hill: University of North Carolina Press, 2018), 64.

20. Described in Ferran Adrià et al., *A Day at elBulli* (London and New York: Phaidon, 2008), 286–89, 298–99.

21. ElBulli menus, July 23, 2002; April 5, 2011.

22. Anthony Bourdain, *Kitchen Confidential: Adventures in the Culinary Underbelly* (New York: Bloomsbury, 2000), 266.

23. Nathan Myhrvold, *Modernist Cuisine: The Art and Science of Cooking* (Bellevue, WA: Food Lab, 2011); Hervé This, *Molecular Gastronomy: Exploring the Science of Flavour*, trans. M. B. Debevoise (New York: Columbia University Press, 2006); Harold McGee, *On Food and Cooking: The Science and Lore of the Kitchen*, 2nd ed. (New York: Scribner's, 2004; first published 1984).

24. Alinea menu, January 7, 2012.

25. Website "Memories of a Gourmand in New York," May 2, 2017, https://memoriesofagourmand .com/2017/05/02/eleven-madison-park-retrospective/, accessed July 16, 2018.

26. Thomas Keller, *The French Laundry Cookbook* (New York: Artisan, 1999), 6–7, 262–63.

27. Hillary Dixler Canavan, "7 Truths About LA Tasting-Menu Sensation Vespertine," Eater, October 20, 2017, https://www.eater.com/2017/10/20/16284480/vespertine-jordan-kahn-interview, accessed July 15, 2018. I'm grateful to my friend Thomas Barton of the University of San Diego for a firsthand report about Vespertine and a copy of his personalized menu.

28. Alison Pearlman, *Smart Casual: The Transformation of Gourmet Restaurant Style in America* (Chicago: University of Chicago Press, 2013), 129.

29. As noted in Pearlman, *Smart Casual*, 128.

30. Keller, *French Laundry Cookbook*, 247; Michael Ruhlman, *The Soul of a Chef: The Journey toward Perfection* (New York: Viking Penguin, 2000), 300–01.

31. Ruhlman, *The Soul of a Chef*, 288–293.

32. Keller, *French Laundry Cookbook*, 35, 214–15.

33. Per Se menu, September 2, 2016.

34. Adam Platt, "The Apotheosis of Fresh: How New York Finally Stopped Importing Cuisines and Invented Its Own," *New York Magazine*, December 6, 2009, http://nymag.com/arts/all/aughts/62491/, accessed June 14, 2018.

35. Pearlman, *Smart Casual*.

36. Bruno Laurioux, *Le règne de Taillevent: livres et pratiques culinaires à la fin du Moyen Âge* (Paris: Sorbonne, 1997), 21–116; Eleanor Scully and Terence Scully, *Early French Cookery: Sources, History, Original Recipes and Modern Applications* (Ann Arbor: University of Michigan Press, 1995).

37. Scully and Scully, *Early French Cookery*, 41–42; Chiquart, *Chiquart's 'On Cookery,' A Fifteenth-Century Savoyard Cooking Treatise*, ed. Terence Scully (New York: Peter Lang, 1986), 22–24.

38. Ken Albala, *The Banquet: Dining in the Great Courts of Late Renaissance Europe* (Urbana and Chicago: University of Illinois Press, 2007), 12–14.

39. On his career, see Ian Kelly, *Cooking for Kings: The Life of Antonin Carême, the First Celebrity Chef* (New York: Walker Books, 2004).

40. His *Memories of My Life* was translated by Laurence Escoffier (New York: Van Nostrand Reinhold, 1997). See also Timothy Shaw, *The World of Escoffier* (New York: Vendome Press, 1995); Kenneth James, *Escoffier: The King of Chefs* (Hambleton and London: Bloomsbury, 2002).

41. "Alex Atala on Creativity and Innovation in Food," talk for the Design Indaba Conference, Cape Town, 2013: http://www.designindaba.com/videos/conference-talks/alex-atala-creativity-and-innovation-cuisine, accessed July 31, 2018.

42. Friedman, *Chefs, Drugs and Rock and Roll*, whose subtitle is "*How Food Lovers, Free Spirits, Misfits and Wanderers Created a New American Profession.*"

43. What follows relies on the magisterial and entertaining book by Allen Salkin, *From Scratch: Inside the Food Network* (New York: G. P. Putnam's Sons, 2013).

44. Kim Severson, "Rachael Ray, Beyond TV," *New York Times*, May 9, 2018, D1, D6.

45. On these enterprises, Patric Kuh, *Finding the Flavors We Lost: From Bread to Bourbon, How Artisans Reclaimed American Food* (New York: HarperCollins, 2016); Amy B. Trubek, *The Taste of Place: A Cultural Journey into Terroir* (Berkeley: University of California Press, 2008).

46. Ligaya Mishan, "When the Restaurants, Home Kitchens and Sidewalks of the City First Embraced Global Ingredients—and the Rest of the World Followed Suit," *New York Times, Style Magazine*, April 22, 2018, 42–44.

47. Jeff Gordinier, "2004, the Year That Changed How We Dine," *New York Times*, December 30, 2013, https://www.nytimes.com/2014/01/01/dining/2004-the-year-that-changed-how-we-dine.html, accessed June 13, 2018. I too have noted the importance of the year 2004, Paul Freedman, *Ten Restaurants That Changed America,* 2nd ed. (New York: Liveright, 2018), 441, 445.

48. Platt, "The Apotheosis of Fresh."

CONCLUSION—FOOD IN THE YEAR 2020 AND BEYOND

1. Rebecca Skloot, "Two Americas, Two Restaurants, One Town," *New York Times Magazine*, October 17, 2004, 78–81.

2. Blake Spalding and Jennifer Castle, *This Immeasurable Place: Food and Farming from the Edge of the Wilderness*, 2nd. ed. (Boulder, UT: HBG Press, 2017), 225–29.

3. Blake Spalding and Jennifer Castle, *With a Measure of Grace: The Story and Recipes of a Small Town Restaurant*, 2nd. ed. (Boulder, UT: HBG Press, 2018); Kathryn Schulz, "Why Two Chefs in Small-Town Utah Are Battling President Trump," *New Yorker*, October 21, 2018, https://www.newyorker.com/magazine/2018/10/01/why-two-chefs-in-small-town-utah-decided-to-sue-president-trump, accessed October 21, 2018.

4. El Celler de Can Roca, menu from August 14, 2012.

5. Restaurant Sant Pau, menu for summer 2017.

6. https://www.youtube.com/watch?v=iUU1BffGon0.

7. Amanda Cohen, "I've Worked in Food for 20 Years. Now Finally You Care about Female Chefs?" *Esquire*, November 6, 2017, http://www.esquire.com/food-drink/restaurants/a13134079/sexual-harassment-sexism-food-industry/, accessed December 22, 2017.

8. Helen Bottomiller Evich and Catherine Boudreau, "The Big Washington Food Fight," Politico, November 25, 2017, https://www.politico.com/story/2017/11/26/food-lobby-consumer-tastes-washington-190528, accessed January 14, 2018.

9. A presentation by Peter McGuinness, Chief Marketing Officer for Chobani, entitled " 'One for All': Chobani's Quest to Give Yogurt to Everyone in America," Association of National Advertisers and Advertising Education Foundation Conference, Yale University, October 30, 2018.

10. Hans Taparia and Pamela Koch, "Real Food Challenges the Food Industry," *New York Times*, November 8, 2015, SR 3

11. Rachel Abrams and Robert Gebeloff, "Overstuffed on Restaurant Row," *Wall Street Journal*, October 31, 2017, B1–B2.

12. Brian Raskin and Anne Gasparro, "Kraft Heinz Fixed Factories, Now It Has to Sell Bologna," *Wall Street Journal*, February 13, 2018, A1, A9. See also David Gelles, "Learn from Old Mistakes, Welcome New Ones" (an interview with Kraft Heinz CEO Bernardo Hees), *New York Times*, May 6, 2018, BU3. On stock price declines for food companies, Aaron Black, "Food Makers Meet with Little Appetite," *Wall Street Journal*, June 6, 2018, B1.

13. Stephanie Strom, "Back to the Kitchen: Campbell Adjusts Soup Recipe to Address Changing Tastes," *New York Times*, November 9, 2015, https://www.nytimes.com/2015/11/10/business/campbell-rethinks-its-recipe-as-consumer-tastes-change.html, accessed January 14, 2018.

14. Taparia and Koch, "Real Food Challenges the Food Industry."

15. Anne Gasparro and Cara Lombardo, "Investors Don't Relish Older Brands," *Wall Street Journal*, August 25, 2017, B1, B6, which begins: "Trouble for packaged-food companies is deepening." See also Nathaniel Meyersohn, "Trouble in Big Food: America's Cereal, Soda and Soup Companies are in Turmoil," CNN Money, May 21, 2018, https://money.cnn.com/2018/05/21/news/companies/campbell-soup-general-mills -hershey-pepsi/index.html, accessed July 28, 2018.

16. Matt Richtel and Andrew Jacobs, "American Still Packing on the Pounds," *New York Times*, March 26, 2018, A13; Jane Black and Brent Cunningham, "No, Americans Aren't Finally Ready to Cook," *Wall Street Journal*, August 4, 2017, https://www.wsj.com/articles/the-problem-with-meal-kits-1501860563, accessed July 20, 2018.

17. Jenette Rowan, "Consumers Continue to Spend More on Restaurants," The Food Institute website, June 6, 2017, https://foodinstitute.com/blog/consumers-spending-more-at-restaurants, accessed July 27, 2018.

18. Livia Albeck-Ripka, "Climate Change Brought a Lobster Boom. Now It Could Cause a Bust," *New York Times*, June 21, 2018, https://www.nytimes.com/2018/06/21/climate/maine-lobsters.html, accessed November 1, 2018.

BIBLIOGRAPHY

Abbott, Elizabeth. "Sugar." In *The Routledge History of American Foodways*, ed. Michael D. Wise and Jennifer Jensen Wallach. New York and Abingdon: Routledge, 2016, 128–50.

Abrams, Rachel, and Robert Gebeloff. "Overstuffed on Restaurant Row." *Wall Street Journal*, Oct. 31, 2017, B1-B2.

Adrià, Ferran, et al. *A Day at elBulli*. London and New York: Phaidon, 2008.

Albala, Ken. *The Banquet: Dining in the Great Courts of Late Renaissance Europe*. Urbana and Chicago: University of Illinois Press, 2007.

Albeck-Ripka, Livia. "Climate Change Brought a Lobster Boom. Now It Could Cause a Bust." *New York Times,* June 21, 2018, https://www.nytimes.com/2018/06/21/climate/maine-lobsters.html, accessed November 1, 2018.

Alexander, Kelly, and Cynthia Harris. *Hometown Appetites: The Story of Clementine Paddleford, the Forgotten Food Writer Who Chronicled How America Ate*. New York: Gotham House, 2008.

Algren, Nelson. *America Eats*. Iowa City: University of Iowa Press, 1992.

Amarillo Cookbook. Amarillo: no publisher listed, 1909.

Apple Jr., R. W. "A Life in the Culinary Front Lines." *New York Times*, Nov. 30, 2005.

Art Institutes. *American Regional Cuisine*. New York: John Wiley and Sons, 2002.

The Art of Cooking in Emporia. Emporia: Boston Grange, after 1963.

Barbas, Samantha. " 'I'll Take Chop Suey:' Restaurants as Agents of Culinary and Cultural Change." *Journal of Popular Culture* 26 (2003), 669–86.

Barr, Luke. *Provence, 1970: M. F. K. Fisher, Julia Child, James Beard, and the Reinvention of American Taste*. New York: Clarkson Potter, 2013.

Batterbury, Ariane, and Michael Batterbury. *On the Town in New York: The Landmark History of Eating, Drinking and Entertainment from the American Revolution to the Food Revolution*. New York and London: Routledge, 1999.

Bauer, Michael. "At $225, Food Needs to Dazzle, Too." *San Francisco Chronicle*, January 31, 2018, L4.

Beahrs, Andrew. *Twain's Feast: Searching for America's Lost Foods in the Footsteps of Samuel Clemens*. New York: Penguin, 2011.

Beaugé, Bénédict. *Plats du jour. Sur l'idée de nouvauté en cuisine*. Paris: Métaillié, 2013.

Bégin, Camille. *Taste of the Nation: The New Deal Search for American Food*. Urbana: University of Illinois Press, 2016.

Belasco, Warren. *Appetite for Change: How the Counterculture Took On the Food Industry, 1966–1988*. New York: Pantheon, 1989.

Belasco, Warren. *Meals to Come: A History of the Future of Food*. Berkeley and Los Angeles: University of California Press, 2006.

Belasco, Warren, and Philip Scranton, eds. *Food Nations: Selling Taste in Consumer Societies*. New York and London: Routledge, 2002.

Bell, David, and Gil Valentine. *Consuming Geographies: We Are What We Eat*. London and New York: Routledge, 1997.

Bentley, Amy, ed. *A Cultural History of Food in the Modern Age*. London: Berg, 2012.

Bilger, Burkhard. "True Grits: In Charleston, A Quest to Revive Authentic Southern Cooking." *New Yorker*, October 31, 2011, http://www.newyorker.com/magazine/2011/10/31/true-grits, accessed July 14, 2018.

Biltekoff, Charlotte. *Eating Right in America: The Cultural Politics of Food and Health*. Durham, NC: Duke University Press, 2013.

Bingham, Emily, and Thomas Underwood. *The Southern Agrarians and the New Deal: Essays after I'll Take My Stand*. Charlottesville: University of Virginia Press, 2001.

Bizier, Hélène-Andrée, et al. *Cuisine traditionnelle des régions du Québec*. Montréal: Gouvernement du Québec, 1999.

Black, Aaron. "Food Makers Meet with Little Appetite." *Wall Street Journal*, June 6, 2018, B1.

Black, Jane, and Brent Cunningham. "No, Americans Aren't Finally Ready to Cook." *Wall Street Journal*, August 4, 2017, https://www.wsj.com/articles/the-problem-with-meal-kits-1501860563, accessed July 20, 2018.

Bonner, Arthur. *"Alas! What Brought Thee Hither?" The Chinese in New York, 1800–1950*. Madison and Teaneck: Rowman and Littlefield, 2005.

Booker, Matthew M., and Charles C. Ludington, eds. *Food Fights: How the Past Matters to Contemporary Food Debates*. Chapel Hill: University of North Carolina Press, in press.

Bottura, Massimo. *Never Trust a Skinny Italian Chef*. London and New York: Phaidon, 2014.

Boudreau, Catherine, and Helen Bottomiller Evich. "The Big Washington Food Fight." Politico, Nov. 25, 2017, https://www.politico.com/story/2017/11/26/food-lobby-consumer-tastes-washington-190528, accessed Jan. 14, 2018.

Bourdain, Anthony. *Kitchen Confidential: Adventures in the Culinary Underbelly*. New York: Bloomsbury, 2000.

Bower, Anne L., ed. *Recipes for Reading: Community Cookbooks, Stories, Histories*. Amherst: University of Massachusetts Press, 1997.

Bracken, Peg. *The I Hate to Cook Book*. New York: Harcourt, Brace and World, 1960.

Britchky, Seymour. *Seymour Britchky's New, Revised Guide to the Restaurants of New York*. New York: Random House, 1976.

Brodie, John. "A Map of Regular Guy Manhattan." *Spy*, October 1988, 106–07.

Brooks, David. *Bobos in Paradise: The New Upper Class and How They Got There*. New York: Simon and Schuster, 2000.

Brown, Dale. *American Cooking*. New York: Time-Life, 1968.

Brown, Edward Espe. *The Tassajara Bread Book*. Berkeley: Shambhala, 1970.

Brown, Edward Espe. *Tassajara Cooking*. Berkeley: Shambhala, 1973.

Brown, Eleanor, and Bob Brown. *Culinary America: 100 Years of Cookbooks Published in the United States from 1860 through 1960*. New York: Roving Eye Press, 1961.

Brunsdon, Charlotte. *The Feminist, the Housewife and the Soap Opera*. Oxford: Oxford University Press, 2000.

Burton, Nathaniel, and Rudy Lombard. *Creole Feast: 15 Master Chefs of New Orleans Reveal Their Secrets*. New York: Random House, 1978.

Campbell's Great Restaurants Cookbook, U.S.A. New York: Routledge, 1969.

Canavan, Hillary Dixler. "7 Truths about LA Tasting-Menu Sensation Vespertine." Eater, October 20, 2017, https://www.eater.com/2017/10/20/16284480/vespertine-jordan-kahn-interview, accessed July 15, 2018.

Cannon, Poppy. *The Can-Opener Cook Book: A Guide for Gourmet Cooking with Canned or Frozen Food and Mixes*. New York: Thomas Y. Crowell and Co., 1951.

The Canyon City Cookbook. Canyon City: no publisher listed, 1909.

Capatti, Alberto, and Massimo Montanari. *Italian Cuisine: A Cultural History*. New York: Columbia University Press, 2003.

Carlson, Allan. *The New Agrarian Mind: The Movement toward Decentralist Thought in Twentieth-Century America*. New Brunswick: Transition, 2000.

Carney, Judith A., and Richard Nicholas Rosomoff. *In the Shadow of Slavery: Africa's Botanical Legacy in the Atlantic World*. Berkeley: University of California Press, 2010.

Casey, Emma, and Lydia Martens, eds. *Gender and Consumption: Domestic Cultures and the Commercialisation of Everyday Life*. Aldershot, UK: Ashgate, 2007.

Castle, Jennifer, and Blake Spalding. *This Immeasurable Place: Food and Farming from the Edge of the Wilderness*, 2nd. ed. Boulder, Utah: HBG Press, 2017.

Castle, Jennifer, and Blake Spalding. *With a Measure of Grace: The Story and Recipes of a Small Town Restaurant*, 2nd. ed. Boulder, Utah: HBG Press, 2018.

Cave, James. "Capri Sun Is Making Organic Juice, but Don't Be Fooled into Thinking It's Good for You." Huffington Post, April 5, 2016, https://www.huffingtonpost.com/entry/organic-capri-sun_us_5703c8ade4b0a06d5806de54, accessed Jan. 29, 2018.

Cecelski, David. *The Art of Making Oyster Fritters*. Durham, NC: no publisher, 2012.

Chaplin, Joyce. *Subject Matter: Technology, the Body and Science on the Anglo-American Frontier, 1500–1676*. Cambridge, MA: Harvard University Press, 2001.

Chapman, Pat, ed. *The Cobra Indian Lager Good Curry Restaurant Guide*. London: Piatkus, 1991.

Chauncey, George. *Gay New York: Gender, Urban Culture, and the Makings of the Gay Male World, 1890–1940*. New York: Basic Books, 1994.

Cheung, C. H. Sidney, and David Y. H. Wu, eds. *The Globalization of Chinese Food*. Honolulu: University of Hawaii Press, 2002.

Chiquart. *Chiquart's 'On Cookery,' A Fifteenth-Century Savoyard Cooking Treatise*, ed. Terence Scully. New York: Peter Lang, 1986.

Cho, Lily. *Eating Chinese: Culture on the Menu in Small Town Canada*. Toronto: University of Toronto Press, 2010.

Cinotto, Simone. *The Italian American Table: Food, Family and Community in New York City*. Urbana: University of Illinois Press, 2013.

Claiborne, Craig, ed. *The New York Times Guide to Dining Out in New York*. New York: Athenaeum, 1964.

Cobb, James C. "From 'Cracklins' to 'Gourmet Bacon Puffs:' The Complex Origin and Shifting Shape of Southern Foodways." In *Citizen Scholar: Essays in Honor of Walter Edgar*, ed. Robert H. Brinkmeyer, Jr. Columbia: University of South Carolina Press, 2016, 165–78.

Coe, Andrew. *Chop Suey: A Cultural History of Chinese Food in the United States*. New York: Oxford University Press, 2009.

Coe, Andrew, and Jane Ziegelman. *A Square Meal: A Culinary History of the Great Depression*. New York, HarperCollins, 2016.

Cohen, Amanda. "I've Worked in Food for 20 Years. Now Finally You Care about Female Chefs?" *Esquire*, Nov. 6, 2017, http://www.esquire.com/food-drink/restaurants/a13134079/sexual-harassment-sexism-food-industry/, accessed Dec. 22, 2017.

Cohen, Amanda, and Ryan Dunlavey. *Dirt Candy: A Cookbook. Flavor-Forward Food from the Upstart New York City Vegetarian Restaurant*. New York: Clarkson Potter, 2012.

Coleman, Arthur, and Bobbie Coleman. *The Texas Cookbook*. New York: A. A. Wyn, 1949.

Conkin, Paul H., and Erwin F. Hargrove, eds. *TVA: Fifty Years of Grass-Roots Bureaucracy*. Urbana: University of Illinois Press, 1983.

Contois, Emily. "Microwave Cookbooks: Technology, Convenience and Dining Alone," on the website "Nursing Clio," October 24, 2014. https://nursingclio.org/2017/10/24/microwave-cookbooks-technology-convenience-dining-alone/, accessed November 4, 2017.

Cook, Margaret. *America's Charitable Cooks: A Bibliography of Fund-Raising Cook Books Published in the United States (1861–1915)*. Kent, Ohio: Kent State University Press, 1971.

Cooke, Nathalie, ed. *What's to Eat? Entrées in Canadian Food History*. Montreal and Kingston: McGill-Queen's University Press, 2009.

Cooking in the Grand Manner. Cleveland: Grand Home Appliance Company, 1950.

Cooley, Angela Jill. *To Live and Dine in Dixie: The Evolution of Urban Food Culture in the Jim Crow South*. Athens: University of Georgia Press, 2015.

Counihan, Carole M., ed. *Food in the U.S.A.: A Reader*. New York, 2002, first published 1985.

C. P. Workers Cookbook. Canyon City: Canyon City News Print, 1903.

Creese, Walter L. *TVA's Public Planning: The Vision, the Reality*. Knoxville: University of Tennessee Press, 1990.

The Creole Cookery Book, Edited by the Christian Women's Exchange of New Orleans, La. New Orleans: T. H. Thomason, 1883.

Croly, J. C. *Jennie June's American Cookery Book*. New York: American News Company, 1866.

Crumpacker, Bunny. *The Old-Time Brand-Name Cookbook: Recipes, Illustrations and Advice from the Early Kitchens of America's Most Trusted Food Makers*. New York: Smithmark, 2011.

Cusack, Igor. "African Cuisines for Nation Building?" *Journal of African Studies* 13 (2000), 207–22.

Dabag, Mihran, et al. eds. *New Horizons: Mediterranean Research in the 21st Century*. Paderborn: Fernand Schöningh, 2016.

Davidson, Donald, et al. *I'll Take My Stand: The South and the Agrarian Tradition, by Twelve Southerners*. New York: Harper & Brother, 1930.

Davis, Adelle. *Let's Cook It Right*. New York: Signet, 1962.

Davis, Nancy, and Kathy Hart. *Coastal Carolina Cooking*. Chapel Hill: University of North Carolina Press, 1986.

Deighton, Len. *Len Deighton's Action Cook Book*. Harmondsworth, UK: Penguin, 1967.

Diamond, Becky Libourel. *The Thousand Dollar Dinner: America's First Great Cookery Challenge*. Westholme, PA: Yardley, 2015.

Diat, Louis. *Louis Diat's French Cooking for Americans: La cuisine de ma Mère*. Philadelphia and New York: J. B. Lippincott, 1946.

Driver, Elizabeth. *Culinary Landmarks: A Bibliography of Canadian Cookbooks, 1825–1949*. Toronto: University of Toronto Press, 2009.

Driver, Elizabeth. "Home Cooks, Book Makers and Community Builders in Canada." *Moving Worlds: A Journal of Transcultural Writings* 6, no. 2 (2006), 41–60.

Durban, Pam, ed. *Cabbagetown Families: Cabbagetown Food*. Atlanta: Patch Press, 1976.

The East Hampton Cookbook of Menus and Recipes, ed. Ruth A. Spear. Bridgehampton, NY: Dan's Papers, 1975.

Edge, John T. *A Gracious Plenty: Recipes and Recollections from the American South*. New York: HP Books, 1999.

Edge, John T. *The Potlikker Papers*. New York: Penguin, 2017.

Edge, John T., Elizabeth S. D. Engelhardt, and Ted Ownby, eds. *The Larder: Food Studies Methods from the American South*. Athens, GA: University of Georgia Press, 2017.

Edington, Ryan. "'Be Receptive to the Good Earth': Health, Labor and Nature in Countercultural Back-to-the-Land Settlements." *Agricultural History* 82 (2008), 279–308.

Edwards, Clarence E. *Bohemian San Francisco*. San Francisco: Paul Elder and Co., 1914.

Egerton, John. *Southern Food: At Home, on the Road, in History*. New York: Knopf, 1987.

El Gammal, Jean. *Tables en vue: trois âges de la gastronomie des années 1950 à nos jours*. Paris: Les Belles Lettres, 2018.

Elias, Megan J. *Food on the Page: Cookbooks and American Culture*. Philadelphia: University of Pennsylvania Press, 2017.

Emerson, Lucy. *The New England Cookery*. Montpelier, VT: Parks, 1808.

Ephron, Nora. *The Most of Nora Ephron*. New York: Penguin Random House, 2013.

Eskridge, Sara K. *Rube Tube: CBS and Rural Comedy in the Sixties*. Columbia: University of Missouri Press, 2018.

Escoffier, Auguste. *Memoirs of my Life*. Laurence Escoffier, trans. New York: Van Nostrand Reinhold, 1997.

Farmer, Fannie Merritt, and Wilma Lord Perkins. *The Boston Cooking School Cook Book*. Boston: Little, Brown & Co., 1896.

Favorite Recipes of Texas. Montgomery, AL: Favorite Recipe Press, 1964.

Favorite Recipes of the Women of Randall County. Amarillo: Canyon News, no date but 1942–1945.

Feirstein, Bruce. *Real Men Don't Eat Quiche: A Guide to All That Is Truly Masculine*. New York: Pocket Books, 1982.

Ferguson, Priscilla Parkhurst. *Accounting for Taste: The Triumph of French Cuisine*. Chicago: University of Chicago Press, 2004.

Ferris, Marcie Cohen. *The Edible South: The Power of Food and the Making of an American Region*. Chapel Hill: University of North Carolina Press, 2014.

Fertel, Rien. "'Everybody Seemed Willing to Help': *The Picayune Creole Cook Book* as Battleground, 1900–2008." In John T. Edge et al., eds., *The Larder*, 10–31.

Fertel, Rien. *Imagining the Creole City: The Rise of Literary Culture in Nineteenth-Century New Orleans*. Baton Rouge: Louisiana State University Press, 2014.

Fischler, Claude, and Estelle Masson, eds. *Manger: Français, Européens et Américains face à l'alimentation*. Paris: Odile Jacob, 2008.

Fitzgerald, Deborah. *Every Farm a Factory: The Industrial Ideal in American Agriculture*. New Haven: Yale University Press, 2003.

Fitzmorris, Tom. *Hungry Town: A Culinary History of New Orleans: A City Where Food Is Almost Everything*. New York: Stewart, Tabori and Chang, 2010.

Fitzmorris, Tom, and Peggy Scott Laborde. *Lost Restaurants of New Orleans and the Recipes That Made Them Famous*. Gretna, LA: Pelican Publishing, 2012.

Fitzpatrick, Sheila. *Everyday Stalinism: Ordinary Life in Extraordinary Times. Soviet Russia in the 1930s*. Oxford: Oxford University Press, 2000.

Fox, Minnie L. *The Bluegrass Cook Book*. New York: Duffield and Co., 1904.

Franey, Pierre. *The New York Times 60-Minute Gourmet*. New York: Fawcett Columbine, 1979.

Frank, Matthew Gavin. *The Mad Feast: An Ecstatic Tour through America's Food*. New York, W. W. Norton, 2017.

Franklin, Sara B. ed. *Edna Lewis: At the Table with an American Original*. Chapel Hill: University of North Carolina Press, 2018.

Freedman, Paul, ed. *Food: The History of Taste*. London: Thames and Hudson, 2007.

Freedman, Paul. *Out of the East: Spices and the Medieval Imagination*. New Haven: Yale University Press, 2008.

Freedman, Paul. *Ten Restaurants That Changed America*. New York: Liveright, 2016.

Freedman, Paul, Ken Albala, and Joyce E. Chaplin, eds. *Food in Time and Place: The American Historical Association Companion to Food History*, Berkeley: University of California Press, 2014.

Fried, Stephen. *Appetite for America: Fred Harvey and the Business of Civilizing the Wild West One Meal at a Time*. New York: Bantam Books, 2010.

Friedan, Betty. *The Feminine Mystique*. New York, W. W. Norton, 1997.

Friedman, Andrew. *Chefs, Drugs and Rock and Roll: How Food Lovers, Free Spirits, Misfits and Wanderers Created a New American Profession*. New York: HarperCollins, 2018.

Fussell, Betty. *I Hear America Cooking: A Journey of Discovery from Alaska to Florida—the Cooks, the Recipes, and the Unique Flavors of Our National Cuisine*. New York: Viking, 1986.

Gabaccia, Donna R. *We Are What We Eat: Ethnic Foods and the Making of Americans*. Cambridge, MA: Harvard University Press, 1998.

Gabaccia, Donna R., and Jeffrey M. Pilcher. "'Chili Queens' and Checkered Tablecloths: Public Dining Cultures of Italians in New York City and Mexicans in San Antonio, Texas, 1870s–1940s." *Radical History Review* 110 (2011), 109–26.

Gaige, Crosby. *Food at the Fair: A Gastronomic Tour of the World, New York World's Fair 1939.* New York: Exposition Press, 1939.

Gaige, Crosby. *New York World's Fair Cook Book: The American Kitchen.* New York: Doubleday Doran, 1939.

Gasparro, Anne, and Brian Raskin. "Kraft Heinz Fixed Factories, Now It Has to Sell Bologna." *Wall Street Journal*, February 13, 2018, A1, A9.

Gasparro, Anne, and Brian Raskin. "Investors Don't Relish Older Brands." *Wall Street Journal*, August 25, 2017, B1, B6.

Gelles, David. "Learn from Old Mistakes, Welcome New Ones." An interview with Kraft Heinz CEO Bernardo Hees, *New York Times*, May 6, 2018, BU3.

Genovese, Eugene D. *The Sweetness of Life: Southern Planters at Home.* Cambridge, UK: Cambridge University Press, 2017.

Gibbons, Euell. *Stalking the Wild Asparagus.* New York: Alan C. Hood, 1962.

Glaser, Milton, and Jerome Snyder. *The Underground Gourmet.* 3rd ed. New York: Simon and Schuster, 1977.

Goldstein, Joyce. *Inside the California Food Revolution: Thirty Years That Changed Our Culinary Consciousness.* Berkeley and Los Angeles: University of California Press, 2013.

Goody, Jack. *Cooking, Cuisine and Class: A Study in Comparative Sociology.* Cambridge, UK: Cambridge University Press, 1982.

Goodyear, Dana. "The Scavenger: Pig's Ears, Octopus and Fish-Kidney Curry with L.A.'s Most Adventurous Eater." *New Yorker*, Nov. 9, 2009.

Gordinier, Jeff. "2004, the Year That Changed How We Dine." *New York Times*, Dec. 30, 2013, https://www.nytimes.com/2014/01/01/dining/2004-the-year-that-changed-how-we-dine.html, accessed June 13, 2018.

Gordon, Bertram M. "Shifting Tastes and Terms: The Rise of California Cuisine." *Revue Française d'Études Américaines* 27–28 (1986), 109–26.

Gottlieb, Dylan. "'Dirty . . . Authentic . . . Delicious': Yelp, Mexican Restaurants, and the Appetites of Philadelphia's New Middle Class." *Gastronomica* 15, no. 2 (2015), 39–48.

Greenman, Barbara, ed. *Church Suppers: 722 Favorite Recipes from Our Church Communities.* New York: Black Dog & Leventhal, 2005.

Grey, Sarah. "A Social History of Jell-O Salad: The Rise and Fall of an American Icon." Serious Eats 2015, http://www.seriouseats.com/2015/08/history-of-jell-o-salad.html, accessed Jan. 29, 2018.

Grimes, William. *Appetite City: A Culinary History of New York.* New York: North Point, 1999.

Grimes, William. "Paul Bocuse, Celebrated French Chef, Dies at 91." *New York Times*, January 20, 2018, https://www.nytimes.com/2018/01/20/obituaries/paul-bocuse-dead.html, accessed July 5, 2018.

Haber, B. "The Mediterranean Diet: A View from History." *American Journal of Clinical Nutrition* 66, no. 4 (1997), 1053–58.

Hadow, Robert H. *Pavilions of Plenty: Exhibiting American Culture Abroad in the 1950s.* Washington: Smithsonian Institution, 1997.

Hagerty, James R. "Founder's Angry Outburst Saved Burger King" [obituary]. *Wall Street Journal*, April 21–22, 2018, A9.

Haley, Andrew P. *Turning the Tables: Restaurants and the Rise of the American Middle Class, 1880–1920.* Chapel Hill: University of North Carolina Press, 2011.

Hardy, Lady Helen Henriques, and Raymond J. Martinez. *Louisiana's Fabulous Foods and How to Cook Them.* Jefferson, LA: Hope Publications, ca. 1939.

Harris, Jessica B. *High on the Hog: A Culinary Journey from Africa to America.* New York: Bloomsbury, 2011.

Harris, Jessica B. *Iron Pots and Wooden Spoons: Africa's Gifts to New World Cooking.* New York: Athenaeum, 1989.

Harsanyi, Doina, and Nicolae Harsanyi. "On the Fringes of History: Food and Eating Habits in the Banat." *Petits Propos Culinaires* 47 (1994), 22–31.

Hartman, Stephanie. "The Political Palate: Reading Commune Cookbooks." *Gastronomica* 3 (Spring 2003), 29–40.

Hatchett, Louis. *Duncan Hines: How a Traveling Salesman Became the Most Trusted Name in Food*, 2nd ed. Lexington: University Press of Kentucky, 2014.

Hazard, Thomas Robinson. *The Jonny-Cake Papers of "Shepherd Tom."* Boston: Merrymount Press, 1915.

Hearn, Lafcadio. *La Cuisine Creole, A Collection of Culinary Recipes from Leading Chefs and Noted Creole House-Wives, Who Have Made New Orleans Famous for Its Cuisine*, 2nd ed. New Orleans: F. F. Hansell & Bro., Ltd., 1885.

Helstoski, Carole. *Pizza: A Global History*. London: Reaktion, 2008.

Henderson, Mary F. *Practical Cooking and Dinner Giving*. New York: Harper and Brother, 1877.

Hensley, Tim. "A Curious Tale: The Apple in North America." Brooklyn Botanic Garden, June 2, 2005, http://www.bbg.org/gardening/article/the_apple_in_north_america, accessed Nov. 21, 2017.

Hess, John L., and Karen Hess. *The Taste of America*. New York: Grossman, 1977.

Hibben, Sheila. *American Regional Cookery*. New York, Crown: 1946.

Hibben, Sheila. *The National Cookbook: A Kitchen Americana*. New York and London: Harper Brothers, 1932.

Hightower, Jim. *Hard Tomatoes, Hard Times: The Failure of the Land Grant College Complex*. Washington, DC: Agribusiness Accountability Project, 1972.

Hine, Thomas. *Populuxe*. New York: Alfred A. Knopf, 1984.

Hines, Duncan. *Duncan Hines' Food Odyssey*. New York: Thomas Y. Crowell, 1955.

Hirbodian, Sigrid, and Tjark Wegner, eds. *Was ist schwäbisch?* Ostfildern: Jan Thorbecke, 2016.

Hobsbawm, Eric, and Terence Ranger, eds. *The Invention of Tradition*. Cambridge, UK: Cambridge University Press, 1983.

Hoffman, Gretchen L. "What's the Difference between Soul Food and Southern Cooking? The Classification of Cookbooks in American Libraries." In *Dethroning the Deceitful Pork Chop: Rethinking African American Foodways from Slavery to Obama*, ed. Jennifer Jensen Wallach. Fayetteville: University of Arkansas Press, 2015, 61-75.

Hogan, Lou Rand. *The Gay Cookbook*. Los Angeles: Sherbourne Press, 1965.

The Home Cook Book, Compiled by the Ladies of Toronto and Chief Cities and Towns of Canada. Toronto: Rose Publishing, 1877.

Hooker, Richard J. *Food and Drink in America: A History*. Indianapolis and New York: Bobbs-Merrill, 1981.

How to Keep a Husband, or Culinary Tactics. San Francisco: Cubery and Co., 1872.

Howland, Esther A. *The New England Economical Housekeeper and Family Receipt Book*. Worcester, MA: S. A. Howland, 1844.

Hunt, Peter ed. *The Food Lovers' Anthology*, 2nd ed. Oxford: Bodleian Library, 2014.

Inness, Sherrie. *Dinner Roles: American Women and Culinary Culture*. Iowa City: University of Iowa Press, 2001.

Ireland, Lynne. "The Compiled Cookbook as Foodways Autobiography." In *The Taste of American Place: A Reader on Regional and Ethnic Food*, ed. Barbara G. Shortridge and James R. Shortridge. Lanham, MD: Rowman and Littlefield, 1998, 111–17;

Isenberg, Nancy. *White Trash: The 400-Year History of Class in America*. New York: Penguin, 2016.

Island Born and Bred: A Collection of Harkers Island Food, Fun, Fact and Fiction Compiled by the Harkers Island United Methodist Women. Atlantic Beach, NC: Weathers Printing Company: 1987.

The Jackson Cookbook. Jackson, MS: Symphony League of Jackson, 1971.

James, Kenneth. *Escoffier: The King of Chefs*. Hambleton and London: Bloomsbury, 2002.

Johnson, Leslie, and Justine Lloyd. *Sentenced to Everyday Life: Feminism and the Housewife*. Oxford: Berg, 2004.

Johnson, Simon. "Haggis Was Invented by the English, Not the Scottish, Says Historian." *Daily Telegraph*, August 2, 2009, http://www.telegraph.co.uk/foodanddrink/foodanddrinknews/5960237/Haggis-was-invented-by-the-English, accessed August 2, 2017.

Kamp, David. *The United States of Arugula: The Sun-Dried, Cold-Pressed, Dark-Roasted, Extra Virgin Story of the American Food Revolution*. New York: Broadway, 2006.

Kander, Lizzie Black. *"The Settlement" Cook Book: The Way to a Man's Heart*. New York: Gramercy Publishing, 1903.

Kaplan, Steven Laurence. *Good Bread Is Back: A Contemporary History of French Bread, the Way It Is Made and the People Who Make It*, trans. Catherine Porter. Durham, NC: Duke University Press, 2006.

Katzen, Mollie. *Moosewood Cookbook: Recipes from Moosewood Restaurant, Ithaca, New York*. Berkeley: Ten Speed Press, 1977.

Kauffman, Jonathan. *Hippie Food: How Back-to-the-Landers, Longhairs, and Revolutionaries Changed the Way We Eat*. New York: William Morrow, 2017.

Keller, Thomas. *The French Laundry Cookbook*. New York: Artisan, 1999.

Kellum, H. Charles et al. *The Southern Cook Book: 322 Old Dixie Recipes*. Reading, PA: Culinary Arts Press, 1939.

Kelly, Ian. *Cooking for Kings: The Life of Antonin Carême, the First Celebrity Chef*. New York: Bloomsbury, 2004.

Kenneally, Rhona Richman. "'There *Is* a Canadian Cuisine, and It Is Unique in All the World': Crafting National Food Culture During the Long 1960s." In *What's to Eat? Entrés in Canadian Food History*, ed. Nathalie Cooke. Montreal and Kingston: McGill-Queen's University Press, 2009, 167–96.

Kennedy, Nancy. *The Ford Times Cookbook: A Traveler's Guide to Good Eating at Home and on the Road*. New York, Simon and Schuster, 1968.

Kennedy, Nancy. *The Ford Treasury of Favorite Recipes from Famous Eating Places*, [vol. 1–3], 2nd ed. New York: Simon and Schuster, 1955.

Kennedy, Nancy. *The New Ford Treasury; The New Ford Treasury of Favorite Recipes from Famous Restaurants*. New York: Golden Press, 1963.

Kennedy, Nancy. *The Second Ford Treasury of Favorite Recipes from Famous Eating Places*. New York: Golden Press, 1954.

Keys, Ancel, and Margaret Keys. *Eat Well and Stay Well*. New York: Doubleday, 1959.

Keys, Ancel, and Margaret Keys. *How to Eat Well and Stay Well the Mediterranean Way*. New York: Doubleday, 1974.

Kimball, Chris. *Fannie's Last Supper: Re-Creating One Amazing Meal from Fannie Farmer's 1896 Cookbook*. New York: Hyperion, 2010.

Koch, Pamela, and Hans Taparia. "Real Food Challenges the Food Industry." *New York Times*, November 8, 2015 p. SR 3

Kraig, Bruce. *A Rich and Fertile Land: A History of Food in America*. London: Reaktion, 2017.

Kroc, Ray. *Grinding It Out: The Making of McDonald's*. Chicago: Contemporary Books, 1977.

Kuh, Patric. *Finding the Flavors We Lost: From Bread to Bourbon, How Artisans Reclaimed American Food*. New York: HarperCollins, 2016.

Kuh, Patric. *The Last Days of Haute Cuisine: The Coming of Age of American Restaurants*. New York: Viking, 2001.

Kun, Josh. *To Live and Dine in L.A.: Menus and the Making of the Modern City*. Los Angeles: Angel City Press, 2015.

Kurlansky, Mark. *The Food of a Younger Land*. New York: Riverhead, 2009.

Langholtz, Gabrielle. *America, The Cookbook: A Culinary Road Trip through the 50 States*. London and New York: Phaidon, 2017.

Lappé, Frances Moore. *Diet for a Small Planet*. New York: Ballantine, 1971.

Larsh, Phyllis. "Duncan Hines." *Life,* July 8, 1946, 17–22.

Latshaw, Beth A. "The Soul of the South: Race, Food, and Identity in the American South." In *The Larder: Food Studies Methods from the American South*, ed. John T. Edge, Elizabeth S. D. Engelhardt, Ted Ownby. Athens: University of Georgia Press, 2017, 99–127.

Laudan, Rachel. *Cuisine and Empire: Cooking in World History*. Berkeley: University of California Press, 2013.

Laudan, Rachel. "A Plea for Culinary Modernism: Why We Should Love New, Fast, Processed Food." *Gastronomica* 1, no. 1 (2001), 36–44.

Laurioux, Bruno. *Le règne de Taillevent: livres et pratiques culinaires à la fin du Moyen Âge*. Paris: Sorbonne, 1997.

Lear, Jane. "What Is Southern: The Annotated Edna Lewis." In *Edna Lewis: At the Table with an American Original*, ed. Sara B. Franklin. Chapel Hill: University of North Carolina Press, 2018, 17–26.

Lee, Heather. "Entrepreneurs in the Age of Chinese Exclusion: Transnational Capital, Migrant Labor, and Chinese Restaurants in New York City, 1850–1943." Doctoral Dissertation, Brown University, 2014.

Lee, Jennifer 8. *The Fortune Cookie Chronicles: Adventures in the World of Chinese Food*. New York: Twelve, 2008.

Leonard, Jonathan Norton. *American Cooking: New England*. New York: Time-Life, 1970.

Lesy, Michael, and Lisa Stoffer. *Repast: Dining Out at the Dawn of the New American Century, 1900–1910*. New York: W. W. Norton, 2013.

Levenstein, Harvey. *Paradox of Plenty: A Social History of Eating in Modern America*. Berkeley and Los Angeles: University of California Press, 2003.

Levenstein, Harvey. *Revolution at the Table: The Transformation of the American Diet*. Berkeley and Los Angeles: University of California Press, 2003.

Levinson, Marc. *The Box: How the Shipping Container Made the World Smaller and the World Economy Bigger*, 2nd ed. Princeton, NJ: Princeton University Press, 2016.

Levinson, Marc. *The Great A&P and the Struggle for Small Business in America*. New York: Hill & Wang, 2011.

Lewis, Edna. *The Taste of Country Cooking*. New York: Knopf, 1976.

Lilienthal, David. *TVA: Democracy on the March*. New York: Harper and Brothers, 1944.

Lindgren, Don, and Mark Germer, eds. *UnXld: American Cookbooks of Community and Place*, vol. 1. Biddeford, ME: Rabelais, 2018.

Little, B. M. "What You Can Eat in Los Angeles." *Los Angeles Times,* Sept. 23, 1934.

Liu, Haiming. *From Canton Restaurant to Panda Express: A History of Chinese Food in the United States*. New Brunswick, NJ: Rutgers University Press, 2015.

Lobel, Cindy R. *Urban Appetites: Food and Culture in Nineteenth-Century New York*. Chicago: University of Chicago Press, 2014.

Lohman, Sarah. *Eight Flavors: The Untold Story of American Cuisine*. New York: Simon and Schuster, 2016.

Longi, Lucy M., ed. *Culinary Tourism*. Lexington: University Press of Kentucky, 2004.

Love, John F. *McDonald's: Behind the Arches*. Toronto: Bantam Books, 1986.

Lukins, Sheila, and Julee Rosso. *The Silver Palate Cookbook*. New York: Workman, 1982.

Lundy, Ronni. *Victuals: An Appalachian Journey, with Recipes*. New York: Clarkson Potter, 2016.

Mackall, Lawton. *Knife and Fork in New York*. Garden City, NY: Doubleday, 1948.

Mariani, John F. *America Eats Out*. New York: William Morrow, 1991.

Mariani, John F. *How Italian Food Conquered the World*. New York: Palgrave Macmillan, 2011.

Markel, Howard. *The Kelloggs: The Battling Brothers of Battle Creek*. New York: Pantheon, 2017.

Marsden, Rhodri. "Rhodri Marsden's Interesting Objects: The Sliced Loaf." *The Independent* (UK), July 5, 2014, https://www.independent.co.uk/life-style/food-and-drink/features/rhodri-marsdens-interesting-objects-the-sliced-loaf-9579661.html, accessed September 29, 2018.

Marshall, Alex. *How Cities Work: Suburbs, Sprawl and the Roads Not Taken*. Austin: University of Texas Press, 2000.

Masterovoy, Anton. "Eating Soviet: Food and Culture in the USSR, 1917–1991." Doctoral thesis, City University of New York, 2013.

McAleer, John. *Rex Stout, A Biography*. Boston and Toronto: Little, Brown, 1977.

McDonald, Michael J., and John Muldowney. *TVA and the Dispossessed: The Resettlement of Population in the Norris Dam Area*. Knoxville: University of Tennessee Press, 1982.

McDonald-Gibson, Charlotte. "No Mr. Bond, I Expect You to Dine." *Independent*, May 18, 2012, https://www.independent.co.uk/life-style/food-and-drink/features/no-mr-bond-i-expect-you-to-dine-7763921.html, accessed June 12, 2018.

McFeely, Mary Drake. *Can She Bake a Cherry Pie? American Women and the Kitchen in the Twentieth Century*. Amherst: University of Massachusetts Press, 2000.

McLean, Alice L. *Cooking in America, 1840–1945*. Westport, CT: Greenwood Press, 2006.

McNamee, Thomas. *Alice Waters and Chez Panisse: The Romantic, Impractical, Often Eccentric, Ultimately Brilliant Making of a Food Revolutionary*. New York: Penguin, 2007.

McWilliams, James E. *A Revolution in Eating: How the Quest for Food Shaped America*. New York: Columbia University Press, 2005.

Meehan, Peter. "Sheila Lukins." *Lucky Peach*, Summer 2017, 49.

Mendelson, Anne. *Chow Chop Suey: Food and the Chinese American Journey*. New York: Columbia University Press, 2016, 54–96.

Mendelson, Anne. "A Fish Story." *Gourmet*, October 2002, 176–83.

Mendelson, Anne. "Food Writing Lives: Sheila Hibben." cookNscribble, 2013, www.onebigtable.com/cooknscribble/2013/06/06/food-writing-lives-sheila-hibben, accessed July 30, 2017.

Mendelson, Anne. "Glossy South: *Gourmet*'s Long-Running Romance with Southern Cuisine and Clichés." *Oxford American* 49, Spring 2005, 128–29.

Metcalfe, Gayden and Charlotte Hays. *Being Dead Is No Excuse: The Official Southern Guide to Hosting the Perfect Funeral*. New York: Hyperion, 2005.

Meyer, Danny. *Setting the Table: The Transforming Power of Hospitality in Business*. New York: HarperCollins, 2006.

Meyers, Ella B. *The Centennial Cook Book and General Guide*. Philadelphia: J. B. Meters, 1876.

Meyersohn, Nathaniel. "Trouble in Big Food: America's Cereal, Soda and Soup Companies are in Turmoil." CNN Money, May 21, 2018, https://money.cnn.com/2018/05/21/news/companies/campbell-soup-general-mills-hershey-pepsi/index.html, accessed July 28, 2018.

Mickler, Ernest Matthew. *White Trash Cooking*. Berkeley: Ten Speed Press, 1986.

Miller, Adrian. *Soul Food: The Surprising Story of an American Cuisine One Plate at a Time*. Chapel Hill: University of North Carolina Press, 2013.

Mintz, Sidney. *Sweetness and Power: The Place of Sugar in Modern History*. New York: Penguin, 1985.

Mintz, Sidney. *Tasting Food, Tasting Freedom: Excursions into Eating, Culture, and the Past*. Boston: Beacon Press, 1996.

Mishan, Ligaya. "The Spread of Filipino Cuisine." *New York Times*, March 14, 2018, D1, D7.

Mishan, Ligaya. "When the Restaurants, Home Kitchens and Sidewalks of the City First Embraced Global Ingredients—and the Rest of the World Followed Suit." *New York Times, Style Magazine*, April 22, 2018, 42–44.

Möhring, Maren. *Fremdes Essen: Die Geschichte der ausländischen Gastronomie in der Bundesrepublik Deutschland*. Munich: Oldenbourg, 2012.

Montagné, Prosper. *Larousse Gastronomique: The Encyclopedia of Food, Wine and Cookery*. New York: Crown, 1961.

Moruzzi, Peter. *Classic Dining: Discovering America's Finest Mid-Century Restaurants*. Layton, UT: Gibbs Smith, 2012.

Myhrvold, Nathan. *Modernist Cuisine: The Art and Science of Cooking*. Bellevue, WA: Food Lab, 2011.

The Negro Motorist Green-Book. New York: Victor H. Green, 1936–1966. New York Public Library, https://digitalcollections.nypl.org/collections/the-green-book#/?tab=about&scroll=18, accessed July 23, 2017.

Nestle, Marion. *Food Politics: How the Food Industry Influences Nutrition and Health*, 2nd ed. Berkeley and Los Angeles: University of California Press, 2007.

Neuhaus, Jessamyn. *Manly Meals and Mom's Home Cooking: Cookbooks and Gender in Modern America*. Baltimore: Johns Hopkins University Press, 2003.

The New York Times Guide to Dining Out in New York: New 1972 Revised Edition. New York: Athenaeum, 1971.

Nora, Pierre. "Between Memory and History." *Representations* 26 (Spring 1989), 7–25.

Oldenziel, Ruthand, and Karin Zachmann, eds. *Cold War Kitchen: Americanization, Technology, and European Users*. Cambridge, MA: MIT Press, 2009.

100 Prize-Winning Recipes from Pillsbury's Grand National $100,000 Recipe and Baking Contest. Minneapolis: Pillsbury Mills, Inc., 1951.

Opie, Frederick Douglass. *Hog and Hominy: Soul Food from Africa to America*. New York: Columbia University Press, 2008.

Our Favorite Recipes: Ladies of the Upper Keys. Bev-Ron Publishing: Kansas City, 1974.

Ozersky, Josh. *Colonel Sanders and the American Dream*. Austin: University of Texas Press, 2012.

Ozersky, Josh. *The Hamburger*. New Haven: Yale University Press, 2008.

Paddleford, Clementine. *How America Eats*. New York: Scribner's, 1960.

Page, Linda Garland, and Eliot Wigginton, eds. *The Foxfire Book of Appalachian Cookery: Regional Memorabilia and Recipes*. New York, E. P. Dutton, 1984.

Panayi, Panikos. *Spicing Up Britain: The Multicultural History of British Food*. London: Reaktion, 2008.

Parkin, Katherine J. *Food Is Love: Advertising and Gender Roles in Modern America*. Philadelphia: University of Pennsylvania Press, 2006.

Parkinson, James W. *American Dishes at the Centennial*. Philadelphia: King and Baird, 1874.

Parkinson, Joe. "Africans Have Heated Views about Rice, Just Ask Mark Zuckerberg." *Wall Street Journal*, August 21, 2017.

Parks, Stella. *BraveTart: Iconic American Desserts*. New York: W. W. Norton, 2017.

Pearlman, Alison. *Smart Casual: The Transformation of Gourmet Restaurant Style in America*. Chicago: University of Chicago Press, 2013.

Pilcher, Jeffrey M., ed. *The Oxford Handbook of Food History*. Oxford: Oxford University Press, 2012.

Pilcher, Jeffrey M. *Planet Taco: A Global History of Mexican Food*. New York: Oxford University Press, 2012.

Pillsbury, Richard. *No Foreign Food: The American Diet in Time and Place*. Boulder: Routledge, 1998.

Pinkard, Susan. *A Revolution in Taste: The Rise of French Cuisine*. Cambridge, UK: Cambridge University Press, 2009.

Pitts, Brent A., trans. *The Fifteen Joys of Marriage: Les XV joies de mariage*. New York: P. Lang, 1985.

Platt, Adam. "The Apotheosis of Fresh: How New York Finally Stopped Importing Cuisines and Invented Its Own." *New York Magazine*, December 6, 2009, http://nymag.com/arts/all/aughts/62491/, accessed June 14, 2018.

Pollan, Michael. *The Botany of Desire: A Plant's Eye View of the World*. New York: Random House, 2001.

Pollan, Michael. *Cooked: A Natural History of Transformation*. New York: Penguin, 2014.

Porterfield, James D. *Dining by Rail: The History and the Recipes of America's Golden Age of Railroad Cuisine*. New York: St. Martin's, 1993.

Powell, Lawrence N., ed. *The New Orleans of George Washington Cable: The 1887 Census Office Report*. Baton Rouge: Louisiana State University Press, 2008.

Powell, Lawrence N. *The Accidental City: Improvising New Orleans*. Cambridge, MA: Harvard University Press, 2012.

Ramanatha, Lavanya. "Why Everyone Should Stop Calling Immigrant Food 'Ethnic.'" *Washington Post,* July 20, 2015, https://www.pinterest.com/pin/145452262936424918/, accessed March 12, 2018.

Rambourg, Patrick. *Histoire de la cuisine et la gastronomie française*. Paris: Perrin, 2010.

Randolph, Mary. *The Virginia Housewife or Methodical Cook*. Washington, DC: Way and Gideon, 1824.

Ranhofer, Charles. *The Epicurean*. New York: Charles Ranhofer, 1893.

Rao, Tejal. "Bloodroot Is 40 and Still Cooking." *New York Times*, March 14, 2017. https://www.nytimes.com/2017/03/14/dining/bloodroot-feminist-restaurant.html, accessed June 12, 2018.

Rawson, Katie, and Eliott Shore. *Dining Out: A Global History of Restaurants*. London: Reaktion, 2019.

Ray, Krishnendu. *The Ethnic Restaurateur*. London and New York: Bloomsbury, 2016.

Richtel, Matt, and Andrew Jacobs. "Americans Still Packing on the Pounds." *New York Times*, March 26, 2018, A13.

Riera i Melis, Antoni. "Jerarquía social y desigualdad alimentaria en el Mediterráneo noroccidental en la Baja Edad Media. La cocina y la mesa de los estamentos privilegiados." *Acta Mediaevalia* 16 (1996), 181–205

Roth, Philip. *Portnoy's Complaint*. New York: Vintage, 1994.

Roth, Rodris. "The New England or 'Olde Tyme,' Kitchen Exhibit at Nineteenth-Century Fairs." In *The Colonial Revival in America*, ed. Alan Axelrod. New York: W. W. Norton, 1985.

Rowan, Jenette. "Consumers Continue to Spend More on Restaurants." The Food Institute website, June 6, 2017, https://foodinstitute.com/blog/consumers-spending-more-at-restaurants, accessed July 27, 2018.

Ruhlman, Michael. *Grocery: The Buying and Selling of Food in America*. New York: Abrams, 2017.

Ruhlman, Michael. *The Reach of a Chef: Professional Cooks in the Age of Celebrity*. New York: Penguin, 2006.

Ruhlman, Michael. *The Soul of a Chef: The Journey toward Perfection*. New York: Viking Penguin, 2000.

Ruiz, Vicki I. "Citizen Restaurant: American Imaginaries, American Communities." *American Quarterly* 60 (2008), 1–21.

Rural Electric Fact Book. Washington, D.C.: National Rural Electric Cooperative Association, 1960.

Sabin, Paul. *The Bet: Paul Ehrlich, Julian Simon and Our Gamble over Earth's Future*. New Haven, CT: Yale University Press, 2013.

Sackett, Lou, and David Haynes. *American Regional Cuisines: Food Culture and Cooking*. Upper Saddle River, NJ: Pearson, 2012.

Salkin, Allen. "Be Yourselves, Girls, Order the Rib-Eye." *New York Times*, August 9, 2007, http://www.nytimes .com/2007/08/09/fashion/09STEAK.html, accessed January 12, 2018.

Salkin, Allen. *From Scratch: Inside the Food Network*. New York, Putnam, 2013.

Schlosser, Eric. *Fast Food Nation: The Dark Side of the All-American Meal*, 2nd ed. New York: HarperCollins, 2002.

Schmidt, Stephen, "When Did Southern Begin?" In Manuscript Cookbooks Survey, posted November 2015, www.manuscriptcookbookssurvey.org/when-did-southern-begin, accessed August 30, 2017.

Schulz, Kathryn. "Why Two Chefs in Small-Town Utah Are Battling President Trump." *New Yorker*, October 21, 2018, https://www.newyorker.com/magazine/2018/10/01/why-two-chefs-in-small-town-utah-decided -to-sue-president-tr, accessed October 21, 2018.

Schulz, Phillip Stephen. *As American as Apple Pie*. New York: Simon and Schuster, 1990.

Schwartz, David. "Duncan Hines: He Made Gastronomes Out of Motorists." *Smithsonian* 15 (November 1984), 86–97.

Scott, Erik R. "Edible Ethnicity: How Georgian Cuisine Conquered the Soviet Table." *Kritika: Explorations in Russian and Eurasian History* 13 (2012), 831–58.

Scully, Eleanor, and Terence Scully. *Early French Cookery: Sources, History, Original Recipes and Modern Applications*. Ann Arbor: University of Michigan Press, 1995.

Seabrook, John. "Crunch." *The New Yorker*, November 21, 2011, 54–64.

Sen, Amarya. *Poverty and Famines: An Essay on Entitlement and Deprivation*. New York: Oxford University Press, 1982.

Sermolino, Maria. *Papa's Table d'Hôte*. Philadelphia: Lippincott, 1952.

Severson, Kim. "Rachael Ray, Beyond TV." *New York Times*, May 9, 2018, D1, D6.

Shapiro, Edward. "The Southern Agrarians and the Tennessee Valley Authority." *American Quarterly* 22 (1970), 791–806.

Shapiro, Laura. *Perfection Salad; Women and Cooking at the Turn of the Century*. New York: Northpoint, 1986.

Shapiro, Laura. *Something from the Oven: Reinventing Dinner in 1950s America*. New York: Penguin, 2004.

Shapiro, Laura. *What She Ate: Six Remarkable Women and the Food that Tells Their Stories*. New York: Viking, 2017.

Sharpless, Rebecca. *Cooking in Other Women's Kitchens: Domestic Workers in the South, 1865–1960*. Chapel Hill: University of North Carolina Press, 2010.

Shaw, Timothy. *The World of Escoffier*. New York: Vendome Press, 1995.

Shenton, James P., et al. *American Cooking: The Melting Pot*. New York: Time-Life, 1971.

Sheraton, Mimi. "I Tasted Everything in Bloomingdale's Food Shop." *New York*, October 16, 1972, 51–75.

Shields, David S. *The Culinarians: Lives and Careers from the First Age of American Fine Dining*. Chicago: University of Chicago Press, 2017.

Shields, David S. *Southern Provisions: The Creation and Revival of a Cuisine*. Chicago: University of Chicago Press, 2015.

Shimbo, Hiriko. *The Sushi Experience*. New York: Knopf, 2006.

Shortridge, Barbara G., and James R. Shortridge, eds. *The Taste of American Place: A Reader on Regional and Ethnic Foods*, Lanham, MD: Rowman and Littlefield.

Sietsema, Robert. *Good & Cheap Ethnic Eats in New York City*. New York: City and Co., 1994; revised ed., 1997.

Simmons, Amelia. *American Cookery or the Art of Dressing Viands, Fish, Poultry and Vegetables . . .* Hartford, CT: Hudson & Goodwin, 1796.

Skloot, Rebecca. "Two Americas, Two Restaurants, One Town." *New York Times Magazine*, October 17, 2004, 78–81.

Smith, Andrew F. *Eating History: Thirty Turning Points in the Making of American Cuisine*. New York: Columbia University Press, 2009.

So Fast Recipes and So Good Too. Washington, DC: National Canners Association, no date but 1930s.

Sokolov, Raymond. *Fading Feast: A Compendium of Disappearing American Regional Foods*. New York: Farrar, Straus & Giroux, 1981.

Spiegel, Alison. "A Brief History of the Crock Pot, the Original Slow Cooker." Huffington Post, January 12, 2015, https://www.huffingtonpost.com/2015/01/12/what-is-a-crock-pot_n_6443398.html, accessed July 6, 2018.

Spring, Justin. *The Gourmands' Way: Six Americans in Paris and the Birth of a New Gastronomy*. New York: Farrar, Straus and Giroux, 2017.

Slattery, Harry. *Rural America Lights Up: The Story of Rural Electrification*. Washington DC: National Home Library Foundation, 1940.

Stanonis, Anthony J. "The Triumph of Epicure: A Global History of New Orleans Culinary Tourism." *Southern Quarterly* 46 (2009), 145–61.

Stavely, Keith, and Kathleen Fitzgerald. *America's Founding Food: The Story of New England Cooking*. Chapel Hill: University of North Carolina Press, 2004.

Stavely, Keith, and Kathleen Fitzgerald. *United Tastes: The Making of the First American Cookbook*. Amherst and Boston: University of Massachusetts Press, 2017.

Steinberger, Michael. *Au Revoir to All That: The Rise and Fall of French Cuisine*. London and New York: Bloomsbury, 2009.

Stern, Jane, and Michael Stern. *500 Things to Eat before It's Too Late and the Very Best Places to Eat Them*. New York: Houghton Mifflin Harcourt, 2009.

Stern, Jane, and Michael Stern. *Blue Plate Specials and Blue Ribbon Chefs*. New York: Lebhar-Friedman, 2001.

Stern, Jane, and Michael Stern. *Chili Nation*. New York: Clarkson Potter, 1999.

Stern, Jane, and Michael Stern. *Eat Your Way across the USA*. New York: Broadway Books, 1997

Stern, Jane, and Michael Stern. *Roadfood*. New York: Random House, 1978; 2nd ed., 1980; 10th ed., 2017.

Stern, Steven. "Based on an Old Family Recipe." *New York Times,* June 8, 2011, D1.

Stewart, Keith. *It's a Long Road to a Tomato: Tale of an Organic Farmer Who Quit the Big City for the (Not So) Simple Life*. New York: Marlowe and Company, 2006.

Stout, Rex, and the Editors of Viking Press. *The Nero Wolfe Cookbook*. New York: Viking, 1973.

Stout, Rex. *Too Many Cooks*. New York: Farrar and Rinehart, 1938.

Strauss, David. *Setting the Table for Julia Child: Gourmet Dining in America, 1934–1961*. Baltimore: Johns Hopkins University Press, 2011.

Strom, Stephanie. "Back to the Kitchen: Campbell Adjusts Soup Recipe to Address Changing Tastes." *New York Times*, November 9, 2015, https://www.nytimes.com/2015/11/10/business/campbell-rethinks-its-recipe-as-consumer-tastes-change.html, accessed January 14, 2018.

Strom, Stephanie. "Is the Supermarket Done For?" *New York Times*, May 16, 2016, published online as "What's New in the Supermarket? A Lot, and Not All of It Good," https://www.nytimes.com/2017/05/16/dining/grocery-book-michael-ruhlman-supermarket-shopping.html?_r=0, accessed Jan. 14, 2018.

Sussman, Gerald. "Welcome to the Cooking of Provincial New Jersey." *National Lampoon* 51 (June 1974), 57–63.

Talbott, Damon. "Recommended by Duncan Hines: Automobility, Authority, and American Gastronomy." Master's Thesis, University of Kansas, 2008.

Talbott, Damon. "Senses of Taste: Duncan Hines and American Gastronomy, 1931–1962." Doctoral Dissertation, University of Kansas, 2013.

This, Hervé. *Molecular Gastronomy: Exploring the Science of Flavour*, trans. M. B. Debevoise. New York: Columbia University Press, 2006.

Thomas, Lately. *Delmonico's: A Century of Splendor.* Boston: Houghton Mifflin, 1967.

Thompson, Derek. "How America Spends Money: 100 Years in the Life of the Family Budget." *The Atlantic,* April 5, 2012, https://www.theatlantic.com/business/archive/2012/04/how-america-spends-money-100-years-in-the-life-of-the-family-budget/255475/, accessed November 19, 2017.

The Three Hundredth Anniversary Cook Book, 2nd ed. East Hampton, NY: Ladies' Village Improvement Society, 1949.

Tipton-Martin, Toni. *The Jemima Code: Two Centuries of African American Cookbooks.* Austin: University of Texas Press, 2015.

Toklas, Alice B. *Aromas and Flavors of Past and Present: A Book of Exquisite Cookery.* New York: Harper & Bros, 1958.

Tower, Jeremiah. *California Dish: What I Saw (and Cooked) at the American Culinary Revolution.* New York: Free Press, 2003.

Tower, Jeremiah. *Start the Fire: How I Began a Food Revolution in America.* New York: Ecco, 2017.

Trillin, Calvin. *American Fried: Adventures of a Happy Eater.* New York: Vintage, 1979.

Trillin, Calvin. *Third Helpings.* New Haven and New York: Ticknor and Fields, 1983.

Trubek, Amy B. *Haute Cuisine: How the French Invented the Culinary Profession.* Philadelphia: University of Pennsylvania Press, 2018.

Trubek, Amy B. *The Taste of Place: A Cultural Journey into Terroir.* Berkeley: University of California Press, 2008.

Tucker, Susan ed. *New Orleans Cuisine: Fourteen Signature Dishes and Their Histories.* Jackson: University Press of Mississippi, 2007.

Turner, Bertha L. *The Federation Cook Book: A Collection of Tested Recipes Contributed by the Colored Women of the State of California.* Pasadena: Applewood Books 2007, original edition 1910.

Twain, Mark. *A Tramp Abroad.* Hartford, CT: American Publishing Co., 1880.

Twitty, Michael W. *The Cooking Gene: A Journey through African-American Culinary History in the Old South.* New York, 2017.

Tyree, Marion Fontaine Cabelle. *Housekeeping in Old Virginia, Containing Contributions from Two Hundred and Fifty Ladies in Virginia and Her Sister States, Distinguished for Their Skill in the Culinary Art, and Other Branches of Domestic Economy.* Richmond: J. W. Randolph & English, 1878.

Ushumirsky, Boris, trans. *Book of Tasty and Healthy Food.* Middletown, DE: Skylark Publishing, 2017.

Veit, Helen Zoe. *Modern Food, Moral Food: Self-Control, Science and the Rise of Modern American Eating.* Chapel Hill: University of North Carolina Press, 2013.

Vester, Katharina. *A Taste of Power: Food and American Identities.* Berkeley: University of California Press, 2015.

Vider, Stephen. " 'Oh Hell, May, Why Don't You People Have a Cookbook?': Camp Humor and Gay Domesticity." *American Quarterly* 65 (2013), 877–904.

Visitor's Guide to the Centennial Exhibition and Philadelphia 1876. Philadelphia: J. B. Lippincott and Co., 1876.

de Vita, Oretta Zanini. *Encyclopedia of Pasta*, trans. Maureen B. Fant. Berkeley and Los Angeles: University of California Press, 2000.

Wall Street Survivor Team. "McDonald's Real Estate: How They Really Make Their Money." *Wall Street Survivor,* October 15, 2015, https://blog.wallstreetsurvivor.com/2015/10/08/mcdonalds-beyond-the-burger/, accessed December 26, 2017.

Wallach, Jennifer Jensen. *Every Nation Has Its Dish: Black Bodies and Black Food in Twentieth-Century America.* Chapel Hill: University of North Carolina Press, 2019

Wallach, Jennifer Jensen, ed. *Dethroning the Deceitful Pork Chop: Rethinking African American Foodways from Slavery to Obama.* Fayetteville: University of Arkansas Press, 2017.

Wallach, Jennifer Jensen, and Michael D. Wise, eds.. *The Routledge History of American Foodways.* New York: Routledge, 2016.

Weiskopf-Ball, Emily. "'Tried! Tested! Proven!': *The Canadian Home Cook Book Compiled by: Ladies of Toronto and Chief Cities and Towns in Canada*, 1877, 384 Pages." *Cuizine* 6, number 1 (2015), www.erudit.org/en/journals/cuizine/2015-v6-n1-cuizine01991/1032258ar/, accessed July 19, 2017.

White, Jasper. *Jasper White's Cooking from New England*. New York: Harper Row, 1989. Reprinted Newton, Mass.: Biscuit Books, 1998.

Wilcox, Estelle Woods. *Buckeye Cookery and Practical Housekeeping: Compiled from Original Receipts*. Minneapolis: Buckeye Publishing, 1877.

Wilson, José. *American Cooking: The Eastern Heartland*. New York: Time-Life, 1971.

Wolfe, Tom et al. *New York Herald Tribune Presents New York, New York*. New York: Delta, 1964.

Woloson, Wendy A. *Refined Tastes: Sugar, Confectionery, and Consumers in Nineteenth-Century America*. Baltimore: Johns Hopkins University Press, 2002.

Woodward, C. Vann. *The Strange Career of Jim Crow*. New York: Oxford University Press, 1957.

Worthington, Diane Rossen. *The Cuisine of California*. Los Angeles: J. O. Tarcher, 1983.

WPA Federal Writer's Project. *The Italians of New York: A Survey*. New York: Random House, 1938.

Wyman, Carolyn. *Better Than Homemade: Amazing Foods That Changed the Way We Eat*. San Francisco: Chronicle Books, 2004.

Wyman, Carolyn. *Jell-O: A Biography*. San Diego: Harcourt, 2001.

Yu, Renqiu. "Chop Suey: From Chinese Food to Chinese American Food." *Chinese America: History and Perspectives* 1 (1987), 87–100.

Zeide, Anna. *Canned: The Rise and Fall of Consumer Confidence in the American Food Industry*. Oakland: University of California Press, 2018.

Zukin, Sharon. *Naked City: The Death and Life of Authentic Urban Places*. New York: Oxford University Press, 2010.

INDEX

Page numbers in *italics* indicate photos, illustrations, or reproductions of menus.